Australia's economic performance, like that of other industrial countries, deteriorated significantly between 1973 and 1983. Compared with the previous decade, annual growth of Australia's gross domestic product declined 60 percent while inflation and unemployment tripled. What explains this? What might be done to alleviate Australia's economic problems? How does Australia differ from other industrial countries? What can other countries learn from Australia's experience?

The eight papers in this book address these and other important questions about the Australian economy. In the first paper Rudiger Dornbusch and Stanley Fischer survey the Australian macroeconomy, emphasizing how the volatility of resource exports and Australia's peculiar wage-setting process affect the management of fiscal, monetary, and exchange rate policy. John F. Helliwell presents a longer-term perspective of the economy in his paper on natural resources. Daniel J. B. Mitchell takes a close look at the Australian labor market and its unique institutional features. Two papers analyze specific Australian government functions: Andrew S. Carron outlines the financial system, and Edward M. Gramlich looks at the state-commonwealth relationship and how it affects the achievement of the basic goals of the tax system. The next two papers look at Australian trade and its industries protected by tariffs: Lawrence B. Krause analyzes changes in Australia's comparative advantage, especially its trade with Japan and with the United States, and Richard E. Caves probes the scale, openness, and productivity of the Australian manufacturing industry. In the last paper Henry J. Aaron discusses Australia's social welfare programs and their provisions for the elderly, the ill, and the disabled.

The papers were originally presented at a conference in Canberra, Australia, on January 9–11, 1984. The conference was sponsored by the Brookings Institution with the cooperation and assistance of the Centre for Economic Policy Research at the Australian National University and was attended by about ninety prominent economists and policymakers from business, government, and the academic community. The book contains an introduction and a summary by the editors.

Richard E. Caves, professor of economics at Harvard University, and Lawrence B. Krause, a senior fellow in the Brookings Economic Studies program, have each written separately about the economic problems of other nations; they jointly edited *Britain's Economic Performance* (Brookings, 1980).

Jacket design by Stephen Kraft

Australian symbol by Catherine Baird

RICHARD E. CAVES AND LAWRENCE B. KRAUSE
Editors

The Australian Economy:
A View from the North

RUDIGER DORNBUSCH AND STANLEY FISCHER

JOHN F. HELLIWELL

DANIEL J. B. MITCHELL

ANDREW S. CARRON

EDWARD M. GRAMLICH

LAWRENCE B. KRAUSE

RICHARD E. CAVES

HENRY J. AARON

THE BROOKINGS INSTITUTION
Washington, D.C.

Library of Congress Cataloging in Publication data:

Main entry under title:

The Australian economy.

Includes bibliographical references and index.
1. Australia—Economic conditions—1945–
—Addresses, essays, lectures. I. Caves, Richard E.
II. Krause, Lawrence B. III. Dornbusch, Rudiger.
HC605.A7765 1984   330.994′063   84-17074
ISBN 0-8157-1326-6
ISBN 0-8157-1325-8 (pbk.)

1 2 3 4 5 6 7 8 9

Foreword

AMERICANS know little about Australia and are often surprised to discover how different the Australian and U.S. economies are. In 1983 the Brookings Institution undertook a study of the Australian economy to improve American understanding of the economic problems faced by Australia and to bring new insights and perspectives to those problems—a view from the North. A team of nine economists from the United States and Canada, headed by Richard E. Caves and Lawrence B. Krause, led the research effort.

Between 1973 and 1983 Australia's economic performance, like that of other industrial countries, deteriorated significantly. Australia's gross domestic product declined, while inflation and unemployment rates tripled. Australia's distinctive physical characteristics have been important in shaping its economic behavior—low population, isolation from its trading partners, and abundance of minerals and pastoral land in relation to its land mass. Policy decisions inevitably reflect these characteristics: Australia has encouraged immigration and defended protectionism; it has preferred government-determined solutions because the country is geographically isolated and contains too few economic actors to ensure efficient market outcomes. Because Australian economic growth has been tied so closely to natural resource developments, changes in resource production have significantly affected prices and the growth of aggregate output. The difficulties in addressing Australia's economic problems have been compounded by the overlapping powers and responsibilities held by state governments and the commonwealth.

This research project could not have been undertaken without the cooperation of the Centre for Economic Policy Research at the Australian National University and its director, Fred H. Gruen. Professor Gruen initiated the study, helped provide financial support, and organized and chaired the Brookings-Canberra Conference held January 9–11, 1984. He and his staff helped make arrangements and appointments for the Brookings team during their research visits to Australia. Professor Gruen was assisted in his role as adviser by a group composed of W. M. Corden, E. A. Evans, V. W. J. FitzGerald, and A. R. Pagan. The project was made possible by financial support from the Australian National University, the Reserve Bank of Australia, ANZ Bank, BP (Australia) Ltd., CRA Ltd., Esso (Australia) Ltd., MIM Holdings Ltd., WestPac Banking Corporation, and the Andrew W. Mellon Foundation of the United States.

The editors thank the eighty-four Australian participants from business, government, and the academic community who took part in the conference. Their contribution is reflected in Dr. FitzGerald's summary presented at the conference conclusion. The staff of the Centre for Economic Policy Research provided research and administrative assistance during the conference. Jenny Anderssen, Catherine E. Baird, Kim Choham, Lynne Gallagher, Eva Klug, Fiona Tully, and Margi Wood were especially helpful.

Karen J. Wirt, Vicky Macintyre, and Carol Cole Rosen edited the manuscript. Julia A. Henel verified the factual content, with the help of Harold S. Appelman, Shannon P. Butler, Alice G. Keck, Carolyn A. Rutsch, Penelope Schmidt, and the Australian embassy in Washington, D.C. Kirk W. Kimmell, Meropi Antoniadou-McCoy, and Susan F. Woollen provided administrative and secretarial assistance during the preparation of the book. Paul E. Morawski and Carole H. Newman of the Social Science Computation Center at Brookings assisted with technical advice. Florence Robinson prepared the index. Catherine Baird designed the conference symbol that appears on the cover.

The views expressed in this book are those of its authors and should not be ascribed to the trustees, officers, or other staff members of the Brookings Institution, to the Centre for Economic Policy Research, or to the foundations and institutions that contributed to the financing of the project.

BRUCE K. MACLAURY
President

July 1984
Washington, D.C.

Contents

Contents

Contents

Figures

Introduction

WHEN VIEWED from the vantage point of an industrial country in the Northern Hemisphere, the Commonwealth of Australia appears to be a familiar country, but one that has three very distinctive physical characteristics: it has a small population for such a large land mass, it is located at a distance from its trading partners, and it is rich in natural resources. At different times these characteristics have been important in shaping Australian concerns and images of themselves. The first characteristic, low population, has been seen as both a societal and a security problem—"populate or perish" was a commonly heard phrase. This led Australia to encourage immigration; it was one reason put forth to defend protectionism based on the correct analytical point that by inhibiting the importation of labor-intensive goods, Australia would encourage the inflow of factors of production that would otherwise have been embodied in those goods. Second, Australia has long suffered from the "tyranny of distance," particularly when the society and economy were oriented toward Europe, a journey of several months by ship. This has added to the sense of isolation brought about by the insularity of the country. The third characteristic is a plus—Australia is extremely well endowed with minerals and pastoral land in relation to its population. Another favorable feature is that the climate varies from mild to tropical, so that the outdoor life style is predominant. This has led Australians to

The editors acknowledge the help received from numerous people. Special thanks go to Fred H. Gruen, who was chairman of the Brookings-Canberra Conference, and to Vince W. FitzGerald, who summarized the proceedings of the conference. Others include Sir Roderick Carnegie, W. M. Corden, John Laird, P. McGuinness, Don Stammer, and James Wolfensohn.

1

think of their nation as the "lucky country," although being an exporter of natural resources has also made the economy sensitive to cyclical developments abroad.[1]

Two other characteristics of Australian society are also striking; namely, a general distrust of markets and a strong endorsement of egalitarianism. The distrust of markets may arise naturally in a geographically isolated country in which the economic actors are too few to ensure efficient market outcomes. However, pervasive distrust seems to suggest that Australians prefer government-determined outcomes in many cases to market solutions even if efficiency is sacrificed. Australians may choose at some cost the seemingly greater control of outcomes that government interference promises. The design and scope of governmental policy and action reflect this distrust.

Australia's endorsement of egalitarianism has deep historical roots. It is manifested in a popular ethos that no one should be poor in Australia and similarly no one should be very rich. While the reality at the upper end of the income distribution differs in some degree from the tenet of egalitarianism, this societal virtue does affect behavior. It is somehow "un-Australian" to be outstanding—as is sometimes said, Australia cuts off its tall timbers. Thus, aggressive persons, whether in business in or politics, tend to be seen as idiosyncratic figures and not widely admired. However, foreign recognition of outstanding qualities of certain Australians somehow legitimizes those persons and makes them acceptable at home. Egalitarianism also affects government policy. The highly developed mechanism for redistributing fiscal resources among the states, as analyzed in the chapter by Edward M. Gramlich, is an example.

Recent Performance of the Australian Economy

Australia's economic performance, like that of other industrial countries, deteriorated significantly during the ten years following fiscal 1973. Compared to the previous decade, annual growth of real gross domestic product (GDP) was reduced by 60 percent, from 5.1 percent to 2.2

1. The phrase came from a book by Donald Horne, *The Lucky Country: Australia in the Sixties* (Melbourne: Penguin Books, 1965). While Horne emphasized the absence of ethnic, cultural, and social divisions in Australia, it has come to refer in popular usage to the generous natural endowment of the country.

Table 1. *Real Growth of Gross Domestic Product, Consumer Price Inflation, and Unemployment, Selected Periods, 1962–63 to 1982–83*
Percent

Item	1962–63 to 1972–73	1972–73 to 1977–78	1977–78 to 1982–83	1972–73 to 1982–83	1982–83[a]
Real GDP (growth rate)	5.1[b]	2.5[c]	2.0[d]	2.2[d]	−2.0[d]
Consumer price inflation (annual average)	3.8	13.2	9.9	11.6	11.5
Unemployment rate[e] (annual average)	1.7	3.6	6.7	5.2	9.0

Sources: W. E. Norton, P. M. Garmston, and M. W. Brodie, *Australian Economic Statistics, 1949–50 to 1980–81: II. Tables,* Occasional Paper 8A (Canberra: Reserve Bank of Australia, May 1982), pp. 92, 117, 118, 145; *National Economic Summit Conference, April 1983: Information Paper on the Economy* (Canberra: Australian Government Publishing Service, 1983), p. 55; and *Budget Statements 1983–84,* Budget Paper 1, prepared by the Treasury of the Commonwealth of Australia (Canberra: AGPS, 1983), pp. 13, 23, 32.

a. Estimate.
b. Based on 1966–67 prices.
c. Based on 1974–75 prices.
d. Based on 1979–80 prices.
e. Data for August only in 1971–72 through 1975–76.

percent; inflation rates measured by consumer prices tripled from 3.8 percent to 11.6 percent on average each year; and unemployment rates more than tripled from 1.7 percent to 5.2 percent (see table 1). In addition, in fiscal 1983 Australia experienced a further worsening of its performance as gross national product actually declined by 2 percent, the consumer price index rose by 11.5 percent, and unemployment reached a postwar record (more than 10 percent at the end of the year). While, as noted, Australia's economy was not alone in performing less well during this period, Australians found very little comfort in this because their country has been a net energy exporter and, therefore, the oil price disruptions of the 1970s should have been less damaging to it.

Inflation was the scourge of all industrial countries in the 1970s and early 1980s. In efforts to counter it, governments adopted restrictive macroeconomic policies that resulted in economic stagnation and rising unemployment. Australia's macroeconomic experience during this period fell well within the mainstream. To be sure, there were differences among countries as to the cause and severity of inflation, although all were affected by rapidly rising oil prices. The differences between Australia and other industrial countries became quite marked in fiscal 1983 as inflation accelerated at home but abated abroad.

Inflation has been one of the major concerns of Australian policymakers, although the public has been more preoccupied with unemployment.[2] What explains Australia's economic performance? How does Australia differ from other industrial countries? What can other countries learn from Australia's experience? What might be done to alleviate Australia's economic problems? In broad outline, these are the questions that each of the chapters of this book addresses.

Australia Compared to Other Industrial Countries

A case can be made to demonstrate that, compared to other industrial countries, Australia's economy has been performing relatively badly for a very long time.[3] According to estimates made by Angus Maddison, Australia's per capita income in 1870 was about 75 percent greater than that in the United States and was the highest in the world, as shown in table 2. By 1929, however, Australian per capita income had fallen to 25 percent below that of the United States, a relationship that has remained more or less the same ever since.

Australia's prosperity of the mid-nineteenth century was not sustainable in its own terms. Gold booms always end in a bust. Also the population was composed primarily of prime-age males, an unnatural condition resulting largely from the prosperous period. Much of the relative deterioration of Australian per capita income occurred in the nineteenth century and reflected the end of the unsustainable factors. Nevertheless, for half a century following 1890, measured per capita income fluctuated greatly and its trend grew relatively slowly compared to other industrial countries. McLean and Pincus argue that the per capita GDP measurement fails to reflect substantial increases in the average Australian's standard of living due to increases in life expectancy, greater leisure, improved (and unmeasured) housing quality, and the like.[4] Such gains were also made in other industrial countries.

2. Voter surveys indicate that unemployment and inflation were the top two concerns in both 1980 and 1983, with strikes being a close third. See B. Carr, "Gallup Poll: Hawke Looks the Winner," *The Bulletin*, vol. 103 (March 8, 1983), pp. 22–25.

3. See discussion in the chapter by John F. Helliwell.

4. Ian W. McLean and Jonathan J. Pincus, "Living Standards in Australia 1890–1940: Evidence and Conjectures," Working Papers in Economic History 6 (Canberra: Australian National University, August 1982). See also Rodney Maddock and Michael Carter, "Hours, Leisure and Wellbeing 1911–1981," Working Paper in Economic History 19 (Canberra: Australian National University, November 1983), who make the same point with respect to leisure for more recent years. Fred Gruen brought attention to this point at the Brookings-Canberra Conference.

Table 2. *GDP per Capita and Economic Growth in Industrial Countries, Selected Years, 1870–1982*

	GDP per capita as percent of U.S. GDP per capita[a]							Annual average growth rate, 1870–1976 (percent)	
Country	1870	1890	1913	1929	1960	1976	1982	GDP	GDP per capita
Australia	173	145	107	74	75	80	80	3.2	1.1
Austria	53	n.a.	58	48	54	69	68	2.6	2.1
Belgium	123	104	82	75	66	84	65	2.1	1.5
Canada	80	77	81	70	78	91	91	3.8	2.0
Denmark	69	66	73	64	66	76	84	2.9	1.9
Finland	52	42	41	39	54	71	77	3.1	2.2
France	87	71	67	66	67	87	76	2.2	1.9
Germany	68	60	58	51	70	81	82	2.5	2.0
Italy	69	46	42	37	43	53	47	2.3	1.6
Japan	35	33	29	32	35	77	69	3.8	2.6
Netherlands	123	87	69	70	69	80	74	2.7	1.4
Norway	63	52	47	50	65	85	105	2.9	2.1
Sweden	54	48	55	61	79	88	90	3.0	2.3
Switzerland	104	88	74	85	85	78	114	2.4	1.6
United Kingdom	124	103	81	67	70	67	65	1.8	1.3
United States	100	100	100	100	100	100	100	3.5	1.9

Sources: Angus Maddison, "Phases of Capitalistic Development," *Banca Nazionale del Lavoro Quarterly Review*, vol. 30 (June 1977), pp. 103–37; and Organization for Economic Cooperation and Development, *Main Economic Indicators* (November 1983), pp. 182–83.

a. Index is calculated from data based on U.S. prices. Data for 1982 are not strictly comparable to earlier years.

After World War II, Australia's population grew more rapidly than that of any other industrial country except Canada, but its per capita income growth was among the slowest. Although other industrial countries managed to close the per capita income gap with the United States during the postwar period, Australia fell from fourth place in 1929 to ninth place in 1976. As Kravis, Heston, and Summers point out, such comparisons of per capita income may not accurately reflect relative real income, which can only be measured after careful disaggregate price comparisons, and such comparisons have not been made for Australia.[5] Nevertheless, the sketchy data that exist through an approximation of the Kravis method suggest that Australian per capita GDP was about 83 percent of that of the United States in 1970 and 1975, and only about 79

5. Irving B. Kravis, Alan Heston, and Robert Summers, *World Product and Income: International Comparisons of Real Gross Product* (Johns Hopkins University Press, 1982).

Table 3. *Industries as a Proportion of GDP, at 1974–75 Prices,*
Selected Periods, 1962–63 to 1980–81
Percent

Industry	1962–63	1967–68	1972–73	1977–78	1980–81
Agriculture[a]	8.5	6.1	5.5	5.9	5.6
Construction	8.3	8.8	8.4	7.3	7.3
Manufacturing	25.7	26.0	25.4	22.4	22.7
Mining	1.6	2.2	3.6	3.6	3.5
Other services[b]	33.5	35.0	35.4	38.9	38.6
Ownership of dwellings	5.4	5.9	6.2	6.7	7.0
Wholesale and retail trade	17.0	16.0	15.5	15.2	15.3

Sources: Norton, Garmston, and Brodie, *Australian Economic Statistics,* p. 120, and *National Economic Summit Conference, April 1983: Information Paper on the Economy,* p. 10.
a. Includes fishing, forestry, and hunting.
b. Electricity, gas, and water; entertainment, recreation, restaurants, hotels, and personal services; finance, insurance, real estate, and business services; public administration; and transportation, storage, and communications.

percent in 1980.[6] During the 1950s and 1960s Australians were reasonably satisfied with their economic growth. Only in recent years have many Australians become aware that other nations have passed them by. At current prices and exchange rates, seven industrial countries had greater per capita income than Australia in 1982.

The Structure of the Australian Economy

For much of the postwar period Australian trade policy was designed to encourage domestic production and employment in manufacturing. As seen in tables 3 and 4, that policy was not entirely successful. Although it is true that tariffs on manufactured imports also restrict exports of manufactures, more people were employed in manufacturing than would likely have been the case if free trade had been in effect. At the same time, the share of the labor force employed and the share of GDP originating in manufacturing declined during the 1960s and 1970s. Australia's share of manufacturing in GDP is among the lowest of all industrial countries.[7] Like other industrial countries, Australians increasingly devoted themselves to producing services. Indeed, Australia

6. The estimate with disclaimers was provided by Irving Kravis.
7. Alan A. Tait and Peter S. Heller, "International Comparisons of Government Expenditure," International Monetary Fund Occasional Paper 10 (IMF, April 1982), table 15, p. 38.

Table 4. *Employment, by Industry, Selected Years, 1967–81*[a]

Percent

Industry	1967	1972	1977	1981
Agriculture	8.7	7.9	6.7	6.5
Construction	8.1	8.3	8.0	7.4
Manufacturing	25.6	23.7	21.3	19.4
Mining	1.3	1.4	1.3	1.5
Other services[b]	36.0	37.8	42.9	45.2
Wholesale and retail trade	20.4	20.7	19.8	19.9

Sources: Norton, Garmston, and Brodie, *Australian Economic Statistics*, p. 101.

a. Employment in the civilian population aged fifteen years or over. Columns may not add to 100 because of rounding.

b. Same as table 3, note b.

has the largest share of employment in services among all the industrial countries with the exception of Canada and the United States. Australia's high degree of urbanization (89 percent of the total population) is second only to that of the United Kingdom among the industrial countries; and Australia's urban areas are concentrated in five state capitals.[8]

Unlike other industrial countries, the agricultural share of Australian output did not decline very much, and the mining share actually expanded during the 1970s.[9] It follows that natural resources have been important in the growth of the economy, but they have not provided significant increases in job opportunities. Only about 8 percent of the labor force is employed in agriculture and mining despite the importance of those sectors for the economy.

An Open or a Closed Economy?

The question of whether Australia is an open or a closed economy is interesting because it is both. Depending on which aspect of the economy

8. World Bank, *World Development Report 1983* (Oxford University Press, 1983), tables 21 and 22, pp. 188–89, 190–91.

9. The measurement of the proportion of GDP arising in mining is sensitive to which year's prices are utilized. If average 1979–80 prices were used in table 3 rather than 1974–75 prices, the mining share would have been 6.2 percent rather than 3.5 percent. Also see discussion in the Helliwell chapter.

is being emphasized, it could be characterized as either largely or minimally influenced by outside events.

Foreign developments have a large influence on Australia, although they may not be dominant at any particular time. Exports of goods and services comprise about 15 percent of the GDP, and about 80 percent of Australian exports are natural resource goods subject to great variance in foreign demand. Hence the contribution of changes in net exports to changes in GDP can be very great. For the eleven-year period from fiscal 1972 through fiscal 1982, the change in the volume of net exports averaged 53 percent of the change in real GDP.[10] The pricing of Australia's natural resource trade is largely set in foreign markets and also fluctuates greatly, and these fluctuations lead to shifts in Australia's terms of trade. Norton and McDonald find that movements in the terms of trade played a large part in determining short-term profitability in Australia, which in turn was a major factor affecting changes in production.[11] Australia's capital markets are integrated with the rest of the world. Australian natural resource development depends on raising a great deal of foreign capital. In addition, foreign entrepreneurship is relied upon heavily in minerals and partially in manufacturing. Short-term banking funds flow in and out, making Australian interest rates responsive to developments abroad, especially those in the United States. Because linkages between Australia and the rest of the world are so strong, Rudiger Dornbusch and Stanley Fischer in their chapter describe Australia as an open economy.

The opponents of this view argue that much of what really matters to the Australian economy is domestically determined and independent of foreign influences, and thus on average the economy is closed. For example, the long-run profit squeeze that has been so important to the operations of the economy and noticeable in recent years is not attributable to movements in the terms of trade.[12] Australian policymakers

10. Changes in exports minus imports divided by changes in GDP (ignoring signs) and averaged over the eleven years. All magnitudes measured in constant 1979–80 prices. Calculated from *National Economic Summit Conference, April 1983: Information Paper on the Economy* (Canberra: Australian Government Publishing Service, 1983), table 2.3, p. 13.

11. W. E. Norton and R. McDonald, "The Decline in Australia's Economic Performance in the 1970s: An Analysis of Annual Data," *Australian Economic Papers*, vol. 22 (June 1983).

12. W. Kasper and P. O'Hara, "Long Waves in Australia and What Can be Done about Them," paper presented at the fifty-third meeting of the Australian and New Zealand Association for the Advancement of Science (ANZAAS), Perth, May 1983.

have designed and implemented policy for domestic needs. Those needs, as interpreted by the policymakers, when combined with the unique labor market institutions in Australia have given the country its own economic rhythm—that of a predominantly service-oriented economy. The high wage settlements of the 1970s pushed up the wage share of GDP from 57.4 percent in the mid-1960s to 63.5 percent in the late 1970s at the expense of profits. Moreover, the share of public expenditures in the economy rose rapidly in the 1970s as in other industrial countries, a factor that may also have contributed to the compression of profits.[13] Thus, while Australia may also reflect world developments, it is believed that most of its economic performance is domestically determined. This view was endorsed by Brian Beedham in a survey article on Australia in *The Economist*:

politics will decide what happens to Australia in the next few years; but the politics are about economics. The heart of the approaching battlefield is a fight about the size of the public-sector deficit, and an even bigger fight about the size of wage increases the unions can wring out of the economy.[14]

Labor markets and institutions, an essential ingredient in the operation of the Australian economy, are described in Daniel J. B. Mitchell's chapter as relying little on international factors. Indeed, the Australian labor market operates as though in a closed economy, even though a round of wage increases could be affected by an external event such as a rise in minerals prices.

Obviously both external and internal factors are important to the Australian economy, thus making it partly open and partly closed. What is significant is how Australian policymakers view the economy and whether they want it to be more open or not. Their choice will help define the scope for domestic policy and may determine the kind of policy instruments that are most appropriate.

Policy Experimentation in the 1970s

The Australian economy was bound to have changed in the 1970s if for no other reason than the rapid growth of a large, highly productive

13. Kasper and O'Hara, ibid.
14. Brian Beedham, "In the Deep End, Bob Hawke's Australia: A Survey," *The Economist* (August 6–12, 1983), p. S-9.

mining sector including iron ore, coal, and bauxite, which reduced the economy's dependency on the vagaries of nature and foreign agricultural protectionism. In addition, the people chose a Labor party government for the first time in thirty-three years. The government under Prime Minister Gough Whitlam that took office in December 1972 immediately made significant policy changes.[15] The exchange rate became more variable.[16] An across-the-board tariff reduction of 25 percent was instituted primarily as part of an attempt to stabilize the economy. The first effort was made to reduce Australia's protectionism since the establishment of the Commonwealth of Australia in 1901.[17] Foreign direct investment came under greater control (although the roots of regulation began in the mid-1960s). The government under Labor Minister Clyde Robert Cameron pressed the Australian arbitration courts to increase wage awards to enhance labor's share of output. Finally, various government social expenditures were increased sharply, as analyzed by Edward M. Gramlich and Henry J. Aaron in their chapters.

All this domestic activity took place within the context of a world economy disrupted by the first OPEC oil shock. Arguably the two most important effects of the oil crisis for energy-rich Australia were the inflation it abetted and the recession in other industrial countries that attempted to contain inflation. In particular, the remarkably high level of Japanese growth was cut in half, with devastating results on resource investment in Australia. The worsening economic situation undoubtedly played a part in convincing Australian voters to return the Liberal-Country party coalition government to power at the end of 1975 with Malcolm Fraser as prime minister. The goal of the Fraser government was to restore the level of prosperity and social-political tranquility of the pre-Whitlam era. As is evident from the data on GDP, inflation, and unemployment shown in table 1, that goal was never achieved.

Following the second oil crisis in 1979–80, the prospect arose for a new resource boom in Australia based on coal, natural gas, petroleum,

15. Ross Garnaut, "Australia's Shrinking Markets," in Lawrence B. Krause and Sueo Sekiguchi, eds., *Economic Interaction in the Pacific Basin* (Brookings Institution, 1980).

16. The exchange rate is analyzed in the chapter by Dornbusch and Fischer.

17. Policies dealing with foreign trade and direct investment are discussed in the chapter by Lawrence B. Krause.

uranium, and energy-intensive alumina and aluminum. Indeed, the Organization for Economic Cooperation and Development rated Australia as having better prospects than any other member nation.[18] In fact, Australia's future looked so bright following 1979–80 that pressures for wage increases mounted. However, the boom fizzled under the weight of the prolonged worldwide recession. The result was a sharp rise in real wages and decline in profits. Controlling domestic sources of inflation and taming irresponsible union action, along with reducing unemployment, were widely believed to be the major imperatives of the country. The March 1983 general election was concerned largely with these issues, and the electorate decided that former union leader Robert James Lee Hawke of the Labor party could do it better. Thus the Labor party was returned to power, but this time without a mandate for massive social change. The people backed the Labor party apparently without endorsing either socialism or unionism.

The first order of business of the new government was to convene a unique National Economic Summit Conference, which brought together government officials and representatives of various political, economic, and social interests for the purpose of forming a consensus on appropriate national goals and policy approaches.[19] Several observers noted that wage inflation and the confrontational nature of Australian industrial relations had advanced to the point that they constituted a barrier to economic recovery and sustained growth. In the aftermath of the summit conference more permanent institutions are being created to bring together labor, business, and the government (both state and commonwealth). The purpose is to devise a plan for forging a societal consensus so that macroeconomic policy can be improved in general and wage pressures be contained in particular. Separate groups are being formed for several industries as well as one for the economy as a whole. Although this development may have been necessary given the particular circumstances, it will increase government intervention in the economy and, in the extreme, lead to corporate statism that would reduce rather than increase the adjustment capabilities of the economy.

18. Organization for Economic Cooperation and Development, *Economic Outlook*, vol. 29 (July 1981).
19. *National Economic Summit Conference, April 1983: Communique* (Canberra: AGPS, 1983).

Australia and Economic Rents

It is possible to argue that the essential point concerning Australia is that it is a rent-seeking society. The concept of rent seeking was advanced by Anne Krueger and was developed to help explain the behavior of developing countries pursuing an import-substituting development strategy.[20] In essence, the hypothesis is that when an economy is constrained by government regulations and controls, contrived economic rents are created, and there are economic incentives to share in these rents by obtaining favorable government decisions such as allocations of foreign currency, import permits, investment licenses, and the like. Thus the best human resources will be devoted to seeking rewards from the political system rather than to increasing the production of goods and services. This is bound to have a negative effect on total real growth.

In the case of Australia, one must recognize that there are real economic rents created from exploiting natural resources. Part of the rent goes to various commonwealth and state governments in the form of royalties and income taxes, which are then spent for general government purposes including transfers. Another part of the rent is absorbed through excessive wage payments to workers in mining who are able to command large wage gains; possibly another part is excess profits (relative to the risk). Australians will inevitably compete for these windfalls because by one way or another they will be distributed.

Australia also resembles developing countries by creating artificial rents through import-substitution policies. Indeed, Australia has adopted trade policies described as "all-around" protectionism.[21] The real net effect of comprehensive protection on particular economic activities is not obvious, but it is certain to make rent seeking an important activity for everyone. It must be seen as an inward orientation of policy and economic activity.

20. Anne O. Krueger, "The Political Economy of the Rent-Seeking Society," *American Economic Review*, vol. 64 (June 1974), pp. 291–303.
21. The phrase is attributed to John McEwen, deputy prime minister and leader of the Liberal-Country party in the 1960s. He was also prime minister for a short time in 1967–68. He believed that it was politically popular for the government to help farmers and therefore it was also desirable to help other industries using the instruments appropriate to the situation. He also held the position that generally Australians should turn to the government for help.

Furthermore, the states in Australia regulate and control economic activity within their domain to such an extent that for many products and services there is no national market, but rather a collection of state markets. Thus there are strong economic incentives for individuals and firms to seek rewards in state capitals. Even labor unions can choose among state arbitration courts, as distinct from the commonwealth court, to pursue a wage-maximization strategy. Finally, state politicians themselves have great incentives to turn to Canberra in search of more grants, to obtain more loans from the Australian Loan Council, and the like. Hence there are several levels of rent seeking in Australia.

There must be tremendous costs involved in all this unproductive rent seeking. Society loses when businesses find import quotas more attractive than becoming internationally competitive, when labor unions lobby for the best court decision rather than producing maximum output and bargaining for a proper share of it with management, or when state officials seek to reinforce their base in Canberra rather than administering their own governments. The loss to society will be reflected in a less efficient and more rigid economy, in more inflation, and possibly in ineffective government. While there may be offsetting political and social benefits from the elaborate rent redistribution mechanism in Australia, they would have to be great to offset the costs.

Policy Alternatives for Australia

Policymakers are forced to think in terms of certain trade-offs. Following a period in which they have been plagued by both high inflation and high unemployment, the most pressing trade-off is between growth and stability. A second type of trade-off is that between economic efficiency and equity, a decision that is necessarily involved in any policy measure that might be adopted. This is a major theme in Gramlich's chapter in this book. In this latter type of trade-off the equity issue is further complicated by concerns about economic justice among employed workers on the one hand and between the employed and the unemployed on the other. It is clear that there are no painless alternatives.

A major choice must be made concerning the basic direction of the economy: should Australia remain an inward-looking economy or should it become substantially more outward looking? Some Australian prime ministers and foreign ministers, several commissions, and numerous studies of the Industries Assistance Commission have pointed to the improvement in economic efficiency and reduction in inflation that could be expected if Australia became more outward looking. Most Australian academics accept these findings and support the policy conclusion. Yet little progress has been made. Indeed, the one real effort in that direction—the 25 percent across-the-board cut in tariffs at the start of the Whitlam government—is viewed as a mistake by many Australians. It is even possible that Australia could become more protectionist in trade matters, less hospitable to foreign investment, and more restrictive in immigration.

Another major decision must be made concerning the proper role of government in the economy: should it be more intrusive or follow a policy of laissez-faire? In the past Australian governments have not intervened in the economy by using the numerous government enterprises but have been content to regulate and control the economy by influencing private markets. It would be more consistent with the ideology of the Labour party, however, if it were to become more intrusive and more direct.

These choices will be made in the process of developing a strategy for economic recovery from the recession. The Fraser government in 1982–83 emphasized fighting inflation and, thus, a "restraint-only" strategy was followed. It is probably not unfair to characterize the early stance of the Hawke government that is now in office as using different instruments to follow a similar strategy. Subsequently a more expansionary policy has ensued. If public expenditures are to be increased further or taxes cut, then a choice must be made between distribution objectives or supply promotion.

Coming to Grips with the Australian Economy[22]

The purpose of this study is to gain some understanding of the Australian economy and of its performance and problems, and to suggest ways of finding solutions or even suggest the solutions themselves. This

22. This section reflects Vince FitzGerald's summary presented in the final session of the Brookings-Canberra Conference.

section presents a chapter-by-chapter overview of the issues investigated.

Macroeconomic Behavior of the Economy

An analysis of recent economic performance and macroeconomic problems is undertaken in the chapter by Dornbusch and Fischer. Although similar in many respects to other OECD countries, Australia has had more inflation following the wage explosion of 1973–75. Thus Australia is seen as an economy with high unemployment, high inflation, and large budget deficits. Four issues are identified as being particularly important for macroeconomic policy discussion: the wage-setting process and the role of the Arbitration Commission, the role of fiscal policy in stimulating demand, the resources boom, and the interaction between monetary policy and exchange rate policy. Each of these issues is analyzed and empirical evidence presented.

Attention is focused on the relation between wages, inflation, and unemployment because the rise in real wages is seen by the authors as the cause of inflation.[23] Dornbusch and Fischer explain the determination of money wages in Australia by an equation using unemployment and expected inflation as variables (an augmented Phillips curve). They also find, as have other researchers, that a simple form of the equation omits some relevant variables or that the structure of the relation shifts over time; however, the authors tend to reject the second explanation based on their econometric results. In their search for omitted variables, they find that support is admittedly weak for the proposition that there is real wage resistance in Australia—that is, workers prefer to remain unemployed rather than accept lower real wages than they previously earned. Dornbusch and Fischer also accept the notion that both Australia's wage policies and the Arbitration Commission have an independent effect on real wages. Evidence is seen in the increase in real wages through the 1972 decision favoring equal pay for women, in the national wage case in 1973, and in the decline in real wages through indexation in the 1975–80 period.

The authors also accept the proposition that part of Australia's unemployment is classical (rather than all Keynesian) because real

---

23. This issue is also addressed in the chapter by Mitchell.

wages have risen faster than productivity gains and have remained higher despite a rise in unemployment. This means that the real wage is too high to permit employment of the entire labor force.

The role of fiscal policy in stimulating demand also received much attention. Dornbusch and Fischer take issue with the Australian Treasury's position, namely that expansionary fiscal policy will fail to stimulate output and will only worsen inflation. The authors conclude that Australia's budget deficit is not excessive when measured on a structural basis, that is, what it would be at full employment; they also believe that the budget deficit is modest when compared to that of other industrial countries, and that the outstanding level of public debt relative to income in Australia will not cause problems anytime in the near future. They contend that inflation can be contained by appropriate monetary policy, which need not be compromised by a higher budget deficit. Dornbusch and Fischer conclude that a more expansionary fiscal policy is appropriate for Australia but that, because of the real wage issue, that policy would have to be combined with vigorous incomes policy.

Natural Resources and the Economy

A longer term perspective of the Australian economy is presented by Helliwell in his chapter on natural resources. He analyzes three issues: the influence of natural resources on Australian economic growth, the macroeconomic effects of resource developments and the policy issues implied, and the main macroeconomic factors determining the overall costs and benefits of different rates of resource development. With respect to the first issue, the point is made that the usual pattern for expansion of natural resources is not steady growth, but a concentrated burst of activity, or a boom. Furthermore, booms do not end on a plateau but in a bust. Significant booms and busts have marked Australian history, and even the largest mineral expansions contemplated in the foreseeable future would not be outside this historical experience. Thus booms and busts should be the expected pattern, but they are rarely anticipated. Governments cannot control the scale and timing of resource booms, but they should seek to dampen them rather than exaggerate their amplitude. Maintaining a stable tax structure and expenditure path would permit automatic stabilizers to have the desired dampening effect.

With large swings in demand for complementary factors of production required to develop natural resources, the rest of the economy will certainly be affected. The level of exports of resources may be permanently raised, and this will affect all traded goods and services. These consequences have been analyzed through existing structural models of the Australian economy. However, such models are incomplete because they do not distinguish among the investment, construction, and production stages of mineral development. Furthermore, they include neither empirical data on the influence of terms-of-trade effects on real wages and other feedbacks nor monetary factors. A Canadian model that may have some applicability to Australia indicates that the construction stage of a resource boom is similar to the comparable stage of other investment booms and that there is little evidence that other industries are crowded out by the expanding minerals sector.

Helliwell recommends a mixed system to tax natural resource production. He believes that some taxation should occur at the beginning of a project—for instance, through competitive bidding for exploration and development rights—and some should come from production revenue—a resource-rent tax, for example. In his view, however, business firms must be given assurance that the tax regime will not be changed to their disadvantage after they have commited huge resources. Another way to gain revenue is to attract productive factors from abroad. Historically resource booms have stepped up immigration, but other considerations are also involved.

The Labor Market

Mitchell undertakes the task of describing the Australian labor market with its unique institutional features and analyzing their economic consequences. The author, in his examination of some critical analytical issues that relate directly to policy, finds that, like other industrial countries, Australia has experienced a rise in female participation rates and a decline in male participation rates in the labor force; the decline is particularly striking for older men. This may well be related to the enactment of social welfare programs in the 1970s. Employment patterns indicate a shift of workers away from agriculture and manufacturing and toward community services (mainly government).

Like other industrial countries, Australia experienced a sharp rise in unemployment in the 1970s and 1980s that was not due to compositional shifts in the labor force. There is some weak evidence to suggest that more generous unemployment benefits did add numbers to the unemployment rolls, but the change in benefits was not the main reason for the rise. Rather, unemployment rose because macroeconomic policy was restrictive in response to inflationary pressures. Inflation was driven by militant unions demanding increases in real wages above productivity gains. Reconciliation of claims in excess of real national income was achieved by constraining the growth of the economy, and this led to higher unemployment. Because unemployment by itself has not been sufficient to induce workers to accept lower real wages, the natural rate of unemployment has risen. Mitchell suggests that widespread use of profit-sharing or other forms of gain-sharing could permit more employment with less inflation.

The Australian wage-determination system is unique with its compulsory arbitration through state and commonwealth tribunals and an Arbitration Commission that sets award wages. Wage awards set the minimum, but larger wage increases can be obtained through collective bargaining if employers will grant them. The higher wages can then become standard by action of the arbitration system enforcing the principle of comparative wage justice. Thus the system pushes wages up, not down. The alternative of free collective bargaining is unlikely to be less inflationary because in Australia most of the labor force is unionized and there are numerous unions that have split along craft lines.

Mitchell believes that Australia needs an incomes policy. Since the arbitration system can affect wages, as seen by the uniformity of wage increases and the compression of the distribution of wages in Australia compared to other countries, the system is functionally capable of being an instrument of incomes policy. The wage pause in 1983 is cited as evidence that it can work. Thus Mitchell recommends that the Arbitration Commission should promote national gain-sharing with less inflation.

The Financial System

The financial system of Australia has been intensively studied as a consequence of the Campbell report.[24] The chapter by Andrew S.

24. Australian Financial System Inquiry (Campbell Committee), *Final Report of the Committee of Inquiry* (Canberra: AGPS, 1980).

Carron outlines the developments, including extensive reviews of applicable government policies and a rethinking of policies and regulations. Since many policy changes are of recent origin (several occurring during the course of this study), all consequences could not be evaluated; however, their likely effects are analyzed in general terms. The major distinction in Australian regulation is that between bank and nonbank financial institutions. Banks have been given special privileges denied others, for instance, to accept transactions deposits and deal in foreign exchange. However, banks must accept greater regulation to guarantee the integrity of the system and also to serve other social purposes such as providing credit to small businesses, farmers, and housing developers. The movement toward less regulation and greater market determination, which is the major thrust of the Campbell report reform process, will increase the efficiency of capital markets, but may raise questions concerning the prudent overseeing of the system.

Carron lists several types of continuing regulation as candidates for reform, including limitations on foreign ownership of banks and rules to ensure captive markets for government securities (both state and commonwealth). He also points out the inadequacy of existing reforms in addressing the problem of extreme seasonal swings in liquidity resulting from uneven tax payments to the commonwealth.

Fiscal Federalism

Australians have been critical of many aspects of their commonwealth tax system, but have tended to ignore the state-commonwealth provisions to equalize differences among the states. The chapter by Gramlich gives careful attention to these neglected matters and includes an examination of the basic goals of the tax system and an assessment of how effectively they are being achieved. Clearly there is great diversity of public expenditures despite fiscal equalization. The three separate instruments in the grant system are scrutinized: tax sharing grants, the Australian Loan Council, and specific-purpose grants. Throughout the chapter the questions addressed are: do the instruments promote the intended goals, and what are the efficiency costs? As Gramlich demonstrates, the goals are achieved by some definitions and not by others, and economic efficiency is sacrificed. The Loan Council in particular is seen to fall short of the ideal.

Gramlich also looks at the more general problem of the structure of Australian taxes, especially in relation to fixing responsibility. From an efficiency point of view, the decision of how much and to whom tax to be paid is often separated from the decision to spend, with unfortunate consequences. The Australian tax structure is marked by high marginal tax rates on earned income and no capital gains tax or death tax. As a result, the tax structure tends to reduce incentives to work, promote the so-called black economy, and divert scarce resources into socially unproductive efforts. The author devotes some attention to taxes on resources and recent proposals to change them.

Comparative Advantage

One major question arising from Australia's interaction with other countries is: what explains changes in Australia's comparative advantage? The chapter by Krause addresses this question by examining Australia's imports and exports to determine their dominant factor characteristics. Australia's comparative advantage is primarily in natural resource products; however, Australia also seems to have improved its position in the development of technological goods. To explore this hypothesis, Krause investigates Australia's trade with Japan and with the United States and finds weak confirming evidence.

In sharp contrast to other industrial countries, Australia's involvement in international trade declined in the early post-World War II period and then failed to increase (measured by either imports or exports as a percentage of GDP). Thus a second major question Krause explores is: what is the cause of the failure of Australia's trade ratios to rise? Several factors are considered but the most important cause seems to be the high level of protection provided at the Australian border and augmented by trade restrictions between the states. The tariff has long been an issue in Australian politics and is seen to be a commanding element in its economy, as is recognized in the chapter.

Australia's policy with respect to direct foreign investment is also examined. Although policymakers are not negative, the door is not wide open to foreign investors as it once was. The basic choice in both trade and international investment policy is whether Australia should become more outward oriented; if changes are to be made, the issue becomes one of implementation. Krause advocates much greater liberalization and distinct, even abrupt moves in that direction.

Scale, Openness, and Productivity in Manufacturing

How efficient is Australia's industry—indeed, how should one measure the efficiency of industry? These are the questions addressed in the chapter by Richard E. Caves. Industrial productivity in Australia is burdened by the relatively small size and geographic fragmentation of the national market and its insulation from international competition by trade restrictions and transportation costs. Producers operating under these constraints naturally choose technologies and management practices that involve small-scale and nonspecialized production facilities.

To investigate these forces, Caves develops a model that relates productivity and plant scale; he tests the model with a sample of Australian manufacturing industries and their counterparts in the United States. He confirms that scale economies and tariffs interact in a complex way to curb Australian productivity: the more formidable the scale economies are, the less likely is inefficient production to be viable for any given level of tariff protection. With these influences controlled, however, he finds few other influences that significantly affect the relative productivity of Australian industries. Similar techniques are used to explain interindustry differences in Australian plant scales. Caves confirms that Australian plants are small when protection is great and the diseconomies of small-scale operation not too onerous. The prevalence of foreign subsidiaries is shown to be positively related to plant scales, but foreign investment also interacts negatively with other influences.

Although these findings are tentative because of deficiencies in the data and various statistical problems, they are consistent with the results of a similar model developed for Canada and Britain.[25] And they contribute to a greater understanding of the effects of tariff policy, competition policy, and policy regarding industrial location and strategy.

Social Welfare

Australia's social welfare programs provide for the elderly, the ill, and the disabled. These programs are examined in the chapter by Aaron.

25. See the chapter by Caves.

A distinctive characteristic is that, unlike most other countries, Australia relies on income-test programs for the aged and the unemployed as well as for assisting the poor. Aaron devotes special attention to assistance for the aged, unemployment insurance, and health care.

The aged in Australia are assisted by a pension system that provides a flat-rate payment; this payment is unrelated to earnings experience but is subject to both a tax and a test for eligibility. As a result, the payment system is very generous to the poor. Australia's tax system also affects the aged by exempting capital gains, gifts, and inheritances from tax. Only recently has the government begun to lightly tax superannuation payments (modestly increasing overtime). Since coverage of superannuation is virtually universal for high earners and government employees but spotty for low earners, the tax system is generous to the aged who are rich. Thus it is the aged who fall in the middle who do not fare as well.

Unemployment insurance is provided to everyone regardless of previous work experience; the insurance subject to an income test can continue indefinitely subject to a willingness to accept a job. These features are believed to reduce the participation rate of both young and old workers in the labor market and contribute to long-term unemployment. This may be particularly disadvantageous for sixteen- and seventeen-year-olds who can qualify for unemployment by leaving school and have little incentive to accept low-paying jobs. Australia has a smaller share of persons aged sixteen to seventeen in school than other industrial countries and also a smaller share of students enrolled in higher education. Thus human capital formation may be being shortchanged in Australia.

Aaron also points out that Australia, unlike other industrial countries, has not seen a rising share of its income absorbed by medical care. It has been doing some experimentation in health care financing, and seems to have devised a system in which all patients are guaranteed access to basic care while hospitals are subject to budget control by states.

Concluding Comments

One observation that comes to mind after reviewing the Australian economy is that all forecasting is difficult and technology forecasting is hardest of all. Nevertheless, current research efforts in materials technology in the United States, Japan, and certain European countries show that a quantum breakthrough in new products is highly likely. The implications for Australia are profound. It is possible that development of ceramics, fiber optics, carbon fiber composites, powder alloys, and super polymers would do to copper, aluminum, and steel (and by implication to bauxite, iron ore, and coal) what synthetic fibers did to wool. Such developments would strain the adjustment capabilities of Australia given the importance of these products to Australia's export basket. There is no way to prepare for this in the short term, but much can be done to prepare for the future. Australia's response could be to hone the adjustment capabilities of its business firms by exposing them to world competition and preparing its young people by relatively large investments in human capital. It is doing neither. If no preparations are made, what will be the outcome for the next generation of Australians? Is the "lucky" country living in a fool's paradise?

Some issues that are taken up in the book cut across several chapters, and these are reviewed in the concluding chapter.

RUDIGER DORNBUSCH AND STANLEY FISCHER

The Australian
Macroeconomy

AUSTRALIA is a small, open economy with unusual wage-setting institutions. During the past twenty years its development has been similar to
that of most nations in the Organization for Economic Cooperation and
Development. Table 1 presents summary data on Australian economic
performance. Australia, like other nations in the OECD, has experienced
a marked deterioration in growth and inflation between the pre- and post-
1973 periods (see figure 1). For most variables shown in table 1,
the deterioration in Australian performance was slightly worse than
average. However, productivity growth fell less in Australia than in the
OECD as a whole.[1]

The similarity between the Australian and OECD experiences extends
to the debate about the causes of the worsened economic performance
after 1973. In Australia, as in Europe, discussion in the latter half of the
1970s centered on the behavior of real wages. The Australian real wage

The authors have benefited from the generous help and guidance offered by many
Australian economists. Financial support from the National Science Foundation is
greatly appreciated. We thank Data Resources, Inc., for making their data banks
available. We also thank Adrian R. Pagan and Peter D. Jonson, the discussants of this
chapter at the Brookings-Canberra Conference. Research assistance was provided by
Jenny Andersen, Patricia C. Mosser, and David W. Wilcox.

1. Norton compares Australian economic performance in the 1960s and 1970s with
that of nine other OECD countries. See W. E. Norton, *The Deterioration in Economic
Performance,* Occasional Paper 9 (Canberra: Reserve Bank of Australia, September
1982).

Table 1. *Economic Performance of Australia and the OECD Countries, Selected Periods, 1960–83*

Item	1960–73		1973–82		1983	
	Australia	OECD countries	Australia	OECD countries	Australia	OECD countries
Gross domestic product						
Growth rate	5.1	5.0	1.7	2.1	−1.3	2.3
Growth rate per employee[a]	2.4	3.9	1.2	1.5	n.a.	n.a.
Consumer price inflation (annual average)	3.5	3.9	11.5	10.1	n.a.	5.1
Unemployment rate (annual average)[b]	1.9	3.0	5.4	5.6	10.3	9.0

Sources: Data through 1981 are from Organization for Economic Cooperation and Development, *Historical Statistics, 1960–1981* (Paris: OECD, 1983), pp. 44, 47, 83. Data for 1982–83 are from *OECD Economic Outlook*, vol. 30 (December 1981), p. 142 and vol. 34 (December 1983), pp. 14, 26, 45, 55, 113, 163.

n.a. Not available.

a. Data are for 1973–80.

b. Standardized OECD definition based on fifteen countries: Australia, Austria, Belgium, Canada, Finland, France, Germany, Italy, Japan, Netherlands, Norway, Spain, Sweden, United Kingdom, and the United States. Data in the second column are for 1965–73; data in the fourth column are for 1974–82.

rose with the wage explosion of 1974, which is shown in figure 2, and did not fall thereafter. By 1983 the focus had shifted to the Treasury's view that expansionary aggregate demand policy could only reignite inflation despite unemployment rates above 10 percent. Here, too, the similarity with Europe is marked.

Four issues stand out in the Australian macroeconomic policy discussion: the wage-setting process and the role of the Australian Conciliation and Arbitration Commission; the scope for fiscal policy to stimulate demand; the resources boom; and questions surrounding the interaction of monetary and exchange rate policy.

The predominant concern in the Australian wage debate is the role of the Arbitration Commission in the wage determination process. The Treasury takes the view that a move to decentralized bargaining is desirable. Alternative views range from acceptance of the commission as a more or less unfortunate fact of life to the belief that the commission could, by putting appropriate flexibility in wage indexation, play a valuable role in maintaining labor peace and macroeconomic adjustment. On the budget question there is sharp disagreement between a Keynesian view that high unemployment warrants all-out fiscal expansion and the

Figure 1. *Growth and Inflation in Australia and the OECD Countries,*
1967–83

Annual percentage change

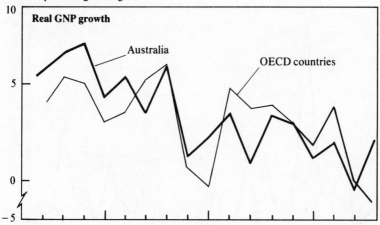

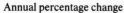

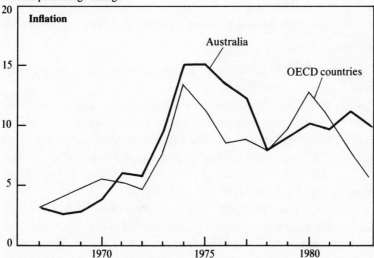

Sources: GDP—International Monetary Fund, *International Financial Statistics,* computer tapes, and *OECD Economic Outlook,* vol. 34 (December 1983), pp. 18–19, 152, inflation—*OECD Economic Outlook,* vol. 34, pp. 14, 104, 161.

Figure 2. *Wage and Price Inflation, 1972:1 to 1983:1*

Quarterly percent change

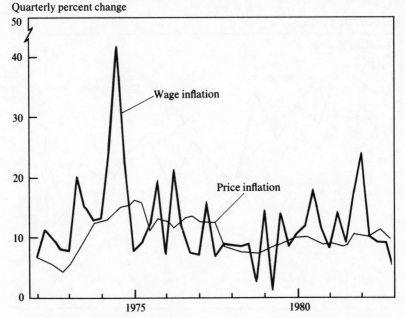

Sources: Price inflation—International Monetary Fund, *International Financial Statistics*, computer tapes; wage inflation—data provided by R. G. Gregory.

highly conservative Treasury view, which questions the sustainability of any expansionary fiscal policy.

In the late 1970s, as a consequence of the oil shock and increased real prices of resources, an investment boom took place in Australian resources. The expectation was that the development and export of resources would have a fundamental impact on the macroeconomy. The policy discussion at the time was about how best to take advantage of resources through exchange rate and trade policy.

Australia saw in December 1983 a dramatic innovation in the exchange rate calculation: exchange controls were removed across the board and the rate was allowed to float. The question now is how to coordinate monetary and fiscal policy under flexible rates and what room to give to foreign exchange market intervention.

We begin this chapter with a brief description of the structure of the Australian economy and its development over the past twenty years. We then take up in turn the issues of wage determination and unemploy-

Table 2. *Structure of Aggregate Demand in Australia and the OECD Countries, 1967–73 and 1974–81*
Percent of GDP

| | 1967–73 | | 1974–81 | |
Item	Australia	OECD	Australia	OECD
Private consumption	60.6	60.3	60.0	60.9
Government consumption	12.5	16.2	16.1	16.8
Government outlays	25.9	32.7	33.1	38.4
Gross fixed investment	25.5	21.8	23.1	21.8
Exports	15.0	13.3	16.1	18.5
Imports	14.9	12.9	17.1	18.8

Sources: OECD, *Historical Statistics, 1960–1980*, pp. 58–60, 62, 63; and OECD, *Historical Statistics, 1960–1981*, pp. 62, 64, 65, 67, 68.

ment, the resource boom, fiscal policy, and monetary and exchange rate policy. The chapter ends with a discussion of policy alternatives.

The Australian Economy: Structure and Trends

Australian GNP in 1982 was $152 billion, just over $10,000 per capita, compared with U.S. per capita GNP in that year that was more than $13,000.[2] Table 2 shows the structure of aggregate demand in the Australian economy and in the OECD as a whole from 1967 to 1981.

Australia's share of consumption expenditures in GDP is almost identical to the OECD average; it is thus somewhat below the U.S. share and well above that for Japan and for Germany. Investment is a higher proportion of GDP in Australia compared to the OECD average, but Australia does not have a large investment share in OECD terms— during 1974–81, eight other OECD countries invested a higher share of their GDP, and another two countries invested about the same amount, despite the Australian raw materials boom. Like OECD countries, Australia has shown a trend toward larger government; Australian government consumption (also shown in table 2) has risen more rapidly than the OECD average, but government outlays in Australia are still well below the OECD average. Indeed, during this same 1974–81 period

2. In 1982 the average exchange rate between the U.S. and the Australian dollar was close to unity. In 1983 the rate was about $0.90 (U.S.) per $1.00 (Australian).

government outlays as a percentage of GNP in Australia were slightly below those of the United States.

The share of agriculture in output has fallen rapidly in Australia during the past twenty years. The share of manufacturing is below the OECD average. Mining output is of course larger than the OECD average, and grew rapidly between 1967–81 and 1974–81. The share of services is slightly below the OECD average.

Trade and the Balance of Payments

The low export and import shares in output in table 2 seem to belie our description of Australia as an open economy: among OECD countries, only the United States, Japan, Spain, and Turkey have smaller shares of trade in GDP. The low trade share is in part a result of Australia's location and transportation costs, and in part a consequence of quotas and high tariffs. Despite the small shares of imports and exports, many of Australia's macroeconomic problems are associated with its openness—for instance, the problems of exchange rate management, resource booms, other foreign-induced demand changes, and foreign interest rate movements.

The shares of Australian trade in GDP fell substantially after the Korean War commodities boom and are still low by the standards of OECD countries except for the United States.[3] Since the mid-1970s Australia's shares of both imports and exports in GDP have risen, with the share of exports fluctuating more. Table 3 provides details of the commodity composition of Australia's exported goods. Both that composition and the destination of exports have changed substantially in the post–World War II period. The percentage of exports and their destinations are shown below.

Destination of exports	1950–51 to 1954–55	1979–80 to 1980–81
United Kingdom	35.6	4.4
Other European Economic Community (EEC) countries	22.4	8.9
Japan	7.5	27.1
South and Southeast Asia	8.6	13.6
United States	9.4	11.0

3. Note that export and import shares for the OECD countries except for the United States are much larger than the shares when the United States is included: for exports the shares excluding the United States are 19.9 percent and 24.1 percent for the two periods, respectively; for imports these shares are 19.2 percent and 24.3 percent.

Table 3. *Commodity Composition of Exports, Selected Periods, 1950–82*
Percent of exports

Period	Wool	Other rural goods	Coal	Iron ore	Alumina[a]	Other metals	All other goods
1950–51 to 1954–55	50.7	31.1	0.1	n.a.	. . .	7.4	10.5
1965–66 to 1969–70	24.3	33.7	3.1	4.2	. . .	14.3	21.3
1970–71 to 1974–75	13.8	33.4	5.6	7.7	2.7	15.2	21.6
1975–76 to 1979–80	10.3	31.0	10.8	7.1	5.0	15.8	19.9
1980–81 to 1981–82	9.9	n.a.	11.3	6.4	n.a.	n.a.	n.a.

Sources: W. E. Norton, P. M. Garmston, and M. W. Brodie, *Australian Economic Statistics, 1949–50 to 1980–81: I. Tables*, Occasional Paper 8A (Canberra: Reserve Bank of Australia, May 1982), tables 1.3 and 1.4, pp. 5–6. Data for 1981–82 are from Australian Bureau of Mineral Resources, Geology and Geophysics, *Australian Mineral Industry Annual Review 1981* (Canberra: Australian Government Publishing Service, 1983), table 6, p. 9; and Australian Bureau of Statistics, "Exports and Imports (Balance of Payments Basis) at Constant Prices: Australia, September Quarter 1983," no. 5332.0 (Canberra: ABS, December 8, 1983), table 2, p. 5.
n.a. Not available.
a. Alumina was included in the "other metals" category before 1970.

Exports of wool have fallen from a little more than 50 percent of exports to less than 10 percent, while coal and metal have increased from less than 8 percent to more than 30 percent of exports. At the same time, exports have been redirected from Europe to Japan and Asia.

Changes in the commodity composition of imported goods have been less marked. Machinery and other manufactured goods made up 37.7 percent of imports in 1950–55 and a similar 38.3 percent in 1976–81. Mineral fuels and lubricants were below 5 percent of imports in 1970–73, increased to about 10 percent in the next few years, and have been about 13 percent from 1980 to the present. The shift in the sources of imports matched that in the destination of exports. Since the early 1960s Australia has had a substantial deficit in its goods account with the United States and a surplus with Japan.

The cyclical behavior of Australian trade can be seen in table 4, which shows the correlation of growth rates in total real GDP, nonfarm real GDP, farm real GDP, real exports, real imports, and net exports. Net exports are negatively related to growth of GDP and nonfarm GDP, but positively though insignificantly related to farm GDP. The correlation between trade and GDP is quite low, suggesting that domestic disturbances and shock absorbers, in the case of external disturbances, are important.[4]

4. Shann has given particular attention to measuring the contribution of the trade sector to macroeconomic stability. See Edward W. Shann, "The Size of the Mineral Sector: Volatility and Macroeconomic Effects" (Canberra: Australian National University, Centre for Resource and Environmental Studies, May 1983).

Table 4. *Cyclical Behavior of the GDP and Foreign Trade,
1970:1 to 1982:4*

Item	GDP	Nonfarm real DGP	Farm real GDP	Real exports	Real imports
Nonfarm real GDP	0.93	...	...	...	...
Farm real GDP	0.45	0.09	...	...	...
Real exports	0.27	0.23	0.17	...	...
Real imports	0.19	0.18	0.06	0.10	...
Net exports	−0.17	−0.20	0.02	−0.12	0.03

Source: Authors' calculations based on series data from Norton, Garmston, and Brodie, *Australian Economic Statistics.*

Figure 3 shows the terms of trade and the current account as a fraction of GDP. From 1950 to 1960, following the Korean War boom, the terms of trade deteriorated by 50 percent; since then there has been fluctuation, and a new peak was reached during the raw material boom of 1973. But even that peak was still 36 percent below the 1950 peak. The current account has been in deficit from 1960 to 1981 in every year with the exception of 1972–73, when a small surplus of less than 1 percent of GDP was posted. The usual pattern is one of current account deficit, and it has been more than 5 percent of GDP in some years. Australia is thus a net borrower in the world capital market. That borrowing is done both by the private sector and the government. In 1981 and 1982 the Australian deficit was more than $8 billion (measured in U.S. dollars), one of the largest current account deficits of the OECD countries aside from the United States and France.

Until 1971 the exchange rate for the Australian dollar was fixed relative to the pound sterling; between 1971 and 1974 the link was to the U.S. dollar; from 1974 to 1976 there was a fixed link to a mixed currency basket; and since then the currency has been on a managed float. Figure 4 shows the U.S.-Australian dollar exchange rate (index 1975 = 100) and an index of Australian competitiveness measured by the real effective exchange rate in manufacturing.[5] The data for the dollar exchange rate

5. The data for the index of competitiveness were kindly provided by R. B. Whitelaw. See also R. B. Whitelaw, "Australia's International Competitiveness: Measurement and Significance," paper presented at the Twelfth Conference of Economists (Hobart, August 1983). We note here that measures of competitiveness in manufacturing vary significantly depending on whether or not manufactured foods are included. The Morgan Guaranty series, for example, focuses on nonfood manufactures and shows peak losses in competitiveness in 1976 and 1982 with a 5 percent real depreciation between 1982 and 1983:3.

Figure 3. *Current Account and Terms of Trade, 1960–82*

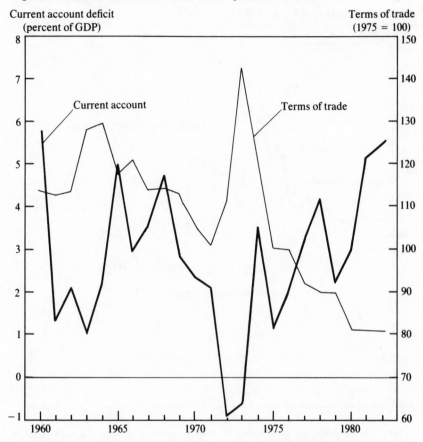

Current account deficit
(percent of GDP)

Terms of trade
(1975 = 100)

show substantial movements, as does the index of competitiveness in manufacturing. It is quite apparent that the dollar exchange rate has moved significantly more than the measure of competitiveness, reflecting in part an exchange rate policy geared to offsetting inflation differentials and in part a policy that recognizes Australia's multilateral trade patterns. Even so there are significant fluctuations in the real exchange rate in the 1978–81 period. The strong appreciation of the U.S. dollar relative to the yen and European currencies starting in 1981 did not enhance Australian competitiveness, even though it compensated for some of the loss in competitiveness that peaked in 1981.

Figure 4. *U.S.-Australian Dollar Exchange Rate and Real Effective Exchange Rate, 1968:3 to 1983:1*

Index, 1975 = 100

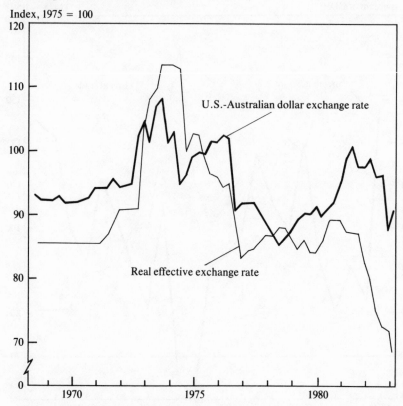

Source: Exchange rate—International Monetary Fund, *International Financial Statistics,* computer tapes; real effective rate—data provided by R. Whitelaw.

Inflation and Unemployment

As table 1 shows, in the 1960s Australia had little inflation and a low level of unemployment; both rose in the early 1970s, but the most rapid increase in inflation in Australia followed the wage explosion of 1973–74. The CPI inflation rate rose above 15 percent in 1974 and only slowly came down to the single-digit range by the end of the decade after a prolonged period of high unemployment. In the 1980s inflation has remained at about 10 percent while the unemployment rate has reached a post–World War II high.

Figure 5 presents Australian and OECD inflation and unemployment

Figure 5. *Inflation and Unemployment in Australia and the OECD Countries, 1967–83*

Inflation (percent)

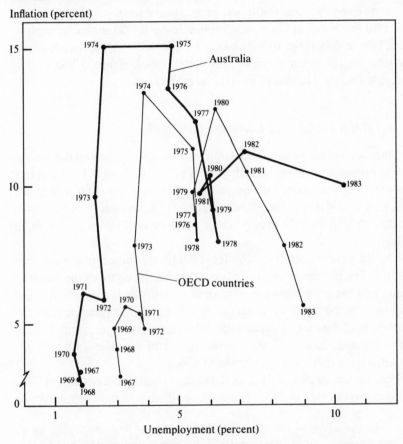

Unemployment (percent)

Sources: Inflation—*OECD Economic Outlook*, vol. 34 (December 1983), pp. 14, 104, 161; unemployment—Organization for Economic Cooperation and Development, *Historical Statistics, 1960–1980* (Paris: OECD, 1983), p. 37, and *OECD Economic Outlook*, vol. 34 (December 1983), pp. 14, 45, 163.

rates for the 1967–83 period. Australian relative performance began to deteriorate in 1971; by 1977 the Australian inflation rate was well above the OECD average, while the unemployment rate had risen to the average OECD level. By 1980 Australia's inflation and unemployment rates were both below OECD averages, but thereafter relative economic performance again deteriorated.

The Australian unemployment rate in figure 5 takes two big jumps. In

1975 it rose from about 2 percent to about 5 percent. Between 1981 and 1983 the unemployment rate increased from 6 percent to more than 10 percent. Even the most optimistic projection of the unemployment rate made for the National Economic Summit in April 1983 shows unemployment falling very little, to 8.7 percent by 1985–86.[6] The discussion thus focuses on the unemployment problem, which figure 5 shows has worsened relative to that of the OECD as a whole.

Monetary, Fiscal, and Exchange Rate Policy

Macroeconomic policy discussion in Australia focuses on the budget that is presented in August each year. The key document in this policy discussion is Statement 2 of the *Budget Statement*, which describes the Treasury's analysis of the economic impact of the budget and communicates the Treasury's views of the wisdom or folly of government policy.[7]

The Reserve Bank is a semi-independent body subject to government control. The Secretary to the Treasury sits on the board of the Reserve Bank, and the government has the right to overrule the board. When it does so, the board is supposed to report on the disagreement to the Parliament. It has not yet made a formal report of a disagreement, though there are descriptions in the annual report of episodes in which the Reserve Bank influenced government policy.[8]

Figure 6 shows annual data for the budget surplus as a percent of GDP and the growth rate of M3.[9] The striking difference between Australia

6. See *National Economic Summit Conference, April 1983: Projections of the Australian Economy to 1985–86* (Canberra: Australian Government Publishing Service, 1983), p. 34.

7. For a review of the development of this budget statement and a comparison between the Treasury and the Reserve Bank analyses of policy, see P. P. McGuinness, "Statement No. 2 and Reserve Bank Annual Report," *The Economic Record*, vol. 58 (December 1982), pp. 303–10.

8. For example, in its 1983 report, the Bank explains how the government did not, in the face of opposition, follow through on a plan to release bank reserves to finance housing. See *Reserve Bank of Australia, Report and Financial Statements 1983* (Canberra: RBA, 1983), p. 7.

9. The budget surplus is the series for net lending of government in the OECD statistics. See, for example, Organization for Economic Cooperation and Development, *Historical Statistics, 1960–1981* (Paris: OECD, 1983), p. 65. The M3 is defined as M1 plus "quasi-money" in the International Monetary Fund statistics.

Figure 6. *Money Growth and the Budget Surplus, 1961–82*

Percent

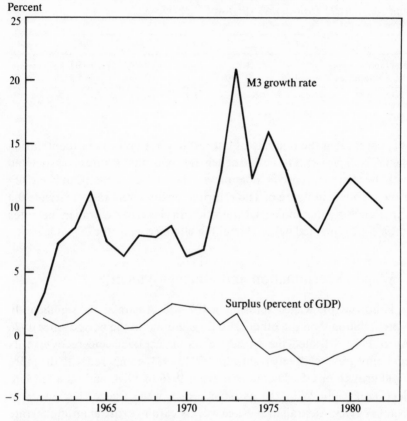

Sources: *OECD Economic Outlook*, vol. 34 (December 1983), pp. 33, 159–60; and International Monetary Fund, *International Financial Statistics*, computer tapes.

and the OECD countries appears in the history of net government lending documented in table 5. Australia has long had much smaller lending deficits than the OECD countries. Only in 1983 and 1984 are Australian lending deficits large, and as large as those of OECD countries. In fact throughout the 1961–75 period net government lending was positive in every single year. Since then, with the exception of 1977 and 1981, there have been lending deficits every year. Money growth, also shown in figure 6, was high in the two periods of instability, 1972–76 and 1979–81. The data immediately raise a major question: are budget deficits and, in particular, money growth the main culprits in the inflation story?

Figure 7 shows the short-term interest rate and the rate of inflation. It

Table 5. *Net Government Lending of Australia*
and the OECD Countries, 1960–84
Percent of GDP

Country	1960–67	1968–73	1974–81	1982	1983[a]	1984[a]
Australia	1.4	1.9	−1.0	0.2	−4.3	−4.3
OECD countries	−0.1	0.1	−1.9	−4.2	−4.3	n.a.

Sources: OECD, *Historical Statistics, 1960–1981*, p. 65; and *OECD Economic Outlook*, vol. 34 (December 1983), p. 33.
a. OECD forecasts, from *OECD Economic Outlook*, vol. 33 (July 1983), p. 34.

is apparent that the real rate of interest has been positive except during the 1972–77 period. The period of negative real interest rates is associated with the sharp increase in inflation and the strong acceleration in money growth shown in figure 6. The return to positive real rates matches the experience of other industrial countries: the level of Australian real rates in 1981–82 remained below that of the United States, for example.

Wage Determination and Unemployment

Following the wage explosion of 1973–75, Australia had significantly more inflation than the other OECD countries. In the period since 1976 Australia has trailed the world trends in recession and recovery; its economy grew relatively fast from 1979 to 1981, compared with the more rapid growth of OECD countries from 1976 to 1978, and then fell into deep recession. With the assistance of a wage freeze that ended in October 1983, Australian average weekly earnings rose at an annual rate of only 4 percent through the first two quarters of 1983 after increasing by 14 percent over the previous four quarters. Despite the lower rates of wage inflation, the Australian CPI increased at an annual rate of more than 8 percent during the first two quarters of 1983, presumably because of lagged responses to earlier wage increases. The OECD projects that the Australian GDP will grow by more than 4 percent in 1984; however, unemployment is predicted to decrease only slowly, and inflation is expected to remain at more than 7 percent.

The Expectations-Augmented Phillips Curve

Central to the discussion about wages in Australia is the issue of stability in the Phillips curve. More specifically, is there a relation

Figure 7. *Short-term Interest Rate and Rate of Inflation, 1961–82*

Percent

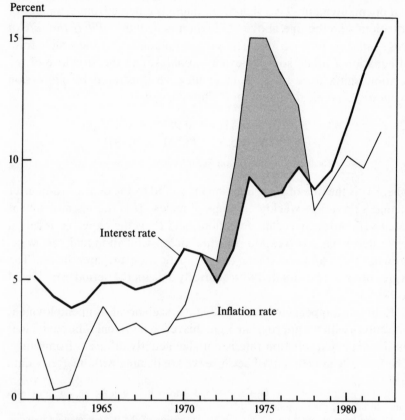

Sources: International Monetary Fund, *International Financial Statistics*, computer tapes; and *OECD Economic Outlook*, vol. 34 (December 1983), pp. 14, 45, 163.

between the rate of increase in money wages, W, and the rate of unemployment relative to the natural rate $(U - \overline{U})$; and between W and the rate of expected inflation, P^*? This relation can be expressed as

(1) $$W = a + b(U - \overline{U}) + cP^*.$$

One would expect unemployment above the natural rate to exert a dampening effect on wage inflation, that is, the coefficient b should be negative. Moreover, expected inflation P^* should translate one-for-one into wage inflation so that the coefficient c should be unity.

The increase in Australian unemployment in the 1970s, combined with the higher inflation of that period, led to reconsideration of the nature and existence of a short-run Phillips trade-off between inflation and unemployment. Two significant findings emerge from estimates of equations like the one above.[10] The first is *demand affects the rate of wage inflation in Australia*. The second finding is that the simple form of equation 1 omits some relevant variables, and the structure of the relation shifts over time. Both results are illustrated by regression equation 2, a typical Australian Phillips curve:[11]

$$(2) \qquad W = -12.18 - 3.51U + 0.95P^* + 0.25Time,$$
$$\qquad\qquad (-1.87)(-4.57) \quad (5.55) \quad\;\; (2.97)$$

$R^2 = 0.43$, Durbin-Watson = 2.07, standard error = 4.56

where W is the rate of wage inflation measured by the quarter-to-quarter change of average weekly earnings of males, U is the unemployment rate (NIF, Australian data definition), and P^* is the expected inflation generated from a regression of actual on past inflation and past wage growth. Here and elsewhere the t-statistics are in parentheses. The regressions were estimated with quarterly data for the period from 1966:4 to 1982:4.[12]

Equation 2 appears to be acceptable at first glance. The unemployment rate enters with the appropriate sign; this result is typical. The coefficient on the expected inflation rate is not significantly different from unity. The low R^2 can be excused because we are dealing with quarterly data

10. We are grateful to R. G. Gregory and Adrian R. Pagan for providing us with data and offering their comments.

11. We present equation 2 mainly as an illustration of the type of relation found in the Phillips curve literature; because it fails to model the natural rate of unemployment, or to include variables reflecting real wage resistance, relative price variables, and award wages, equation 2 is almost certainly misspecified. We note also that the unemployment rate on the right-hand side should be treated as endogenous; when we calculated the unemployment rate, with government spending and the growth rate of M3 as instruments, the results changed very little.

12. When the time trend is omitted the equation becomes

$$W = 6.68 - 1.46U + 1.06P^*.$$
$$(4.38)(-4.06) \quad\;\; (6.00)$$

$R^2 = 0.35$, Durbin-Watson = 1.88, standard error = 4.84

The coefficient of unemployment changes appreciably, but remains significant. The coefficient of expected inflation remains insignificantly different from unity. These findings differ from those of Kirby, who finds a coefficient on P^* well above unity. See Michael G. Kirby, "An Investigation of the Specification and Stability of the Australian Aggregate Wage Equation," *The Economic Record*, vol. 57 (March 1981), pp. 35–46.

in which the underlying variation is itself large. However, the significance of the trend term implies that other relevant variables are omitted. We discuss below candidates for the role of shift variables. Researchers working with equations like 2 have employed a variety of demand indicators, including unemployment, weighted unemployment rates, vacancies, overtime hours, actual relative to potential output, and no doubt others.[13] From the standpoint of policy the key question about the Phillips curve is of course the nature of the trade-off—particularly in the short run—between unemployment and inflation. From this perspective the most important issue to emerge from the discussion of the appropriate demand indicator is that pursued by Gregory, who argues that unemployment (or conditions in the labor market in general) has no effect on wages, but that labor tightness *within the firm* does affect the rate of wage change.[14] The tightness of demand for labor within the firm is measured by overtime hours.[15]

The Gregory argument that the demand for labor within the firm rather than the excess demand in the marketplace determines the rate of wage change is buttressed by reference to implicit contracts between firms and workers, in which firms agree, among other things, not to reduce real wages during recessions or hire new workers at lower wages. Workers on their part agree not to push for increases in real wages when profits are low. The argument is motivated particularly by the increase in the inflation rate from 9.7 percent in 1981 to 11.2 percent in 1982, while the unemployment rate rose from 5.7 percent to 7.1 percent, and by the continued high inflation in 1983 even with an unemployment rate above 10 percent (see figure 5).

Gregory and Smith estimate a conventional Phillips curve for the 1966:4 to 1982:4 period and allow the coefficient on the unemployment

13. Challen describes the wage (and output) equations in five econometric models. See D. W. Challen, "The Wages-Employment Relationship in Australian Macro-Econometric Models" (Hobart: University of Tasmania, July 1983).

14. R. G. Gregory and Ralph E. Smith, "Unemployment, Inflation and Job Creation Policies in Australia" (Canberra: Australian National University, September 1983). See also Peter Scherer, "Insubstantial Compliance: Changes in Composition and Distribution of Earnings under Wage Indexation 1975–1980" (Canberra: Australian National University, August 1981).

15. An alternative interpretation of Gregory's results is that the *change* in the unemployment rate rather than the level affects the rate of wage increase. We examine this possibility below in the discussion of determinants of the natural rate of unemployment.

Table 6. *Wage Equation, 1966:4 to 1982:4*

| | Independent variable[a] | | | | Summary statistic | | | |
Equation	U1	U2	P*	Constant	Durbin-Watson	Standard error	Rho	R^2
6-1	−2.13	−1.64	1.20	7.29	1.98	4.81	n.a.	0.36
	(−3.51)	(−4.31)	(5.95)	(4.62)				
6-2	−1.16	−1.00	0.75	32.2	1.92	4.15	−0.16	0.52
	(−2.23)	(−3.08)	(3.95)	(6.1)				
6-3	−1.50	−1.54	0.80	37.3	1.96	3.70	−0.29	0.62
	(−3.70)	(5.19)	(6.28)	(9.18)				

Source: Data provided by R. G. Gregory, L. Defris, and R. Williams.
n.a. Not available.
a. The variable U1 is equal to the actual employment rate for 1966:4 to 1978:2 and zero thereafter; U2 is zero until 1978:3 and equal to the actual unemployment rate thereafter. The P* denotes the inflation prediction as in the previous equation. Equations 6-1 and 6-2 include a dummy variable that is zero except during the wage explosion of 1974:3, when it was unity. In equation 6-3 the P* denotes the expectation from surveys; see the text description.

rate to differ between two subperiods, with the second subperiod starting in 1978:3. The results of a similar procedure are shown in equations in table 6. They leave little question that there appears to be a *stable* Phillips curve with unemployment and expected inflation as the determinants of the rate of wage inflation. These results clearly differ from those of Gregory and Smith. In the first two equations of table 6, 6-1 and 6-2, the unemployment coefficients do not change significantly and expected inflation has a coefficient not significantly different from unity. Moreover, the equations explain a significant part of the variation in wage inflation.

The question then arises whether the difference with the findings of Gregory and Smith is merely due to the inflation prediction. Gregory and Smith use lagged actual inflation whereas we use a forecast from a prediction equation. A third alternative would be to use the actual expectations as they are reported in Defris and Williams.[16] This is done in equation 6-3 in table 6. The use of this expectations variable again yields stable unemployment coefficients and a coefficient for expected inflation that is not significantly different from unity.

16. L. Drefis and R. Williams, "The Formation of Consumer Inflationary Expectations in Australia," *The Economic Record*, vol. 55 (June 1979), pp. 136–48. The survey data start in 1973:1. Before that date we use the lagged average inflation rate for the preceding four quarters. We use the series of Defris and Williams that excludes expectations of negative inflation and inflation in excess of 100 percent. Updated data were provided by R. Williams.

The alternative series for expected inflation produces divergent regression results just as the overtime and unemployment variables do (see appendix to this paper for further details). They therefore can explain a number of differences in empirical findings. But we note that Gregory's Phillips curve based on overtime, unlike our formulation in table 6, is not stable. This is shown in the appendix table; using overtime as the cyclical variable leads to a shift in coefficients between the pre- and post-1978:2 periods and also leads to a coefficient on expected inflation that is significantly smaller than unity. Using overtime in place of unemployment is not a way of establishing a stable wage equation.

Gregory concludes, on the basis of his work, that there is little connection between the rate of unemployment and the rate of wage inflation. Although we are in sympathy with the view argued by Solow that employers do not push their short-run advantage to cut wages when unemployment is high, the Gregory-Smith argument is not watertight.[17] In the first place, the empirical evidence presented by Gregory and Smith is weak. The hypothesis that the coefficient on the unemployment rate remains the same over the entire period is not rejected.[18] Further, while firms are no doubt reluctant on morale grounds to take on workers willing to work for less than those they already employ, we find it difficult to imagine that unemployed individuals willing to work for less than those currently working do not exert some downward pressure on the rate of wage increase. Some of the effect could come through product markets, with firms—new or existing—willing to hire the unemployed at lower wages in order to undercut firms faced with higher labor costs. In addition, the argument puts considerable weight on the notion of implicit contracts, which are likely to have flexible terms that adjust to the realities of the marketplace. Explicit contracts do allow for periodic wage readjustments, and it is difficult to see why implicit contracts

17. Solow's argument is presented in Robert M. Solow, "On Theories of Unemployment," *American Economic Review*, vol. 70 (March 1980), pp. 1–11.

18. Trivedi notes that Gregory and Smith apparently did not experiment with forms of the Phillips curve in which unemployment or vacancies entered nonlinearly before reaching the conclusion that the overtime rate was a more appropriate demand indicator. The nonlinearity needed would have to imply that the effects of an extra percentage point of unemployment on wages are weaker at high unemployment rates (as in 1980–82) than at lower rates. Entering the unemployment rate in the form $1/u$ would have this property. See P. K. Trivedi, "Unemployment, Inflation and Job Creation Policies in Australia: A Comment" (Canberra: Australian National University, September 1983).

should be more rigid in renegotiating or resetting the wage rate when willing workers are available and when it is difficult to sell goods.

The Natural Rate of Unemployment

Increases in the natural rate of unemployment, the U in equation 1, would also help account for the high inflation of the last decade. Trivedi and Baker estimate equilibrium unemployment rates that correspond to equality between the unemployment rate and the vacancy rate—one possible interpretation of the condition that requires excess demand for labor to be zero.[19] Their estimated full employment rate of unemployment is 1.0 percent in 1968–69 and only 1.6 percent in 1976–77. Thus this measure of the natural rate of unemployment does not account for any substantial shift in the Phillips curve.

Similarly, Kalisch estimates that the weighted full employment rate of unemployment rose from 1.6 percent in 1966 to 1.7 percent in 1980.[20] This last result might seem surprising in light of the emphasis in the literature on changes in the composition of the labor force during the 1970s. Although there has been a clear increase in the proportion of women in employment and in the proportion of part-time workers, the structure of the labor force has not changed sufficiently to generate large changes in the weighted unemployment rate.

Under these interpretations the natural rate of unemployment does not show any substantial increase. It should be noted that Trivedi and Baker include in their estimates the rate of unemployment benefits and the rate of increase of the working-age population as determinants of the natural rate. An alternative approach argues that the notion of a natural rate is incorrect. Indeed, as pointed out by Trivedi, one interpretation of the Gregory-Smith premise is that the natural rate of unemployment fluctuates with the current rate of unemployment.[21] Since there is a connection between the amount of overtime and the unemployment rate

19. P. K. Trivedi and G. M. Baker, "Equilibrium Unemployment in Australia: Concepts and Measurement" (Canberra: Australian National University, Centre for Economic Policy Research, October 1983).

20. David Kalisch, "The Output Loss from Unemployment: Okun's Law Revisited," Working Paper 10 (Canberra: Bureau of Labor Market Research, August 1982).

21. Trivedi, "Unemployment, Inflation and Job Creation Policies in Australia: A Comment."

in the short run, the force of the Gregory argument must be that firms will in the long run choose a labor force of optimal size that is independent of the overall rate of unemployment. Any shifts in demand will alter overtime hours and produce changes in the rate of wage inflation that look exactly like a short-run Phillips trade-off; in this view, however, there is no mechanism for bringing the system back to any particular natural rate of unemployment.[22]

This argument is virtually equivalent to saying that it is the *change* in the unemployment rate, or the deviation of the unemployment rate from a distributed lag on past unemployment rates, that drives the rate of wage change. Our evidence is not strongly supportive of any simple version of the argument. We did not find a significant role for the change in the unemployment rate in the equations we investigated with quarterly data.

Taking an alternative approach, we modeled the natural rate, $\overline{U}$, as a three-year average of past unemployment rates. In that formulation the difference, $(U - \overline{U})$, does not play any significant role in the Phillips curve; nor does $\overline{U}$ when it is entered separately. A slow, moving average of the unemployment rate thus does not capture the shifts picked up in a time trend.

Real Wage Resistance

The discussion thus far has rejected or provided very little support for one interpretation of the view that the natural rate of unemployment shifts over time. An alternative hypothesis is that the natural rate fluctuates with the unemployment rate because workers, employed and unemployed, are unwilling to take real wage cuts; in other words, workers suffer from real-wage resistance. It is obvious that employed workers who can avoid having their real wages cut would prefer higher to lower wages. Thus we should certainly expect to see real wage resistance from the employed.

The question immediately raised by the real-wage resistance of the unemployed is whether such persons should be viewed as involuntarily

22. James Tobin, "Stabilization Policy Ten Years After," *Brookings Papers on Economic Activity, 1: 1980*, pp. 19–90, expresses the view that the natural rate may be substantially determined by recent history.

unemployed. If the unemployed prefer to continue searching for jobs with higher pay, we can either say that there is real wage resistance on their part or that the natural rate of unemployment is higher than we first thought.[23]

To test for real-wage resistance we created a variable measuring the current real wage relative to its last peak. We would expect real wages that are low relative to past peaks to lead to an acceleration of wage inflation in the presence of real-wage resistance. The evidence for such an effect, however, is not strong. The discrepancy between current and peak real wages is indeed significant, but it has the effect of lowering the significance of overtime or unemployment and reducing the coefficient of expected inflation. Real-wage resistance thus does not appear to be the missing variable. The significance of the variable does suggest, though, that it may play an important role in the wage process.

Award Wages and the Arbitration Commission

The Arbitration Commission is the most striking feature of the Australian wage-determination process. Treasury economists and those in the Australian industrial sector tend to believe that the origins of Australia's inflation and unemployment problems are in the commission's use of legalistic reasoning and concepts of fairness, equity, and worth in wage setting. Others consider the commission to be an ideal institution through which to administer a flexible, intelligent incomes and indexation policy. The extreme of such enthusiasm is expressed in a much quoted 1969 statement by E. H. Phelps Brown:

It may be an accident of history that long before the need for a national incomes policy was apprehended, Australia came to adopt procedures so propitious to

23. Trivedi and Baker include the level of the real wage as a determinant of the equilibrium unemployment rate in their neo-Keynesian (disequilibrium) and search-theoretic models. These can be viewed as models of the natural rate. They find a significant role for both the level and lagged rate of change of the real wage in determining the unemployment rate in their neo-Keynesian model. They do not explicitly estimate a Phillips curve in their work, but the approach that argues that the natural rate, U (in their equation 14'), is a function of current and lagged wages is not far from an alternative that does not allow the real wage to influence U but assumes the aspiration wage affects the rate of nominal wage change. See Trivedi and Baker, "Equilibrium Unemployment in Australia."

one; but that they should now be available to meet the needs of the hour seems to me a precious legacy of their history for the Australian people.[24]

It is noted almost as frequently, though apparently without justification, that this author's enthusiasm had waned by 1977.[25]

A major concern from the macroeconomic viewpoint is whether the Arbitration Commission merely reproduces decisions on nominal and real wages that would in any event be reached if the commission did not exist or whether it has independent effects on wages. There is an extensive literature on the effects of the arbitration system on *relative* wages; typically analysts compare the Australian wage structure with that of other countries. Mulvey describes the evidence as inconclusive.[26] Evidence that the commission affects relative and real wages would suggest that it also influences the inflation process. But the commission could have a powerful impact on the overall rate of nominal wage increase while having no persistent effects on the structure of relative wages.

The macroeconometric models of Australia's wage-determination process also have to deal with the role of the wage tribunals. Nevile includes the rate of increase of award wages in his Phillips curve for prices and models award wages as determined by lagged output, but he needs dummy variables to account for the 1973–75 wage explosion.[27] Further, he is unable to find a satisfactory equation to describe award wage determination for the 1954–67 period. The implication is that the Arbitration Commission can have an independent effect on wage setting and thus on inflation. NIF-10, an Australian model and data base, includes an explanation of the level of award wages based on the decision in the national wage case and the award to the metals trades, which are treated as exogenous.[28] Similarly, award wages are exogenous in the

24. Quoted in J. P. Nieuwenhuysen and J. Sloan, "Wages Policy," in F. H. Gruen, ed., *Surveys of Australian Economics* (Sydney: George Allen & Unwin, 1978), p. 117.

25. We owe the qualification to Joseph Isaac.

26. Charles Mulvey, "Arbitration, Collective Bargaining and the Wage Structure: A Review of Some Empirical Evidence" (Nedlands: University of Western Australia, 1983).

27. J. W. Nevile, "Monetary and Fiscal Policies against Stagflation," Centre for Applied Economic Research, paper 19 (Kensington: The University of New South Wales, June 1983).

28. The wage-price sectors of the major models are described in Challen, "The Wages-Employment Relationship in Australian Macro-Econometric Models."

model developed by the Reserve Bank of Australia, RBA 2, and feed back into actual wages.

Contributions to this literature have also been made outside the context of macroeconomic models. Jonson, Mahar, and Thompson examine data for the 1960–72 period and find that award wages affect earnings, but they are relatively unsuccessful in fitting an Arbitration Commission reaction function.[29] Trivedi and Rayner model award wages during the period 1964–74 as determined mainly by lagged real wage growth, "wage drift," and productivity. They typically explain 60 to 70 percent of the variation in wage awards, thus leaving room for the award process to add autonomously to inflation.[30]

On balance it appears that the Arbitration Commission does make a difference in the wage-setting process, as suggested by econometric evidence, anecdotal evidence, the apparent effectiveness of the 1972 decision supporting equal pay for women, and the fact that indexation was formally introduced across the board in Australia (for example from 1975 to 1981, and in 1982–83) and then rapidly abandoned.[31,32]

Because of the importance of the first wage explosion, we next examine the role of the commission from 1973 to 1975. The explosion began in 1973, in part as a result of increased food prices. The wage increases were also fueled by a national wage case in May 1973, in which the government stated: "It is the Commonwealth's opinion that there is

29. P. D. Jonson, K. L. Mahar, and G. J. Thompson, "Earnings and Award Wages in Australia," *Australian Economic Papers*, vol. 13 (June 1974), pp. 80–98. Related studies are surveyed in Nieuwenhuysen and Sloan, "Wages Policy." See also J. J. Pincus and G. A. Withers, "Economics of Regulation," in F. H. Gruen, ed., *Surveys of Australian Economics*, vol. 3 (Sydney: George Allen & Unwin, 1983).

30. The Trivedi-Rayner work develops and estimates a model of the labor market in which there are overlapping contracts well before this approach became fashionable in the United States. P. K. Trivedi and J. Rayner, "Wage Inertia and Comparison Effects in Australian Wage Determination, 1964–74," *The Economic Record*, vol. 54 (August 1978), pp. 195–218.

31. Barry Hughes, while generally placing little of the blame on the Arbitration Commission for the 1973–75 wages explosion, remarks on the 1974 May national wage case decision (to award an amount that was well below the likely increase in the cost of living), "It must rank as the daftest decision of the decade by a full bench. Presumably it was signalling that it was still alive amidst the wage explosion. It was a costly signal." See Barry Hughes, *Exit Full Employment* (Sydney: Angus and Robertson, 1980), p. 81.

32. One can contrast this indexation decision with, for example, the United States system, in which indexation enters in an uncoordinated fashion at the industry level.

scope in the capacity and the flexibility of the Australian economy for an appreciable increase in wages without undesirable inflationary consequences."[33]

Nieuwenhuysen and Sloan attribute some of the wage explosion to increases in the pay of female workers. This suggests that the Arbitration Commission helped the wage explosion by adding momentum to the process in 1973.[34] We also regard the period of indexation from 1975 to 1981, including episodes in which indexing was made partial rather than complete, as providing evidence that the commission can influence wage behavior—because we think that it would have been impossible not to pass on price increases resulting from changes in the exchange rate without the coordinating mechanism of the commission.[35]

One measure of the effectiveness of the commission is to study the impact of indexation on real wages. Our empirical evidence clearly points to a dampening effect of this indexation on real wages (relative to previous peaks) during the period from 1975 to 1980. Indexation appears to have reduced real wages relative to their peaks. The size of the real wage containment is estimated to be a little more than 2 percent.

The Treasury shares the view that the commission affects real and nominal wages and consistently opposed indexation during 1975–80 because it appeared to be responsible for keeping real wages high. The Treasury's preferred solution is to decentralize the wage-setting process, in the belief that the final outcome will be a system similar to that of the United States. Similarly, Corden refers to two principles of wage determination, comparative wage justice and bargaining power, and states, "As long as the Arbitration Commission and the State tribunals

33. Nieuwenhuysen and Sloan, "Wages Policy," p. 112.
34. The opposing view is taken by Hughes, who by and large absolves the commission from blame in this episode that so marked subsequent developments in the 1970s. He does this by asserting that the explosion occurred in 1974 rather than 1973—Australian wage increases in 1973 were high though not out of line with those of the rest of the OECD. But labor markets in 1974 were excessively tight and wages rose rapidly. Hughes blames employers for their willingness to grant wage increases in the 1974 boom, with the result that "the wage scene was one mad scramble" (see Hughes, *Exit Full Employment*, p. 81). Presumably the argument would be that the views expressed by the government in the 1973 national wage case would have influenced wages with or without the Arbitration Commission.
35. Details of the extent of indexation are presented in Indecs Economics, *State of Play 2, The Indecs Economics Special Report* (Sydney: George Allen & Unwin, 1982), p. 50.

play their part and yet are unable to discipline the strong unions the competition between the two principles will be worse than if they stayed right out."[36]

It is difficult, however, to restructure the Australian unions by industry, particularly when the aim of the government undertaking the restructuring is to reduce union power to affect wages. It is more likely that, if the commission were somehow abolished, Australian wage determination would reflect the discipline of the British system.

The Arbitration Commission is sometimes seen as the ideal arena in which to tame inflation through incomes policy. The basic argument for incomes policies is that there is an externality in the wage-setting process in which efforts by one group to raise relative wages increase nominal wages and eventually worsen inflation. Of course, a government that resolutely controls the level of nominal aggregate demand can prevent inflation, if necessary, by creating unemployment. But modern governments faced with a choice between inflation and unemployment will typically choose a little of each. Incomes policies, to which governments often turn despite their repeated failures, can make the trade-off more favorable but cannot substitute for noninflationary aggregate demand policies, which are the most important part of any program that seeks to maintain reasonable price stability.

The Arbitration Commission is not enthusiastic about the prospects of an incomes policy. In the May 1976 National Wage Case, it stated: "The Commission is a body independent of governments, unions and employers. It should not be seen as an arm of government which formulates wage decisions simply to 'fit in' with economic policy."[37] Thus the Commission does not now stand in an ideal position from which to direct an incomes policy.[38] It may nonetheless be "the best wheel in town at which to play regularly."

36. W. M. Corden, "The Wages Push and Macroeconomic Policy: The Dilemmas Ahead," *The Economic Record*, vol. 58 (June 1982), p. 116.

37. Gerard Henderson, "The Industrial Relations Club," *Quadrant*, vol. 27 (September 1983), p. 23.

38. For a discussion of the requirements for success of a more centralized wage policy see J. E. Isaac, "Economics and Industrial Relations," *The Journal of Industrial Relations*, vol. 24 (December 1982), pp. 495–516. Isaac, one of the commissioners and an economist, writes, "an institutional machinery for centralisation exists in Australia. However, the course for the future will be set not so much by wage tribunals as by the attitudes and actions of unions, employers and governments. There is, of course, no perfect solution to the wage problem" (ibid., p. 515).

The Role of Real Wages

We turn now to unemployment to discuss the role of the real wage in determining the levels of employment and unemployment in the 1970s and 1980s. This issue, above all others, has divided Australian macroeconomists—policy views range from the demand-expansion view of "full speed ahead and damn the torpedoes," a position taken by the Melbourne Institute, to the dour "real-wage overhang" pessimism that the Australian Treasury shares with the West German and other European policymakers.

The theoretical issues in the real-wage debate have been lucidly stated by Corden;[39] both theoretical and empirical aspects have been pursued by economists too numerous to mention.[40] In this section we briefly discuss the significance of high real wages for employment, and examine measures of the real-wage overhang.

The following diagram shows the regions in a disequilibrium real wage.[41] Combinations of spending and real wages are along the line $Y'Y'$ such that the goods market is in equilibrium: the lower the real wage is, the more labor firms will hire and the more output they will supply; to clear the goods market at lower real wages, higher levels of spending are required. Points to the right of $Y'Y'$ correspond to excess demand. Here spending exceeds the level of output that firms choose to supply. The line $N'N'$ shows full employment, points to the left corresponding to unemployment. We use this figure to discuss whether unemployment is due to a lack of demand—Keynesian unemployment—or due to exces-

39. W. M. Corden, "Wages and Unemployment in Australia," *The Economic Record*, vol. 55 (March 1979), pp. 1–19. See also Corden, "The Wages Push and Macroeconomic Policy: The Dilemmas Ahead."

40. For the flavor of the empirical disputes, see Reserve Bank of Australia, *Conference in Applied Economic Research* (Canberra: Reserve Bank of Australia, 1979), chap. 5, with a contribution by R. G. Gregory and R. C. Duncan suggesting that supply—participation of females in particular—was as important a factor in the unusual labor market situation in the 1970s as the real wage overhang, and commentaries and discussion by several other participants. C. I. Higgins makes a particularly forceful presentation of the Treasury view. A recent survey paper is Paul A. Inglis and Paul A. Volker, "Unemployment in Australia: An Overview of the Issues" (Canberra: July 1983).

41. A similar analysis is developed in Rudiger Dornbusch and others, "Macroeconomic Prospects and Policies for the European Community," Centre for European Studies Paper 1 (Brussels: CES, 1983).

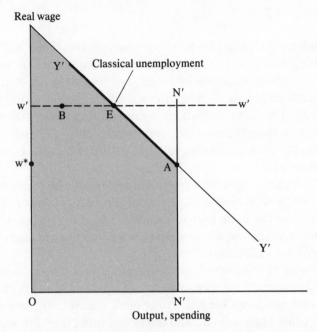

sive real wages—classical unemployment. In Corden's terms this would
be "union-voluntary unemployment."

Any point to the left of $Y'AN'$ is a point at which, at the given real
wage, an increase in spending would raise employment. In this shaded
region firms cannot sell the output that they wish to produce at current
wages and prices. By contrast, along the segment $Y'A$ there is classical
unemployment. Because real wages (except at A) are too high, firms do
not find it profitable to hire all the available labor. At points along $Y'A$,
unlike those in the Keynesian unemployment region, an expansion in
nominal demand will lead to higher prices, not greater output.

Wage cutting achieves nothing of first-order importance to restore
full employment in the Keynesian region.[42] Because firms cannot sell as
much as they want, the marginal value of the product of labor exceeds
the real wage in this region; cutting real wages does not eliminate that
problem. What is needed is an expansion of demand. Expansionary
policies can increase output, along line $w'w'$ from B, say, as far as E. But

42. Reducing real wages may, because of distributional effects, also reduce demand
and output.

further demand expansion does not increase output as one moves to the right of E. Beyond E, firms are in labor-demand positions; they can sell all they want, but the real wage is too high for them to produce more.

The real-wage overhang debate has pitted those in favor of expansionary demand policies against others who believe it is essential to reduce the real wage. The debate thus apparently has focused on the question of whether the economy was after 1975 in a Keynesian or classical unemployment situation. Before proceeding, though, we note that, even if the economy were in the Keynesian region on $w'w'$, a policy of demand expansion could not return the economy back to full employment as long as the real wage remained above w^*, the equilibrium level. Thus if the real wage were above the equilibrium level, there would be a rationale for policies that reduce the real wage to w^*—and at the same time adjust the level of demand appropriately to restore output to the full-employment level. The difficulty is, of course, that demand-side policies aimed at reducing real wages also reduce aggregate demand.

The most direct test for whether the economy can be characterized as having Keynesian or classical unemployment is to compare the marginal value product of labor with the real wage paid by employers. In the absence of direct measures of the marginal product of labor, the production function can be used to deduce the marginal product of labor relative to the real wage.[43]

The trouble with judging real wages relative to their full employment levels is that labor productivity depends on the technology, which changes over time, on the amount and prices of factors such as energy and capital, and on employment itself. It is therefore necessary to determine the warranted wage, but the necessary information is not available, at least not in any precise form. One possibility is to use rough

43. We have not seen direct production-function estimates of the relation between the real wage and marginal product during the 1970s. Several studies assume that the real wage is equal to the marginal product and thus that unemployment is classical. See, for instance, P. D. Jonson, R. Battellino, and F. Campbell, "Unemployment: An Econometric Dissection," Research Discussion Paper 7802 (Canberra: Reserve Bank of Australia, December 1978); and C. W. Murphy and R. J. Brooker, "Real Wages and Employment" (Department of the Treasury, May 1983). Symons estimates a standard demand function for labor (including raw materials as an input) but tests for Keynesian unemployment by including the level of output in the labor-demand function. He finds weak support for the existence of Keynesian unemployment. See J. Symons, "Employment and the Real Wage in Australia," Working Paper 513 (Centre for Labour Economics, March 1983).

approximations: movements of real wages relative to productivity trends or to movements in the share of labor in output. Typically if the share of labor rises, unemployment would be classical. But these rough measures can lead to seriously misleading real-wage increases and to assumptions that the elasticity of substitution in production is high. In these circumstances one would expect to observe a fall in labor's share together with a decline in employment. Yet unemployment would clearly be classical. Suppose, by contrast, there were a reduction in demand that reduced output and employment at unchanged real wages. If productivity declined, as is usual in a recession, one would expect to see growth in labor's share even though unemployment is Keynesian.[44]

Identification of unemployment as Keynesian or classical does not automatically imply the appropriate policies to restore the economy to full employment. Consider two different calculations that could be made if the economy's production function is known. First, compare the marginal product of labor with the real wage. If the former exceeds the latter, the economy has Keynesian unemployment; policies of demand expansion can reduce unemployment, and can continue to do so as long as the marginal product of labor remains above the real wage. Second, compare the current real wage with the real wage that would prevail if the labor force were fully employed. If the current real wage exceeds the full employment real wage, the economy could not return to full employment purely through demand-expansion policies.

The first three columns of table 7 show measures of the real wage. Real wages rise a minimum of 10 percent over the two years from 1973 to 1975 and continue rising thereafter. This shock to real wages was accompanied by the first substantial rise in unemployment, as can be seen in figure 5. Was this Keynesian or classical unemployment? We do not know, though because the real wage rose rapidly at a time of increasing unemployment, it was quite likely classical unemployment. The last three columns provide measures of the wage gap, the amount

44. If the actual production function is known and we assume there is a Cobb-Douglas function, we have a simple relation to use. Let x be the marginal product of labor; Y, output; w, real wage; and N, employment. With a Cobb-Douglas production function $a = xN/Y$ is constant. The actual labor share is $a' = wN/Y$. Combining the two expressions yields $a'/a = w/x$. Thus if the actual share is below the equilibrium share, the marginal product exceeds the real wage and unemployment in Keynesian economics.

Table 7. *Measures of Real Wages and the Wage Gap, 1972–82*

	Real wage			Wage gap		
Year	Real hourly earnings in manufacturing	Nonfarm average real labor costs	Average real hourly earnings	Ratio of wages to productivity in manufacturing	Nonfarm unit-labor costs	Wage share
1972	100	100	100	0.0	100	54.1
1973	104	105	99	−3.1	101	54.1
1974	117	111	104	1.9	106	54.2
1975	124	115	117	8.9	107	56.7
1976	126	117	119	3.6	106	57.8
1977	125	120	118	0.8	106	56.8
1978	124	121	121	−2.5	105	56.7
1979	122	120	118	−8.7	103	55.7
1980	122	122	n.a.	−9.6	103	54.1
1981	123	126	n.a.	−11.1	104	54.2
1982	127	131	n.a.	n.a.	105	55.6

Sources: Real hourly earnings—OECD, *Historical Statistics, 1960–1981*, table 9.2, p. 90; and OECD, *Economic Outlook* (December 1983), table 19, p. 51; average real labor costs—*National Economic Summit Conference, April 1983: Information Paper on the Economy* (Canberra: AGPS, 1983), p. 82 (number for a given year is the average of data for the two fiscal years within which it falls); average real hourly earnings—average hourly earnings divided by CPI, from Norton, Garmston, and Brodie, *Australian Economic Statistics*, pp. 204, 214; wages relative to productivity—earnings from first column, real value added per worker from OECD, *Historical Statistics, 1960–1981*, p. 48; and calculation of average hours worked from Norton, Garmston, and Brodie, *Australian Economic Statistics*, pp. 101, 107. Unit-labor costs are from *Budget Statements 1983–84*, Budget Paper 1 (Canberra: AGPS, 1983), p. 28; wage share is based on *National Summit Conference, April 1983: Information Paper*, p. 85.
   n.a. Not available.

by which the wage has grown relative to productivity during the period since 1972. The first measure of the wage gap is for the manufacturing sector, in which the wage gap grew rapidly until 1975 and then disappeared fast as productivity caught up and overtook real-wage growth. During this period the labor force in manufacturing was reduced. The behavior of this measure reflects one of the difficulties of using the conventional wage-gap data: productivity can be made to outstrip the rise in the real wage by reducing the labor force. Each of the remaining two measures of the gap rises rapidly to about 10 percent above the base level and then falls slowly until the latter part of the 1970s.[45]

45. Bruno and Sachs present unpublished OECD wage gap data—which they describe as unreliable—that show the Australian real wage gap to be 15 percent in 1974, the highest for all the OECD countries. This suggests that if there were classical unemployment anywhere in the OECD, it was quite likely to have been in Australia. From an unpublished paper by Michael Bruno and Jeffrey Sachs, "Wages, Profits, and Commodity Prices: Macroeconomics of Stagflation" (October 1983), table 11.4.

Under the hypothesis that the real wage is exogenous, the series in the first three columns of table 7 show how much the marginal product of labor *at full employment* would have had to rise to maintain full employment. Increases in the full-employment marginal product could have come from investment or from technological progress. Murphy and Brooker estimate this technological progress to have taken place at the rate of 1.2 percent a year during the 1970s. This would have still left an increase of 10 percent in wages to be adjusted during the 1972–80 period.

If the production function is Cobb-Douglas, with a labor share of 0.75 and capital the only other factor, the elasticity of the real wage with respect to the capital stock is 0.25.[46] Thus it would take an increase of more than 40 percent in the capital stock to raise the employment level of the real wage by 10 percent. This suggests that the high-investment approach to controlling excessive real wages is not viable in any reasonable time period. There seems to be little choice but to try to lower real wages. We examine the policy options below.

The Resource Boom

Australia has on several occasions been the testing base for the macroeconomics of natural resource issues. Cairnes invented the notion of nontraded goods in the context of the nineteenth century gold boom, and commodity prices were central to the trade and debt questions of the 1930s and to the commodity boom and bust that followed the Korean War.[47] These issues are once again of interest after world oil price increases and resource development have created an enhanced role for resources in the Australian economy.

The first natural resource boom occurred in Australia in 1970–71 with the development of a coal supply for export to Japan, where it was used in the Japanese steel industry. A second Australian investment boom

46. More generally, the elasticity of the real wage with respect to the capital stock is higher the lower is the elasticity of substitution. If the production function is CES with elasticity of substitution s, then the elasticity of the real wage with respect to the capital stock is $(1 - a)/s$, where $(1 - a)$ is the share of capital.

47. E. J. Cairnes, *Some Principles of Political Economy Newly Expounded* (Harper & Brothers, 1974).

Table 8. *Profile of the Resource Boom, Selected Years,*
1982–90
Index 1981 = 100

Development stage	1982	1984	1986	1988	1990
Employment	144	191	216	267	252
Investment	144	101	76	74	34
Export	111	141	182	240	275

Source: Derived from Stephen Derrick, Daina McDonald, and Phyllis Rosendale, "The Development of Energy Resources in Australia: 1981 to 1990," *Australian Economic Review* (Third Quarter 1981), table 34, p. 51.

got under way in 1980–82; resources affected were alumina, uranium, oil and gas, and coal. An estimate by the OECD places investment in Australian resource sectors in the 1980–82 period at an annual rate of 3 percent of GDP.[48] The investment part of the resource boom is expected to taper off during the early 1980s when the export stage is to begin. Table 8 gives a profile of the expected path of constant-price export earnings, investment, and employment as of mid-1981. The world recession has set the projections back a few years.

Table 8 shows clearly the investment and export stages of the resource boom. The rising trend in employment suggests a growing demand for labor due to resources, but that must be interpreted with caution. The data do not show the labor demand associated with the investment stage. In fact it is possible that the investment stage should require more labor, in particular where infrastructure development comes into play, than the exploitation, or export stage.

How significant are these resource developments as part of the Australian macroeconomy? Table 9 offers a historical perspective. The table shows exports of minerals and metals both as a percent of total exports and of GDP. The size of the resource sector in 1981 and its expected growth at twice the rate of GDP—7.2 percent export growth versus 3.6 percent for GDP—imply that the resource sector is and will increasingly be important in the macroeconomy. Resource development is particularly significant in two respects. On the resource side the absorption of factors of production for resource development and exploitation poses intersectoral issues. But at the same time the export

48. OECD, *Economic Surveys, 1981–82: Australia* (Paris: OECD, January 1982), p. 27.

Table 9. *Importance of Minerals and Metals*
in the Macroeconomy, Selected Periods, 1960–91
Percent

Measure	1960–61	1970–71	1980–81	1982–83	1990–91[a]
Percent of exports	10.6	31.0	37.1	47.8	n.a.
Percent of GDP	1.4	4.0	5.3	5.9	6.6

Sources: Australian Bureau of Mineral Resources, Geology and Geophysics, *Australian Mineral Industry Annual Review 1981*, table 6, p. 9; Norton, Garmston, and Brodie, *Australian Economic Statistics*, pp. 3–5, 116; International Monetary Fund computer tapes on international financial statistics; and Australian Bureau of Statistics, "Exports and Imports (Balance of Payments Basis) at Constant Prices: Australia, September Quarter 1983," table 2, p. 5.
  a. The 1990–91 data are based on a 1981–91 trend GDP growth of 3.6 percent and a forecast of 7.2 percent real growth of exports.

growth raises the question of the appropriate policy for external balance. These questions are at the center of the Gregory thesis. Neville Norman summarizes the issue as follows:

The essential finding of Gregory's work is that the emergence of a mineral export sector tends to revalue our currency and to make for competitive disabilities for our import-competing and other export industries. Further, he argues, attempts by Government policy to offset the damage done to any one of these disadvantaged sectors can only be to the detriment of other sectors not so specifically assisted, or to the mining industry itself. Accordingly the inevitability of inter-sectoral conflict emerges as the main theme in Gregory's explanation.[49]

The following diagram develops the analytical issue. The figure shows the Australian model of real wages and unemployment in the Salter-Swan tradition. The real exchange rate is the price of traded goods (exports and imports) relative to home goods. The line *HH* shows equilibrium in the home goods market. A real depreciation or a rise in the real exchange rate shifts demand from traded to home goods, while moving productive resources toward the traded goods sector. The resulting excess demand for home goods is eliminated by a cut in spending. Hence *HH* is negatively sloped with points to the right denoting excess demand and points to the left, excess supply. The value of output measured in terms of home goods is shown along *YY*. A real depreciation raises the value of output in terms of home goods so that *YY*, drawn for given technology and resources, is positively sloped. We assumed that an initial equilibrium in the real exchange rate, *e*, occurs at point *A*.

49. See N. R. Norman, *Mining and the Economy: An Appraisal of the Gregory Thesis* (Australian Mining Industry Council, September 1977), p. 3.

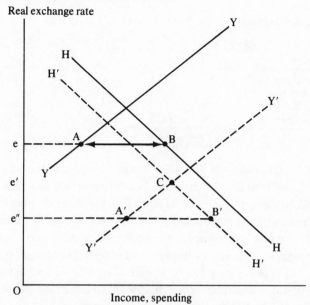

Real exchange rate

Income, spending

Typically in Australia that equilibrium will be replaced by a deficit in the external balance as spending exceeds income.

Resource development raises the value of income and is shown in this diagram as a rightward shift of the *YY* line. At the same time, the high-productivity resource industries compete successfully to capture resources from the home goods industries. This implies excess demand for home goods and a need to cut spending to maintain the home goods market equilibrium at an unchanged real exchange rate. Thus the *HH* line shifts left to *H'H'*.

It is clear from the diagram that the Australian economy has alternative options for adjustment, all of them combinations of trade deficit and appreciation strategies. Whatever happens to the economy, there will be a need for some appreciation. Real appreciation implies that in traditional exporting industries and in the import-competing industries prices fall relative to costs and competitiveness disappears. That is the channel, familiar from the work of Cairnes, through which factors of production are diverted to resources. Of course real appreciation means that the traditional sectors are the losers, even if on balance some positive spillover effects occur through resource processing.

The extent to which the traditional sectors lose depends on the precise

Table 10. *Adjustment to the Post–Korean War Bust,*
1950–54

Item	1950	1951	1952	1953	1954	1955
Inflation (percent a year)	9.2	20.1	17.0	4.4	0.7	...
Unemployment (percent)	0.4	0.3	1.1	1.5	0.6	...
Terms of trade (index)	100	142	91	99	98	88
Real wage (index)	100	105.8	105.7	105.5	109.2	113.7

Sources: Norton, Garmston, and Brodie, *Australian Economic Statistics*, pp. 20, 108, 110, 144, 214. Data for terms of trade and real wage are for fiscal years. Real wage is average weekly earnings divided by CPI.

appreciation-spending mix that policymakers choose in the adjustment. One possibility is to use the resource boom to stop external borrowing. This would be shown by a move to point C in the diagram where income is equal to spending and hence there is external balance. But if the initial deficit, AB, were maintained, the economy would move to a real exchange rate, e'', at point A', implying an even larger real appreciation.

The question of policy adjustment in the face of external disturbances is a traditional Australian concern. Swan summarizes the inherited wisdom (the 1945 White Paper "Full Employment in Australia") as follows:

"Minor fluctuations in export income" should be borne by international reserves.

A loss of export income which, "although prolonged and severe, is not permanent" should be met by quantitative import restrictions (which would incidentally help maintain employment in Australia, but would only be imposed if the balance of payments required them).

A "permanent" loss of export income should be met by exchange depreciation.

And he further comments,

It is not an automatic mechanism: "conscious action by the authorities" is required to prevent over-spending, to keep real wages in line with long-run movements of productivity and the terms of trade, and to impose temporary quantitative restrictions during (and only during) middle run troughs of the terms of trade.[50]

The adjustment to the post–Korean War bust, shown in table 10, involved slowing real wage growth according to the deterioration in the terms of the trade. From the perspective of the 1970s, that adjustment was quite rapid.

50. T. W. Swan, "Longer-Run Problems of the Balance of Payments," in H. W. Arndt and W. M. Corden, *The Australian Economy* (Melbourne, Canberra, Sydney: F. W. Cheshire, 1963), pp. 384–85.

By contrast, the adjustment to an export boom allows gains in real wages. In the diagram it is shown that a resource boom leads to a real appreciation. Discussion in Australia in the past ten years has explored how best to achieve that adjustment. There are two main choices: exploit the export boom to make structural adjustments, in particular changes in tax collection and in protection, or make the adjustment through lower inflation or currency appreciation. It is apparent from the statement by Swan above that the themes are entirely those of the 1950s; however, the signs are now reversed.

The adjustment through a reduction in protection is based on the notion that any tariffs, and especially quotas, that were motivated by balance-of-payments constraints become redundant when net exports show increased growth. Thus it is a good time to reduce protection, thereby reducing the payments surplus while at the same time freeing resources for export.[51] This is the position advocated by Stone and endorsed by Corden in the case of quotas.[52]

Fiscal policy is also affected because the Australian export boom makes it possible to increase tax collection. Indeed, if most of the increased profitability of the export sector were absorbed by taxation, no boom would occur at all. The collection of export tax revenue would allow improvements in the public sector budget and would make retirement of domestic and external debt possible.[53] When reduced protection or increased taxation do not fully offset the need for real appreciation, there are two options available—allow wages to rise at a given exchange rate or allow the exchange rate to appreciate with unchanged domestic wages. The former option corresponds to fixed rates and the monetary mechanism, the latter to a flexible or managed rate. There has been little

51. The gain in real wages occurs whether or not protection is removed. In one case, labor enjoys high real wages in terms of imports because of lower tariffs, in the other case, wages increase because the external terms of trade improve.

52. J. O. Stone, "Australia in a Competitive World: Some Options," paper presented at the twenty-first General Management Conference of the Australian Institute of Management, Sydney, 1979; W. M. Corden, "Booming Sector and Dutch Disease Economics: A Survey," Working Paper in Economics and Econometrics 079 (Canberra: Australian National University, 1982).

53. Stone emphasized resource allocation decisions for the private versus the public sector; at the time Australia was in the midst of a resource-sector boom. See J. O. Stone, "Australia in a Competitive World: Some More Options," Stan Kelly Memorial Lecture, presented to the Victorian Branch of the Economic Society of Australia and New Zealand (Melbourne, November 1981).

disagreement in the discussion of these options. Appreciation of the exchange rate is clearly seen as the favored option. This is not surprising because for manufacturing, which will be squeezed, it matters little whether prices fall or wages rise. But the balance sheet effects favor the appreciation; firms that have borrowed in foreign currency find that the domestic currency value of their external debts declines. The adjustment thus favors external debtors rather than domestic currency debtors.

The resource boom is sufficiently interesting analytically to generate a large literature independent of its empirical significance.[54] But will the resource boom be as significant as table 9 suggests, given the more pessimistic outlook for world growth and energy prices that we have today compared with 1979–80?

There are unlikely to be significant gains to employment from the investment phase, and shifting to production will not generate much more direct employment, if any. Important macroeconomic effects must stem then from the export or income effects. These are limited because the resource development has called on foreign capital, which will share in the incomes and will directly bring an external balance offset in the form of dividend and interest payments.

There will be some surplus left, provided that the world demand for resources remains strong. Does the extra income and export revenue suggest excess demand for labor and a need for real appreciation? Perhaps so, if the economy had started from equilibrium or a labor shortage. But it did not start from equilibrium. On the contrary, unemployment is high and thus an expansion in demand due to export growth would be a healthy stimulus to employment and to budget revenues. For macroeconomic reasons, allowing deindustrialization through appreciation would be poor policy, particularly because resource booms have a way of collapsing.

Fiscal Policy

In this section we discuss the current fiscal problems of Australian policymakers. We support the emphasis on the real wage and disagree

54. The chapter by John F. Helliwell in this volume assesses research on the effects of the resources boom and suggests that its macroeconomic impact may have been exaggerated because the models used did not embody relevant international adjustment mechanisms.

with the Treasury's fixation on the budget deficit. Barry Hughes summarizes the Treasury's viewpoint as follows:

Treasury has . . . invented a brand new economics—strictly speaking a rediscovery of old propositions—which asserts that present unemployment is caused largely by factors other than measures taken to hold down inflation, and that Keynesian expansionary policy no longer works in any case. This is the economics of the Stone Age.[55]

Hughes goes on to cite the essence of the argument:

unemployment is the result of excessive real wages; and attempts to expand the economy through fiscal policy will fail because higher deficits create expectations of inflation that lead to higher consumer saving and lower investment. Stone explains in current economic circumstances in Australia, [that is in 1979] a policy of expanding the budget deficit, whether by increased government spending or by reduced taxation would *not* achieve the ends to which it would presumably be directed. That is it would not lead to expanded output and employment and reduced unemployment, at least in any sustained sense, but rather would darken prospects in those areas.[56]

Turning to the budget, Stone argues in the same work that increases in the deficit are inflationary—and therefore contractionary for real output—because they create pressure for higher money growth and because they adversely affect expectations. Any conventional model agrees that expansionary fiscal policy is expansionary and tends to raise both real output and prices in proportions that depend on the Phillips curve trade-off. The expansion will be larger if monetary policy accommodates the fiscal expansion by maintaining a constant domestic interest rate, but there is no reason that monetary policy has to be accommodating.

We therefore suppose that the money stock is held constant when the deficit is increased. Domestic interest rates will tend to rise, investment will be reduced, and there will be a capital inflow. The Treasury believes that at this stage private spending is crowded out more than one for one by government spending—or if the deficit was created by cutting taxes, that private spending falls rather than rises. The blame is assigned not

55. Barry Hughes, *Exit Full Employment*, p. 153. Stone is of course J. O. Stone, Secretary to the Treasury, a dominant figure in Australian economic policymaking in the 1970s and early 1980s. For more details, see Hughes, ibid., pp. 153–54.

56. J. O. Stone, "The Budget Deficit and the Economy," in J. W. Nevile, ed., *Policies against Stagflation*, Readings in Australian Economic Policy 1 (Melbourne: Longman Cheshire, 1981), p. 256.

to the higher real interest rate, but rather to higher actual and expected rates of inflation.

Empirical work tends to show that consumption in Australia falls when the rate of inflation increases, and that investment demand is likewise adversely affected by inflation.[57] But we have not seen evidence supporting the view that crowding out would be more than one for one.[58] Further, part of the reduction in investment is caused by the unwillingness of the Treasury to adjust corporate taxation for inflation, and thus is avoidable.[59]

In any event we doubt that, given the money stock, increased deficits could be shown to reduce aggregate demand in a rational expectations version of the Treasury argument. The Treasury's starting point is the fact that the increase in the deficit increases aggregate demand and thus puts pressure on prices. Consequent fear of inflation may dampen the increase in aggregate demand produced by the deficit. But if aggregate demand were to drop to a lower level than it was initially, there would be no cause to fear inflation other than pressure from the adverse expectations associated with the deficit itself rather than those associated with the induced inflation. This would be a case of deficit hysteria, rather than a rational calculation based on the actual effects of deficits on demand. If such hysteria were universal, the United States would not have enjoyed the rapid recovery it did in 1983.

We turn now to the characteristics of the deficit. Table 11 presents data on public sector borrowing, on the commonwealth government

57. The effects of inflation on the Australian economy are reviewed in A. R. Pagan and P. K. Trivedi, eds., *The Effects of Inflation: Theoretical Issues and Australian Evidence* (Canberra: Australian National University, Centre for Economic Policy Research, 1983).

58. J. W. Nevile notes in his comments on R. K. Anstie, M. R. Gray, and A. R. Pagan, "Inflation and the Consumption Ratio," in Pagan and Trivedi, *The Effects of Inflation*, p. 356, that the estimated effects of inflation on the consumption ratio are smaller than those implied by the Treasury; A. R. Pagan and M. R. Gray, "Inflation and Investment: An Historical Overview," find that inflation reduces investment, with much of the effect being attributed to the interactions between taxes and inflation.

59. The Treasury is opposed to the indexation of business taxation, presumably in the belief that inflation is so pervasive that anything that reduces its costs is a useless effort. Even if the base inflation rate were brought down to zero, it is quite likely that there would still be periods of years with an inflation rate of 5 to 10 percent, a range at which nonneutralities of the tax system with respect to inflation become serious. There is thus a case for indexing taxes, and particularly corporate taxes, so that inflationary bouts do not cause more damage than necessary.

Table 11. *Actual and Structural Budget Deficits and Debt, 1965–84*
Percent of GDP

| Year or period | Public sector borrowing require- ment | Commonwealth budget deficit | | | | Common- wealth debt |
| | | Actual | Estimates of structural deficit | | | |
			Treasury	Nevile	Blandy- Creigh	
1965–75	2.6	1.5	n.a.	1.3	n.a.	38.8
1976	5.5	4.9	n.a.	2.3	5.0	24.2
1977	4.9	3.3	n.a.	1.0	2.5	22.9
1978	6.1	3.7	n.a.	0.3	2.7	25.0
1979	5.4	3.4	n.a.	0.1	3.0	25.3
1980	4.1	1.8	n.a.	−2.5	0.5	24.0
1981	3.6	0.8	n.a.	−3.6	−0.3	21.3
1982	3.3	0.4	−0.3	−4.7	−1.2	14.9
1983	6.4	2.8	0.8	−3.1	−0.5	16.9
1984[a]	n.a.	4.7	2.6	−1.5	1.5	n.a.

Sources: The 1965–75 average for the first and second columns is from Norton, Garmston, and Brodie, *Australian Economic Statistics*, pp. 39, 49, 116. Public sector borrowing requirement—*Budget Statements 1983–84*, p. 350; actual and Treasury estimate—*Budget Statements 1983–84*, p. 341, and *National Economic Summit Conference April 1983: Projections of the Australian Economy to 1985–86* (Canberra: AGPS, 1983), app. 4, p. 104; Nevile and Blandy-Creigh estimates—based on data kindly provided by John Nevile; and commonwealth debt—debt outstanding minus holdings by the Reserve Bank of Australia, based on Norton, Garmston, and Brodie, *Australian Economic Statistics*, pp. 52, 54, 204, and for 1982 and 1983, "Australia," *International Financial Statistics*, vol. 37 (January 1984), pp. 82–85.

deficit, and on the ratio of the commonwealth debt to GDP. The first point to be made is that the Australian public sector had a current-account surplus throughout the period shown. The second point is that, except in the years 1974–78 and 1982–84, the deficit was a small percentage of GDP. Indeed, as the data on the debt show, the deficit was sufficiently small that the ratio of the debt to GDP fell during most of the post–World War II period—to the extent that by 1983 the debt was less than 20 percent of GDP, a little below that of the United States and down from a level of 70 to 80 percent in the 1950s.[60] The OECD data in table 12 show that Australia has had small deficits by international standards.

60. Several points are germane to this discussion. First, it is frequently argued that the deficit should be adjusted to reflect government capital gains on its outstanding debt. This adjustment is accomplished by examining the ratio of the debt to GDP. Second, of course, some of the fall in this ratio occurred as a result of inflation that was not correctly anticipated and incorporated in interest rates. Third, inclusion of the debt of local governments and public corporations would not change the basic pattern shown in table 11. Such debt amounted to 18.7 percent of GDP in 1949–50 and 14.1 percent in 1979–80, according to W. E. Norton, P. M. Garmston, and M. W. Brodie, *Australian Economic Statistics, 1949–50 to 1980–81: I Tables*, Occasional Paper 8A (Canberra: Reserve Bank of Australia, 1982), p. 57. The last point is that part of the commonwealth debt (10 percent in 1981) is held by public authorities. We have adjusted the series to exclude Reserve Bank holdings of this debt.

Table 12. *Net Government Lending*
of Selected Industrial Countries, 1960–81
Percent of GDP

Country	1960–67	1968–73	1974–81
Australia	1.4	1.9	−1.0
European Economic Community	−0.2	−0.6	−3.3
Germany	0.8	0.2	−3.2
Japan	−1.6	0.0	−3.6
United Kingdom	−1.1	−0.4	−3.8
United States	0.0	0.1	−0.4

Source: OECD, *Historical Statistics, 1960–81*, tables 6 and 7, p. 65.

Table 11 shows three estimates of the structural deficit, that is, the total deficit less the component due to the decline in economic activity. These estimates differ from one another because of varying assumptions about the "full employment" level of output and the cyclical responsiveness of tax collection.[61]

Given the difference in assumptions, Nevile represents a larger part of actual deficits as cyclical, followed by Richard Blandy and Stephen Creigh. The Treasury, predictably, views deficits as structural, as can be seen from a comparison of the data for 1983: in 1983 Nevile and Blandy-Creigh estimate structural surpluses, while the Treasury estimates a deficit.

It could be argued that whatever may have been the case in the past, table 11 shows that the *current* deficit problem is extremely serious because deficits of nearly 5 percent of GDP are not sustainable. But this argument can be made only by ignoring the distinction between the actual and the full-employment deficits. There is no reason to think that the full-employment rate of unemployment in Australia exceeds—to choose a large number—6 percent, and thus there is no case for believing that the 1983–84 projected deficit of 4.7 percent of GDP will last. Nor is

61. The Treasury estimates are based on an elasticity of 0.7, those of Nevile assume a unit elasticity, and those by Blandy and Creigh assume an elasticity of 1.1. (This information was provided by John Nevile; we did not actually have access to the underlying research.) The Treasury estimates are based on a full-employment unemployment rate of 6.3 percent, which was obtained in 1979 with a trend growth of potential output of 3.5 percent. (See *National Economic Summit Conference: Projections of the Australian Economy to 1985–86*, appendix 4.) Nevile takes 1973–74 to represent full employment with subsequent trend growth of potential output of 4.3 percent, declining toward 4 percent. Blandy and Creigh base their estimates on a potential output growth of only 3.4 percent with 1970–71 representing full employment.

Figure 8. *Ratio of Debt to GDP, 1960–83*

Percent

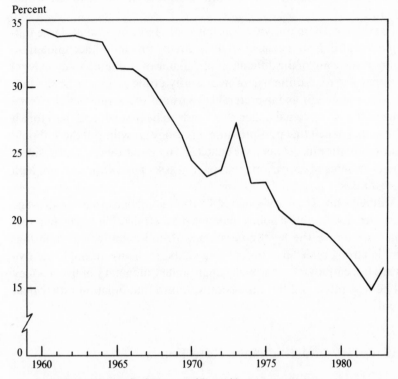

Source: International Monetary Fund, *International Financial Statistics*, computer tapes.

there any reason to believe that deficits of such magnitude do any serious harm at times of deep recession. The refusal of the Treasury to work with a sensible full-employment figure or structural deficit makes no sense, except as a means of frightening the bourgeoisie by exaggerating the deficit problem.

The relevant consideration in evaluating the long-run effects of short-run deficits must be what happens to the public debt relative to GNP. Table 11 shows that by 1982 the debt had declined toward 15 percent of GDP, way below the levels for most other advanced countries (see figure 8). The initial conditions for the present deficits are thus exceptionally favorable, and deficits do not appear to be a threat to economic and financial stability for some time. Indeed, the situation is so unusually favorable in terms of the debt-income ratio that the Treasury has avoided phrasing the discussion in these terms (as a professional treatment would require).

To summarize, in our view it is unwise to have persistent, large full-employment deficits because of their effects on capital accumulation. We are also aware of the difficulties of defining the full-employment level of output but regard the use of necessarily crude estimates of the full-employment deficit as far preferable to use of the actual deficit. Some argue that it is the actual deficit that needs to be funded, and therefore it is the actual deficit that puts pressure on money growth. But there should be no automatic link between the deficit and money growth—and besides, deficits at times of recession are typically associated with low, not high interest rates.

Although the Treasury's deficit fixation is inappropriate, real wage resistance does create a policy dilemma in Australia. If it is true that real wages are above the level consistent with full employment, and that there is strong resistance to real wage cuts, then any attempt to move toward full employment through expansionary monetary or fiscal policy will be frustrated and the expansion will turn into inflation rather than output.

Monetary and Exchange Rate Policy

Although there is little controversy on the technical details of the functioning of the financial markets, policy questions generate considerable disagreement. The most significant policy issues arise from institutional innovations over the past decade. In this respect, too, Australia does not differ from the rest of the OECD.

Financial innovations have made the interpretation of the monetary aggregates difficult. The resulting apparent instability of money demand raises two empirical issues. The first is whether, interest rates apart, there are significant determinants of velocity that have been left out of consideration and can account for the observed instability.[62] The second

62. Davis and Lewis review studies of the demand for money of the standard form suggesting that there are clear signs of instability in the standard demand function. See K. T. Davis and M. K. Lewis, "The Demand for Money," in J. W. Nevile, ed., *Policies against Stagflation*. Porter presents an estimate of the standard form of the demand for money function. He claims that there was no marked secular deterioration of the fit of the conventional money-demand function through 1979, though quarter-to-quarter

is whether there is an important role for regulatory changes in the payments system and administered rates to affect money demand. This second issue is of continuing importance as financial markets become more competitive and could become especially significant for monetary policy if the recommendations of the Campbell Committee are substantially implemented.[63] The Australian practice of concentrating on M3, which is a relatively broad definition of money, makes it more likely that the function will remain stable in the face of institutional change than would concentration on M1.

The money supply process links the nominal money stock to the stock of high-powered money, H, via the money multiplier, m. High-powered money is equal, on the "sources" side, to foreign exchange reserves, R, plus domestic credit of the monetary authorities, DC. Thus

$$(3) \qquad M = m(\quad)H(\quad) = m(\quad)(R + DC).$$

Australian practice in describing the determination of the money supply varies between the base approach shown in equation 3 above and the "formation of liquidity and money" tabulation introduced by the Reserve Bank.[64] This latter approach, the money-formation tabulations, begins with the sources, assets of the private sector that come from the foreign sector, the commonwealth government budget deficit, and the Reserve Bank; all of which can be viewed as potentially acquired by banks and therefore as increases to the stock of bank assets. Bank loans and advances are added to this total, and purchases of government securities by the nonbank public are subtracted, the final result being an increase in the volume of bank assets plus currency equal to the increase in the stock of money. As presented by the Reserve Bank, the final total is the increase in M3, which includes the assets (or liabilities) of both the trading and savings banks. As noted by Davis and Lewis, the usefulness

---

prediction errors were large. Lagged adjustment, or monetary disequilibrium, is central to the Reserve Bank of Australia's RBA 2 model, in which equations for the desired stock of money are functions of several interest rates, along with sales rather than output. See Michael G. Porter, "Monetary Targeting," in Australian Financial System Inquiry (Campbell Committee), *Commissioned Studies and Selected Papers*, pt. 1: Macroeconomic Policy: Internal Policy (Canberra: AGPS, 1982).

63. See Australian Financial System Inquiry (Campbell Committee), *Final Report of the Committee of Inquiry* (Canberra: AGPS, 1980).

64. See, for example, Reserve Bank of Australia, *Bulletin*, July 1983, p. 24. A similar table is presented in Statement 2 of the *Budget Statement, 1983–84*, p. 40.

of the approach depends on the predictability or controllability of the components of the increase in the money stock.[65]

Since both equation 3 and the money-formation tabulations of the Reserve Bank are statistically valid, the question of which approach—if either—to use must be made on pragmatic grounds. There is no clear evidence on this issue.[66] One difficulty with using the base approach in Australia is that there are two reserve requirements, one for a statutory cash-reserve deposit, the other for liquid assets and government securities. We nonetheless prefer to emphasize the base approach of equation 3 because it more clearly focuses on the Reserve Bank as the potential source of monetary control. By giving the budget deficit a prominent role, the approach that relies on money-formation tabulations may mistakenly give legitimacy to the notion that monetary policy is necessarily tied to the government deficit in the short run.

Monetary growth forecasts (they are not officially targets) have been published during the past six years; actual monetary growth has exceeded the forecast in each year. However, the growth rate of M3 has not come close to the very high levels of 1973–76 when money growth undoubtedly contributed to the great excess demand that fed the wage explosion. The Australian approach to monetary targeting, which retains flexibility to adjust money growth in response to exchange rate developments, has much to recommend it in an economy in which the exchange rate matters. The successful inflation-fighting European central banks of Germany and Switzerland have allowed their money growth to diverge from target in response to exchange rate movements. Monetary forecasts are useful also if they disprove the assumption that there is necessarily a link between the budget deficit and money growth.

Three important sets of issues arise regarding the base approach and the underlying money-supply equation 3. First is the question of the relative effectiveness of controlling the money supply by policies, such

65. K. Davis and M. Lewis, "Monetary Policy," in F. H. Gruen, ed. *Surveys of Australian Economics* (Sydney: George Allen & Unwin, 1978).

66. Both Purvis and Sharpe provide evidence indicating shortcomings of the base approach in the Australian context. See Douglas D. Purvis, "The Role of the Monetary Base in Australia," in K. T. Davis and M. K. Lewis, eds., *Australian Monetary Economics* (Melbourne: Longman Cheshire, 1981); and Ian G. Sharpe, "Australian Money Supply Analysis: The Relationship between the Monetary Base, Secondary Reserves and the Money Supply," *Journal of Banking and Finance*, vol. 4 (September 1980), pp. 283–300.

as changes in statutory cash-reserve deposits, that affect the money multiplier rather than the monetary base. Second is the issue of the potential endogeny of the money stock via fiscal or exchange rate policy, and the related question of the authorities' ability to sterilize the effects of the external balance. This set of issues perhaps emerges more clearly from the money-formation tabulations than from the money-multiplier approach. Third is the broader policy question of whether money-stock control is essential, desirable, or both as the central instrument in a disinflation effort and how it affects efforts to maintain low rates of inflation over the longer term. This latter question, which needs to be studied from a broader perspective in which the stability of velocity, the stability of the Phillips curve, and the nature of expectations formation play essential roles, is examined below.

Asset Markets and Transmission Channels

Another important empirical issue concerns the tightness of links between interest rates in Australia and the exchange depreciation-adjusted returns abroad. Two questions arise: first, whether asset markets in Australia are appropriately modeled as being "always in equilibrium"; and second, whether Australian and foreign assets are approximately perfect substitutes or the contrary, very imperfect substitutes.

The formulation of asset markets raises still another question: whether a stock-equilibrium approach to the financial sector is appropriate, or whether a disequilibrium dynamic formulation is preferable, such as one that generalizes the lagged adjustment typically included in money-demand specifications. Here we distinguish the possibility that asset holdings are adjusted slowly to target levels from the assumption that asset prices do not move rapidly to clear markets dependent on the demand functions for assets; we see no reason to believe that asset prices are sluggish in the absence of intervention that seeks, for example, to stabilize the exchange rate or the interest rate.

The second issue in the specification of conditions for asset-market equilibrium is that of substitutability between real and nominal assets, and substitutability between assets denominated in Australian currency and in foreign securities. The degree of substitutability matters because it determines whether Australia can pursue an independent policy on interest rates. This is the question of the ability to sterilize the effects of the external balance on the money supply when fixed rates prevail.[67] Under flexible rates the issue concerns the effects of monetary and fiscal policies on the exchange rate. Substitutability thus has a bearing on the transmission channels between financial markets and real activity and on the linkages among domestic financial markets, the balance of payments and the exchange rate, and foreign capital markets.[68] The degree of asset substitutability also has implications for debt-financed budget deficits.

The discussion of the linkages between domestic and foreign interest rates obviously assumes that capital can move. Capital controls may severely limit the scope for such flows or, at a minimum, regulate the terms under which capital flows take place. In particular, embargoes, minimum-time borrowing constraints, and reserve requirements on foreign borrowing all potentially affect the extent of international linkage.[69] The removal of almost all controls in December 1983 means that for now these impediments do not stand in the way of capital flows.

67. Macfarlane summarizes the results of several studies of the extent to which capital inflows offset monetary policy changes, finding offset coefficients varying between 0.3 and 0.7. The implication is that capital flows offset but do not completely undo the effects of open market operations on the money stock. See I. J. Macfarlane, "The Balance of Payments in the 1970's" in *Conference in Applied Economic Research* (Canberra: Reserve Bank of Australia, 1979), p. 22. J. R. Hewson, in his comments on the Macfarlane paper (pp. 40–43), raises some doubts about the reliability of these estimates.

68. In an empirical study, Sharpe firmly rejects the existence of a tight, short-run, link between interest differentials and forward premiums. See Ian G. Sharpe, "Covered Interest Rate Parity: The Australian Case" (Newcastle, New South Wales: University of Newcastle, June 1983). There is certainly no closer link between short-term interest differentials and the realized rate of depreciation. The implications of alternative combinations of exchange rate regimes and degrees of capital mobility are studied for the RBA 2 model in P. D. Jonson, W. J. McKibbin, and R. G. Trevor, "External and Domestic Interactions: A Sensitivity Analysis," Research Discussion Paper 8104 (Canberra: Reserve Bank of Australia, September 1981).

69. Chapter 8 of the Campbell report describes the history of the exchange controls and recommends that the set of controls should be gradually dismantled. See Australian Financial System Inquiry, *Final Report of the Committee of Inquiry*. Polasek and Lewis describe Australia's growing financial integration with world markets and evaluate the costs and benefits of same. See M. Polasek and M. K. Lewis, "Foreign Exchange Markets and Capital Inflow," in M. K. Lewis and R. H. Wallace, eds., *Australia's Financial Institutions and Markets* (Melbourne: Longman Cheshire, 1984). See also *Reserve Bank of Australia, Report and Financial Statements, 1983.*

The Policy Mix

Another important policy question at present is how to strike a balance between a stance of monetary policy that favors disinflation and the need to accommodate the recovery in economic activity. The flexible exchange rate reinforces the difficulty of that policy choice because different monetary-fiscal policy mixes have rapid, large effects on nominal and real exchange rates and therefore on inflation and unemployment. The flexible rates pose additional policy questions—whether or not to intervene and whether intervention should be sterilized or not (monetary aggregates being held constant). No sterilization of intervention, of course, is just exchange rate-oriented monetary policy.

The first point to make is that unemployment is intolerably high in Australia and that dramatic inflation fighting should not be the priority. Therefore a trend rate of money growth consistent with significant real growth at roughly the projected rate of inflation is broadly the right policy. This has to be translated into operational terms by taking into account trend and cyclical changes in velocity. But beyond that the question becomes how to cope with velocity surprises. We believe that a velocity-adjusted or nominal income growth-oriented monetary policy is appropriate. Surprise declines in velocity should be offset by increased monetary growth and should not be allowed to cut into real growth. Similarly, surprise increases in velocity should not be permitted to lead to excessive inflationary pressures and should be offset by reduced money growth.

Is there any room left for the exchange rate in this target setting for nominal income? Specifically, should short-term fluctuations in exchange rates lead the monetary authorities to change their path? We believe it is unwise to allow the exchange rate too much independence in a small, open economy. On the contrary, the exchange rate should be kept closely in line with the target of raising employment in a noninflationary manner. Deviations of the exchange rate thus should be resisted by intervention. Because real depreciation is inflationary in the absence of explicit incomes policy, it should not be used to create employment and real appreciation, and although tempting as a control for disinflation, it should be banned on the grounds of its effects on employment.

But should exchange rate policy work through changes in money growth relative to the target of nominal income growth, or should sterilized intervention be used to change the currency denomination composition of the public debt? Here the relevant issue is the degree of substitutability between Australian and foreign assets. If substitutability is exceedingly high, sterilized intervention accomplishes little if anything and exchange rate-oriented monetary policy must accomplish the task. If substitution is very imperfect, sterilized intervention is appropriate. It is worth noting that if the latter were the case, the currency composition of deficit finance would be an important macroeconomic consideration. These intervention principles can also be stated as appropriate responses to disturbances. If disturbances to the exchange rate originate in financial markets—for example, portfolio shifts between domestic and foreign securities or between money and securities—then full accommodation is appropriate. Full accommodation implies that interest rates and exchange rates will not change because asset supplies change instead to meet the changed demands, and therefore undesirable spillover effects on inflation and economic activity are avoided.

Monetary policy assumes a special importance in the context of a fiscally led recovery. For a given money growth path a more expansionary fiscal policy implies higher income growth and therefore rising interest rates together with currency appreciation. The U.S. expansion in 1982–83 serves as an example. The real appreciation helps stop a cyclical upswing of inflation, but of course it is unsustainable and hence is ultimately not welcome in view of the unemployment it must create. Therefore expansionary fiscal policy should be accompanied by monetary accommodation, at least as long as unemployment exerts a strongly dampening effect on wage and price inflation. Better yet, strong incomes policy should reinforce (and replace) the discipline that unemployment imposes on wage setting.

Conclusions: Policy Alternatives

The Australian economy finds itself in early 1984 with high unemployment, high inflation, and large budget deficits. The resource boom has not materialized in any significant way and the outlook is by all accounts discouraging. It is all the more discouraging because the leeway for policy action is obscured by disagreements among economists and, as a matter of strategy, arguments raised by fiscal conservatives.

Michael Parkin has suggested the most radical solution to the current difficulties: monetary, fiscal, and public-sector wage policies are all simultaneously moved to a setting that supposes zero inflation.

I am advocating a policy of *concerted* but total disinflation which is implemented with sufficient forewarning to enable maximum rearrangement of private contracts. This is certainly not to say that the Australian government can announce that inflation will disappear, will be believed because there is a small full employment deficit, and will in fact banish inflation at no cost. Rather it is to say that Australia has the preconditions for a major political effort to eradicate inflation. It has fundamentally sound public finances and it is poised on the edge of the rest-of-the-world's recovery from the deepest recession since the 1930s.[70]

There is not much precedent for how such a disinflation program might work. But there is little doubt that with flexible exchange rates, the currency would dramatically appreciate. Money would be tight at the outset, even if the program were effective (if only because velocity would decline sharply) and the limited ability to sterilize would force the authorities into appreciation. Once the appreciation has occurred it would certainly help the disinflation, just as it did in Argentina, Chile, Britain, and the United States. But the overvaluation would create such a severe unemployment problem that the success of the program would become problematic. Radical ends to inflation require, at a minimum, incomes policy if they are to be effective. We discuss incomes policy below.

An alternative possibility has been vigorously promoted by Perkins. He argues that a low-tax (particularly indirect tax), tight money mix that is in general expansionary can increase output while reducing inflation because expansionary fiscal and monetary policies have differential effects on output and prices.[71] It is difficult to believe that changes in the policy mix alone can achieve major reductions in inflation and unemployment. Nonetheless, Perkins's emphasis on the effects of taxes on take-home pay is an important one, for it focuses attention on the wage issue.

The real wage issue and the potential for expansionary fiscal policy

70. "The Bank and Treasury Views of Australia's Macroeconomic Problems: An Appraisal," *The Economic Record*, vol. 58 (December 1982), pp. 315–316. Parkin wrote this before the severity of the 1983 Australian recession was clear.

71. See, for instance, J. O. N. Perkins, "Using the Macroeconomic Policy Mix to Stop Stagflation," in J. W. Nevile, ed., *Policies against Stagflation*, pp. 267–76. This view has also been associated with Mundell and, less coherently, with the Reagan administration.

are at the center of most analyses and proposed solutions of the Australian problem. Some diagnoses and prescriptions offered for the Australian economy are shown below.

	Are there fiscal problems?	
	Yes	*No*
Real wage is too high	Balanced budget, real wage cut (Treasury view)	Fiscal expansion, real wage cut
Real wage is not a problem	. . .	Fiscal expansion (Melbourne school)

The question is whether Australian unemployment is primarily Keynesian, in which case it can be alleviated by an expansion of aggregate demand, or whether it contains a significant classical component resulting from real wages that exceed what is needed to produce full employment within a few years. Policymakers must decide whether fiscal policy can afford to be expansionary, or whether the problem of the sustainability of fiscal expansion is so great that even now fiscal restraint rather than expansion is appropriate.

Our view is that in Australia fiscal expansion is appropriate but that unemployment can be characterized largely as classical and that fiscal expansion therefore cannot be expected to drive unemployment below 6 to 7 percent without a reduction in real labor costs. We argued above that the real wage has grown relative to productivity, although we recognize that this point is difficult to establish definitely. We also do not believe that increasing returns to labor associated with a fiscal expansion would raise productivity sufficiently to warrant the current wage.[72]

Accordingly there is a case for joint policy on both demand and supply sides of the economy. Policy should concentrate on a medium-term reduction in labor costs to firms by means of both a cut in payroll taxes and transitory investment subsidies. These measures will have direct stimulatory supply effects on employment but will also affect demand through increased disposable income and after-tax profits. Given Aus-

---

72. Burns and Mitchell argue that current and expected sales, not wages, determine employment. See Michael E. Burns and William F. Mitchell, "Unemployment: Is There a Case against Expansion?" (Clayton, Victoria: Monash University, August 1983). We do not share that view and attach a central role to the real wage.

tralia's strong fiscal position (as measured by the ratio of debt to income) the policy program should be looked at as a two-to-three-year investment in restoring high employment and growth.

Real wages fell sharply in the recent recession. By the middle of 1983, Australia was only 4 percent above its 1978 level. Nonetheless, fiscal expansion—even concentrated on the supply side—might not be sufficient to restore the economy to an unemployment rate of about 5 percent. Simulations of the ORANI model and rough calculations both suggest that real wage costs would have to fall 10 percent or more to increase employment by the 6 percent needed to bring unemployment down to 5 percent.[73] Over half of this amount could come from fiscal policy, the remainder from wage cuts relative to the rate of productivity increases.

Fiscal policy should not be expected to carry the entire expansionary burden. Exchange depreciation would provide a needed additional boost to demand. The inflationary effects can perhaps be reduced by persuading the Arbitration Commission to provide—and unions to accept—only partial indexation, as they did in the face of devaluation in the 1970s. Foreign growth and depreciation, combined with appropriate incomes policies and tax policies, would help make the return to full employment more rapid and less inflationary than the projections of the National Economic Summit Conference indicated.[74]

Even assuming that some initial real wage contraction can be achieved, the problem remains of containing wage pressures as the rapid growth of the economy occurs. The presumption here must be that incomes policy is used to prevent real and money wage pressures that would bring the expansion to an early end. Incomes policy in Australia now

73. See Peter B. Dixon, Alan A. Powell, and Brian R. Parmenter, *Structural Adaptation in an Ailing Macroeconomy* (Clayton, Victoria: Melbourne University Press, 1979); and W. M. Corden and P. B. Dixon, "A Tax-Wage Bargain in Australia: Is a Free Lunch Possible?" *The Economic Record*, vol. 27 (September 1980), pp. 209–21.

74. The National Economic Summit projections treat wage growth as exogenous. Projection A, which is implicitly the forecast most likely to represent the future, features unemployment that is still at 9.7 percent in 1985–86 with inflation down only as far as 6.5 percent. The optimistic projection C features 2.8 percent growth of average weekly earnings in 1983–84, followed by 3 percent and 4.5 percent in subsequent years. Inflation is only 3.7 percent in 1985–86 with unemployment at 8.7 percent. Real household disposable income is shown as rising each year in all scenarios, thereby presumably avoiding the real wage problem. The way to produce a positive association between inflation and unemployment across the projections is to treat nominal wage growth as exogenous.

takes the form of wage indexation, which follows the example of the successful wage freeze that ended in October 1983. The return to indexation by removing the threat of real wage cuts is designed to reduce the pressure on nominal wages that arises from attempts to maintain real wages when contracts are made in nominal terms. The hope is that in the meantime productivity growth will proceed to the point that the real wage is once more consistent with full employment.

For the longer term, wage indexation alone is not the entire answer to the Australian wage problem. There have now been two episodes in which some exaggerated settlements were reached with one union—the metal workers—resulting in wage explosions and recessions as full employment came nearer. Perhaps the memory of the severity of the recessions of the mid-1970s and early 1980s will suffice to prevent such episodes for years to come. Alternatively the government could try to put in place mechanisms to discourage large nominal wage increases. One approach that is in principle attractive, though politically perhaps not viable, is to use a wage-penalty tax-based incomes policy that penalizes the firms, unions, or both that agree to high nominal wage settlements. If no solution is found, the Australian government might be tempted to try to weaken the unions through a policy of unemployment that is more persistent than that of the mid-1970s. The British example—which is more relevant to Australian unions than the American counterparts—does not recommend this course of action. Living with inflation is not the ultimate evil.

Appendix: The Wage Equation

This appendix reports further findings on the wage equation issue. Table 13 shows estimates of a wage equation. The equations here differ from those in table 6 in the cyclical variable (unemployment versus overtime) and the inflation expectations variable.

Although the overall performance of these equations is quite similar to that of the Phillips curve, there are important differences. First, in each case the coefficient on expected inflation is significantly below unity. Second, in each case there is a shift in the coefficient of overtime between the two periods. The coefficients of *OT1* and *OT2* in each

RICHARD E. CAVES and LAWRENCE B. KRAUSE

Editors

The Australian Economy

A VIEW FROM THE NORTH

Table 13. *Gregory-Smith Wage Equation, 1966:4 to 1982:4*

	Independent variable[a]				Summary statistic			
Equation	OT1	OT2	P*	Constant	Durbin-Watson	Standard error	Rho	R²
13-1	9.07 (4.26)	7.27 (3.40)	0.74 (5.68)	15.77 (2.88)	1.98	3.85	−0.27	0.59
13-2	7.68 (4.34)	4.57 (2.64)	0.636 (6.87)	23.98 (4.44)	1.98	3.61	−0.32	0.64
13-3	9.20 (4.48)	7.21 (3.52)	0.72 (6.08)	20.8 (3.43)	2.01	3.77	−0.27	0.61

a. Each equation includes a dummy variable for the 1974:3 wage explosion. The variables *OT1* and *OT2* denote overtime in the period from 1966:4 to 1978:2 and the period from 1978:3 to 1982:4, respectively. The *P** in equation 13-1 denotes inflation expectations from a prediction equation; in equation 13-2 the Defris-Williams series is used; and in equation 13-3, the lagged inflation rate over the preceding year is used.

equation are significantly different. Thus the overtime formulation is not the complete answer to obtaining a stable wage equation.

The instability of the wage equation also appears when we include, in addition to the cyclical variable, inflation expectations and the 1974:3 dummy, a time trend. This time trend is significant when the overtime variable represents labor utilization, but is not when the unemployment rate is used. Thus overtime alone does not solve the instability in the wage equation.

JOHN F. HELLIWELL

Natural Resources
and the Australian Economy

How have natural resources influenced the economic growth of Australia and how is this pattern likely to change in the future? What are the macroeconomic effects of resource developments, and what policy issues do they pose? What are the microeconomic factors determining the overall costs and benefits of different rates of resource development?

This chapter tries to answer the first question by using historical data from the past 120 years, coupled with projections of likely developments in the 1980s. It shows, by a variety of evidence, that large and variable expenditures on resource development and large changes in the volumes and prices of resource exports are well-established features of the Australian economy. New resource projects and likely exports are still well within the range of past experience and thus are unlikely to create unusual stresses.

The second question is answered in two ways. The first is to survey the various models and results that have been used to show the aggregate

I am grateful to many Australian research collaborators and sponsors for data, advice, and hospitality. For assistance in obtaining documents and data, I am grateful to Bruce R. Bacon, Eva Klug, and Fred H. Gruen of the Australian National University, and to John Taylor and Nola McMillan of the Reserve Bank. In preparing the paper, I have had welcome research assistance from Cindy Papso and Alan Chung. In revising my initial drafts, I have been especially aided by the comments of my discussants at the Brookings-Canberra Conference, Ken W. Clements and H. N. Johnson, the other conference participants, the editors and other authors, and Chris Higgins, Peter D. Jonson, E. W. Shann, Tony Scott, and K. W. Witney.

effects of Australian natural resource projects and exports. This survey exposes some gaps in the available information. To fill these gaps, I draw on comparable results from research on the Canadian economy.

The answers to the first question and most of the available answers to the second question suggest that changes in natural resource production and prices raise some important issues in macroeconomic policy and have been responsible for significant changes in the rates of growth of aggregate output and prices. However, the overall assessment of the costs and benefits of particular projects needing government approval requires consideration of a much wider range of factors, including the level and efficiency of resource taxation, environmental and aboriginal issues, and the pricing of roads, rail transport, electricity, and other public services to the resource sector. On many of these issues, there are overlapping powers and responsibilities held by the state and commonwealth governments. Edward M. Gramlich deals with some aspects of resource taxation and revenue sharing in his chapter on fiscal federalism; in this chapter I shall raise some of the same issues, but with emphasis on their effects on the overall size, location, and efficiency of resource developments. I shall also deal, to some extent, with the consequences of interstate competition for resource developments and resource revenues.

The material dealing with my third major question is thus more diverse than the macroeconomic evidence. Nonetheless, both the microeconomic and macroeconomic effects need to be considered if effective policy decisions are to be made. In the final analysis, resource development decisions, whether for particular projects or for a whole new export industry, should not be seen as decisions by particular governments, but as the result of a whole series of decisions—often without an eye to their overall consequences—by domestic and foreign enterprises and governments, heavily conditioned by the state of commodity markets and the rate of growth of the world economy. State governments mainly set the terms under which access is granted to their resource deposits. Put differently, resource deposits are for them chips to be played in return for some combination of short-term and long-term revenues, employment, and production, where the other players in the game include other governments, foreign and domestic investors, and industries whose prospects are helped or hindered by resource projects.

Thus, even though the commonwealth government has the primary responsibility for macroeconomic policy (as analyzed in the chapter by Rudiger Dornbusch and Stanley Fischer), it does not have the power to choose the aggregate scale and timing of resource developments, beyond its one-way power (also possessed by the state governments for resources in their jurisdiction) to set taxation and other policies so tight that new projects do not take place. The changing distribution of initiative and stopping power among enterprises and governments and the diversity of project-specific issues embrace more material than can be included here; this chapter will make general points about the three questions posed at the outset rather than deal equally fully with all resource industries and policies. The closing sections deal with government policies influencing the rate and structure of resource developments and draw together the main conclusions of my investigation.

Natural Resources and the Economy in the Long Run

Australian economic growth has been tied to natural resource developments for all of this century and for most of the previous history of the six colonies that federated in 1901 to form the Commonwealth of Australia. The population of the Australian colonies trebled in the 1850s, as one in every fifty British citizens was drawn south by Victoria's gold rushes at Ballarat and Bendigo. In the next forty years the ebb and flow of gold rushes moved counterclockwise around the continent, arriving at Coolgardie and Kalgoorlie in Western Australia in 1892 and 1893. In this century, the major natural resource booms and slumps have been spurred less by the pace of new mineral discoveries than by changes in world markets and technology, whether for mining or agriculture. Each major boom has been followed by a slump, and each has had important effects on other industries and on the economy as a whole.

Over the past decade, there has been much discussion of the impact of increased mineral production and exports on employment, prices, and output in the rest of the economy. I shall attempt to deal with these and other major contemporary issues, but first I wish to set these questions in their historical context. From a historical perspective, the projected doubling of mineral exports during the 1980s appears less dramatic. The gold rushes of the 1850s not only trebled the population but at their peak quadrupled the wage rate for carpenters in Victoria,

Figure 1. *Real Output per Capita in Five Industrial Countries, 1861–1981*

Real output per capita (1970 U.S. dollars, log scale)

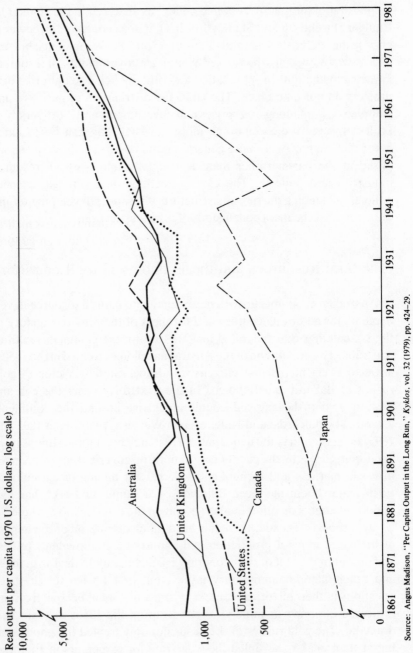

Source: Angus Madison, "Per Capita Output in the Long Run," *Kyklos,* vol. 32 (1979), pp. 424–29.

trebled the price of nontradable goods, and raised the prices of import-competing goods by 50 percent.[1] Thus the contemporary issues and events have ample precedents.

This section starts with international comparisons of per capita output and population growth and then considers the long-run movements in the development and export of Australian natural resources. The concluding parts of the section detail the role of foreign investment and show changes in the composition of Australia's mineral sector.

Resource Rich and Resource Dependent

Figure 1 shows why Australia acquired its luster for migrants in the mid-nineteenth century. Even after the mass immigration of the 1850s, Australian real output per capita in 1861 was more than twice as high as that in Canada and five times as high as that in Japan. Those emigrating from Great Britain to Australia in 1861 could expect to find real per capita output 40 percent higher than they had known back home.

Thanks largely to gold, wool, and the good conditions for agriculture in Victoria and New South Wales, Australian income per capita was at the top of the heap in 1861. A British migrant in the 1980s could still expect to find higher real incomes in Australia, but to a lesser degree than 120 years earlier. Real income per capita is now higher in the United States and Canada than in Australia, while in Japan it had almost caught up by 1981. A full explanation of these international comparisons lies well beyond this chapter, but the data do show why Australia was such a magnet for migration. When gold was no longer available for the picking, when the farmers and pastoralists started to test the productive limits of the arid outback, and when the terms of trade began their long slide against wool, then the United States and Japan, with less immigration, larger populations, and more central locations, started to close the gap.

Resource Booms and Migration

Figure 2 shows population growth for the same five countries whose per capita outputs were shown in figure 1. Of the five countries, Canada

1. The data are from the appendix table of Rodney Maddock and Ian McLean, "Supply-Side Shocks: The Case of Australian Gold" (Canberra: Australian National University, 1982).

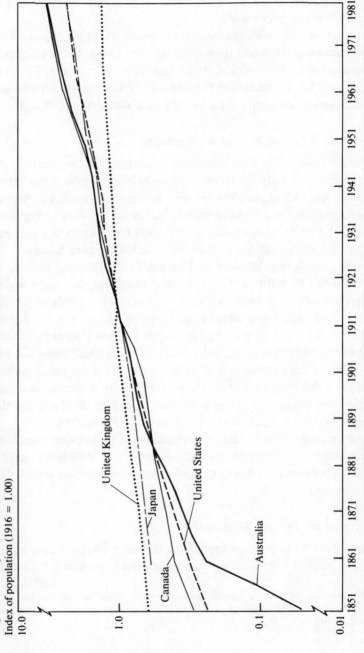

Figure 2. *Population Growth in Five Industrial Countries, 1851–1981*

Index of population (1916 = 1.00)

Sources: For Australia: Australian Bureau of Statistics, *Yearbook of Australia* (Canberra: ABS), various years. For Canada: M. C. Urquhart and Kenneth A. H. Buckley, eds., *Historical Statistics of Canada* (Toronto: Macmillan, 1965); and Canada Statistics Bureau, *Canada Year Book* (Ottawa: Statistics Canada), various years. For the United States: U.S. Bureau of the Census, *Statistical Abstract of the United States* (Washington, D.C.: Government Printing Office), various years, and Bureau of the Census, *Historical Statistics of the United States* (GPO, 1975). For the United Kingdom: Brian R. Mitchell with H. G. Jones, *Second Abstract of British Historical Statistics* (Cambridge University Press, 1971), and Central Statistical Office, *Annual Abstract of Statistics* (London: Her Majesty's Stationery Office), various years. For Japan: Japan Statistics Bureau, *Japan Statistical Yearbook* (Tokyo: Japan Statistical Association), various years. Author's estimates for data before 1876.

and Australia are the two with the greatest immigration. In both countries, the pre-1945 surges of immigration were due to either the prospect or the reality of major natural resource developments. In the Canadian immigration boom of the first decade of this century, which was based on the opening of the prairie wheat lands, settlers were given land grants. In the Australian gold rush of the 1850s, migrants had the prospect of finding record-breaking nuggets as well as the more certain if less lustrous prospect of financial assistance with passage money. Money was given first to pastoral workers who were needed to replace the shepherds who had left in search of gold; after them it was given mainly to women.[2]

In this century, the links between population growth and resource developments have been less obvious than in the previous century, but it remains clear that changing prospects for resource development alter the attractiveness of Australia, and changes in labor market pressures arising from natural resource projects remain a key determinant of Australian immigration policy. The use of natural resource wealth to attract immigration has sometimes been regarded as a way of gaining permanent benefits from resource developments[3] or as a way of securing sovereignty over Australia's vast and sparsely populated northern and western frontiers.[4] If immigration is to succeed in raising per capita income over a long period, economies of scale must be large enough to offset the diluting effects of sharing the richest nuggets and the most arable land among the larger number of citizens.

Changes in the Importance of Resource Production

Figure 3 shows annual changes in mining, agricultural, and total resource output in relation to gross domestic product (GDP). The jagged peaks and troughs reflect droughts and, to a lesser extent, movements in the international wool market. Total resource output exceeded 30

2. Of the 181,000 male migrants from the United Kingdom to Victoria between 1852 and 1861, 18 percent received assisted passage, as did 48 percent of the 116,000 females; ibid., p. 21. Pastoralists and farmers were offered favorable leases and land grants, on terms that varied from one colony and one period to another.

3. Maddock and McLean make this case for various incentives offered to migration in the 1850s; ibid.

4. W. A. Beattie and M. deLacy Lowe make this case for large-scale development of the Kimberley region in their *Australia's North-West Challenge* (Melbourne: Kimberley Publishing, 1980).

Figure 3. *Resource Production, 1861–1981*
Percentage of gross domestic product

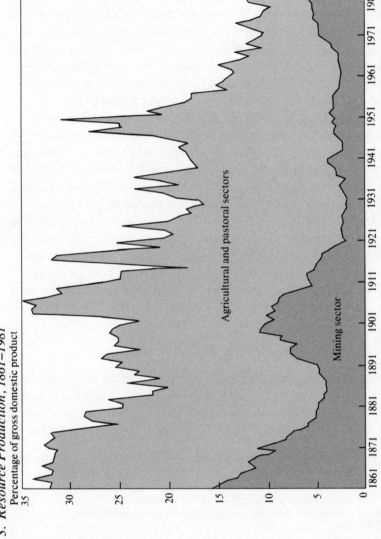

Sources: Gross domestic product: for 1861 to 1938–39, N. G. Butlin, *Australian Domestic Product, Investment and Foreign Borrowing* (Cambridge University Press, 1962), pp. 10, 11; for 1939–40 to 1948–49, *Yearbook of Australia, 1980*, p. 788: for 1949–50 to 1980–81, W. E. Norton, P. M. Garmston, and M. W. Brodie, *Australian Economic Statistics, 1949–50 to 1980–81: I. Tables*, Occasional Paper 8a (Sydney: Reserve Bank of Australia, 1982), p. 125. Agricultural and pastoral sectors: for 1861 to 1938–39, Butlin, *Australian Domestic Product*, pp. 12, 13; for 1939–40 to 1948–49, *Yearbook of Australia*, various years; for 1949–50 to 1980–81: Norton, Garmston, and Brodie, *Australian Economic Statistics*, p. 116. Mining: for 1861 to 1938–39—Butlin, *Australian Domestic product*, pp. 12, 13; for 1939–40 to 1980–81, *Yearbook of Australia*, various years, and Australian Bureau of Statistics, *Mineral Production in Australia*, catalog no. 8405.0 (Canberra: ABS), various years.

percent of GDP in much of the pre-1914 period and has followed an uneven downward trend since. Mining output exceeded 15 percent of GDP in 1861, fell below 5 percent in the 1880s, and exceeded 10 percent again when Western Australian gold production was at its peak in the early 1900s. From 1921 to 1961 mining production averaged about 2.8 percent of GDP. In the twenty years after 1961 it more than doubled to 6.2 percent, and some projections have it exceeding 10 percent by the end of the 1980s. This would bring mining production back to match the greatest relative importance it has had in this century but would leave total resource production far below its earlier peaks. Indeed, the continuing drop in the relative position of the agricultural export sector is one of the most likely consequences of the recent and forecasted future growth in mining output.

Capital Expenditures for Resource Projects

Figure 4 shows the dominance of agricultural investment in the last third of the nineteenth century and the generally increasing size and share of nonresource investment, especially after 1950. Mining investment has generally been about 0.5 percent of GDP, rising briefly to almost 2 percent in 1902 and again in the mining investment boom of the late 1960s and early 1970s. Some forecasts of mining investment (including oil and gas, pipelines, and aluminum) in the early 1980s suggested that it might exceed 3 percent of GDP in 1982, a level never reached previously.[5] Like all its predecessors, the early 1980s "investment boom" fell far short of projections being made during the immediately preceding years. The 1983 recession has been sharp enough to suppress most references to a 1980s mining boom. Many planned black coal, natural gas, and aluminum projects have been canceled, shelved, delayed, or scaled down in the face of cost increases, soft world markets, and tighter and more realistic financial appraisals of their prospects.

Natural Resource Exports

Figure 5 shows the changing role of mineral and agricultural exports in Australia's foreign trade over the past 120 years. Mineral exports are

5. Stephen Derrick, Diana McDonald, and Phyllis Rosendale, "The Development of Energy Resources in Australia: 1981 to 1990," *Australian Economic Review* (Third Quarter 1981), p. 52.

Figure 4. *Resource Investment, 1861–1981*
Percentage of gross domestic product

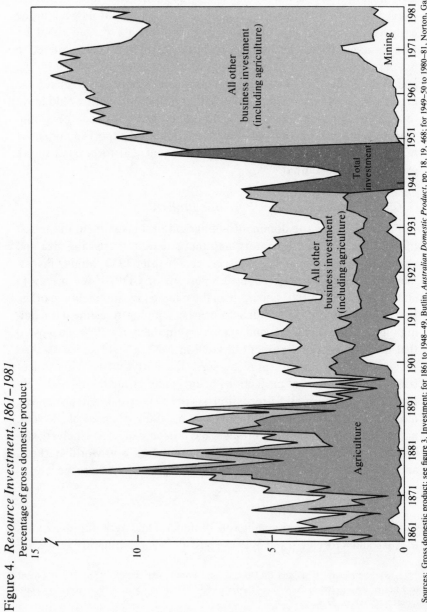

Sources: Gross domestic product: see figure 3. Investment: for 1861 to 1948–49, Butlin, *Australian Domestic Product*, pp. 18, 19, 468; for 1949–50 to 1980–81, Norton, Garmston, and Brodie, *Australian Economic Statistics*, p. 136.

never again likely to match their peak of 15 percent of GDP in the early 1860s. Some projections, however, have energy-related exports (including aluminum, coal, uranium, and gas) almost trebling in real terms over the 1980s. If this happened, these exports alone would be about 4 percent of GDP at the end of the decade.

For all of this century and certainly before (although fully comparable statistics are not available), natural resources have been more than two-thirds and usually more than four-fifths of total Australian exports. There are probably no other industrial countries with such a complete specialization in natural resource exports.

Although the degree of specialization in resource exports has changed from year to year, because of weather conditions, world markets, and new projects, it has not shown any strong trend. The mix of resource exports has changed markedly, however, and total exports themselves have generally not grown as fast as GDP. Agricultural and pastoral exports, mainly wool, had their greatest relative importance in 1950, when they were more than 90 percent of total exports and 25 percent of GDP. By the late 1970s pastoral and agricultural exports were down to 40 percent of total exports and 6 percent of GDP. Most of this drop is due to changes in wool exports, which fell from half of total exports in 1950 to less than a tenth in 1980. Over the same period, total exports fell from 29 percent to less than 15 percent of GDP, so that in 1981 a smaller share of GDP went into exports in Australia than in any other country in the Organization for Economic Cooperation and Development (OECD) except the two largest—the United States and Japan—and the four poorest—Greece, Portugal, Spain, and Turkey.

Increasing industrialization has made most countries more open to and dependent on world trade, while in Australia the reverse has happened. Distance and tariffs combine to give Australian manufacturers a higher degree of effective protection than in most other countries.[6]

To an extent that is surprising to outsiders, the tariff has become so pervasive a part of economic policy discussion in Australia that almost every resource policy issue somehow manages to get linked to the size or structure of the Australian tariff. The most widely quoted article on the macroeconomic effects of mineral exports emphasized the potential

6. Effective rates of protection are reported in table 7 of the chapter in this book on comparative advantage by Lawrence B. Krause and in the chapter on scale, openness, and productivity by Richard E. Caves.

Figure 5. *Resource and Nonresource Exports, 1861–1981*

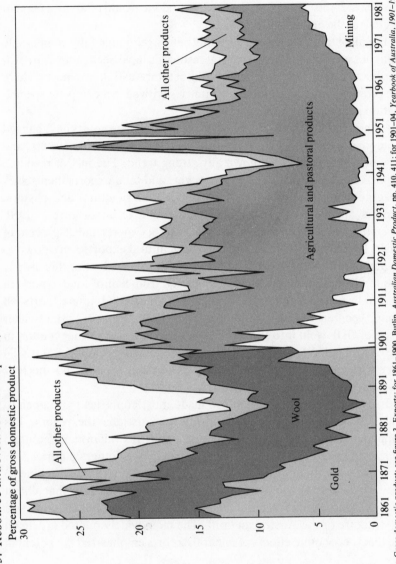

Sources: Gross domestic product: see figure 3. Exports: for 1861–1900, Butlin, *Australian Domestic Product*, pp. 410, 411; for 1901–04, *Yearbook of Australia, 1901–1907*, p. 510; for 1905 to 1937–38, Butlin, *Australian Domestic Product*, p. 212; for 1938–39 to 1948–49, Commonwealth Bureau of Census and Statistics, *Australian Balance of Payments, 1928–29 to 1951–52* (Canberra: Australian Government Publishing Service, n.d.), p. 94; for 1949–50 to 1980–81, Norton, Garmston, and Brodie, *Australian Economic Statistics*, p. 4.

impact of mineral exports by calculating that they would affect the other export- and import-competing sectors more than a 25 percent general reduction of tariffs.[7] The purpose of presenting the comparison in terms of recently completed tariff reductions might have been to lessen concern about the tariff cuts. In fact, the likely effect was instead to heighten concern about the structural adjustments required to accommodate a large expansion of mineral exports. I shall discuss this issue further in the section dealing with macroeconomic effects.

Capital Inflows and Debt Service Payments

The role of capital inflows in financing resource projects has varied sharply over the decades, depending principally on the type and scale of the projects, as well as on the development of international capital markets and of Australian policies toward capital inflows. The gold rushes of the 1850s attracted individual gold seekers, and large blocks of foreign capital were neither needed nor sought. By the 1880s a substantial interest had been created in the United Kingdom for Australian mining shares, especially for the shares of gold mines; net capital inflows amounted to almost half of total fixed capital expenditures in the 1880s.[8] Most of that capital inflow went into other than mining shares, but in the 1890s more and more Australian mines, whether gold, copper, lead, or tin, were quoted or floated in London. The average return on these ventures is said to have been small, but the inflow of capital certainly accelerated the pace of exploration and development.[9] In the last twenty years of the century, mining output was increasingly from large, rich

7. R. G. Gregory, "Some Implications of the Growth of the Mineral Sector," *Australian Journal of Agricultural Economics*, vol. 20 (August 1976), pp. 71–91. A second, and essentially unrelated, example of resources being linked to tariff questions is provided by P. J. Higgs and A. A. Powell, "The Scope for Tariff Reform Created by a Resources Boom: Simulations with the ORANI Model," impact project general paper G-40 (University of Melbourne, IMPACT Centre, September 1982).

8. E. A. Boehm, *Twentieth Century Economic Development in Australia* (Melbourne: Longman Cheshire, 1979), p. 136.

9. G. Blainey, *The Rush That Never Ended: A History of Australian Mining* (Melbourne University Press, 1963), p. 250.

Figure 6. *Net Capital Inflows and Debt Service Payments, 1861–1981*

Percentage of gross domestic product

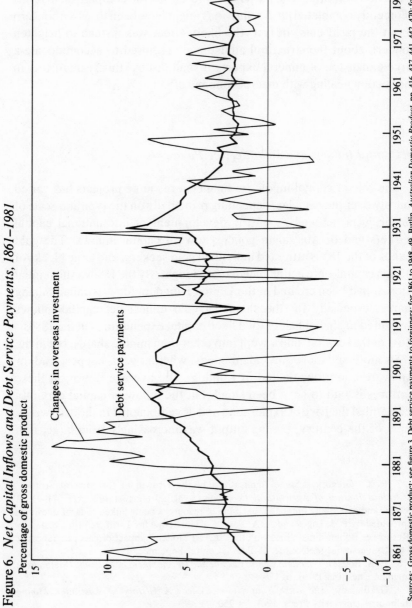

Sources: Gross domestic product: see figure 3. Debt service payments to foreigners: for 1861 to 1948–49, Butlin, *Australian Domestic Product*, pp. 416, 437, 441, 442, 470; for 1949–50 to 1980–81, Norton, Garmston, and Brodie, *Australian Economic Statistics*, p. 13. Net capital inflows: for 1861 to 1929–30, Butlin, *Australian Domestic Product*, pp. 422, 441, 444; for 1930–31 to 1948–49, Bureau of Census and Statistics, *Australian Balance of Payments*; for 1949–50 to 1980–81, Norton, Garmston, and Brodie, *Australian Economic Statistics*, p. 22.

mines.[10] Some of these companies, like Mount Morgan, paid large dividends to foreign shareholders, as shown in figure 6. Many other large companies that attracted capital inflows were less profitable, with dividends being deferred until much later or not paid at all.

The two mining booms in the second half of the twentieth century each attracted considerable foreign capital. Many of the mining projects involved foreign firms as partners who wished, or were required, to put up some equity capital. Optimism and publicity about the developments attracted additional foreign equity capital in search of everything from lone shares to takeovers. Furthermore, in the latest boom, large, capital-intensive energy projects relied heavily on bank loans, often from syndicates of international banks. The increasing relative importance of international debt finance in Australian resource projects is due to several factors: the large size and capital intensity of the projects, the prevailing international financial practices, and the Australian policies aimed at keeping 50 percent or more of the equity interest in the hands of Australian companies.

The Past and Future Structure of Mining

Figure 7 illustrates the early predominance and long-lasting importance of gold in Australian mining. In the long period when the price of gold was fixed while other prices rose and fell with world activity, gold provided a valuable countercyclical force. For example, when international commodity prices and domestic costs all fell during the 1930s, gold mining became increasingly profitable, and the increasing gold production and revenues helped to insulate Australia from the worst effects of the depression.[11] Even in the 1930s, gold did not regain the dominant role it had played in the nineteenth century, as the industrial

10. Sixteen of these paid dividends over 1 million pounds sterling: the Mount Morgan gold and copper mine in Tasmania, the Mount Lyell mine, five separate companies working the Broken Hill silver-lead-zinc ore body, seven gold mining companies working the "golden mile" at Kalgoorlie, and two other gold mines in Western Australia; ibid, p. 256.

11. The value of gold output rose from 2 million to 5 million pounds sterling from 1929 to 1932, while the value of GDP was falling by almost 30 percent, from 795 million pounds sterling in 1928–29 to 553 million pounds sterling in 1931–32.

Figure 7. *Mining Output, 1861–1981*

Percentage of gross domestic product

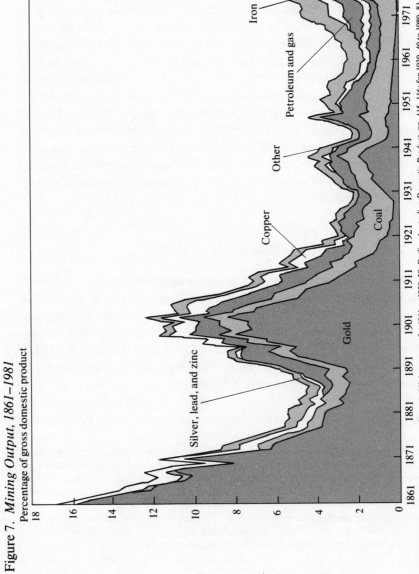

Sources: Gross domestic product: see figure 3. Mining output: for 1861 to 1938–39, Butlin, *Australian Domestic Product*, pp. 115, 116; for 1939–40 to 1980–81, *Yearbook of Australia*, various years, and Bureau of Statistics, *Mineral Production in Australia*, various years.

metals, especially lead and zinc, and the energy minerals, especially coal, had already become more important.

The minerals boom of the late 1960s and early 1970s was more broadly based than previous expansions, with most of the increased production coming from oil and gas, coal, iron ore, nickel, and alumina. The main projects for the early 1980s are either for energy minerals—coal, uranium, oil, and gas—or for minerals that use energy heavily—alumina and, especially, aluminum.

The aluminum case is interesting because it presumes that Australia's thermal coal deposits are a low-cost source of electricity. Aluminum production, because it is electricity intensive, provides an indirect way of exporting thermal coal, as well as a direct way of using Australia's large supplies of bauxite. The softness of world demand and the presence of substantial excess capacity in aluminum smelting combined to make these prospects appear less attractive in 1983 and 1984 than they seemed in 1980 and 1981.[12]

Even though Australia produced no bauxite at all before 1963, it was catapulted by 1980 into the position of being the world's third largest exporter of bauxite and the largest exporter of alumina and could become perhaps the largest exporter of aluminum by 1985. It is not surprising that the aluminum industry's expansion plans have attracted much attention. Their very magnitude is enough to cause, in different quarters, awe, alarm, and competing claims for a share of the potential revenues. Industry representatives caution that they face a brief "window of opportunity" to capitalize on the critical combination of bauxite and thermal coal, in a context of high world oil prices.[13] They fear that high and rising labor costs, high construction costs, high state charges for rail freight and electricity, and high taxes and royalties could close the

12. In 1981 it was projected by the Senate Standing Committee on Natural Resources that "based on projects either underway or for which firm announcements have been made, Australia's annual aluminium capacity will be increased from 280,000 tonnes at present to more than 1.3 million tonnes by 1985. Nearly all of the increased capacity will be used to supply export markets." Even this projected 1985 capacity, thirteen times as large as the 1965 capacity, was only expected to use 25 percent of Australia's projected 1985 alumina output of 9.5 million tonnes per year. Senate Standing Committee on National Resources, *The Development of the Bauxite, Alumina, and Aluminium Industries* (Canberra: Australian Government Publishing Service, 1981), pp. 58–59, 61.

13. M. R. Rayner, "The Economics of the Australian Aluminium Industry," paper delivered to the Australian Institute of Mining and Metallurgy Conference, Melbourne, 1982.

window. The forecast requirements for new power plants are so great,[14] and electricity costs are such an important part of aluminum smelting costs, that the expansion of aluminum smelting capacity has become the focus for much concern about electricity pricing, environmental damage, and macroeconomic dislocation.[15]

Total capital expenditures on aluminum and alumina have been estimated at about 0.35 percent of average real GDP over the 1980s. Adding the capital expenditures for related electricity generation would bring the total to 0.5 percent of GDP over the decade.[16] Investment in oil and gas is also projected to be 0.5 percent of GDP, with two-thirds of that in the Northwest Shelf natural gas project.

The Northwest Shelf project has attracted much attention because of its very large scale and its reliance on large sales of liquefied natural gas to Japan. The project has three components: the platforms and gathering system off the northwest coast of Western Australia, a 1,500-kilometer pipeline from Dampier to Perth to supply natural gas to Western Australian markets, and the construction of a liquefied natural gas plant on the northwest coast and a fleet of tankers to ship the liquefied natural gas to Japan. The initial offshore platform, the gathering system, and the pipeline to Perth are all under construction, while the liquefied natural gas project, which was to have used 80 percent of the projected flow of gas, continues to be held in abeyance because of unpromising profitability and weak demand.

Another major element of the projected 1980s minerals investment is black coal for export, about half from New South Wales and half from

14. A capacity of 7,000 megawatts of electricity would be required to service planned smelter expansion over the 1980s, according to the Senate Standing Committee on National Resources, *Development of the Aluminium Industry*, pp. 18–19. The Department of National Energy and Development, *Forecasts of Energy Demand and Supply— Primary and Secondary Fuels, Australia: 1980–81 to 1989–90* (Canberra: AGPS, 1981), p. 122, forecasted that more than half of the total increase in electricity demand from 1980–81 to 1989–90 would come from base metal production, mostly in aluminum, even though that category was responsible for only 16 percent of total electricity demand in 1980–81.

15. Even the relatively energy-efficient new smelters are estimated to use 14,000 kilowatt-hours per tonne of metal (Senate Standing Committee on National Resources, *Development of the Aluminium Industry*, p. 15). A change of one cent per kilowatt-hour would, therefore, alter costs by $140 per tonne, more than 10 percent of the Australian dollar market price of aluminum in mid-1983.

16. Using the capital cost and GDP projections reported in Derrick, McDonald, and Rosendale, "Development of Energy Resources in Australia," pp. 35, 51–52.

Queensland. Total black coal exports in 1990 are projected to be over 100 million tonnes, two and one-half times as much as they were in 1979.[17] Total capital expenditures are projected to be roughly the same as for aluminum and alumina (excluding capital expenditures for power plants) but export revenues are forecasted to be somewhat larger, averaging 1.8 percent of GDP for coal and 1.4 percent of GDP for alumina and aluminum.[18] The main issues that have arisen in connection with the current and projected coal projects relate to interstate competition for coal markets, state royalties and railway charges, tax conflicts between the commonwealth and state governments, environmental effects of coal mining and transport, loading costs, and macroeconomic effects of coal export revenues.

The final component of the energy-related export expansion of the 1980s is uranium. Objections to uranium mining have been based on aboriginal land claims, the environmental effects of the mining and the subsequent foreign use of radioactive materials, and the level and structure of taxation. In macroeconomic terms, the projected expenditures and activity levels in uranium mining are relatively small.[19]

Macroeconomic Effects of Changes in the Size of the Mining Sector

When large quantities of bauxite were discovered in Australia, it was bad news for bauxite producers elsewhere, bad news for copper miners everywhere, and good news for potential aluminum refiners. Everyone understands these simple effects, while appreciating that there may be some important indirect effects that may offset the initial impacts. But what about the car makers and the graziers? Are they gainers or losers?

If new discoveries, whether of ore or technology, happen on a fairly regular basis and if world market conditions change in a fairly stable and predictable way, then the myriad adjustments occur almost unnoticed in the blur of daily events. When there is a real upheaval in relative prices, as there was for the price of oil in 1973–74 and again in 1979–80, there are major problems of adjustment that pervade the economy.

17. Ibid., table 22.
18. Ibid., p. 51.
19. Ibid., pp. 51–52.

Australia, with its large resources of coal, uranium, oil and gas, and bauxite, was generally favored by the rising price of oil, as were a number of other similar energy-rich industrial countries: Norway, the Netherlands, the United Kingdom, Canada, and Mexico. Yet in all of these countries the increasing revenues and potential riches of the energy sectors gave rise to many disputes over the division of the benefits and to objections from other sections of the economy that they would be squeezed between rising domestic costs (sometimes described, in the shorthand of the Australian literature, as the price of nontradables) and the falling, or more slowly rising, prices for their output of tradable goods. The results of this squeeze have been labeled "deindustrialization" in the United Kingdom, the "Dutch disease" in reference to the impact of natural gas revenues in the Netherlands, and the "Gregory thesis" in application to the prospect of rising mineral export revenues in Australia.

In most of the discussion, it is assumed to be bad for a sector to contract, or to grow slower than it would otherwise. This assumption overlooks the fact that it is usually necessary, if new opportunities are to be picked up, for less to be done of something else. These opportunity costs are always relevant, but especially so in the full employment models that are usually used to study such problems. To assess the overall effects of resource development, it is helpful to distinguish the costs of adjusting to the construction of a project, the costs of adjusting to the new pattern of trade flows after the project becomes functional, and the underlying economics of the project.

In a purely competitive environment, the underlying economics of resource projects could be left for the invisible hand to sort out, but in the modern world of infrastructure, acid rain, and competing uses for state-owned sites and resource deposits, it is often the case that one project looks better than another because it has a more favorable package of taxes, royalties, subsidies, and environmental regulations. If the profitability of a project depends on state-owned natural resource deposits, the mechanism for pricing those deposits can be a key factor in the investment decision.

For huge resource projects organized by companies or consortia under limited liability, the government is often drawn in as the implicit guarantor of employment, completion, debt repayment, and financing of infrastructure. A state government may, for example, build a power plant especially to supply an aluminum smelter project. If the project is postponed or canceled, who pays? The answer, usually, is other electricity users and taxpayers; hence their lively interest in the economic prospects underlying major resource developments.

The apparent shifts of comparative advantage in favor of energy-related resource projects have led to the prospect of such a large slate of proposals as to require major accommodating adjustments in other industries. The size of these adjustments, as well as the number of projects simultaneously planning to tap the same foreign markets, has raised questions about the projects' feasibility and desirability. On this line of reasoning, elephants are more likely to be white if they are acquired in herds.

This section first considers the applicability of the Gregory thesis in a fully employed economy. It then examines the macroeconomic issues posed by unemployed resources, capital inflows, and the foreign exchange market and reviews the available empirical evidence.

The Gregory Thesis

The basic idea of the Gregory thesis is simple but compelling. By making the "small country" assumptions whereby Australia's terms of trade are held fixed, R. G. Gregory was able to put on the same graph Australia's supply curve for mineral exports, a supply curve for other exports, and a demand curve for imports.[20] The price, in all cases, is the price of traded goods in relation to nontraded goods. The latter is sometimes taken to be the output price of the service industry and sometimes a fixed wage rate. In either case, it is held fixed for Gregory's analysis.

The price of traded goods relative to nontraded goods is then determined to be the point at which the sum of the two export supply curves intersects the import demand curve. A mineral discovery increases the supply of mineral exports, at any given price, and is represented by a rightward shift of the total export supply curve. This will move the point of intersection to a lower price of traded goods (relative to nontraded goods), thus implying a larger quantity of imports and a smaller quantity of traditional nonmineral exports.

20. Gregory, "Some Implications of Growth of the Mineral Sector."

Since a tariff creates a wedge between the price of imports and the price of exports, it can be made equivalent to a shift in the supply curve for mineral exports. Given estimates of the shapes of the export supply and import demand curves, it is possible to find tariff equivalents for the increase in mineral exports. For the traditional rural exporters, Gregory estimated that Australia's mineral exports (compared with a hypothetical alternative having no mineral exports) are equivalent to a doubling of average import tariff rates. For the import-competing industry, the growth of mineral exports was found to be equivalent to a tariff reduction that exceeded the 25 percent general tariff reduction of 1973.

These calculations suggest that it takes a substantial relative price change (of which the tariff is a special case) either to replace or to make room for any substantial exogenous change in trade flows. While a tariff increase would lessen the effects on the manufacturing sector of expanded mineral exports, it would do so by increasing the amount of adjustment required in the rural exports sector.

The analysis fails to show that the average Australian is necessarily worse off with larger mineral exports. To do that requires comparison of the rents generated in the new minerals sector with those lost in the smaller rural and manufacturing industries. In general, incomes are presumed to rise as mineral exports increase, or the mineral sector would not have been able to attract labor and capital away from other activities. In fact, considering the spending of the higher incomes potentially available from the mineral exports and the interindustry flows of goods, it is no longer clear that the rural sector or the manufacturing sector must contract as the mineral industry grows.[21] However, some sector's output

21. Many papers have been written on this topic. R. H. Snape, "Effects of Mineral Development on the Economy," *Australian Journal of Agricultural Economics*, vol. 21 (December 1977), pp. 147–56, added the spending effects of the higher incomes; A. Stoeckel, "Some General Equilibrium Effects of Mining Growth on the Economy," *Australian Journal of Agricultural Economics*, vol. 23 (April 1979), pp. 1–22, added terms-of-trade effects, the distinction between demand increases and discoveries, the effects of interindustry purchases, and some more refined estimates of the likely magnitudes. W. M. Corden, "Booming Sector and Dutch Disease Economics: A Survey," Australian National University working paper in economics and econometrics 79 (Canberra: Australian National University, 1982), surveys some of the more recent papers and emphasizes the important distinction between the investment and production phases. G. L. Murray summarizes the effects of expanding the number of sectors and internationally mobile factors in "Sectoral Response to an Export Expansion: General Equilibrium Model," paper delivered to the Fifty-third Congress of the Australian and

must be reduced if any labor and capital are needed in the mineral industry, unless the required labor and capital are drawn from abroad. If no domestic labor and capital are required, then the additional mineral exports need not force other industries to contract. In an extreme case such as Saudi Arabia, where the additional mineral export revenues are all invested in foreign assets, the mineral exports may be regarded as a portfolio switch, with mineral ores being traded for claims on foreigners. If some of the revenues are immediately spent domestically, there will be some redistribution of activity among industries, but the pattern cannot be determined without empirical analysis.

The Importance of Mobility of International Factors

To analyze the case where factors are free to move internationally, it is useful to distinguish the investment from the production phase of a mineral export project. During the construction phase, capital goods must be obtained and put in place. The construction labor or the capital goods or both may be imported. Typically, Australian resource projects involve some domestic and some foreign financing. If the project is entirely foreign financed and foreign built, then there will be no direct effects on the Australian economy. If the direct import content and the direct foreign financing are roughly in balance, then the impact of the project on the domestic economy depends on the extent of unemployed resources and the industry mix of the expenditures.[22] If the industry mix of spending is roughly like that of any exogenous shift in spending, the project will increase or decrease the exchange rate depending on whether the induced capital flows are greater or less than the induced imports.[23]

New Zealand Association for the Advancement of Science, Perth, 1983. P. J. Forsyth, "The Australian Mining Boom and British North Sea Oil: A Comparison of Their Economic Effects" (Sydney: University of New South Wales, 1982), emphasizes the distinction between highly profitable and highly factor-using mineral development. The empirical work on Australia will be referred to later.

22. Detailed analysis of a proposed Canadian arctic natural gas pipeline in the early 1970s found it to have direct foreign financing that roughly matched the imported content of the capital spending. J. F. Helliwell, "Impact of a Mackenzie Pipeline on the National Economy," in P. H. Pearse, ed., *The Mackenzie Pipeline: Arctic Gas and Canadian Energy Policy* (Toronto: McClelland and Stewart, 1974), chap. 8.

23. In terms of the investment savings, *IS*, liquidity money, *LM*, and balance-of-payments, *BP*, curves usually used in textbooks to explain the balance-of-payments effects of spending changes, there will be no pressure on the exchange rate if the *LM* and the *BP* curves have the same slope.

During the operations phase of a resource project, the net additions to export revenues are equal to total export sales less current payments for imported labor and materials, and less the interest and profits accruing to foreign owners and lenders. If the project is a rich one, with output large in relation to the capital and labor employed, then the current account effects will more closely resemble those in Gregory's analysis.

For a rich project that produces substantial economic rents, the macroeconomic impact depends entirely on who collects the rents and how they are spent. If the lucky owners are governments or domestic residents who treat the sale as an asset switch, the effects follow the Saudi Arabian example mentioned before. If the owners live overseas, as with some of the richer Australian gold and copper mines in the 1890s, then the exports of ore are matched by investment income flowing to foreigners.

If the project is a poor one, with much labor and capital required to win ore from a difficult deposit, then the results will depend on the source of the labor and capital. The essential point is that when labor and capital are mobile internationally, there is little pressure for other industries to alter their production patterns. In the Australian case, with distance, tariffs, and migration policies limiting the flows, the operations phase provides markets for domestic suppliers of labor and materials. To the extent that the project uses local labor and materials, it will produce a net export surplus, thus inducing a readjustment in other industries, with relatively less output and factors going directly into foreign markets (the Gregory effect) and more being used to meet the needs of the mineral project. The extent of this readjustment depends on the nature of economic policies, the rate of capacity utilization, and the empirical nature and rigidity of the industrial structure.

Fiscal, Monetary, and Exchange Rate Policies

Four types of fiscal policies come into play in resource booms (and slumps): changes in public infrastructure investment, changes in tariffs, changes in resource taxation, and changes in government spending or taxes to maintain overall macroeconomic balance.

Because of their long lead times, infrastructure investments often must be started when the resource projects themselves are subject to delay or cancellation. Alternatively, if the infrastructure investments are delayed to coincide with the project itself, they tend to exacerbate the bottleneck problems that so often accompany the construction phase. If the government gets swept up in the boom-time euphoria about the scale and richness of resource developments, then there is a risk that its infrastructure investments will exacerbate the expenditure pressures at peak times and create excessive capacity on average, that its other expenditures will move too much in response to the swings in natural resource revenues, and that its tax policies will change so often as to create an uncertain investment climate and thus lessen the average benefits available from natural resources.

A general tariff reduction was used in 1973 with the objectives of offsetting some of the inflationary effects of the increase in world mineral prices and of improving structural efficiency. As Gregory makes clear, a tariff reduction eases the adjustments required in the rural sector, while increasing those in the tariff-protected manufacturing sector. The same argument has been made for tariff reductions to accompany the mid-1980s expansion of mineral exports,[24] but since the argument for tariff reform is essentially independent of the resource boom, it is not surprising that others have argued for an increase in the tariff to offset the possible effects on the manufacturing industry.[25]

Changes in resource taxation are sometimes suggested to smooth the pace of mining booms. They are more frequently used to alter the distribution of surpluses arising from higher prices or from rich deposits. These issues will be discussed later.

The arguments for and against the uses of general fiscal policy to dampen resource booms and slumps, either through the so-called automatic stabilizers or through discretionary changes in spending or tax rates, prompt the same arguments as do countercyclical policies generally. The special feature of natural resource revenues, especially those from profits taxes or resource rent taxes, is that they are subject to world

24. For example, J. O. Stone, "Australia in a Competitive World—Some Options," paper presented to the Twenty-first General Management Conference, Australian Institute of Management, Sydney, 1979; and Alan Powell, "Resources and Resource Allocation Policy," *Australian Bulletin of Labour*, Supplement No. 3 (March 1982), pp. S 24–25.

25. See the chapters on the United Kingdom and Mexico in T. Barker and V. Brailovsky, eds., *Oil or Industry? Energy, Industrialization and Economic Policy in Canada, Mexico, the Netherlands, Norway and the United Kingdom* (London: Academic Press, 1981).

market booms and slumps. For governments to keep their budgets balanced in the face of big cyclical changes in resource revenues, they must cut spending and increase taxes just when the resource industries are cutting spending. The benefits of keeping the automatic stabilizers in action, and of accepting boom-time surpluses and slump-time deficits, are especially great for the governments of the resource-dependent states, since resource revenues are a larger fraction of their total revenues and their employment, wages, and prices already are more affected by the cycles in resource activity and revenues.

The potential role for monetary and exchange rate policies to ease the strains of resource booms in Australia is probably overstressed in public policy discussions and understressed in the theoretical literature, which typically is concerned only with the "real" economy on the assumption that the overall price level is either fixed exogenously or is irrelevant. It has been argued that the inflationary effects of the 1971–73 improvement in Australia's export prices could have been reduced or eliminated by letting the Australian dollar revalue and running a correspondingly tighter monetary policy.[26] This is really part of the general debate about monetary policy under alternative exchange rate systems and does not have a direct application to resource booms. However, if wages or other domestic costs and prices are sticky, then a depreciation of the domestic currency, or a slower appreciation than would otherwise take place, can be thought of as a form of protection for domestic manufacturers.[27]

Most analysts would agree that a long-term export of minerals eventually requires some real adjustment, unless all the net export receipts are saved. An exchange rate depreciation, unlike a tariff increase, provides only temporary protection for manufacturers because it must be accompanied by a more expansionary monetary policy that will eventually increase domestic costs to erode the competitive advantage.

The temporary nature of exchange rate protection, coupled with the possibility of speculative funds running into the Australian "coal dollar"

26. For example, M. G. Porter, "External Shocks and Stabilization Policy in a Small Open Economy: The Australian Experience," *Weltwirtschaftliches Archiv*, vol. 114 (1978), pp. 709–35.

27. See L. H. Cook and E. Sieper, "The Minerals Sector and Structural Change in Australia—Some Economic Issues," discussion paper (Clayton, Victoria: Monash University Centre of Policy Studies, 1983); W. M. Corden, "Exchange Rates Policy and the Resources Boom," *The Economic Record*, vol. 58 (March 1982), pp. 18–31.

in anticipation of a future export boom, have led some to suggest that "some 'leaning against the wind' intervention in the foreign exchange market may be appropriate in response to sudden expectations-determined appreciation, the aim being to moderate rather than avoid the required changes."[28]

Others with more faith in the rationality of exchange market participants argue that any exchange rate appreciation that occurs in advance of the mineral export boom is merely that required to provide the imported goods demanded as domestic residents start to spend a small but stable portion of the present value of the newly recognized addition to their wealth.[29] The post-1973 experience seems to suggest that exchange market participants are not as consistently far-sighted as this analysis assumes, but there is other evidence that efforts to smooth exchange rates have themselves frequently been subject to speculative rout.

Empirical Evidence

Most of the Australian evidence on the economy-wide impact of resource booms relates to the interindustry shifts of output that would take place if there was an expansion of mineral exports. In part this kind of evidence reflects the fact that there is no split between resource and nonresource industries in the official macroeconomic models of the Australian economy.[30] Such evidence also reflects the existence of several interindustry models of the Australian economy.[31]

28. Corden, "Exchange Rates Policy," p. 23.

29. A. O. Krueger and M. G. Porter, "The Asset Theory of Exchange-Rate Determination and the Resources Boom," discussion paper (Clayton, Victoria: Monash University Centre of Policy Studies, 1982).

30. The main official models are the Treasury's National Income Forecasting model and the Reserve Bank's series of RB models. To date, neither model has been extensively used for studies of the effects of energy price shocks, mining export booms, and other resource-based macroeconomic issues. This may be in part because of the model changes required and in part because of institutional specialization.

31. Even the existence of these models reflects the prevalence of the tariff in Australian policy discussion. The ORANI model, which has been the most widely used model for the study of resource booms, is part of the IMPACT project. The IMPACT project is officially an interagency model but has its main support from the Industries Assistance Commission, the body set up in 1973 to study and recommend policy on subsidy and protection policies. The nature and role of the IAC are discussed more fully in the chapter by Caves on scale, openness, and productivity.

Following the lead of the Gregory article, most of the studies have been of the operations phase of the mining projects, with an increase of mining export revenues achieved either as a gift of foreign exchange or by means of a shift in the mining industry supply function. I shall try to summarize these results, both with and without the assumption of full employment, and shall then briefly discuss the more limited evidence on the construction phase.

There are four sources of reasonably comparable information about the interindustry and aggregate employment and output effects of mineral exports: the Stoeckel model;[32] the ORANI interindustry model[33] as run by members of the IMPACT project team;[34] a more aggregated revision of ORANI run at Monash University;[35] and a simplified version of the IMP model of the Melbourne University Institute of Applied Economic and Social Research.[36]

All of the models have an interindustry structure, with fixed input-output weights. None of the models makes the "small country" assumption about traded goods; terms-of-trade effects therefore arise in all cases. All make allowance for the higher levels of national income and spending permitted by the additional mineral exports, although the size of the total increase in income depends on whether there is any scope

32. Stoeckel, "Some General Equilibrium Effects of Mining Growth."
33. The fullest description of the model is in P. B. Dixon, B. R. Parmenter, J. Sutton, and D. P. Vincent, *ORANI: A Multisectoral Model of the Australian Economy* (Amsterdam: North-Holland, 1982).
34. P. B. Dixon, A. A. Powell, and B. R. Parmenter, *Structural Adaptation in an Ailing Macroeconomy* (Melbourne University Press, 1979); P. B. Dixon, J. D. Harrower, and A. A. Powell, "Long Term Structural Pressures on Industries and the Labour Market," *Australian Bulletin of Labour*, vol. 3 (June 1977), pp. 5–44; and P. B. Dixon, B. R. Parmenter, and J. Sutton, "Some Causes of Structural Maladjustment in the Australian Economy," *Economic Papers*, no. 57 (January 1978), pp. 10–25.
35. The methodology and results of the empirical work are described in four working papers issued by the Centre of Policy Studies at Monash University: L. H. Cook, "Quantifying the Effects of Changes in the Minerals Sector: Background Notes" (1982), and "Some Quantitative Estimates of the Effects of Changes in the Minerals Sector" (1982); L. H. Cook and E. Sieper, "The Minerals Sector and Structural Change in Australia—Some Economic Issues" (1983); and M. G. Porter, "The Minerals Sector and the Australian Economy: A Broad Overview" (1983).
36. The results are from chapters 12 and 14 of P. J. Brain and G. P. Schuyers, *Energy and the Australian Economy* (Melbourne: Longman Cheshire, 1981). The authors employ the energy demand and supply modules coupled to an eighteen-sector long-run model of the Australian economy, which is reproduced in their appendix 4.

for increasing total employment, the capital stock, or the rate of capacity utilization. I shall describe briefly how the four models treat these issues.

The Stoeckel model assumes full wage flexibility, full employment, free mobility of labor and capital between industries to equalize marginal returns, output balance between industries to equalize marginal returns, and foreign trade balance both with and without the minerals exports. No changes are permitted in either the total level of employment or the total size of the capital stock, so that increases in some industries must be balanced by reductions elsewhere.

The IMPACT team's ORANI-based studies of mineral exports have included experiments in long-run, short-run, and mixed modes. In the long-run mode, full employment and adjustments to the capital stock are assumed at industry and aggregate levels.[37] In the short-run mode, industry capital stocks and all real wages are held fixed, and adjustment comes from interindustry and aggregate changes in employment and profit rates.[38] In the mixed mode, capital is held fixed in each industry; employment is held fixed in the aggregate but is free to move among industries and occupations; and occupational wage relativities are held fixed, with wages moving so as to maintain full employment.[39] In all three modes, mining export revenues are treated as transfer payments or gifts of foreign exchange; there is thus no labor or materials required for the additional mining output. Prices, output, and employment in the various industries then adjust so that the higher incomes are spent and trade balance is restored.

The Monash group has run their version of the ORANI model under five different modes.[40] In all five modes, capital stock is held fixed in each sector, except where the mineral sector expansion is achieved by an increase in its capital stock. In two modes, real wage flexibility and aggregate full employment are assumed; in the first of these the mineral sector expansion is treated as a gift of foreign exchange;[41] in the second it is achieved by an expansion of the mineral sector's capital stock, thus

37. Dixon, Harrower, and Powell, "Long Term Structural Pressures."
38. Dixon, Parmenter, and Sutton, "Some Causes of Structural Maladjustment."
39. Dixon, Powell, and Parmenter, Structural Adaptation.
40. The results discussed are from the appendix of Cook and Sieper, "Minerals Sector and Structural Change."
41. The first mode thus uses the same framework as the IMPACT group's mixed mode, since capital is immobile, employment is mobile, real wages are flexible, trade balance is restored, and no inputs are needed to get the extra mining output.

requiring additional mining employment, and purchases of goods and services from other industries in order to achieve the additional output. In the third and fourth modes the nominal wage is held rigid, and aggregate as well as sectoral employment is therefore permitted to change. In the fourth mode the nominal exchange rate is flexible and nominal national income is held fixed, thus forcing any increase in real income to be offset by a reduction in the aggregate price level. The fifth mode is like the third mode except that the real wage rather than the nominal wage is held fixed.[42]

The Melbourne Institute modeling is done in three modes, one with the real wage held fixed, one with full employment, and one with the nominal wage adjusted so that aggregate wage income is a constant share of nominal national income.[43] Aggregate employment is therefore free to change, as is its distribution among sectors. Aggregate and sectoral capital stocks also adjust; foreign capital inflows are assumed to finance a constant proportion of aggregate business fixed capital expenditures. This induced capital inflow increases the expansion of income that accompanies an expansion of mineral exports.[44]

In addition to being less constrained by supply than the other models, the Institute model has an additional demand-side stimulus. This comes from the policy rule used for setting the income tax rate, which is changed so as to adjust aggregate demand up or down by enough to restore balance in international payments. Under the Institute's third mode, the supply curve for labor is downward sloping and prices actually fall with

42. The fifth mode is like the short-run mode used by Dixon, Parmenter, and Sutton, "Some Causes of Structural Maladjustment."

43. Most of the emphasis is on the third alternative, which has the effect of lowering the nominal wage rate in the face of any expansionary shock that increases employment by more than nominal income. For given nominal income, the aggregate labor supply function is thus downward sloping.

44. Aside from the fact that both aggregate capital and total employment are variable in the Institute model, there is a further difference in aggregate output in the Institute model compared with all the other models examined here. All of the other models have output that is rigidly restricted by explicit production functions; hence output cannot rise without a corresponding rise in land, labor, and capital. The Institute model uses a three-factor production structure as a basis for deriving consistent cost-minimizing demands for capital, labor, and energy, but there is no explicit use of the production structure to determine either output or capacity utilization. Thus there is the possibility that even over extended periods industry and aggregate output could rise faster than factor inputs without facing supply constraints.

an expansion of mineral exports,[45] thus increasing international competitiveness and increasing the scope for further expansionary fiscal policy to absorb the balance-of-trade surplus created by natural resource projects.[46] The result of these structural features of the Institute model is that any increases in mineral or energy export revenues, whether or not they require inputs of capital, labor, and materials from other industries, produce a much-magnified increase in income and employment.[47] To make the Institute model's results more comparable with those of the others and to downplay the implausible results from the most unconstrained versions, I shall restrict my subsequent discussion to the fixed real-wage and full-employment cases.[48]

So much for the basic structure of the models. What of the results? In all of the models, expansion of mineral exports leads to expansion of the service sector relative to the manufacturing and rural sectors. In all the full-employment cases there is an absolute increase in the gross output of the service sector and a decrease in the gross output of the rural sector.[49] Manufacturing output is generally down, but by less than rural

45. Tables 12.2A and 12.2B, pp. 225–26, of Brain and Schuyers, *Energy and the Australian Economy*, show, for example, that an oil shale development of 400,000 barrels per day (19.1 million tonnes per year) would decrease the price level by 14 percent.

46. The income tax rate is 22 percent of household receipts in the base case and falls to 17.3 percent with the oil shale projects in place; ibid., pp. 212, 228.

47. Since the "pessimistic base case" projects an unemployment rate of 25 percent of the potential work force (ibid., p. 210), even the very large employment increases associated with individual energy projects do not drive the unemployment rate below 3 percent. If this target rate is broached, then tariffs are reduced as an alternative way of restoring balance-of-payments equilibrium.

48. The Institute model might be regarded as an application of E. Shann's view, "Policy Issues in Mineral Sector Growth: A Keynesian Model," discussion paper 60 (Canberra: Australian National University, Centre for Economic Policy Research, 1982), that the balance-of-payments adjustment to mineral exports comes from expansion of national income rather than intersectoral movements triggered by relative prices. This parallel should not be overstressed, however, as all of the four empirical models surveyed here have multiplier effects in all but their full-employment cases, and all have relative prices influencing foreign trade and industrial structure. The main reasons for the Institute model's differing results are the labor supply conditions and the lowering of income tax rates in the face of increases in mineral export revenues.

49. Stoeckel, "Some General Equilibrium Effects of Mining Growth," p. 21, provides the only near exception with an insignificantly small reduction in services output in the case where the increase in mining output comes from a shift in the demand curve. The other results are from Dixon, Powell, and Parmenter, *Structural Adaptation*, pp. 49–51; Cook and Sieper, "Minerals Sector and Structural Change," pp. 45–46; and Brain

output. Where a split is made between export-oriented and import-competing manufacturing, the output of the latter is generally up while the former is down.

When real wages, rather than aggregate employment levels, are held fixed, the result of the models is an increase in employment and higher output than in the full-employment case. This is because in all models the real wage rises in the full-employment case.

The effect of the increase in mining exports with fixed real wages is to raise real output everywhere except in most of the rural sector and in the export-oriented manufacturing sector.[50] When nominal wages are held fixed, as in one of the Monash cases, aggregate output and employment increases are larger than in the case of fixed real wages, and no sectors show output declines.[51]

The overall impression given by the supply-constrained models is that allowance for terms-of-trade gains, income increases, the purchases of the mining sector, and some degree of initial unemployment and real wage stickiness are sufficient to reduce to modest size the adjustments required in most sectors in response to expansions of mineral exports of the sort envisaged for the 1980s. Even in the rural sector, the adjustments are very small compared with the average year-to-year variations in agricultural output.

In the Institute model, where attainable output is constrained by the balance of payments rather than factors of production, any expansion of

---

and Schuyers, *Energy and the Australian Economy*, p. 262. The Dixon, Powell, and Parmenter results are at a very disaggregated level and show profits rather than output, so inferences about aggregate sectoral output cannot be made with precision, but the broad pattern is clearly consistent with the other models.

50. Dixon, Parmenter, and Sutton, "Some Causes of Structural Maladjustment," table 2, show (often substantial) output declines in most of the rural sector, in the rest of the mining industry, and in some of the metal industries, especially basic iron and steel. Cook and Sieper, "Minerals Sector and Structural Change," table A6, show a 1.5 percent decline in agricultural output and a 0.1 percent drop in total manufacturing, compared with declines of 2.0 percent and 0.7 percent in agriculture and manufacturing, respectively, in the full employment case. The shock, in both cases, is a net increase of about 9 percent in the total output of the mineral sector. Brain and Schuyers, *Energy and the Australian Economy*, p. 248, in their version of real wage stability, report large increases in real GDP (14 percent from the oil shale project), so large as to imply output increases in all sectors. Since their real wage grows with average output per worker, which itself has risen substantially, the case is really one of real wage increase. This result emphasizes the large quantitative difference between this model and the others.

51. Cook and Sieper, "Minerals Sector and Structural Change," table A4.

net export revenues, whether from mineral exports, energy production, or whatever, yields an output increase several times as large.

What about the construction phase? Most of the evidence is too specific to particular projects or models to be very helpful. The four models assessed here are not well suited to analyze dynamic macroeconomic effects and therefore have not been used much to analyze the boom-and-slump features of the construction phase. The history of resource booms since 1850 suggests that international movements of population, financial capital, and capital goods are especially important in the Australian case. To ignore those movements is bound to exaggerate the impact of investment booms.

Agenda for Further Research

What is missing from the current empirical evidence on the macroeconomic effects of major resource developments in Australia? Evidence has been amassed on the equilibrium changes in output for different industries. The tricky issue is how it can be used to aid investment decisions and avoid speculative bubbles of building and bankruptcy. At the aggregate level, the results depend very heavily on labor supply conditions, on wage and price determination, and on the international mobility of labor and capital. None of the models surveyed deals well with these issues; the ORANI-type models must assume either fixed wages, fixed employment, or some arbitrary compromise,[52] while the Institute model uses an unrealistic simulation rule.

What is needed is empirical feedback from factor-based potential output and capacity utilization to the determination of wages and prices. To address the issues of crowding-out and the role of foreign capital, a model must permit interest rates and monetary conditions to influence investment, savings, and capital flows. None of the models surveyed here has any role for monetary factors.

An especially important issue in the Australian context is how changes in world resource prices, and hence changes in Australia's terms of trade, influence domestic wage levels. To what extent was the resource-

---

52. For example, Cook, "Quantifying the Effects of Changes in the Minerals Sector," assumes full employment and wage flexibility for skilled labor and wage rigidity and variable employment for unskilled labor.

based improvement in the terms of trade in the early 1970s responsible for the wage explosion in 1974? To what extent did the anticipation of a resource boom in the 1980s fuel the wage bubble of 1982? The latter question is especially difficult because events did not fulfill the government and industry projections of rapid growth in resource investment, production, exports, and revenues.

Another topic for investigation is whether there are ratchet effects, with terms-of-trade improvements leading to wage increases larger than the wage reductions following terms-of-trade deterioration. If the terms of trade trigger large changes in money wages, especially asymmetric changes, macroeconomic policy is likely to face serious problems. Any long-run improvement in the terms of trade can support corresponding increases in real incomes, but wage bubbles in response to higher resource prices are likely to exacerbate the difficulties faced by other industries and to increase the unemployment rate.

Also to be established is the extent to which a fiscal policy that absorbs, but does not spend, a large fraction of temporary changes in resource revenues would help to reduce the changes in wages that might otherwise follow changes in natural resource prices. The empirical issue is whether wages respond differently to resource-based changes in the terms of trade if the terms-of-trade changes influence tax revenues rather than profits. If wages do respond differently, there is a clear link between resource taxation policies and macroeconomic strategy.

What might such a research agenda show? Consider what the application to Canada of the type of modeling I am recommending for Australia shows about the consequences of changes in energy investment, output, and prices.[53] Despite the likely differences in wage behavior in the two countries, their similarities of size, income, political structure, and resource dependence probably make the Canadian evidence more relevant to Australia than that from any other country.

The Canadian evidence supports the importance of distinguishing the investment and production phases and of treating resource price changes differently from changes in production volumes. All of the results depend on the monetary policy followed. In general, the macroeconomic effects of the construction phase are not very different from those of any other

53. The model and results are described in detail in J. F. Helliwell and others, "Energy and the National Economy," in A. D. Scott, ed., *Progress in Natural Resource Economics* (Oxford University Press, 1984).

surge in capital spending. Changes in the volume of resource exports do not apparently give rise to the "Dutch disease" because the higher aggregate income and demand are sufficient to increase total output of the nonresource sectors in the face of the real appreciation. Nonenergy exports are reduced, and hence there are likely to be some specialized industries with falling demand and output.

Effects of resource prices are more complicated than they would be in an Australian model based on a resource-nonresource split, since it is energy that is singled out for special treatment in the Canadian model. Canadian energy use is a larger fraction of Canadian production than would be true of the typical Australian natural resource industry. Thus increases in world energy prices are more likely to cause stagflation in Canada,[54] even without foreign income effects, than would a rise in the average price of Australian natural resources. For a rise in energy prices alone, however, the results would likely be similar for Canada and Australia.

Microeconomic Factors in Resource Development

Much of the preceding discussion pays a lot of attention to changes in industrial structure and none to changes in location. Yet even casual evidence suggests that it is more costly to close down a town than a widely dispersed industry of equal size. Natural resource projects frequently combine industrial specialization with geographic remoteness, so that they create and destroy communities as they come and go. One approach to these issues is to have all the infrastructure costs treated as part of the project itself, so that the mining companies would take account of the start-up and shut-down costs. Internalizing these costs entirely is impossible, of course. Taxpayer-financed unemployment and other assistance programs bear many of the costs. And who is to say whether a ghost town should be regarded as a tourist attraction or a blot on the environment?

Whoever may bear the costs of adjustment, there is often a choice to

54. The results are analyzed in some detail in J. F. Helliwell, "Stagflation and Productivity Decline in Canada, 1974–1982," *Canadian Journal of Economics*, vol. 17 (May 1984).

be made between a large-scale, relatively short-lived project and a smaller-scale project with a longer expected life. The arguments for the former are usually based on expected economies of scale in extraction combined with uncertainty about future market opportunities, land tenure, and tax systems. The arguments for the latter are based on the difficulty of internalizing the costs of mine closure, coupled with a different approach to uncertainty. If the size and shape of an ore body are uncertain, if the costs and details of new technology are best worked out by practical experiments, and if the environmental consequences and the best methods for controlling them are unknown, then total costs may be lowered and the present value of the entire project increased by starting small and learning by doing.[55]

Environmental and Aboriginal Issues

These issues have assumed increasing importance in Australia in the past twenty years. This chapter is not the place, however, to review the issues and the way they have been handled; here I wish only to sketch the links between them and the scale and type of natural resource projects proposed for the 1970s and 1980s. One obvious point is that the immense scale of many of the mining and smelting projects has heightened their potential impact and has amplified potential objections. Large scale has also made the projects focal points for the discussion of aboriginal rights to receive mineral revenues and to keep exploration and mining out of historic or sacred sites. Many of the prospective uranium deposits, in particular, are located in traditional aboriginal areas.

Environmental concerns have been strongly linked to some of the new resource projects that are close to large centers of population—especially projects for mining and shipping of coal and aluminum in New

55. The case for this approach has been made in the context of uranium mining in northern Australia by A. D. Scott and H. Campbell, "Policies towards Proposals for Large-Scale Natural Resource Projects: Attenuation versus Postponement," *Resources Policy* (June 1979), pp. 113–40. Scott and Campbell argue that attenuation may permit managers to find less costly or more effective ways of avoiding environmental damage and may enable aboriginals and other local residents to play more substantial roles in planning and operating the projects.

South Wales and Queensland. In these areas environmental concerns are greater and the pollution carrying capacity of air and water is already under greater strain than in more sparsely settled parts of Australia.

Uranium mining has also aroused strong environmental concerns. Although Australia is likely to continue to rely on coal rather than nuclear energy for its new power stations, there is substantial concern in Australia not just about the possibility of radioactive traces at mine sites, but also about the safety of peaceful uses and the risk of military uses of uranium after it is exported.

Division of Resource Revenues and Powers

The uneven geographic distribution of mineral deposits and the location of many of the recent developments far from centers of population have meant that interregional shifts of activity and income are more important than the interindustry movements that have been the focus of so much attention. In the early days, the agricultural and mineral resources of New South Wales and Victoria drew people there and provided the base for industrial development. Now there is a geographic split between the resource producers (especially the mineral producers) and the manufacturers.

These facts would have created regional pressures whatever political form had been adopted when the Commonwealth of Australia was formed in 1901. The federal form that was chosen has contributed to those pressures. The constitution enumerated the powers of the commonwealth government and left residual powers to the states. No specific mention was made of natural resources, which therefore continued to be owned and controlled by the state governments. The commonwealth government has broad taxing powers, however, as well as powers to regulate foreign trade.[56] Until the early 1970s, the states tended to use their resource deposits as means of attracting industry and growth rather

56. Intergovernmental fiscal relations are dealt with in detail in Gramlich's chapter. A chronology of intergovernmental issues relating to natural resources up to the mid-1970s may be found in G. Stevenson, *Mineral Resources and Australian Federalism*, Research Monograph 17 (Canberra: Australian National University, Centre for Research on Federal Financial Relations, 1976).

than as sources of revenue; state royalty rates were kept low.[57] The rise in resource prices in the early 1970s, especially for energy resources, changed the focus of attention toward potential mineral revenues. The federal government imposed export controls over all minerals, with the intent of increasing export prices, of sharing markets among states, and of using export permission to obtain some commonwealth control over the foreign ownership, environmental standards, and state-controlled features of resource projects.[58] This was a controversial use of commonwealth powers, as was the later introduction of a federal export tax on coal.

Offshore oil and mineral resources were held in a 1975 court decision to fall under commonwealth ownership and control, although in 1979 there was an agreed resolution under which the states have the same rights and powers in the territorial sea as they do onshore.[59] The main offshore production, in Bass Strait off the coast of Victoria, is outside the territorial limit and hence remains under commonwealth control. Since the early 1960s, there has been an agreed sharing of the Bass Strait royalty revenue, with Victoria receiving roughly 60 percent and the commonwealth 40 percent. However, the commonwealth levy keeps the wellhead price low and thereby puts almost all of the revenue into commonwealth hands.[60] The government of Victoria responded to the situation by levying a flat rate license fee on the two pipelines used to transport the Bass Strait oil and gas.[61] In late 1982 the companies operating the oil pipeline, supported by the commonwealth government,

57. In states with substantial mineral resources and few other sources of revenues, as in the cases of South Australia and Western Australia at the beginning of the century, mineral revenues were up to one-half as large as state tax revenues. Subsequently, this fraction has been much smaller, averaging less than 10 percent for all states. See A. D. Scott, *Central Government Claims to Mineral Revenues*, Occasional Paper 8 (Canberra: Australian National University, Centre for Research on Federal Financial Relations, 1978), table 2, p. 4.

58. Stevenson, *Mineral Resources and Australian Federalism*, pp. 48–49. Export controls had been used previously to control exports of minerals thought to be scarce; for example, the export of iron ore was prohibited from 1938 until 1960.

59. See Commonwealth Attorney-General's Department, *Offshore Constitutional Settlement: A Milestone in Cooperative Federalism* (Canberra: AGPS, 1980).

60. According to *The Budget and the Victorian Economy 1982/82* (Melbourne: Government of Victoria, 1982): "In 1981–82, for instance, Victoria received $107 million or 3.2 percent of total returns and the Commonwealth $3,215 million or 96.8 percent."

61. The fees were set at $10 million for each of the two pipelines in the 1981–82 fiscal year and raised to $33 million in the 1982–83 fiscal year.

challenged the fee on the grounds that it is an excise tax, which only the commonwealth government is empowered to levy. The commonwealth-state dispute over resource revenues goes well beyond party politics, as the state license fee was introduced by a Liberal government and raised by a Labor government, while both federal parties have raised objections to the tax. All of the other state governments, regardless of party, supported the position of Victoria. In August 1983 the High Court ruled that the levy was an excise and therefore beyond the state's power. The commonwealth government has since rejected the imposition of a similar levy on the state's behalf on the grounds that it would entail a large reduction in commonwealth receipts from the company tax.

The rapidly changing price and the sometimes uncertain availability of imported oil has led to much attention in Australia, as elsewhere, to the development of secure indigenous alternatives.[62] Australian oil production provides an increasing majority of the oil consumed domestically, and there are potentially large exportable surpluses of coal, natural gas, and natural gas liquids. The development of these energy resources has increased interest in energy pricing and revenue sharing. Between 1973 and 1978 Australians paid less than the world price for oil, by dint of commonwealth regulation of the prices of domestically produced oil. Any oil discovered since September 14, 1975, receives the import parity price, and since August 1978 all domestically produced oil is sold to consumers at the import parity price. A commonwealth levy is collected on the production of oil discovered before August 17, 1978.[63]

To one versed in the Canadian experience, it is surprising that the state governments so easily accepted a large federal levy. One possible reason is that the levy was implicit in the bargain for state powers over offshore resources. A second is that Victoria, a populous eastern state with a large manufacturing base, does not share the needs of the more resource-dependent states, such as Queensland and Western Australia.

62. For example, Senate Standing Committee on Natural Resources, *The Replacement of Petroleum Based Fuels by Alternative Sources of Energy* (Canberra: AGPS, 1980); and J. Black, ed., *Liquid Fuels in Australia* (Sydney: Pergamon Press, 1982).

63. The levy differs by size and location of field. The import parity pricing policy is described and advocated on efficiency grounds in *Energy Markets—Some Principles of Pricing*, Treasury Economic Paper 5 (Canberra: AGPS, 1979). See also F. H. Gruen and A. L. Hillman, "A Review of Issues Pertinent to Liquid Fuels Policy," *Economic Record* (June 1981), pp. 111–27; and the appendix to *Budget Papers*, Statement 4 (Canberra: AGPS, 1979).

Those states want to develop and use their resource revenues to offset the tariff-supported manufacturing power of Victoria and New South Wales.

A third possible reason is that Australia is unusual among federations in the amount of revenues raised by the central government and distributed to other governments. This power of the purse is likely to have influenced state resource policies in two ways. First, states may be tempted to rely on transferred rather than directly levied taxes to minimize the political costs of meeting expenditure goals. Second, the fiscal equalization system provides, in principle, a more equal distribution of revenue among states than in any other federation. The Commonwealth Grants Commission, which administers the equalization system, attempts to maintain the financial incentive for states to tax their own natural resources, but this is difficult to accomplish with so many different types of mineral deposits.[64] For example, there may still be a financial incentive for states to encourage otherwise uneconomic downstream processing, since the reduction of potential revenues will trigger increased entitlements to equalization payments.

Taxing of Resources

Recent debates about the level and form of resource taxation have taken an unusual form in Australia. Most recognizable is the industry position that mining should be taxed no more than other industries and no more than mining in other countries.[65] Before the early 1970s the Australian income tax system did give concessional treatment to the mining industry, and state royalties were very low. During the 1970s there were attempts to reduce tax concessions to the industry,[66] and

---

64. The procedures are spelled out in detail in the chapter by Gramlich.

65. As S. Harris points out in his survey article, "Resources Policies in Australia," *Resources Policy* (June 1980), pp. 179–91, this neglects the fact that state royalties and taxes include the price paid to buy the right to extract the Crown-owned deposit. That mining taxes are on average the same as those in other industries would imply that the resource rights have no value or that they are being distributed at less than their market value.

66. The focal point for commonwealth efforts was probably the 1974 report done by T. M. Fitzgerald for the commonwealth government, *The Contribution of the Mineral Industry to Australian Welfare* (Canberra: AGPS, 1974).

especially at the end of the decade the states began to look for more revenues from the anticipated bulge of export-oriented projects. The industry felt that it was likely to be caught with increasing government claims, wage costs, excess capacity, and international competition for projects and for world markets.[67]

The unusual feature of the Australian discussion is the extent to which it has been dominated by particular forms for mining taxation, especially the resource rent tax (RRT)[68] and competitive bidding for exploration and development rights.[69] The RRT is a tax that comes in at a high rate on profits above a threshold rate of return, where the threshold rate of return is set to approximate the cost of capital to projects of equivalent risk.[70] While some industry representatives would apparently prefer an RRT to a straight royalty, since it allows for deposits of differing costliness,[71] others reject the RRT on grounds that it dampens incentives and discriminates between industries.[72]

At the end of 1983 the commonwealth government proposed an RRT as a replacement for existing excise taxes and royalties in the petroleum sector. The discussion paper containing the proposal expresses the hope

67. For example, C. T. Gibbons, "The Effect of Taxation on New Mining Projects," paper presented to the Silver City Accountants Silver Anniversary Convention, Broken Hill, September 1979; D. W. Barnett, "The Cost of Australian Export Coal," mimeographed (Sydney: Minec Pty, 1982).

68. R. Garnaut and A. Clunies Ross, "Uncertainty, Risk Aversion and the Taxing of Natural Resource Projects," *Economic Journal*, vol. 85 (June 1975), pp. 272–87; R. Garnaut and A. Clunies Ross, "The Neutrality of the Resource Rent Tax," *Economic Record*, vol. 55 (September 1979), pp. 193–201; and W. Mayo, "Rent Royalties," *The Economic Record*, vol. 55 (September 1979), pp. 202–13.

69. For example, see R. Dowell, "Resources Rent Taxation," *Australian Journal of Management*, vol. 3 (October 1978), pp. 127–46; and M. G. Porter, "Australian Resource Development: Some Opening Comments," *Economic Papers*, no. 67 (August 1981), pp. 1–6.

70. The idea, if not the name, will be familiar outside Australia, as similar rules are used in the Alberta profit-sharing royalty on synthetic oil production, the progressive incremental royalty on the Canada lands, and the royalty systems used in the United Kingdom and Norwegian sectors of the North Sea. Many conventional royalty systems come close to the RRT by permitting recovery of capital costs before payments of royalties.

71. As quoted by R. Dowell in "Auctions and Investment Dilution Alternatives to the Resource Rent Tax," *Economic Papers,* no. 67 (August 1981), pp. 43–55.

72. J. Brunner, "Resource Rent Taxation: Some Comments," *Economic Papers,* no. 67 (August 1981), pp. 56–59.

that the proposed RRT for petroleum would be a model for later application in other parts of the mining sector.[73] The paper also raises the possibility of a later move toward a cash bids system operated jointly with the RRT.[74]

There are many attractions to a mixed system of resource taxation in which an RRT, or some other form of agreed-in-advance royalty rate, is used to distribute net revenues, with the rates set low enough that firms are prepared to bid for the rights to develop the project.[75] The bidding process would reduce the pressures placed on the choice of the tax rate and the threshold rate of return, by ensuring that the sharing system passed the market test of being neither too harsh nor too soft. Such a mixed system is not novel, of course, even in Australia; it was used in the copper mines of South Australia more than a century ago.[76] Probably the most important feature of its success then was that the rent-sharing included the miner at the pit face.

Early Australian mining history also shows the pitfalls of relying only on front-end payments, especially if they are fixed entry fees that do not take account of different extraction costs. The Ballarat rebellion of 1854 arose from resentment over per-miner license fees that penalized the deep Ballarat diggings, which required many men and many days to reach the gold-bearing leads. Miners felt there was too great a prospect that funds would run out before gold was found.[77] Six months after the

73. *Discussion Paper on Resource Rent Tax in the Petroleum Sector* (Canberra: AGPS, 1983), p. 1.

74. Ibid., p. 12.

75. For example, C. Emerson and P. Lloyd, "Improving Mineral Taxation Policy in Australia," discussion paper 36 (Canberra: Australian National University, Centre for Economic Policy Research, 1981); P. L. Swan, "A Review of the Northern Territory Government's 'Green Paper on Mining Royalty Policy for the Northern Territory,'" discussion paper 39 (Canberra: Australian National University, Centre for Economic Policy Research, 1981); R. Garnaut, "The Role of Resource Rent Tax in Fiscal Arrangements for the Australian Mining and Petroleum Industries," *Economic Papers*, no. 67 (August 1981), pp. 31–42.

76. Blainey, *The Rush That Never Ended*, pp. 123–24, describes the Cornish tribute system as it was applied to the South Australian Moonta copper mines in the last third of the nineteenth century. On every ninth Saturday the company would post a number of "pitches," or areas of the underground pit up for auction. The miners then made bids of the amount of "tribute" they would pay to obtain any particular pitch. In return the miners would get a specified fraction of value of the ore they mined, the fraction being higher for ore dug from unpromising areas.

77. In the 1850s, as now, many of the rents went to the suppliers of scarce goods

rebellion had its bloody end at Eureka, Victoria's mining laws were changed to permit the miners to make and administer their own mining laws and to change the revenue charge from an up-front entry fee to a royalty equivalent to about 3 percent of the value of the gold exported.[78] This change permitted smaller miners to come in and removed some of the discrimination against the search for the deeper deposits.

There are other reasons why exclusive reliance on front-end bid payments is likely to be inefficient. Firms are likely to undervalue their expectation of high revenues because they fear that the tax rules would be changed at their expense if they found an especially rich deposit or if world prices increased dramatically.[79] A mixed system may reduce these fears and hence increase the total revenues from the resource, since the RRT would give the government an automatic share in any abnormally high or low revenues and would thereby reduce the political risk of changes in the tax system when a bonanza appears.

Further elements of uncertainty are injected by the overlapping commonwealth and state taxing powers and by the interaction of Australian and foreign taxes for foreign-financed projects. Total Australian and foreign revenues are likely to be greatest if there is a stable and clearly agreed division of taxing powers and revenues between the two levels of government, if there is a predictable set of tax rules facing resource developers, and if a high proportion of the tax is collected in a form that is creditable against taxes payable elsewhere by foreign shareholders. The first two factors also increase the overall efficiency of resource development, while the third relates chiefly to the distribution of tax revenues between Australia and other countries and to the relative tax burdens faced by foreign and domestic investors in Australian resource projects.

If there were to be a mixed system, what would be the most appropriate way to allocate revenues and responsibilities between the commonwealth and state governments? In the case of onshore resources,

---

and skills. A license fee was therefore levied on tradesmen as well, a policy not popular with either the tradesmen or the miners.

78. Blainey, *The Rush That Never Ended*, pp. 49–56.

79. The pervasive changes in petroleum taxation rates and regimes in the 1970s provide ample evidence for the point, which was raised by John MacLeod of CRA, Ltd., and supported by other conference participants. It is also noted by David Nellor in "Taxation of Australia's Resources," in J. G. Head, ed., *Taxation Issues of the 1980s* (Sydney: Australian Tax Research Foundation, 1983), pp. 306–07.

which belong to the states, it would seem most appropriate for the bidding process and revenues to be under the control of the states, with care taken to ensure that efforts to collect such revenues should not lead to largely offsetting reductions in equalization entitlements. As for the RRT or any equivalent, there is much to be said for a system that is common across states, whichever level of government sets the conditions and whoever receives revenues. It would also seem appropriate that commonwealth revenues from state resources should be offset by changes in equalization entitlements. If they were, joint commonwealth and state agreement on a mixed system would be much easier to achieve. Given recent Australian precedents favoring more centralized control of resources and resource revenues, such an outcome is not likely.

Conclusions

I have tried to cover a broad range of issues and have treated many of them sketchily. There are, fortunately, other surveys that help to fill my gaps on environmental issues;[80] on the structure, ownership, and attitudes of the contemporary resource industries;[81] and on the aspirations, problems, and issues in the faster-growing resource-rich states, especially Western Australia and Queensland.[82]

I would have liked to study further the pricing and taxing incentives designed to encourage downstream processing of mineral resources. I suspect that in Australia, as in most other countries with substantial resources and small populations, these efforts are more likely to dissipate

80. These are well surveyed, however, by Ben Smith in his chapter, "Resources and Australian Economic Development," in F. H. Gruen, ed., *Surveys of Australian Economics*, vol. 3 (Sydney: George Allen & Unwin, 1982).

81. This gap is filled by Brain and Schuyers, *Energy and the Australian Economy*, and H. Saddler, *Energy in Australia* (Sydney: George Allen & Unwin, 1981), for energy; and by D. W. Barnett, *Minerals and Energy in Australia* (Stanmore: Cassell Australia, 1979), and S. Bambrick, *Australian Minerals and Energy Policy* (Canberra: Australian National University Press, 1979), for the minerals industry as a whole.

82. Some of the important issues in Western Australia are raised in the collection of papers edited by E. J. Harman and B. W. Head, *State, Capital and Resources in the North and West of Australia* (Nedlands: University of Western Australia Press, 1981).

potential economic rents than to create a stable industrial base in the long run. I also worry about large expansions of resource-producing capacity to fill a supposedly substantial but temporary "window of opportunity"; such goods often have to be heavily marked down before they are sold from the window.

I have instead dealt mainly with three main themes. First, I tried to set Australia's resource riches and resource dependence in historical context. The main conclusion was that current and projected changes in resource exports and prices were well within the range of past experience. The longer view may help to avoid overreaction to what would otherwise seem to be forbiddingly large changes.

Second, I reviewed the theoretical and empirical evidence about the effects of the two most recent resource booms on the size and structure of the national economy. While being skeptical (as most now are) of estimates made in the early 1980s of the growth of mineral exports during the decade, I found that most evidence from Australia and Canada suggested that the overall adjustments required in the national economy are not likely to be very large in relation to those that have been made in the past. The changes and pressures are greatest, of course, in close proximity to the projects, where the desire to maximize the "local content" frequently conflicts with the limited scale of the local economy and the temporary nature of the construction activity. I recommended stable tax structures and expenditures in the face of swings in resource revenues, especially to reduce the effects of resource price changes on aggregate wage levels.

Finally, I discussed some of the microeconomic policies relating to Australian natural resources. The most important policy decisions on resource developments probably have to do with the terms and conditions under which resource rights are issued, electricity is sold, goods are transported, environmental and aboriginal rights are protected, schools and roads are built, and resource income is taxed. Some individual projects, or groups of projects, are so large that errors or lucky breaks in a few of the supposedly microeconomic decisions can have a bigger impact on a regional or national economy than would a fair range of typical macroeconomic factors. I provided a brief survey of some of those issues, highlighting the difficulties of getting things right in a federal structure where the states have most of the expenditure powers and responsibilities but do not have a correspondingly stable and certain access to tax revenues. My main conclusion on resource taxation was that a mixed system of RRT plus bidding was likely to be much more effective than either on its own and that the RRT should be common across states and the bidding system under state control.

DANIEL J. B. MITCHELL

The Australian Labor Market

To a foreign observer, conditions in the Australian labor market are in some ways familiar and in other ways quite different. The basic trends in industrial and occupational employment and in the participation of women in the work force come as no surprise to an economist from the United States. In absolute terms, the numbers of employees in Australia are small, inasmuch as the population of the country is smaller than that of the United States. But, expressed as rates and ratios, similar trends are evident in both countries. These trends are examined in the first two sections of this chapter.

Unemployment rates in Australia were so low during the 1960s that even higher-than-average rates among subgroups in the population attracted little attention. But by the mid-1970s the rates were close to those of the United States for the first time in many years, and the question of what to do about unemployment began to be widely debated. Not surprisingly, as unemployment rose, concerns about immigration policy increased.

The second half of this chapter deals with Australia's incomes policy, beginning with the unusual wage-setting system in this country and its

Many helpful comments and suggestions were received from the following individuals: Frank Campbell, Ian Castles, Richard E. Caves, W. M. Corden, Richard Curtain, Braham Dabscheck, Daryl A. Dixon, E. A. Evans, N. W. F. Fisher, Edward M. Gramlich, Robert Gregory, Fred H. Gruen, David S. Harrison, J. E. Isaac, Peter D. Jonson, Michael S. Keating, Lawrence B. Krause, Charles Mulvey, Keith Norris, Adrian R. Pagan, David H. Plowman, Don W. Rawson, P. A. Scherer, Keith Sloane, Peter Stebbing, Pravin K. Trivedi, and Glenn A. Withers. Catherine E. Baird and Fiona Tully provided important research materials. I am also grateful to all those who provided useful information during a visit to Australia in June and July 1983.

influence on industrial relations. The foreign analyst is on least familiar ground here, although at first glance the labor institutions may not look that different. Australia has, for example, a large union federation, the Australian Council of Trade Unions (ACTU), and most of the country's union members belong to its affiliates. Its counterpart on the employer side is the Confederation of Australian Industry, the nation's most prominent management group. At that point similarities with most other countries fade rapidly. In Australia, labor and management deal with each other primarily through an unusual system of quasi-judicial compulsory arbitration that has both state and federal components. Periodically, however, the leading wage decisions at the national level are made by the Australian Conciliation and Arbitration Commission. The system was originally created so that labor disputes could be resolved through arbitration, not through strikes.

Because wage decisions in Australia are inherently centralized, concerns about inflation inevitably lead to the discussion—and sometimes implementation—of incomes policy. Stagflation in the early 1980s increased the tempo of this debate, and in early 1983 a new Labor party government was elected on a platform of using incomes policy and social accord to resolve Australia's macroeconomic difficulties.

As important as incomes policy and wage restraint are to economic policy, they are not the only concerns of labor and management. Another worry is that centralized wage mechanisms have a tendency to overwhelm industrial relations at the local level. The discussion closes by emphasizing the need to improve relations at this level as well as to address the macroeconomics of wage determination.

Employment

The trends that have occurred in Australia's labor market will be familiar to students of virtually any advanced industrial country. Although agricultural products constitute a large fraction of exports, agricultural employment constitutes a small and declining fraction of the employed work force. Agriculture and related industries accounted for only 6½ percent of total employment in 1982 (table 1). The industrial sector of the work force has also declined, although not in absolute terms. Employment in mining, manufacturing, construction, and trans-

Table 1. *Growth and Composition of Employment, by Industry and Occupation, 1966–82*

Category	Employment (thousands)		Employment growth, 1966–82 (annual rate, percent)	Composition of employment (percent)	
	1966	1982		1966	1982
Industry					
Agriculture, services to agriculture, fishing, forestry, hunting	429.6	410.0	−0.3	8.9	6.5
Mining	58.0	90.5	2.8	1.2	1.4
Manufacturing	1,232.5	1,192.7	−0.2	25.5	18.8
Construction	406.0	464.2	0.8	8.4	7.3
Wholesale and retail trade	993.5	1,239.9	1.4	20.6	19.5
Transport and storage	270.0	373.9	2.1	5.6	5.9
Finance, insurance, real estate, business services	294.4	582.9	4.4	6.1	9.2
Community services	486.0	1,050.2	4.9	10.1	16.5
Entertainment, recreation, restaurants, hotels, personal services	287.0	399.7	2.1	5.9	6.3
Other industries	366.9	543.6	2.5	7.6	8.6
Occupation					
Professional, technical, and related	472.8	978.1	4.6	9.8	15.4
Administrative, executive, managerial	330.1	429.9	1.7	6.8	6.8
Clerical	729.0	1,117.7	2.7	15.1	17.6
Sales	397.7	552.2	2.1	8.2	8.7
Farmers, fishermen, timber gatherers	464.8	444.0	−0.3	9.6	7.0
Transport and communication	302.5	333.1	0.6	6.3	5.2
Tradesmen, production-process workers, miners, quarrymen	1,731.3	1,892.6	0.6	35.9	29.8
Service, sports, recreation	395.7	600.0	2.6	8.2	9.5
Total	4,823.9	6,347.6	1.7	100.0	100.0

Source: Australian Bureau of Statistics, *The Labour Force*, catalog nos. 6203.0, 6204.0 (ABS), and various issues. Columns may not add to totals because of rounding.

port and storage accounted for more than 40 percent of employment in 1966; by 1982 this fraction had fallen to one-third. In particular, employment in manufacturing—hit by both recession and tariff cuts in the mid-1970s—was virtually stagnant during 1966–82.

Employment has grown primarily in the "service" areas. In particular, community services (the sector containing much of the government's work force) expanded rapidly over the period covered by table 1. Of the jobs added during 1966–82, 37 percent were in community services, which initially accounted for only 10 percent of total employment. Financial and business services also increased rapidly, providing almost one out of five jobs created.

Given these trends, it is not surprising that professional, technical, and clerical occupations accounted for almost three-fifths of the job growth. In contrast, only one out of eight jobs was created in traditional blue-collar, industrial occupations (transport and communication workers, tradesmen, and the like), which in 1966 had accounted for more than four out of ten jobs.

The employer mix also changed during this period. It should first be pointed out that, unlike the United States, there is in Australia substantial government ownership of enterprises in such industries as rail and air transport, public transit, utilities, telecommunications, broadcasting, and banking. Thus the government provides employment both within and outside the traditional civil services. About 22 percent of all employed persons worked for the government in 1971. Up to that time, the proportion of public employees had not increased significantly, as it had in the United States, but the proportion rose rapidly to 25 percent during 1972–75 under Gough Whitlam's Labor party. However, even these figures understate the significance of government as an employer. If only wage and salary earners are considered, the proportion working for the various levels of government in 1981 was approximately 30 percent. By contrast, the American equivalent figure would be about 18 percent.[1] Government is indeed a major employer in Australia and is

---

1. Australian estimates are from Australian Bureau of Statistics, *Year Book Australia 1982*, catalog no. 1301.0 (Canberra: ABS, 1982), p. 163, appendix table 15; estimates for the United States are from U.S. Bureau of Labor Statistics, *Earnings and Other Characteristics of Organized Workers, May 1980*, Bulletin 2105 (Government Printing Office, 1981), p. 28.

therefore capable of influencing wage determination and industrial relations directly.

A number of inferences can be drawn from the shift in the structure of employment in Australia. For one thing, expanding professional and technical occupations requires higher-than-average levels of education and human capital. Compared with other workers, employees in these occupations may well have different expectations about employment conditions, relations with employers, and so on. They may also have greater interest in fringe benefits and other forms of noncash compensation than has been usual in Australia. Although the labor movement has succeeded in entering the newer areas of employment, the character of industrial relations may well change. Employees in the newer sectors have been less militant than workers in areas such as mining and manufacturing have been in the past. Thus, over the long run they may be more willing to use the arbitration system to settle disputes, particularly since a 1983 High Court decision expanded the reach of the federal arbitration authorities into areas previously not considered "industrial."[2]

Trends in Composition of the Labor Force

Australia's labor force has two characteristics in common with its counterparts in other English-speaking countries: participation of men is declining and participation of women rising. The rate of increase for women, especially married women, was rapid before the mid-1970s, after which the increase continued at a more moderate pace (table 2).

Women in the Labor Market

As in the United States and in other countries, women in Australia have tended to be crowded into certain occupations such as clerical work. Although this situation appears to have been changing in certain

2. In a significant case the High Court of Australia ruled in 1983 that social workers employed by the Australian Social Welfare Union were engaged in an "industrial dispute" with their employer. It is widely assumed that other groups—such as teachers who were previously excluded from federal arbitration—will now be covered.

Table 2. *Labor Force Participation Rates, 1966–82*
Percent

Category	1966	1974	1982
All categories	59.8	61.4	60.0
Males	83.9	81.0	77.6
Females	36.2	42.2	43.9
Married	29.0	40.7	42.0

Source: Australian Bureau of Statistics, ibid., and various issues.

respects—in particular, women have been shifting to "mixed-sex" jobs rather than jobs dominated by men—a line of demarcation still exists between the labor markets for men and women in both public and private employment. In the early 1970s, married women who worked were estimated to contribute about 18 percent of total family income, a proportion that reflected both lower wages compared with those earned by men and a greater propensity to work part-time. By the late 1970s, the figure was said to be closer to one-third.[3] In May 1981, 45 percent of married women worked part-time (less than thirty-five hours a week) compared with 21 percent of other women and 5 percent of men.

Econometric efforts to explain the participation of women in the labor force in Australia—most notably on the basis of wage variables—have not been particularly successful. One argument, for example, is that supply is in chronic excess because historically women's wages have been kept above market-clearing levels by the wage arbitration system.[4] Level of education, however, does appear to be positively associated with participation by women.

Attitudes toward women and work may not have changed as rapidly in Australia as they have in the United States. Equal employment

3. The estimate for the early 1970s appears in Martin Rein, "Women and Work—The Incomplete Revolution," *Australian Economic Review*, no. 3 (1980), p. 14. Ian Castles of the Department of Finance (letter to Fred Gruen of January 13, 1984) suggests the later figure on the basis of the income distribution for 1978–79. That survey showed a mean income of $10,170 for men and a mean income of $4,720 for women, the sum of which approximates the mean income of a married couple. Thus if the average man married the average woman, her contribution to family income would be roughly one-third. See *Year Book Australia 1982* (Canberra: ABS, 1982).

4. R. G. Gregory, P. McMahon, and B. Whittingham, "Women in the Labour Force: Trends, Causes and Consequences," paper prepared for the Conference on Trends in Women's Work, Education, and Family Building, Department of Economics, Australian National University and Bureau of Labour Market Research, June 3, 1983.

opportunity (EEO) legislation exists in Australia—the protected groups are women, Aborigines, and immigrants. However, such legislation, at least up to 1983, did not appear to have the profound influence on personnel management that it did in the United States, where initially it was rooted in the racial problem. Aborigines account for only about 1 percent of Australia's population, so that EEO did not become a burning issue on racial grounds. Furthermore, limits on female employment in certain types of work still appear in awards of the arbitration system and in various kinds of "protective" laws. However, new EEO legislation— still under consideration at the time of this writing—would push Australia toward the U.S. model in terms of sex discrimination policy.

Australia did embark on one notable experiment with regard to women in the work force: it introduced significant changes in the relative wages of men and women. As in the United States, a considerable gap existed between the average pay of men and women in Australia during the 1960s. Standardizing for personal characteristics accounts for some of the differential but still leaves much of it unexplained. In the United States the only legislative response to this situation was the Equal Pay Act of 1963, which requires equal pay rates for men and women on the same job. Since men and women typically find themselves in different jobs, however, the law has had limited effect on the overall wage differential. As a result, "comparable worth" became a salient issue in the United States in the late 1970s, its proponents arguing that women's skills are systematically undervalued in jobs dominated by women, and arguing—in essence—for pay increases in "women's" occupations through various court challenges under existing EEO legislation. Since courts in the United States are not normally geared to wage determination, they were initially reluctant to jump into the issue, but that attitude appeared to be changing in some recent litigation.

Australia, on the other hand, does have a system of wage courts, and the job of its federal and state arbitration mechanisms is precisely to set pay rates. In 1969 the federal arbitration authorities adopted the principle of "equal pay for equal work." This decision, which was to be implemented in stages by 1972, was roughly analogous to the Equal Pay Act passed by the United States. A second decision in 1972—which was to be implemented in stages by mid-1975—established the principle of "equal pay for equal value," an idea roughly equivalent to the "comparable worth" notion currently under debate in the United States.

The effect of these decisions on wages is discussed later in this chapter in the analysis of the arbitration system and its influence on labor costs. Suffice it to say here that the ratio between official minimum rates for women and rates for men rose from 74 percent in 1970 to 94 percent by the end of the decade. The ratio based on earnings rose from 65 percent to about 86 percent. These adjustments are remarkable because there was no profound change in occupational structure to explain them— they were not "market" results—and because they stand in contrast to the experience of the United States where the earnings ratio between women and men was virtually unchanged during the 1970s.

Economists are prone to believe that significant changes in relative prices or wages will lead to important changes in resource allocation, and they have struggled to find symptoms of such effects after the equal pay decisions. Yet the gross numbers show that the proportion of women in Australia's labor force and in total employment kept rising in the late 1970s, and that the ratio between unemployment rates for women and those for men did not rise (it fell). Researchers have had to "tease" the data to come up with any signs that the demand for women relative to men was reduced.

Some have noted, for example, that the ratio of female employees to total employees rose about 1.9 percent a year from 1966 to 1970, and that if that rate had been maintained, the ratio should have reached a little over 40 percent by 1982. Instead it reached only 36.7 percent.[5] Was the shortfall due to the relative wage effect, or was it due to other factors that slowed down the growth in employment rates for women? Did the increase in part-time employment among women (relative to full-time) reflect a wage effect, or did it reflect preferences for flexible hours? (In the United States, the slowdown in the growth of employment-to-population ratio for women was even less marked, and the shift toward part-time work was not a significant trend; these observations are consistent with a negative relative wage effect in Australia.) Whatever the reasons for the slowdown in Australia, economists no doubt were surprised (disappointed?) that it was not larger.

Some attribute the employment pattern in Australia to change in industrial structure—that is, a shift toward industries hiring women—a change that occurred as a deus ex machina (albeit bearing part-time

5. Ibid.

work) to prevent a decline in total work opportunities for women. Others point to the segmented labor markets, arguing that, since men and women are not highly substitutable under current institutional arrangements, changes in their relative wage levels have little impact on their relative rates of employment.[6] In any case, the episode is likely to draw considerable foreign interest as word of it spreads.

Young and Old

Teenagers, both male and female, experienced declining participation until the mid-1970s, after which—despite increased slackness in the labor market—their participation rates increased. This phenomenon contributed to growing concern about youth-related problems in the labor market and the transition from school to work. The participation of older workers, especially men, has dropped sharply, particularly since 1974. The participation rate for males aged sixty to sixty-four dropped from 72 percent to 48 percent during 1974–82, whereas in the previous eight years it had declined only 8 percentage points.[7] These declines may be associated with the enhancement of various social welfare programs such as old-age pensions and disability benefits in the early 1970s. Private retirement schemes also have become more commonplace in recent years.

The Issue of Unemployment

Many countries found themselves unable to reduce their unemployment rates after the worldwide recession of the mid-1970s—a recession triggered by the OPEC oil price shock, its inflationary consequences, and the macroeconomic policies adopted in response to these conditions. In terms of its earlier performance, Australia seemed to be particularly hard hit by this problem. During the late 1960s Australia's unemployment rate averaged less than 2 percent, but in 1973–75 it jumped to almost 5

6. Sandra Eccles, "Female Employment: Real and Apparent Gains," *Australian Bulletin of Labour*, vol. 6 (June 1980), pp. 172–85; R. G. Gregory and R. C. Duncan, "Segmented Labor Market Theories and the Australian Experience of Equal Pay for Women," *Journal of Post Keynesian Economics*, vol. 3 (Spring 1981), pp. 403–28.

7. Data are drawn from appendix table 16.

Table 3. *Trend in Unemployment and the Ratio of Employment to Population, 1965–81*
Percent

Period or year	Unemployment rate	Ratio of workers employed to population
1965–70	1.7	60.0
1971	1.9	61.1
1972	2.6	60.6
1973	2.3	61.2
1974	2.7	61.3
1975	4.9	60.1
1976	4.8	59.7
1977	5.6	59.2
1978	6.3	58.1
1979	6.2	57.9
1980	6.1	58.4
1981	5.8	58.4

Source: U.S. Bureau of Labor Statistics, "Statistical Supplement to International Comparisons of Unemployment," Bulletin 1979 (BLS, June 1982). The last column refers to the civilian population aged fifteen years or over.

percent (table 3). After 1976 the rate never fell below 5 percent, and by early 1983 it soared beyond 10 percent.

The Natural or Structural Unemployment Rate

Although changes in the overall unemployment rate are usually associated with macroeconomic policy, rising unemployment tends to trigger a search for other possible causes. Consider, for example, that wage equation studies in Australia before the experience of the late 1970s and early 1980s focused on the "natural" rate of unemployment, which is estimated to be around 2 percent.[8] Subsequently, however, many

8. Michael Parkin estimates the natural rate at 1½ to 2 percent. See Parkin, "The Short-Run and Long-Run Trade-Offs between Inflation and Unemployment in Australia," *Australian Economic Papers*, vol. 12 (December 1973), pp. 127–44. In a subsequent paper, written after the mid-1970s wage explosion, he raises the estimates slightly to 2½ percent. See Michael Parkin, "Yet Another Look at Australia's Short-Run and Long-Run Trade-Offs between Inflation and Unemployment," *Australian Economic Papers*, vol. 15 (June 1976), pp. 128–39. Other estimates in the 1½ to 3 percent range can be found in Michael G. Kirby, "An Investigation of the Specification and Stability of the Australian Aggregate Wage Equation," *Economic Record*, vol. 57 (March 1981), pp. 35–46; and B. Bhaskara Rao, "Inflationary and Efficiency Effects of Relative Wage Distortions: The Australian Case," *Australian Economic Papers*, vol. 19 (June 1980), pp. 68–77.

Table 4. *Hypothetical Unemployment Rate Derived from 1980 Base Unemployment Data and 1966–82 Labor Force Weights, Selected Years, 1966–82*
Percent

Year	Hypothetical unemployment rate
1966	5.3
1970	5.2
1974	5.2
1978	5.3
1982	5.3

Source: Australian Bureau of Statistics, *The Labour Force*, catalog nos. 6203.0, 6204.0 (ABS), and various issues. Unemployment base figures as of November 1980.

analysts questioned whether the natural rate might not be affected by structural shifts in the work force or in institutional arrangements.

Demographic Shifts

Observers of the employment scene in the United States have suggested that the changing demographics of the labor force may account for structural shifts in the unemployment rate there. However, this explanation does not appear to be applicable to Australia. If demographic factors are to blame for the upward shift in Australia's unemployment rate, then the groups experiencing high unemployment rates must have grown drastically as a proportion of the work force. This has not been the case in Australia, where conflicting tendencies have been at work.

When, for example, a hypothetical unemployment rate was calculated solely on the basis of the changes in the proportions of nineteen demographic groups in the labor force from the mid-1960s to the early 1980s, weight shifts alone appeared to have virtually no effect on the unemployment rate (table 4).[9] It is assumed that each group consistently exhibited its November 1980 unemployment rate over the period covered by table 4. Young people—who had relatively high unemployment rates—tended to decline as a fraction of the work force. Middle-aged married women, with below-average unemployment rates, increased

9. The groups used were males aged 15–19, 20–24, 25–34, 35–44, 45–54, 55–59, 60–64, 65 and older; females 15–19, 55–64, 65 and older; married females 20–24, 25–34, 35–44, 45–54; and other females aged 20–24, 25–34, 35–44, 45–54.

their representation over the period. But older workers, with below-average rates, declined as a proportion of the work force. Obviously, different base periods or weighting schemes would change the results somewhat. Nonetheless, it seems unlikely that rising unemployment could be attributed to demographics on the basis of the data.

Unemployment Benefits

Others have suggested that institutional change might explain some of the increased unemployment. Such a change is reflected in the various social welfare programs instituted by the Whitlam Labor government during the early 1970s. In theory, social welfare programs could push unemployment rates up if they discouraged job seekers from accepting employment or if they brought people into the labor force who could not find work. On the other hand, they could well push the rates down. Programs to provide income assistance to the sick and disabled, for example, might take from the labor force people whose job-finding prospects would otherwise be limited. Moreover, job-creation schemes might add to the stock of employment opportunities, although substitution effects (the use of subsidies to finance existing jobs) could limit the net effect.

The factor most likely to be considered the catalyst here is unemployment benefits, which in Australia are financed by general revenue, not by payroll or other employer taxes. As such, they do not have the "experience rating" feature of the typical U.S. unemployment program, under which employers who lay off workers frequently pay higher taxes. In the absence of experience rating, unemployment benefits could provide a marginal subsidy to employers whose employment and layoff patterns are erratic, especially since part-time earnings are heavily "taxed" under Australia's system. The availability of benefits could also lengthen job search by the unemployed, thus lengthening the duration of the average spell of unemployment. Finally, individuals might be attracted into the labor force by the availability of benefits and might exhibit job-search behavior to establish eligibility. The unemployment rate could rise under any of these conditions.

Notwithstanding these possible effects of unemployment benefits, they will have no bearing on the question of whether the natural rate of unemployment changed in the late 1970s unless the unemployment benefit program changed during this period. Indeed, under the Whitlam Labor government, benefits rose relative to earnings. In late 1972 a married man with a spouse could have received about 26 percent of his average weekly earnings, but by 1977 this ratio had climbed to 39 percent (but slipped slightly thereafter). Replacement ratios are higher for workers with below-average earnings.

Youth Unemployment

There has been special interest in the effects of unemployment benefits on the labor market behavior of teenagers, especially those who leave school at a relatively young age. Youth unemployment rates rose relative to adult male rates after the mid-1970s recession. Young people are eligible for unemployment benefits even if they have no previous work experience, since the unemployment benefit scheme does not require a past history of work. However, those under eighteen years of age receive lower benefits. In late 1976 the ratio of benefits to average weekly earnings for juniors rose from 16 percent for males and 18 percent for females to 37 percent for both males and females. Thereafter, the benefit payment for juniors was frozen at $36 (Australian), although the rate for adults continued to be adjusted upward. By early 1981, the ratio of benefits to earnings for juniors had fallen to 21 percent for males and 23 percent for females.[10] Changes were made in the implicit "tax" on partial earnings so as not to discourage young people from accepting part-time work opportunities. This policy was based on the (not unreasonable) supposition that high unemployment benefits could aggravate unemployment problems among young people.

Despite these concerns, most econometric studies have failed to establish that unemployment benefits substantially affect the behavior of teenagers in the labor market (or of the work force as a whole), although some studies have reported an effect on younger males. Studies that use general data on the labor force are less likely to detect such an effect than those that use data on benefits received, as is shown below. These ambiguous findings indicate that the matter needs more careful review.

10. Data are from Australian Bureau of Statistics, *Year Book Australia*, various years.

First, the increased participation of teenagers in the work force after 1974 needs to be explained. The increase in award wages for this group relative to the award wages set for other workers by the arbitration system could have could been responsible for the greater participation. Documentation of the reasons for this general increase in relative wages is limited. It appears that localized shortages of entry-level personnel in the early 1970s, before the recession, may have sparked the movement. There is some evidence that the increase in junior-to-adult wage ratios had an adverse effect on youth employment prospects, especially for girls who experienced both the junior-to-adult and female-to-male relative wage adjustment.[11] However, neither the government nor other employers have asked to lower the relative wage of youth.

Second, Australian youngsters drop out of school at substantially younger ages than their counterparts in the United States and several other countries. In Australia in the mid-1970s, about 37 percent of seventeen-year-olds were enrolled in school compared with 85 percent in the United States and 69 percent in Canada. It has been argued that Australian secondary schools focus excessively on advancement to a university and fail to provide vocational training. Recent evidence suggests, however, that the financial return to higher education in Australia has been declining.[12] Efforts have been made to reform the school system with employer needs in mind, but these reforms have received mixed reviews. However, even if educational credentials simply provided a better place in the queue for job opportunities—and did not increase the productivity of employees—it would still pay to stay in school, particularly as the queue grew longer. Thus it is difficult to understand why enrollment in schools has failed to increase more than it has, especially in the case of males, whose enrollment rate stagnated in the mid-1970s.

Third, in the work force as a whole, the proportion of those counted as unemployed in the regular labor-force surveys who received unem-

11. Bureau of Labour Market Research, *Youth Wages, Employment, and the Labour Force*, Research Report 3 (Canberra: AGPS, 1983).

12. J. R. Niland, "Who Gets What Job: The Changing Job Rules in Ownership and Control of Labour Market Activities," paper prepared for the Sixth World Congress of the International Industrial Relations Association, Kyoto, Japan, March 27–31, 1983, p. 7; Richard B. Freeman, "The Changing Economic Value of Higher Education in Developed Economies: A Report to the O.E.C.D.," Working Paper 820 (National Bureau of Economic Research, December 1981), pp. 4–15.

ployment benefits has increased. In 1970 the ratio of recipients to those recorded as unemployed was only 14 percent. This ratio increased sharply after 1971, and by 1981 it had reached 79 percent.[13] A possible (partial) explanation of this increase is that with the increase in the duration of unemployment, a larger fraction of the unemployed passed through the waiting period for benefits. (Workers who experience very short spells of unemployment are not eligible for benefits.) This—combined with the increased value of benefits—not only made more people eligible, but also made it more worthwhile to apply. Some have said that during the period of the Whitlam government, it became more socially acceptable to claim benefits. In any case, unemployment benefits now seem to be much more a part of the unemployment "experience" than they were when payments were substantially lower.

Macroeconomic Policy

Although unemployment benefits are of interest for particular groups, such as teenagers and those who leave school early, they do not seem to explain much of the upward shift in the overall unemployment rate during the late 1960s, the 1970s, and early 1980s. The behavior of the employment-to-population ratio shown in table 3—an index less subject to the vagaries of the definition of unemployment, or to tendencies to exhibit unemployment behavior to claim welfare benefits—suggests a slackening in the labor market. This ratio continued to rise until 1974, when it peaked at over 61 percent. It then drifted downward, settling at about 58 percent.

The behavior of employment suggests that macroeconomic policy, rather than changes in social policy or the composition of the work force, was at the root of the unemployment problem. Moreover, the relative lack of success in bringing the inflation rate down from the peak of 15.1 percent in 1974–75 (measured by the consumer price index) to a level even remotely close to the 2–4 percent range of the 1960s suggests that the restrictive macroeconomic policy was aimed primarily at fighting inflation. That policy was not a completely exogenous influence, as is

13. Data on the number of unemployed are from "Statistical Supplement to International Comparisons of Unemployment," Bulletin 1979 (BLS, June 1982); data on the number of recipients of unemployment benefits are from Australian Bureau of Statistics, *Year Book Australia 1982*, p. 738.

demonstrated later in the chapter; it interacted with, and was partly a product of, developments in wage determination.

Training and Job Programs

The macroeconomic explanation has implications for microeconomic employment and training policies that might be, or have been, adopted to deal with the overall unemployment problem. That is to say, if this explanation is correct, then programs that address microeconomic inefficiencies in the labor market are unlikely to have any substantial effect on overall unemployment. Many such programs were introduced in Australia. With the sharp rise in unemployment in 1974–75 came a proliferation of job, training, and vocational programs, often aimed at young people, whose unemployment rate had risen especially rapidly.

Although the labor market behavior of young people in Australia is not well understood, the reason for much of their unemployment may simply be that entry-level workers tend to be at the end of the hiring queue. Training programs and employment subsidization programs are more likely to rearrange the order of the queue rather than lower the overall rate of unemployment. Some programs, however, may pull trainees out of the active labor market for a time and possibly lower the unemployment rate in that way. To have a substantial effect, however, these programs would have to be enlarged considerably.

In 1980–81, for example, about 97,000 were admitted into various federal employment and training programs, the duration of which was less than half a year. Hence, a generous estimate would be that about 40,000 people were involved in these programs at any one time. If it is assumed that all 40,000 came out of the ranks of the unemployed, and that the number of unemployed fell on a one-for-one basis with the number of enrollees, the unemployment rate for 1980–81 would have been about 6.4 percent without the programs, rather than the actual 5.8 percent. The actual circumstances are likely to produce substantially less than a one-for-one reduction in unemployment. It has been estimated that the unemployment rate will remain close to 10 percent through

14. Data taken from *National Economic Summit Conference, 11–14 April 1983, Documents and Proceedings*, vol. 1: *Government Documents* (Canberra: AGPS, 1983), pp. 40, 55, 61. See also discussion of table 5.

1985–86.[14] To reduce such rates to the levels of the late 1970s would require massive job-creation programs far exceeding anything mounted or contemplated thus far.

Such employment and training programs may have sectoral use once the overall employment picture improves, however. The trends away from traditional manufacturing mentioned at the outset are likely to be accelerated by the increased slackness in the labor market since 1982. Reductions in plant capacity that might have occurred more gradually may be accelerated and thus may cause irreversible displacements. Programs that facilitate movement to other industries can help the labor market adapt to such developments.

Although training programs will be effective mainly in rearranging the queue, that is not inherently a bad thing; it may lead to a more equitable sharing of the unemployment burden. Moreover, trainees may achieve a more favorable position in the queue by having their productivity raised. Even so, modest programs cannot be expected to produce substantial macroeconomic results.

The Special Issue of Immigration

Immigration policy in Australia has fluctuated greatly because of conflicting goals. For many years before World War II Australia seemed to want population growth, but it also wanted the "right" sort of immigrant in terms of race and country of origin. Thus Australia's tariff policy in the 1920s was justified as a way of raising real wages and attracting immigrants. Even today, a positive correlation exists between the degree of protection afforded industries and their use of immigrant labor.[15] By the 1960s, immigration—now shifting toward southern and eastern European sources—functioned as a labor market policy because it relieved the shortage of labor (the extent of which is reflected in the low unemployment rates of the period). Immigration accounted for 37 percent of total population growth in 1961–65. This figure rose to 47 percent in 1966–70, when the demand for labor peaked. In 1971–75 the

15. Glenn Withers, "Labour Markets in Australia: Implications for ASEAN-Australia Economic Relations," paper prepared for the Labour Market Behaviour Workshop, National University of Singapore, July 30–31, 1983, figure 2.

labor market softened and the ratio fell to 31 percent. In 1976–80, the period of chronically high unemployment after the recession of the mid-1970s, it remained at 32 percent.[16]

Government assistance to immigrants shows an even more marked change. In 1966–70, 107,000 foreigners a year—about two-thirds of total immigrants—received government financial assistance for their relocation expenses. This rate fell to 58,000 in 1971–75 (about half of the total) and to less than 20,000 (roughly one-fourth of the total) in 1976–80.[17] It appears that the mix of immigrants changed, too. A larger fraction of immigrants in the 1970s arrived because of "humanitarian" programs such as refugee resettlement and family reunification. The fact that those who entered the work force in the 1970s now earn higher wages than those who entered in the 1960s suggests that on the average more recent entrants have higher skills.

In a highly publicized agreement on economic and social policy reached by organized labor (the ACTU) and the Labor party before the 1983 elections, immigration policy is mentioned in rather general terms. However, the tone of the statement emphasizes humanitarian types of immigration as the priority for the future and suggests that other types of immigration programs should be reviewed.[18] Clearly, as long as the unemployment rate remains high, government policy is likely to avoid encouraging "economic" immigrants.

Wages and Inflation

Although Australia has unique labor market institutions, its foremost problem with respect to the labor market is not an uncommon one. The determination of wages—in Australia and elsewhere—is intimately bound up with macroeconomic performance. Price inflation has a significant wage component, even in an economy with important elements of import and export goods in its price level. Similarly, wage determination will inevitably reflect the rate of price inflation. The interrelationship between wages and prices—the real wage at any point in time—is closely

16. Australian Bureau of Statistics, *Year Book Australia 1982*, pp. 87, 113.
17. Ibid., p. 87.
18. *National Economic Summit Conference, April 11–14, 1983, Documents and Proceedings*, vol. 1, p. 419.

connected with the determinant of another variable of key macroeconomic concern, the level of unemployment.

Much of the discussion in Australia, as in other countries, has centered on the question of whether there is a stable trade-off between inflation and unemployment, or, more precisely, whether the short-run trade-off that may exist evaporates in the long run. Those who subscribe to the view that the trade-off evaporates in the long run describe the ultimate unemployment rate to which the economy tends to move as the "natural rate." As noted earlier, some consider this rate to be a structural-frictional rate that reflects such influences as the personal characteristics of job seekers. Another view, however, emphasizes the wage-determination process itself. In this view, increases in the real wage pressed (effectively) by militant unions can raise the natural rate.

Another important issue over the long term is whether traditional macroeconomic policy can cope with inflation efficiently. Traditional policies of demand restraint, in all countries, have an initial impact on real output rather than on the main target—the inflation rate. If a policy operates inefficiently—that is, if it affects real output strongly and inflation only mildly—the country will find itself in a difficult predicament. To reduce inflation to a given level, it must endure a prolonged and costly period of unemployment. If that is too painful, it may not succeed in reducing its inflation rate at all.

To the extent that unemployment reflects such factors as the personal characteristics of job seekers, the remedies are easy to suggest in the abstract but difficult to implement successfully. For example, programs could be established to help match workers and employers through such devices as subsidized training, relocation subsidies (for both workers and employers), and so on. Alternatively, jobs could be created and targeted for particular groups. As already mentioned, some programs of this type have been used in Australia since the recession of the mid-1970s, but in the absence of a sufficiently tight labor market, training programs and other forms of subsidies tend to be queue rearrangers. In essence, Australia needs to achieve a tight enough labor market to make its employment and training policies succeed.

Certain social programs might even raise the level of unemployment. The possible effects of unemployment benefits have already been discussed. It is unlikely, however, that such programs can account for the degree to which the Australian unemployment rate became stuck at recession levels *after* the recession of the mid-1970s. Even if unemployment is narrowly defined as the unemployment rate of adult males employed on a full-time basis, the same upward drift as that in the overall rate is apparent. The rate for these workers stood at 0.9 percent in 1966, 0.8 percent in 1971, but 2.4 percent in 1976 and 4.2 percent in August 1982.[19] Adult males employed full-time constitute the group that is most firmly attached to the labor force and that has the lowest unemployment rate. It is unlikely that the behavior of that group will be altered by changes in unemployment benefits, since their participation rate is already high and since they are more likely than other groups to have primary responsibility for the support of dependents.

If the natural rate of unemployment rises under the influence of the wage determination process itself, however, inventing new training programs or "fiddling" with unemployment benefits will not address the principal problem. In fact, in 1983 both the outgoing Liberal government and the incoming Labor government concluded that wage determination was at the heart of the macroeconomic problem. The rhetoric of the two parties was quite different, of course. But the central policy was similar; both governments opted for a reduction in the level of real wages. Neither party, however, explicitly addressed the issue of how to increase the efficiency of macroeconomic policy, although a faction of the Liberal government appeared to want to do so through a move toward "market" wage setting.

Real Wages and Unemployment

Trends in several macroeconomic indicators from September 1966 to September 1973 and September 1973 to September 1982 are of considerable interest in Australia (table 5). The earlier period is one of (comparatively) low inflation; the latter is characterized by high inflation and general economic sluggishness. Similar results were experienced by a number of other countries. In the earlier period, real wages and productivity rose at the same rate. The ratio of real wages to productivity—an index that Australian economists decorously call "real unit-labor costs," but that is really a proxy for labor's proportionate share of

---

19. Bureau of Labour Market Research, *Youth Wages, Employment, and the Labour Force*, p. 12.

Table 5. *Nonfarm Productivity and Related Trends, September 1966 to September 1982*
Annual rates of change, percent

Item	September 1966 to September 1973	September 1973 to September 1982	September 1966 to September 1982
Productivity[a]	3.6	1.9	2.7
Labor costs[b]	9.7	15.1	12.7
Unit-labor costs[c]	5.9	12.9	9.8
Real labor costs[d]	3.6	2.8	3.1
Real unit-labor costs[e]	0.0	0.7	0.4
Price inflation[f]	5.9	12.0	9.3

Source: Data provided by Australia's Department of the Treasury.
a. Gross nonfarm output at 1979–80 prices per hour worked by nonfarm employees.
b. Nonfarm labor compensation (wages, salaries, supplements, payroll taxes) per hour worked.
c. Labor costs divided by productivity.
d. Labor costs divided by implicit price deflator for gross nonfarm product.
e. Unit-labor costs divided by implicit price deflator for gross nonfarm product.
f. Implicit price deflator for gross nonfarm product.

output—was constant.[20] In other words, the division of income was stable. Such stability does not prevent inflation; however, attempts to push up the shares of wage and nonwage incomes simultaneously can be inflationary unless halted by either demand restraint or some form of incomes policy.

During the second period covered by table 5, the situation with regard to the shares was different. Real wages rose faster than productivity; that is, real unit-labor costs (or labor's relative share) increased. Two hypotheses have been put forth to explain these results. One is that labor's relative share increased because the government depressed demand deliberately (labor's share tends to rise during periods of recession). The other is that a real wage push—and subsequent pressure to keep real wages "too" high—led the government to keep the economy more slack than it had been in the earlier period. From table 5 alone it is

20. Unit-labor costs can be defined as WL/Q, where W is the cost of labor compensation per unit of time; L, the number of time units of labor; and Q, output. This measure is equivalent to the ratio of wages, W, to productivity, Q/L. If unit-labor costs are deflated by a price index, P, the result is WL/PQ, that is, the wage will be divided by the total value of output or labor's relative share of output. The published indexes of real unit-labor costs obscure the connection between this concept and labor's share by using somewhat inconsistent data. For example, labor costs used refer only to payroll employees while productivity is measured for all workers, including the self-employed.

Figure 1. *Strike Activity and Labor Costs, 1966–82*

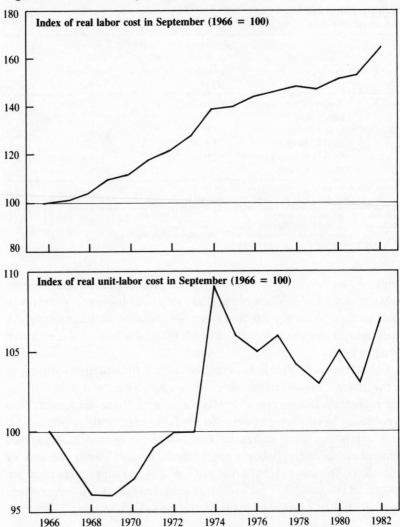

Figure 1 (*continued*)

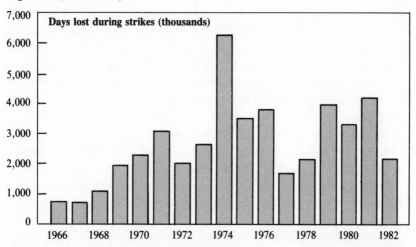

Sources: Data on real labor cost and real unit-labor cost were provided by the Department of the Treasury. Data on number of days lost during strikes are from International Labour Office, *Yearbook of Labour Statistics*, (Geneva: ILO), 1975 to 1981 issues; and Australian Bureau of Labour Statistics, catalog nos. 6321.0, 6322.0 for more recent data.

difficult to conclude which hypothesis is valid. Other evidence, however, suggests that the latter view is the correct one.

First, the jump in real wages came suddenly; it was heavily concentrated in 1974, a year in which Australia's unemployment—if one is to believe the studies cited earlier—stood at about its "natural" rate. Second, the jump came at a time of an upsurge in strike activity (see figure 1), a phenomenon suggesting increased labor militancy. Third, soon after the jump, demands were made to restore quarterly indexation of arbitration wage awards (it was restored in 1975). These demands suggest a shift toward real wage (rather than nominal wage) bargaining; that is, they suggest a loss of money illusion. Fourth, wage increases were initially encouraged by the 1972–75 Labor government, both for special purposes such as raising the female-to-male pay ratio and for general increases to raise labor's share. As inflation rose, of course, the government became concerned and called for restraint. But by then the momentum could not be easily reversed.

Behavior after 1974 is also revealing. Although real unit-labor costs declined somewhat from the high levels they had reached, they never returned to earlier levels. The economy was permitted to expand, but it never returned to full employment. Indexation was continued, in various forms, until 1981; hence, erosion of the level of real unit-labor costs that might have occurred depended on productivity improvement. (A fixed real wage and an increasing level of productivity will lower real unit-labor costs.) Compared with the U.S. record during that period, Australia's productivity performance was good, although it did slow down during the latter part of the 1970s, probably at least partly in response to the climate of economic slackness.

As concern about the real wage issue mounted, the federal arbitration authorities first shifted to partial indexation (less-than-full price protection), sometimes cloaking the decision with an egalitarian mantle consisting, for example, of flat-dollar increases or ceilings on indexed increases. However, increased militancy—as reflected in the strike data—accompanied the renewed upward pressure on real wages. And various channels existed for endorsement by the arbitration authorities of above-indexation increases: "anomalies," increases in "work value," and the like. As settlements outran the official wage determinations, the federal arbitration authorities abandoned "centralized" wage fixing and indexation—this move took place in 1981—and awaited guidance from the parties, including government, on how to proceed. In the interim, bargained settlements were the norm.

A key settlement in the metal industry was endorsed by the arbitration authorities in late 1981 and its terms quickly were spread to other workers. As a result, unions in the metal sector and other industries pushed for reduced hours as well as wage increases. By late 1982, the (Liberal) government proposed that a wage "pause," that is, no further ratification of settlements, be imposed, and it froze the wages of its own employees. It had been arguing for such a move since 1976, but to no avail. However, soaring unemployment in 1982 added strength to the argument.

Why, it may be asked, didn't Australian unions exercise self-restraint, given the experience of the mid-1970s? Indeed, the centralization of the industrialization system and the high unionization rate might have made unions sensitive to externalities and macroeconomic effects. The failure to exercise self-restraint might be explained in a number of ways. First, unions may have expected the resources boom to sustain "ability to pay" increased real wages. The psychology of the boom may have outlived the boom itself.[21] Second, since real wage movements during the mid-1970s triggered macroeconomic policies of demand restraint, it may have been difficult in that period to distinguish the effects of government policy from the effects of wages directly—mainly because the wage effects operated through macroeconomic policy reactions. Third, it is not clear that giving up real wages voluntarily would have been a rational decision. As already noted, unemployment tended to be concentrated among entry-level potential workers, that is, among non-members of the employed work force and of unions. As a high union official put it, "I don't want to sound cynical about this . . . but while there are 10 percent of workers unemployed, there are 90 percent in employment."[22] As the U.S. experience has indicated, wage concessions occur voluntarily when core members of the union work force have been displaced, or are in danger of being displaced. In Australia the core members did not really begin to feel threatened until the economic deterioration of 1982–83. It took several years under such a threat to produce a substantial volume of concessions in the United States. There may be similar lags in Australia.

The Overhang Debate

Australia is no stranger to debate about the effects of real wages. In the early 1930s, for example, federal wage authorities made a deliberate 10 percent cut in award wages in response to the depression. In the early 1950s, the authorities abandoned indexation of the basic wage (which had been in effect since the early 1920s) because they considered it potentially inflationary. In the mid-1970s, the debate reopened, this time under the heading of the "real-wage overhang." The basic issue in the overhang debate was whether real wages—particularly the sudden rise in real wages—had anything to do with the subsequent increase in the unemployment rate along the lines suggested above.

The debate tended to go off course, however, with discussions about capital-labor substitutions. It is natural for economists to think of such substitutions as a reaction to a change in any relative price. Once

21. I am indebted to E. A. Evans for this suggestion.
22. "All Their Own Work," *The Bulletin*, February 1, 1983, p. 85.

substitution becomes the center of the debate, attention focuses on the empirical significance of the effect. Inherently, in the short run—when it is easiest to make before-and-after comparisons—there is little scope for changing cyclically corrected capital-to-labor ratios. The capital stock is large and is expanded only slowly. Once in place, the capital-to-labor ratio of a given plant may be fixed, that is, locked into the technology of the plant.

When employment falls as a result of a recession, the measured capital-to-labor ratio will rise simply because the numerator stays in place while the denominator drops. Although reliable measures of capital are not readily available for Australia, the indexes that are available indicate that the ratio rose in the mid-1970s—probably in large part because of the recession—and that it fell thereafter.[23] This drop—in contrast to what the substitution effect would suggest—is most likely the result of a decline in the general propensity of business to invest in an already slack economy.

The issue is not one of substitution, nor does it have anything to do with theories of pricing behavior. Ultimately, it is a question of adding up the relative shares of wage and nonwage income. As noted earlier, labor's share and real unit-labor costs are essentially equivalent. If real wages rise faster than productivity, labor's relative share will increase. For this to occur, the relative share of nonwage income must decrease.

Starting from a point at which the shares, which are determined by wage and nonwage claims, are consistent with the exhaustion of total output (income), an upsurge in the real wage will accelerate the rate of inflation. Nominal wages will push prices up, but as prices catch up nominal wages will attempt to outpace them in an effort to maintain the real gain. This does not mean that without pressure on real wages there will be no inflation. Nominal wages and prices can chase each other in a wage-price spiral at any distribution of income. But such a spiral need not accelerate. If real claims are continually asserted as more than exhausting the real income available, however, accelerating inflation will occur as the price mechanism vainly attempts to reconcile the competing claims.

In theory, a push on real wages can be accommodated by a decline in the nonwage relative share. If, for example, empirically the nonwage

23. Withers, "Labour Markets in Australia," table 10.

share in relative terms declined with economic expansion, it would be possible for real wages to be pushed up and employment growth to occur simultaneously without having inflation accelerate. Some argued in the late 1970s that if the economy had been rapidly stimulated, productivity would have risen fast enough to satisfy labor with a rising absolute, but falling relative, share of income. But there is little empirical evidence to show that this would have happened. All that was known for sure was that economic expansion did tend to raise the relative nonwage share. Thus, it seemed clear that to prevent accelerating inflation in the face of a real-wage push strong enough to raise labor's share, government policy had to aim at squeezing the nonwage share.

The nonwage share might be squeezed in two possible ways. First, direct intervention, that is, price controls or guidelines, might be used to depress price markups. In fact, in 1973, a Prices Justification Tribunal (PJT) was established to implement a form of "voluntary" price guidelines for larger firms. There is some empirical evidence that margins were squeezed by this program.[24] Thus, the price policy may have accommodated—to a small extent—the increase in the wage share. However, price controls tend to produce shortages if pushed very hard. Although shortages were reported here and there, they certainly do not appear to have been widespread during the time that the Prices Justification Tribunal was in operation (1973–81). Moreover, real world product markets do not always clear, even in the absence of price controls, with the result that occasional order backlogs can be expected during expansions. Because such shortages did not occur, the PJT's efforts could not have substantially reduced the relative share of nonwage income.

Since there is likely to be a positive association between economic expansion and the size of the relative share of nonwage income, the other means—the main means—of reducing the nonwage share is an induced economic contraction. If the push on real wages is sufficient to raise labor's relative share, monetary and fiscal restrictions must be imposed simply to prevent inflation from accelerating. Moreover, to the extent that the pressures on real wages are such that at full employment the sum of the relative shares of labor and nonwage income would

24. D. R. Chapman and C. W. Junor, "Profits, Variability of Profits and the Prices Justification Tribunal," *The Economic Record*, vol. 57 (June 1981), pp. 128–39.

exceed 100 percent of available income, the economy must be kept depressed. Thus, by acting through monetary and fiscal policy, pressure on real wages can raise the natural rate of unemployment. There need be no capital-labor substitutions.

The Appeal of Incomes Policy

In many countries, a push on real wages may not be possible, or likely, given their labor market institutions. Australia's labor market arrangements, discussed below, do permit such a push. It is possible for wage claims to be made sufficient to raise the natural rate of unemployment. In these circumstances an incomes policy carried out through a social accord or compact is obviously appealing. The parties need to be confronted with a menu of the economic choices available. To the extent that a slack economy is not desired, it may be possible to reduce the level of pressure on real wages.

The results of just such an exercise are summarized in table 6. In early 1983, shortly after taking office, the Hawke Labor government called an economic summit conference. Table 6 shows the results of three scenarios of economic outcomes, C being the least inflationary and featuring a continued wage pause, B being the most inflationary, and A being the government's intermediate and preferred option—an end to the pause, with moderate wage increases thereafter.

The projections in table 6 can be used to calculate the implied trade-off between the growth in real wages and in unemployment. This trade-off is, of course, built into the model underlying the estimates. But it expresses an official viewpoint accepted by the conference as well as by many private economists.

The growth in real wages over a three-year period in option B in table 6 is 2.7 percent per annum. In option C it is − 0.2 percent. Option B raises the unemployment rate by 1.6 percentage points from 1983–84 to 1985–86; option C lowers it by 1 percentage point. A rough comparison of the two options suggests that an extra push on real wages of about 3 percent raises the unemployment rate by about 2½ percentage points.

Under option B the real money supply grows at an annual rate of 1.3 percent; under C it grows at a rate of 3 percent. Hence, because the push on real wages is less in C, macroeconomic policy is more stimulative.

Table 6. *Summary of Economic Projections Presented to April 1983 National Economic Summit Conference, 1982–86*
Percent

Projection and measure	1982–83	1983–84	1984–85	1985–86	1983–86
Projection A					
Wage inflation[a]	11.7	5.5	5.3	8.8	6.5
Price inflation[b]	11.3	6.2	4.9	6.5	5.9
Employment growth	-1.6	0.4	2.0	2.7	1.7
Unemployment rate	8.9	10.0	10.1	9.7	9.9
Real GDP growth	-1.4	2.7	3.9	4.8	3.8
Money supply growth[c]	10.5	8.5	8.3	10.0	8.9
Projection B					
Wage inflation[a]	11.7	18.1	15.6	15.8	16.5
Price inflation[b]	11.3	13.0	13.8	13.4	13.4
Employment growth	-1.6	-0.4	0.2	0.8	0.2
Unemployment rate	8.9	10.6	11.7	12.2	11.5
Real GDP growth	-1.4	1.7	1.6	2.4	1.9
Money supply growth[c]	10.5	14.5	15.0	15.0	14.8
Projection C					
Wage inflation[a]	11.7	2.8	3.0	4.5	3.4
Price inflation[b]	11.3	5.3	2.0	3.7	3.7
Employment growth	-1.6	0.7	2.6	3.3	2.2
Unemployment rate	8.9	9.7	9.5	8.7	9.3
Real GDP growth	-1.4	3.0	4.5	5.3	4.3
Money supply growth[c]	10.5	8.0	5.8	7.5	7.1

Source: *National Economic Summit Conference, April 11–14, 1983: Documents and Proceedings,* vol. 1: *Government Documents* (Canberra: Australian Government Publishing Service, 1983), pp. 332, 339, 341.
a. Average weekly earnings.
b. Measured by consumer price index.
c. M3

Not surprisingly, the relative share of labor in nonfarm income rises under option B, but falls under C. Even the intermediate option, A—the Labor government's favored course—provides for a drop in labor's relative share. In effect, the official projections provided to the parties at the summit conference were entirely consistent with a real-wage overhang model.

Apart from the menu of choices available to an exercise of incomes policy by social compact, there is the problem of persuasion. The seemingly unpalatable option B provides real-wage growth, net employment growth (although not enough to hold down the unemployment rate), and an expansion of labor's relative share of income. Labor's *absolute* share grows more rapidly under B than under the other two options.[25] Even though the gross domestic product (GDP) grows more slowly under B—so that there is relatively less to share—labor's percentage share of a smaller "pie" grows fast enough to more than offset the loss of overall potential income. In short, it is not obvious why labor should not prefer B to either A or C.

However, the high level of unemployment in all the projections is revealing. It is true that a disproportionate number of unemployed workers come from groups that are not likely to have much direct influence on union policy. Nevertheless, as the queue lengthens, more and more core union members become threatened, particularly as time passes and layoffs and plant closings receive continuing publicity. The 10 percent unemployment rate reached in 1983 was remarkable by Australian standards. In the United States, where unemployment rates had historically been higher than the rates in Australia, unemployment in the 10 percent range still provoked a series of union wage freezes and cuts to save jobs. Job security had also become a prominent issue in Australia by early 1983. As in the United States, unions in Australia pressed state governments to enact legislation aimed at limiting layoffs and plant closings. Greater job security arrangements were also sought through the arbitration system. High unemployment made B an undesirable option, at least in formal conference proceedings.

Incomes policy has long been debated in Australia; it was an issue even in the halcyon days of the 1960s. The wage arbitration system makes such debate inevitable since a policy of sorts is always being pursued, even if unconsciously. Prime Minister Hawke—who initiated the 1983 summit conference—proposed in the mid 1950s that a board dominated by government economists (but with representatives from labor and management) formulate a policy on wages.[26] This board would have displaced the arbitration system in most matters regarding wages.

Much of the debate over the return of indexation in the 1970s—that

25. Movements in the absolute shares were not mentioned at the conference. However, these movements can be approximated either by adding the growth in the real wage to the growth in employment or by calculating the level of real GDP at the end of the period and multiplying by labor's share.
26. R. J. Hawke, "The Growth of the Court's Authority," in J. R. Niland and J. E. Isaac, eds., *Australian Labour Economics: Readings* (Melbourne: Sun Books, 1975), pp. 46–47.

is, the linkage of wages to prices—involved incomes policy. The argument against indexation was basically that it would lock in the real-wage overhang at its peak level. But the counterargument was that a guaranteed real wage would mean that a social accord could be negotiated. The acceleration in inflation could be broken, according to this view, and the rate of inflation would gradually decelerate as productivity increased. Some research suggests that the 1975 return to indexation did produce reduced wage pressures, but only for a limited time.[27] Efforts at consultation between government and labor after indexation was restored ultimately petered out. In the 1983 discussion of wages policy, however, a return to indexation was again advocated as a way of maintaining a social accord.

The prices and incomes policy proposed by the incoming Labor government in 1983 was surrounded with items designed to entice union cooperation, indexation being but one. What has been called "industrial policy" in the United States was to be achieved through an Economic Planning Advisory Council, whose role would be to participate in "broad indicative planning." The council was to include representatives from unions and other groups. Other items in the accord were taxation policy, social welfare policy, and the reestablishment of a voluntary price surveillance mechanism that would "operate in a less legalistic manner than the former PJT."[28]

Although these programs are quite different from what the outgoing Liberal government would have advocated had it remained in office, some striking similarities in the economic policies of the two governments should be noted. First, the Labor government continued the wage pause it had inherited. Although this was officially viewed as a temporary measure while it awaited a formal wage decision from the Arbitration

---

27. J. E. Isaac, "Wage Determination and Economic Policy," *Australian Economic Review*, no. 3 (1977), pp. 16–24; J. P. Nieuwenhuysen and J. Sloan, "Wages Policy," in F. H. Gruen, ed., *Survey of Australian Economics*, vol. 1 (Sydney: George Allen & Unwin, 1978), pp. 103–06; R. I. Downing, "Inflation: Incomes, Prices and Social Policies," *Australian Quarterly*, vol. 46 (September 1974), pp. 9–19; Anne Romanis Braun, "Compulsory Arbitration as a Form of Incomes Policy: The Australian Case," *IMF Staff Papers*, vol. 21 (March 1974), pp. 176–77; A. J. Phipps, "The Impact of Wage Indexation on Wage Inflation in Australia: 1975(2)-1980(2)," *Australian Economic Paper*, vol. 20 (December 1981), pp. 333–49.

28. *National Economic Summit Conference, 11–14 April 1983, Documents and Proceedings*, vol. 1, pp. 389–401, 407–26.

Commission, the commission appeared to be under no pressure to make a quick decision.

Second, high levels of unemployment were promised by the Labor government, even under its recommended option A. That is, the unemployment rate would still be 9.7 percent in 1985–86, according to the projection presented at the summit conference. Thus, severe economic pressure to live up to the terms of an incomes policy was to be present for an extended period. The move toward demand restraint and higher unemployment was also initiated by the outgoing Liberal government.

Ultimately, the effectiveness of the wages side of the proposed incomes policy depends on the degree to which individual unions can be kept in compliance. With unemployment at record levels, it will never be possible to prove—even if compliance is maintained—whether it was the extreme softness of the labor market or the terms of the social accord that produced the results. Some elements in the institutional arrangements in Australia suggest that unemployment alone might not be sufficient. These same elements, however, give reason for concern about the long-term viability of an incomes policy.

Improving the Efficiency of Demand Restraint

Since demand restraint is an important element of Australia's anti-inflation policy—even with an incomes policy in place—it is important to consider the degree to which wage determination is responsive to such restraint. Even if various policies were to succeed in lowering the natural rate of unemployment, inflation could continue at previously high levels unless the actual rate of unemployment remained above the natural rate for some period. The crucial issue here is how long such a period is likely to last. Would a short dose of demand restraint be sufficient to scale down inflation quickly? Or would a prolonged, costly, and painful exercise be required?

Put another way, it can be said that wage determination in Australia is really concerned with two goals. The first is to lower the natural rate of unemployment by altering elements in the wage-setting process that keep the rate high. Basically, what is at stake here is the real wage and certain relative wage rigidities. The second goal is to ensure that—

regardless of the natural rate of unemployment—if inflationary pressures develop or if the rate of inflation has simply been too high in the past, demand restraint will quickly correct the problem. At stake here is the *short-run* slope of the Phillips curve. Incomes policy discussion in Australia has been concerned with the first goal more than the second.

The Effect of Indexation

To some extent, indexation does help to achieve the second goal, although it has not been viewed quite in this fashion. Indexation makes wage setting sensitive (quickly) to price developments. It can have some perverse effects (these are the ones usually emphasized in the literature) that carry into wages "exogenous" price shocks from such events as increases in world prices, agricultural prices, and excise taxes. Such increases do not reflect increased "ability to pay" of employers; if they are reflected in wage setting, the result is equivalent to an increase in pressures on real wages. (Of course, downward adjustments in exogenous price elements can have the reverse effect.) However, to the extent that price markups in the endogenous sector of pricing reflect general economic conditions (that is, the level of demand), indexation—by conveying these responses quickly into wage setting—enhances the efficiency of demand restraint.

In short, apart from the argument that indexation may help to achieve a social compact, it might also be said to strengthen traditional demand-restraint policy. In this case, two main drawbacks must be weighed. First, the perverse effects of external (positive) price shocks may overpower the reinforcement of demand restraint. In principle, this problem can be surmounted by using an "adjusted" price index, for example, an index that takes account of pricing only in the nonfarm, domestic sector. It is difficult, however, to win acceptance for such an index since it does not necessarily reflect movements in worker purchasing power because of the omissions. Indexation in Australia is historically rooted in the arbitration system, which developed indexation as a means of protecting minimum living standards. As long as the indexation is associated solely with purchasing power (that is, consumer prices), "adjusted" price indexes or ad hoc partial indexation decisions will appear to conflict with the very concept of indexation.

Second, even if the potential problems of a purchasing-power index (such as the traditional consumer price index) are neglected, it matters a great deal at what base level real wages are protected. The danger is that real wages will be indexed at a level that is incompatible with low unemployment. Indexing in the 1970s was introduced at the peak of a wage explosion; had it been introduced much earlier as part of an incomes policy, the real-wage overhang problem might conceivably have been averted.

The difficulty is that Australia's discussion of indexation has been too narrow. It is generally assumed that if there is to be indexation, the index must be exclusively a *price* measure. But other gain-sharing indexes can be suggested that are more closely associated with economic conditions.

Greater Reliance on "The Market"

During the period of Liberal party rule (1975–83), two conflicting views emerged with regard to wage determination. The group that became the dominant voice, as signified by the wage pause of 1982–83, advocated that the arbitration system be used to promote wage restraint. The other group favored scrapping the system, or at least downgrading it, in favor of "market" wage determination. This latter approach, often identified as the "Treasury view," was usually kept muted in public discourse. Public opinion in Australia tends to favor the arbitration system—61 percent of those polled (including 73 percent of Liberal party voters) favored arbitration over private collective bargaining for setting wages.[29] An attempt to tinker with the arbitration system brought down a government in the 1920s, a lesson politicians and government officials are not likely to forget. Hence, it is difficult to find clear-cut public statements of the Treasury position.

To some extent, the Treasury was concerned with *relative* wages and the possible effects of rigid wage differentials on resource allocation. However, inasmuch as the concern was over movements in average wage levels, there is an obvious connection with the effectiveness of demand restraint. Thus the question is, what would be the method of

29. Leonard Radic, "Majority Backs Arbitration Commission," *The Age* (October 5, 1981), p. 17.

wage determination if the arbitration system was eclipsed? In particular, would wages under some successor system show greater sensitivity to demand restraint than they do under arbitration?

One possibility is that the successor system might be some form of collective bargaining. Bargaining tends to become popular when the arbitration system's wage awards fall well behind the rate of inflation. For example, during the late 1960s and early 1970s, bargaining became a common form of wage determination.[30] There is nothing illegal about bargaining per se in Australia. Larger firms with multinational connections, in particular, know how bargaining is conducted abroad and which procedures can be imported into Australia. When the arbitration system "caught up" with bargained wages and introduced indexation in the mid-1970s, interest in private bargaining eroded, but it arose again in the early 1980s when indexation was abandoned.

It is not certain, however, that deliberately restraining the arbitration system—so that bargaining became more prevalent—would produce an environment in which aggregate wage determination would show greater sensitivity to demand restraint than is the case with arbitration. If the example of the United States is any guide, collective bargaining does not resemble the auction-style labor markets of the textbooks. If Australia followed the U.S. example, it would find itself with long-term union management contracts, but they would cover a much larger segment of the work force than is the case in the United States. Such contracts would probably not exhibit substantial wage sensitivity to demand.

Still another approach would be to move away from both arbitration and collective bargaining. During various stages in its administration after 1975, the Liberal government introduced bills to amend the complex laws regulating industrial relations, in particular those laws regulating union security (that is, compulsory union membership). These moves were mirrored to some extent at the state level, especially in Western Australia. Although various motives were behind the proposals for changes in the labor law, one effect might have been a contraction of the union sector. For example, one survey in Western Australia indicated

---

30. It was argued in the early 1970s that firms based in the United States were importing their collective bargaining practices into Australia. See Dianne Yerbury and J. E. Isaac, "Recent Trends in Collective Bargaining in Australia," *International Labour Review*, vol. 103 (May 1971), pp. 421–52, especially pp. 446–47.

that as many as one-third of union members and former union members reported that they were (or had been) members on an involuntary basis.[31]

Even if union membership were to drop substantially to current levels in the United States, and the arbitration system were made to disappear, the resulting degree of wage sensitivity to demand restraint might not be markedly different. A predominantly nonunion labor market—like the one in the United States—is still far removed from idealized auction wage setting. Indeed, in the late 1970s and early 1980s, there developed in the United States a considerable body of literature on "implicit contracting" in the labor market. In essence, this literature purports to explain wage stickiness in nonunion firms—where no contract is available to explain it—on the basis of the theory that an implicit contract exists between employer and employee that has much the same effect as an explicit contract. Regardless of the validity of the explanations offered in the implicit contracting literature, the fact remains: wage stickiness seems to exist regardless of institutional arrangements. A move to the "market" might not change the slope of Australia's Phillips curve, but it might shift its location toward lower average unemployment.

The Australian Wage Equation

In the 1960s, economists in many countries began to make econometric studies of the determinants of wage change. The original paper to apply the Phillips curve to wage setting in the United Kingdom found the level of unemployment to be an important determinant for the rate of wage inflation over a long period.[32] Subsequent studies in a number of countries, especially studies covering the postwar era, suggested that other variables were involved as well, particularly the rate of price inflation, productivity, and profitability.

The original Phillips specification implied a long-term trade-off between wage inflation and unemployment. But researchers later ques-

31. N. F. Dufty, "Conscripts and Volunteers," *Australian Bulletin of Labour*, vol. 7 (March 1981), pp. 88–104. Survey estimates of involuntary union membership varying from one-fourth to one-third are cited in Don Rawson, *British and Australian Labour Law, The Background to the 1982 Bills*, Industrial Relations Paper (Canberra: Australian National University, Research School of Social Sciences, 1982), pp. 26–27.

32. A. W. Phillips, "The Relation between Unemployment and the Rate of Change of Money Wage Rates in the United Kingdom, 1861–1957," *Economica*, vol. 25 (November 1958), pp. 283–99.

tioned—initially on theoretical grounds—whether a trade-off could exist in the long run. In essence, they argued that such a trade-off suggested that an increase in the inflation rate could permanently reduce the real wage and could thus expand employment and reduce unemployment. They pointed out, however, that if wages were ultimately determined in real terms, the trade-off—which might exist in the short run because of lags in perceiving or catching up with inflation—would evaporate.

In Australia, with its long history of debate over, and periodic implementation of, wage indexation to price inflation, the existence of a long-term trade-off is certainly questionable. The principal actors in the wage-determination process appear to be aware of the need to "correct" nominal wage decisions for subsequent movements in prices. This is not to say that decisions to curtail real wages are never made; the wage pause of 1982, the partial indexation decisions of the late 1970s, and the wage cut in the early 1930s are all examples of such decisions. The point is, however, that such decisions are made consciously, not because of money illusion.

Of the substantial literature on wage equations for Australia, some studies take account of the arbitration system explicitly. Award wages are distinguished from actual earnings in the estimation process. Wage award decisions are usually seen as inputs into the determination of actual wage change. Problems do arise, however, if award wages are viewed as totally exogenous decisions, except in short-run forecasting exercises. Nevertheless, many studies have viewed shifts in the actual wage-award wage differential as reflections of demand pressures. Given the readily apparent association between strike activity and wage change in the mid-1970s, it is not surprising that some researchers include strike data as indexes of union militancy in modeling wage change. However, the evidence of a positive association between strike activity and wage change long predates the 1970s.

Although most studies consider demand or unemployment an explanatory variable, since the early 1970s the issue has been whether demand variables play only a short-term role, or whether a long-term trade-off exists along the lines of the Phillips curve.[33] The evidence seems to point to a short-run rather than a long-run trade-off. Such a conclusion does

---

33. One of the first discussions of this issue can be found in Michael Parkin, "The Short-Run and Long-Run Trade-Offs between Inflation and Unemployment in Australia," *Australian Economic Papers*, vol. 12 (December 1973), pp. 127–39.

not necessarily mean that the natural rate of unemployment is rigidly fixed. Some researchers find evidence of a shifting natural rate. As was noted earlier, the natural rate could shift as a result of changes in wage-setting institutions themselves. At least one study suggests that the natural rate was higher after indexation returned in the mid-1970s than before, as might have been expected when the previous effects of the wage explosion became locked in. Still another suggests that increases in award wages can adversely affect employment levels and squeeze profits.[34]

Only a few studies have compared wage equations for Australia with those for other countries. The only way to do this consistently is to run the same regression equation across a group of countries having different institutional arrangements and peculiarities of data. In one study of this type the unemployment rate was assumed to influence the change of wage *inflation* rather than the rate of change of wages.[35] Under this specification, wage setting in Australia seemed more sensitive to unemployment than it did either in the United Kingdom or the United States, but markedly less sensitive than in other countries, notably Japan.

Another study suggested that the price sensitivity of wage setting in Australia and the United Kingdom rose relative to that in the United States during the late 1970s, a time when exogenous price inflation was especially influential. This relative shift, in turn, provided a reason for a comparatively worse case of "stagflation" in Australia and the United Kingdom than was experienced in the United States.[36] These compari-

---

34. B. Bhaskara Rao, "An Analysis of the Short- and Long-Run Trade-offs between Unemployment and Inflation and Estimates of the Equilibrium Steady State Unemployment Rate in Australia," *Australian Economic Paper*, vol. 16 (December 1977), pp. 273–84; and T. J. Valentine, "The Effects of Wage Levels on Prices, Profits, Employment and Capacity Utilization in Australia: An Econometric Analysis," *Australian Economic Review*, vol. 1 (1980), pp. 13–22.

35. Dennis Grubb, Richard Jackman, and Richard Layard, "Wage Rigidity and Unemployment in OECD Countries," *European Economic Review*, vol. 21 (March-April 1983), pp. 11–39. The authors' basic equation explains wage change. However, it includes a right-hand side term in which lagged wage change is constrained to have a unitary coefficient. In the actual estimation, therefore, this term is shifted to the left-hand side, making the dependent variable the change in the rate of wage inflation (see p. 23). Different interpretations can be made of the result; the text simply describes the actual form of the equation.

36. L. J. Perry, "Inflation in the USA, UK, and Australia: Some Comparisons," *The Economic Record*, vol. 57 (December 1981), pp. 319–31.

sons, it should be noted, were complicated by the fact that the wage equations for the three countries used different specifications.

Limited Lessons from Empirical Studies

Unfortunately, the literature discussing wage equations for Australia—extensive as it is—does not provide much guidance for policy-makers. Even if it could be shown that the sensitivity of wage change in Australia to demand or unemployment was lower or higher than that in most other countries, this would say nothing about whether that sensitivity might be *changed* through policy modification. Most countries have faced macroeconomic problems similar to Australia's. Thus, to say that one country is slightly ahead of, or behind, the pack does not indicate whether improvements should be sought. A lower natural rate of unemployment is better than a higher one, and when inflation is too high, more short-term sensitivity of wage change to real economic conditions is better than less. The issue is whether policies that will accomplish these ends can be formulated and implemented.

The nature of wage-equation studies themselves raises another problem. A simple wage equation explaining earnings change with lagged price inflation and unemployment does not produce encouraging statistical results for Australia.[37] The fact that published studies tend to obtain "good" results, often with more complex specifications, suggests that they searched for the best equations. Even if the searching approach is combined with some testing for accuracy of prediction outside the estimation period, it raises questions about the significance of the coefficients and their interpretation.

Information about Australian wage determination in recent years can

37. If an annual regression of the percentage change in weekly earnings per employed male unit, $\%W$, is run over 1959–81 against the annual change in the consumer price index lagged one period ($\%P_{-1}$) and the inverse of the unemployment rate (U^{-1}), the following equation emerges:

$$\%W = 1.37 + 1.04\,\%P_{-1} + 10.35\,U^{-1}$$
$$R^2 = 0.69;\ \text{Durbin-Watson} = 0.17.$$

The strong presence of serial correlation exaggerates the significance levels of the regression coefficients. Nonetheless, the coefficient of the inverted unemployment rate is not significant at conventional levels, although minor changes in period of observation and specification could change this result.

largely be derived from institutional knowledge and an "eyeballing" of available data. Wage setters "think" in real terms, as can be seen in the debates over indexation. From time to time, shifts in union militancy affect the real wages that are obtained. The causes of these shifts, especially the shift that occurred in the late 1960s and the 1970s, are not well understood. Strike activity is apparently influenced by real economic conditions, but the shift during that period seemed to go beyond what could easily be explained by unemployment rates and the like.

Although the abandonment of penalties for striking *may* have played a role in the buildup of militancy, the precise relationship of the two events in terms of cause and effect is difficult to establish; penalties are hard to sustain in the face of widespread strikes. It is also possible that the increased militancy was related to the slippage in real unit-labor costs (labor's relative share) in the late 1960s; inflation—and catching up with inflation—may play a role in strike activity. However, the level of militancy persisted after the catch-up period.

On the surface, the wage data from Australia suggest something like a short-run Phillips curve, but with a shift to the right in the 1970s. The wage bubble of the mid-1970s was followed by high unemployment by Australian standards *and* a slippage in real unit labor costs. However, as the unemployment rate came down in the early 1980s—although it remained absolutely high—wage pressures resumed. With the sharp surge in unemployment in 1982–83, the pressures subsided to the point that a wage pause could be implemented.

Gain Sharing to Steepen the Short-term Trade-off

To achieve macroeconomic control of inflation, Australia would be better off aiming for a steeper short-run trade-off between wage change and unemployment (or some other real-demand proxy). However, wage-fixing discussions in Australia tend to focus more on inflation as an obvious input into wage decisions than on other relevant factors. As noted earlier, the debate over indexation was concerned only with indexation to the consumer price index, not to other measures of economic conditions. Yet, other measures should be considered. Such alternative indexation could steepen the trade-off by linking wages to real economic conditions.

The idea that inflation is not the only variable to which wages might be indexed is not completely new. Alternative arrangements were advocated as early as 1925 in Australia.[38] At the enterprise level, a small number of firms do have such alternative indexation in the form of profit sharing or other types of gain sharing. Such arrangements do not appear to be a recent innovation in Australia. Some of the plans go back to the 1940s. Furthermore, the mining sector has had some experience with bonus systems. Yet relatively few Australian workers are covered by such arrangements, which many consider to be executive compensation only.

To the extent that Australian employers even consider employee participation in the economic gains of their enterprises, they are more likely to create some form of employee stock ownership plan. Often the motivation for such programs is to improve morale—by encouraging employee identification with the employer—or to "teach" the employee about the realities of the marketplace. Whatever the merits of such ideas, they fail in a critical respect.

The creation of more shareholders, even if they be employees, does not by itself make labor costs more sensitive to demand conditions. (In contrast, a gain-sharing bonus builds in such sensitivity automatically.) Hence, share ownership need not affect the pricing behavior of firms. If pricing is not affected within individual firms, then overall inflation will not be affected, either. Only in the case where workers own the entire enterprise, and hence where there is no practical distinction between wages and profits, does share ownership necessarily have the desired macroeconomic effect. Although there are a few examples of complete worker ownership in Australia, the enterprises involved tend to be small, and only a small fraction of the work force is covered by such arrangements.

If gain-sharing plans were to become widespread in Australia, there would be important macroeconomic benefits in the form of increased effectiveness of macroeconomic demand restraint. While each enterprise's gain-sharing arrangement would reflect the conditions within that enterprise, the general ups and downs of the economy would greatly influence the average firm's situation. Labor costs would thus reflect general economic conditions on the average, helping to steepen the

38. J. T. Sutcliffe, "Wages and Production," *The Economic Record*, vol. 1 (November 1925), pp. 63–72.

short-run Phillips curve. It is widely believed, for example, that Japan's bonus system—a form of gain sharing—helps to explain that country's steeper Phillips curve and avoidance of stagflation.

Since the benefits from gain sharing are largely at the level of the overall society, deliberate encouragement by public policy would be required to make it a significant element of Australian wage determination. Even then, some obstacles would have to be overcome, the first of which is the Australian labor movement's lack of enthusiasm for profit sharing and similar arrangements on the grounds that they "are merely guises for improving the return to owners and consolidating the powers of management elites."[39] Second, such programs would have to mesh with the system of multiemployer wage awards through the arbitration system since, if implemented by the employer, they would provide different compensation levels for workers covered by common awards. Third, small employers might lack the sophistication—or the willingness to make the necessary data available—to implement such plans. And fourth, public opinion—at least according to survey questions—seems to eschew profitability as a wage-setting criterion. In a 1981 poll, 80 percent of respondents thought that workers should receive the same wage across industries despite significant variation in profitability levels among industries.[40]

Although these barriers would all have to be overcome to make gain sharing more widespread in Australia, their existence should not be a deterrent to such an effort. The scope of the compensation package—apart from the simple wage element—would obviously have to be addressed in arbitration awards and bargaining, as is discussed in the next section. Even if the barriers to changing the structure of compensation at the microlevel proved insurmountable, a form of national gain sharing could be implemented.

The Australian Conciliation and Arbitration Commission has broad discretion in determining the relevant criteria for establishing the national wage decision, which filters into wage awards throughout the labor market. Just as it can index wage setting to price inflation if it chooses to do so, the commission could index to other relevant economic

39. Brian Sheehan, *Employee Financial Participation* (Canberra: Australian Government Publishing Service for Department of Science and Technology, 1981), pp. 31–32.
    40. Radic, "Majority Backs Arbitration Commission," p. 17.

measures of ability to pay such as overall profitability, the ratio of actual to potential output, unemployment, and so on.

In effect, the commission can write a desired Phillips curve slope into award-wage rates. But, according to the procedures of the commission, any request to consider gain-sharing measures must be part of the submissions of the parties involved and the government. Hence, before gain sharing could be implemented, it would have to become part of general economic policy and, perhaps, even part of a social accord.

It is worth noting that gain sharing, whether implemented at the microeconomic or macroeconomic level, can be made part of an overall package of "industrial democracy." Unlike simple profit sharing, this concept does have appeal for the ACTU. There is a logic in giving workers who participate in the financial fortunes of their employers a voice in the decisions that contribute, in part, to those fortunes (or misfortunes). If workers are given a voice in decisions, there is a logic in allowing them to participate in the fruits (sweet or bitter) of those decisions. Dressed in the right clothing, gain sharing might be a more attractive approach than initial union skepticism would make it appear.

Wage Determination and the Industrial Relations System

Australia's unique industrial relations arrangements, particularly its system of compulsory arbitration of industrial disputes, have received widespread attention. In principle, such disputes are to be settled by a quasi-judicial process through federal, state, or—in certain cases—industry tribunals. Tribunal awards are supposed to substitute for strikes as a method of settling disputes, but penalties for striking have not been applied since the late 1960s. Although the arbitration system sets minimum wages and other conditions of employment for most occupations, nothing prevents the negotiation of higher wages or better conditions through private bargaining.

Private bargaining can occur entirely outside the arbitration system. A few examples of American-style contracts with fixed durations, grievance and arbitration mechanisms, and so on can be found in certain industries. Such unregistered agreements have ambiguous legal status somewhat like the uncertain legal standing of union contracts in the

United States before the passage of the Taft-Hartley Act of 1947. Agreements may be given firmer legal status by "registering" them with the appropriate authorities or by obtaining consent awards. In the latter case, the arbitration authorities essentially "bless" the terms of the agreement by incorporating them into an official arbitration award, thus making them the binding minimum standard for all employers covered by the award. On some occasions, however, the authorities may decline to bestow a blessing on settlements outside appropriate norms.

Although industrial relations matters occupy a key place in Australian politics and economic policy—far more so than in the United States— data on the frequency of industrial relations practices are sadly lacking. There appears to be no ongoing collection of information on the contents of arbitration awards, except for indexes of wage rates. Even the available indexes do not distinguish between decisions that have been reached wholly through the arbitration process, those that have been made privately and then endorsed by the authorities, and those reached entirely outside the system—either by bargaining or through purely unilateral decisions of employers. Only limited information is available on the incidence and cost of fringe benefits.

The need for more comprehensive information in Australia cannot be stressed enough, particularly in view of the frequent changes in its basic labor law—which has been amended more than sixty times since it was enacted in 1904. By way of contrast, the American Wagner Act, the heart of labor relations regulation in the United States, has been significantly amended only five times since its enactment in 1935, and only two of these amendments involved substantial changes.

Available data do make clear the comprehensiveness of the arbitration system: in 1974 only 12 percent of the paid work force was truly nonunion in the sense of being unrepresented by *any* organization and having wages set by unilateral employer decision (table 7); 87 percent were covered by either federal or state arbitration awards. Moreover, fewer than 1 percent bargained, American-style, totally outside the arbitration system.

The year 1974—when the data of table 7 were collected—was generally viewed as a period in which bargaining had previously been the dominant mode of wage setting and in which the arbitration authorities were trying to have their wage decisions catch up with "market" levels.[41] Two years

41. Arbitration awards accounted for about 60 percent of the increase in weekly

Table 7. *Percentage of Employees Covered by Arbitration Awards or Unregistered Collective Bargaining Agreements, May 1974*
Percent

Employee category	Federal awards	State awards	Unregistered agreements	Not covered by awards or agreements
All wage and salary earners	39.2	47.8	0.9	12.2
Males	43.7	40.6	1.1	14.6
Females	30.2	62.0	0.5	7.3
Manufacturing	53.6	32.7	0.8	12.9
Nonmanufacturing	32.6	54.6	0.9	11.9
Public administration	20.7	73.1	1.0	5.2

Source: Australian Bureau of Statistics, *Incidence of Industrial Awards, Determinations and Collective Agreements, May 1974*, cat. no. 6.5 (ABS, November 14, 1975).

later, the truly nonunion sector dropped from 12 percent to 10 percent.[42] Hence, impact of arbitration decisions does not appear to be directly related to the coverage of those awards, which is always comprehensive. Rather it depends on the degree to which the awards are influencing actual wages paid.

The Arbitration Framework

A larger proportion of those covered by arbitration awards are under state rather than federal tribunals (see table 7). Some of the state arbitration systems predate the Australian Conciliation and Arbitration Commission. In certain respects, state tribunals have—or can be given— broader authority than the commission owing to the constitutional limitations placed on the federal government. Therefore, the arbitration system is not monolithic. Nonetheless, in matters of national wage trends, the commission is considered the prime agent in the system.

National wage decisions are generally followed by state and industry tribunals. For example, the Metal Industry Award of late 1981 provided for an initial adjustment in December 1981 and a second adjustment in

---

earnings of males during 1972–74, but 132 percent in 1974, as official wages caught up with actual, and earnings drift declined. In contrast, in 1976 arbitration awards accounted for 79 percent of increases in weekly earnings of males. "Summary of the Economic Situation," *Australian Economic Review*, vol. 4 (1981), p. 7.

42. Bureau of Labour Market Research, *Youth Wages, Employment, and the Labour Force*, p. 36.

June 1982. A study tracking the speed with which the second adjustment spread to other awards—the Metal Industry Case has often served as a pattern-setting settlement—found that 79 percent of workers under "major" awards and 65 percent of workers under small awards had received comparable adjustments by August 1982.[43]

Basically, the arbitration process is triggered by a "dispute," which need not mean an actual strike. It may simply mean that a union has served claims on an employer—or, more likely, employers—and that the claims have not been accepted. The process by which the dispute is resolved—a hearing in which union and management advocates present their respective positions—is often viewed by Australian industrial relations experts as excessively legalistic.

The centralization and legalism of the process, it is said, tend to undermine private settlement of disputes. The lack of private relationships, in turn, is said to limit resolution at the plant and shop level of what in the United States would be minor grievances. In essence, Australia has "nationalized" part, but not all, of the personnel and industrial relations department of each employer, leaving the remaining part—the part that might deal with local issues—in a poor position to handle its responsibilities. It is also said that short strikes are triggered simply to obtain the quick attention of the tribunals to cases that might otherwise sit in the queue. In discussions of compulsory arbitration in the United States, it is tempting to point to the incidence of strikes in Australia, the moral being that a system that bans strikes and provides for arbitration as an alternative neither prevents strikes nor produces a particularly good strike record.

There is something to be said for these criticisms, but the arguments can easily be overstated. Consider how Australia's strike record for 1972–81—a period that includes the unrest of the early and mid-1970s—compares with that of three other English-speaking countries (table 8). In terms of number of strikes per year, Australia seems to have the worst record, although differences in national definitions of a strike significantly affect the figures. Union members in Australia seem to be far more prone than their foreign counterparts to participate in strike actions. The ratio of strikers to union members in Australia was 48 percent in an average

43. "Summary of the Economic Situation," *Australian Economic Review*, vol. 4 (1982), p. 19.

Table 8. *Mean Strike Indicators in Four Industrial Countries, 1972–81*

Strike indicator	Australia	Canada	United Kingdom	United States
Number of disputes[a]	2,388.5	974	2,251	4,813
Number of strikers (thousands)	1,347	558	1,553	1,875
Days lost in disputes (thousands)	3,351	8,166	12,040	33,762
Civilian employees (millions)	6.0	9.6	24.4	91.5
Union members (millions)[b]	2.8	3.1	12.5[c]	22.6
Strikers per dispute	564	573	690	390
Strikers as a percent of total employees	22.5	5.8	6.4	2.0
Strikers as a percent of union members	48.1	18.0	12.4	8.3
Days lost per striker	2.5	14.6	7.8	18.0
Days lost per employee	0.6	0.9	0.5	0.4
Days lost per union member	1.2	2.6	1.0	1.5

Sources: Data on strikes and employment are from International Labour Office, *Yearbook of Labour Statistics, 1982* (Geneva: ILO, 1982), tables 3A and 28A; data on union membership are from Great Britain, Central Statistical Office, *Annual Abstract of Statistics, 1982* (London: HMSO, 1982), p. 185; Labour Canada, *Directory of Labour Organisations in Canada, 1980* (Hull, Quebec: Canadian Government Publishing Centre, 1980), p. 18; David Plowman, *Australian Trade Union Statistics,* working paper (University of New South Wales, Department of Industrial Relations, n.d.), p. 4; and U.S. Bureau of Labor Statistics, press release USDL 81-446, September 18, 1981, p. 3.

a. U.S. data exclude disputes lasting less than one day or one shift; data for the United Kingdom exclude strikes of one day or those involving fewer than ten workers, unless they involve more than 100 man-days; data for Canada and Australia exclude strikes of less than ten man-days.

b. Mean of 1976 and 1977 figures.

c. Adjusted to exclude members in Ireland and other areas outside the United Kingdom.

year during the period shown, compared with substantially lower ratios in the other three countries.

At that point, however, the unfavorable comparison ceases. On the basis of days lost per striker, Australia's average of 2.5 days puts it well below the averages in the other nations being compared. And, in terms of days lost per employee, or—what may be a more relevant measure of the climate of industrial relations—days lost per union member, Australia's record appears comparable to the U.S. and U.K. records and somewhat better than Canada's.

Although Australia has not eliminated strikes, apparently it has succeeded in changing the form of the strikes that do occur. The incidence of long, bruising strikes has been reduced, at the cost of more frequent, minor disruptions. On the other hand, the inability to improve local-level industrial relations and grievance handling and the fact that fixed-term, no-strike guarantees in the American style are comparatively rare are symptomatic of a problem in the current approach to arbitration that needs correcting. In principle, nothing prevents the parties from addressing these issues, for example, by creating grievance processes or agreeing not to push further claims for fixed periods. But the compartmentalization of the current system does not encourage such behavior.

Arrangements such as grievance and (private) arbitration systems, fixed-duration contracts with no-strike clauses, and other features commonly found in U.S. labor-management agreements developed from a series of trade-offs. What unions in the United States first want from an employer is recognition. Even after winning a representation election, they may not be fully recognized until a contract is signed. Unions, in short, have a strong motivation to obtain a written agreement in a system in which management is the ultimate dispenser of recognition and status.

But management also expects to achieve certain objectives with such an agreement. Since strikes are costly and disruptive, it wants a guarantee of fixed periods of labor peace; that is, it expects the contract to be of definite duration and to contain a no-strike clause. In turn, a union expects a contract restricting the right to strike to provide some alternative method for handling the complaints of its members that will inevitably arise during the life of the contract. It wants a dispute-settling mechanism—a grievance and arbitration clause—to be included in the contract. The process is one of give and take: something is offered in exchange for something else.

At present, the arbitration system in Australia simply grants certain types of claims and considers others individually. In other words, unions achieve recognition by establishing a recognized jurisdiction. The recognition comes from the arbitration system, not the employer. Once established, the union's jurisdiction is protected from the encroachments of other unions. A union so recognized can then submit claims against employers, even employers who do not employ its members. The eventual wage award will cover all employers recognized as coming within the defined jurisdiction. Although it cannot be said that the system deliberately impedes the resolution of day-to-day problems, the arbitration process offers *little* incentive to establish an ongoing, close relationship between union and employer.

Compartmentalization makes it difficult to improve not only day-to-day industrial relations, but also the overall wage-determination process. The problem is that cases that have a bearing on one another nevertheless come before the arbitration system as separate issues. For example, during the third quarter of 1983, the ACTU pursued two cases before the Conciliation and Arbitration Commission that could have been treated together. One was the national wage case, in which a wage increase was requested at the end of the wage pause. The other was an employment security case that was filed and heard separately. All parties concerned were aware of both cases. What is more to the point, wages and job security are obviously connected. First, inasmuch as employment security translates into costs to employers as well as benefits to workers, the costs need to be considered in granting an overall wage increase. Employment security can be viewed as a fringe benefit; if more is given in fringes, less can be given in wages. Second, and more important, the provision of employment security is related to the form the compensation adjustment takes.

The weekly payroll of an employer—or, for that matter, of the economy as a whole—can be expressed as the product of three variables: wages per hour, W; hours per week, H; and the number of employees, E. Left to their own devices, employers deal with up-and-down shifts in demand by varying H first (raising or lowering overtime or possibly going to short workweeks). However, the scope for varying the payroll through H alone is limited. Typically, the next step is to vary E (new hires or layoffs). Only as a last resort is W varied. The insulation of W from economic conditions poses a key problem for macroeconomic policy.

One way to introduce variability in W would be to add a gain-sharing element to the wage-setting system. Typically, the variation is introduced through a bonus rather than the straight-time hourly wage, but the effect is much the same. Hence, an obvious trade-off for *less* variability in E— the target of the employment security case—is *more* variation in W, a possibility that could have been considered in the wage case. Isolating the two approaches limits both the opportunity for compromise and the scope for improving macroeconomic performance. To the extent that workplace relations influence productivity, the existing compartmentalization may also have an adverse microlevel effect.

Unions and Employers

The union movement in Australia has two prominent characteristics. First, the number of unions is large, given the small size of the labor force; there were more than three hundred unions in Australia in 1982

Table 9. Union Membership, Selected Years, 1891–1981

Year	Number of unions	Number of union members (thousands)	Union members as percentage of total employment		
			Males	Females	Total
1891	124	54.8	n.a.	n.a.	4
1901	198	97.2	n.a.	n.a.	6
1911	573	364.7	n.a.	n.a.	28
1921	382	703.0	58	32	52
1931	361	740.8	47	35	45
1941	374	1075.6	53	39	50
1951	359	1690.2	66	42	60
1961	355	1894.6	63	41	57
1971	341	2436.6	59	39	52
1981	324	2994.1	60	48	56
1982	322	3012.4	62	49	57

Sources: David Plowman, *Australian Trade Union Statistics;* data for 1981 and 1982 are from Australian Bureau of Statistics, *Trade Union Statistics, Australia, December 1982,* cat. no. 6323.0 (ABS, June 24, 1983); number of unions in 1971 is from D. Plowman, S. Deery, and C. Fisher, *Australian Industrial Relations* (Sydney: McGraw-Hill, 1980), p. 192. This last source appears to refer erroneously to males only for recent years.
n.a. Not available.

(table 9). Second, the rate of unionization is quite high; 57 percent of wage and salary earners belonged to unions in 1982 (table 8). Self-reports of employees in 1982 suggest a somewhat lower rate of 49 percent, which is still quite high, especially by U.S. standards.[44]

One factor in this high rate of unionization is the arbitration system; the various tribunals can grant "preference clauses" in awards under which employers must give preference to union members in hiring. Even so, if it is assumed that arbitration awards cover about nine out of ten wage and salary workers, the estimates in table 7 suggest that at least one-third of these employees are covered by awards initiated by union claims, but that they are not necessarily union members. Still another factor in the high unionization rate appears to be the relative ease with which workers in the public sector (including those in government-owned enterprises) can be organized. According to the self-reports cited earlier, the rate of unionization in the public sector runs at about 73 percent versus 39 percent in private employment.

Many people believe that Australia has "too many" unions and that

44. Australian Bureau of Statistics, *Trade Union Members, Australia, March to May 1982,* catalog no. 6325.0 (Canberra: ABS, April 19, 1983), pp. 6–7. I am indebted to Don Rawson for this alternative source.

mergers between unions should be encouraged. However, legislation enacted in 1972—which was prompted by the fear that merger would lead to the formation of a large, left-wing union—hindered the process of merging. In a preelection accord in early 1983, the ACTU and the Labor party pledged to remove this legal barrier to mergers. Certain barriers were lifted as a result, but current policy still does not actively encourage mergers.

In any case, it is not clear what the "optimum" number of unions should be. If the United States had the same ratio of unions to members as Australia has, there would be well over two thousand unions in the United States. Roughly a tenth of that number report to the U.S. Bureau of Labor Statistics. However, these estimates do not include the many small local independent unions, single-firm unions, and municipal employee associations in the United States, which would raise the U.S. count considerably. Moreover, U.S. national unions are divided into locals that exercise varying degrees of autonomy; in some industries such as construction, bargaining is carried out largely at the local level. There were roughly 50,000 locals in the United States in the mid-1970s.[45] Thus, it is extremely difficult to compare the number of "unions" in the two countries.

The concern about the size of unions in Australia has to do more with the structure of union representation than with union numbers. Because of the workings of the arbitration system, existing jurisdictions and union institutions are perpetuated along craft lines, a pattern that has been dominant ever since the system came into being at the turn of the century. Craft unionism means that firms must often deal with several unions in an atmosphere of interunion rivalry, competition, unstable industrial relations, and wage pressures.

This craft structure poses special problems for incomes policy. Because craft unions cross industry lines, wage breakthroughs in one sector readily spread to other sectors. An incomes policy built on a coordinated "hold the line" approach can easily be imperiled by such a structure.

Although it is more difficult to obtain information on employer characteristics in Australia, apparently the number of employer groups

45. U.S. Department of Labor, Labor-Management Services Administration, *Union Financial Statistics 1976* (GPO, n.d.), p. 4.

is also large: 81 employer groups were registered with the federal arbitration authorities in 1980; at the state arbitration level there were 296 employer groups in New South Wales, 39 in Queensland, 9 in South Australia, and 14 in Western Australia.[46] (Tasmania and Victoria have no procedure for registration.)

The strength of both the unions and employers is somewhat offset at the national level by the ACTU, which plays a much more active role in wage determination—by representing the national union case before the Arbitration Commission—than, say, the American Federation of Labor and Congress of Industrial Organizations (AFL-CIO) would play in the United States. Most union members are in organizations affiliated with the ACTU, especially after several important white-collar organizations joined the fold in the early 1980s. This merger put into the ACTU one of the fastest growing segments of union membership of the previous decade. Similarly, by virtue of its role in national wage cases on behalf of employers, the Confederation of Australian Industry is influential in wage determination; this group has no counterpart in the United States. Hence, both sides have diversity at the bottom but significant potential authority at the top. This authority can be helpful to the operation of a centralized incomes policy.

At the same time, diversity in size of both unions and employers limits the number of significant "players." Consider, for example, that 47 percent of Australia's unions had fewer than 1,000 members in December 1982, and that only about 3 percent of all union members belonged to these organizations. At the same time, 4 percent of the unions had more than 50,000 members, and these contained about 45 percent of all union members.[47]

Data on size of the firms are less readily available. It is known, however, that 48 percent of all firms in manufacturing had work forces of less than ten employees, and these firms accounted for less than 6 percent of total employment in 1980–81. On the other hand, less than 2 percent of manufacturing firms had more than 500 employees and accounted for almost 50 percent of manufacturing employment. In 1981, moreover, the twenty largest employers in all sectors accounted for over 12 percent of wage and salary employment. Large firms not only pay higher

46. *Year Book Australia 1982*, p. 173.
47. Australian Bureau of Statistics, *Trade Union Statistics, Australia, December 1982*, catalog no. 6323.0 (Canberra: ABS, June 24, 1983), p. 4.

average wages than small ones do, but they are probably "leaders" in other aspects of personnel management and labor relations.[48] In particular, this employer concentration suggests that the adoption of particular personnel policies such as gain sharing by a relatively small number of enterprises could have a significant "demonstration" effect on the entire labor market.

Politics and Industrial Relations

The term *politics* as applied to industrial relations in Australia has several meanings. To some, it means the ideologies that separate factions within the trade union movement and that sometimes lead to fascinating internecine conflict. In recent years the ideological component has had limited effect on ongoing industrial relations, except for occasional disruptions such as the "green bans" in Sydney, during which union members refused to participate in construction projects in certain historical areas, and the controversy over the export of uranium. Now and then strikes are organized in reaction to government policy—for example, a 1976 protest was directed against changes in Medibank—but they often meet with only limited success.

There is another meaning of politics: the union interaction with the electoral process, with government policymakers, and with government agencies. The ACTU and most of its constituent unions are closely associated with the Australian Labor party. When the Labor party is in office, the union movement expects to be "consulted" and expects a favorable legislative climate. Although the notion is difficult to quantify, some observers believe that the Labor government of the early 1970s played a part in reversing the downward drift in the unionization rate shown in table 9.

The interplay between the ACTU and the government (even when the Labor party is not in office), and between the ACTU and the arbitration commission, creates a need for a professional staff, and gives the staff significant status. For example, Prime Minister Hawke rose through the ranks of this staff to reach the presidency of the ACTU; at

48. Australian Bureau of Statistics, *Enterprise Statistics: Details by Industry Subdivision, Australia, 1980–81 (Preliminary)*, catalog no. 8107.0 (Canberra: ABS, February 21, 1983), table 2; *Australian Business*, April 15, 1982, pp. 70–71.

one time he held the post of ACTU advocate before the Arbitration Commission. Although the authority of professionals in a rank-and-file movement can create internal tensions, during a period of incomes policy there is a need for individuals who can interact with government policymakers. It is not surprising, therefore, that union professionals have been anxious to have a successful incomes policy under a Labor government. This attitude helps explain the accord in 1983—centered on an incomes policy—between the ACTU and the Labor party.

The position of employers in the political arena is different from the union position in some respects, and similar in others. Employer organizations are not typically affiliated with political parties. But they have an obvious interest in influencing legislation or having a voice in economic policy. Like the unions, employers need to interact with government and with the arbitration system and thus need a professional staff, particularly at the top. Such a staff elevates the importance of the major organizations. Employer representation is essential to an incomes policy. Hence the Labor government must persuade the key employer groups if it is to achieve a social accord.

An Incomes Policy?

The existence of a centralized wage arbitration system has long suggested to some observers that Australia has a ready-made incomes policy, or at least the institutions to implement one. Moreover, there appears to be significant support for the arbitration system itself. Unions receive various protections from the system and they do not need to worry about achieving employer recognition. Furthermore, preference awards help to maintain and boost membership. And, as long as they do not excessively expand their overaward margins, wages are taken out of competition. Employer organizations have grown up largely to mirror unions in the arbitration mechanism; thus, they too are dependent in large part on the system for their existence. And, of course, the functionaries who operate the system generally prefer the current arrangements. Thus, it might be supposed that if the system was accustomed to implementing an incomes policy, it could withstand the inevitable tensions such a policy entails.

Two other important factors must be considered, however, in evaluating the prospects of an incomes policy in Australia. First, the system provides for minimum awards; there is nothing illegal about a payment above the official scale. Hence, the arbitration system is not a wage-control mechanism, and constitutional limitations rule out wage ceilings, except during wartime, at the federal level. The presence of overaward payments raises the question of whether the arbitration system is "really" influencing wages at all. If wages are largely determined apart from the system, then an incomes policy that affects only official wage rates may have form rather than substance.

The second point is that the principle of "comparative wage justice" is used in setting arbitrated wages. As a result, wage decisions spread from award to award on grounds of equity. Thus, incomes policy can be upset if any significant group succeeds in violating the policy; once a violation occurs, there will be pressures for imitation throughout the work force. Australians generally assume that the demand for comparative wage justice emanates from social mores, which in turn are reflected in arbitration decisions. In fact, these pressures may emanate from the arbitration system itself, and may then be transmitted into social mores.

Does the Arbitration System Affect Wages?

It is always tempting for academics to debunk widely held beliefs. The average Australian believes that the arbitration process sets wages and he or she turns to the newspapers for information about wage decisions and the drama that surrounds them. What could be more enticing for an academic than to prove that all of this interplay is merely a show that produces what the "market" would generate anyway?

It is true that in Australia, as in other parts of the world, bank presidents earn more than ditch diggers, more educated people earn more than less educated people, large firms pay more than small firms, and so on. In that sense, the arbitration system does not change anything. However, it has affected Australia's wage structure.

Consider, first, wage awards themselves. Do the awards look like decisions that a relatively unregulated wage-determination system would produce? That question can be answered in part by comparing the dispersions of wage-rate *awards* in Australia, expressed as annualized percentage rates of change, with comparable data for market-produced earnings changes in the United States. Award decisions across the fifteen

182   Daniel J. B. Mitchell

Table 10. Variation in Wage Change, Australia
and the United States, Selected Industries,
December 1969 to December 1980

Coefficient of variation	December 1969 to December 1974	December 1974 to December 1980	December 1969 to December 1980
Award wage changes for adult	0.04	0.08	0.04
males, Australia[a]	(0.04)	(0.08)	(0.04)
Average earnings changes,	0.16	0.15	0.13
United States[a]	(0.14)	(0.14)	(0.12)

Source: See the text description of this table and note 38.
a. Standard deviation of rate of wage adjustment divided by mean of rate of wage adjustment. Numbers in parentheses use a simple mean of fifteen industries as the denominator rather than a mean of economy-wide adjustment. See note 49 for list of industries.

industries compared in table 10 are substantially more uniform in Australia than in the marketplace of a country without an arbitration mechanism.[49]

Many believe that Australian award decisions tend to compress the wage structure because the system attempts to be equitable, thereby protecting the weak at the bottom of the wage ladder. If "market" forces can be said to work against this effect, then both an observation and a question spring to mind. The observation is that the award-wage decisions "oppose" the forces of the market. The question is whether the market succeeds in completely offsetting the compression effect.

Occupational data on award wages and overaward premiums for workers in the metal industry are of interest here (table 11). When the occupations are ranked by their level of award pay in the state of

49. The fifteen industries for Australia were mining and quarrying; engineering, metals, and vehicles; textiles, clothing, and footwear; food, drink, and tobacco; sawmilling and furniture; paper and printing; other manufacturing; building and construction; railway services; road and air transport; shipping and stevedoring; communications; wholesale and retail trade; public authority; community and business services; and amusements, hotels, and personal services. These industries could not be matched exactly with U.S. industries because of differences in national industrial classification schemes. The following corresponding industries from the United States were used: mining; primary metals; textile mill products; food and kindred products; lumber and wood products; paper and allied products; miscellaneous manufacturing; construction; railroads; trucking and warehousing; West Coast longshoring; communications; wholesale and retail trade; city government, noneducational; hotels, motels, and tourist courts.

Table 11. *Award Wages and Overaward Premiums, Early 1982*

	Victoria		All Australia	
Occupation	Award wage (Australian dollars)	Overaward premium (percent)	Award wage (Australian dollars)	Overaward premium (percent)
Process worker, female	211.30	5.9	217.00	7.6
Machinist, third class	225.30	10.3	225.20	9.5
Welder, third class	231.20	14.1	231.60	14.2
Process worker, male	232.30	14.4	232.10	13.7
Sheetmetal worker, second class	248.40	13.5	251.90	14.0
Other, nontradesmen	252.10	21.1	241.40	17.0
Machinist, second class	253.60	15.3	254.70	14.9
Welder, second class	264.20	23.1	256.80	20.4
Machinist, first class	285.20	15.0	285.40	14.5
Sheetmetal worker, first class	295.30	17.9	292.00	16.5
Other tradesmen	299.80	19.1	303.40	19.6
Motor mechanic	300.80	19.4	286.10	14.8
Fitter	303.30	20.1	300.50	18.8
Toolmaker	307.80	16.3	306.80	15.6
Tradesmen's assistant	312.60	34.9	270.90	24.4
Boilermaker	322.40	24.8	305.50	20.2
Welder	343.00	29.3	313.80	22.3
Rigger	400.10	43.5	350.00	34.8

Source: Amalgamated Metal Workers and Shipwrights' Union, *National Wages and Conditions Survey* (AMWSU, June 1982), p. 7.

Victoria, the effect is not uniform, but the overaward premium clearly tends to be higher, in percentage terms, at higher pay levels. That is, award wages appear to be more compressed in distribution than the market would provide, and overaward payments *tend* to offset the effect. But do they offset it altogether?

Because the data in table 11 suggest that overaward payments tend to offset award compression, comparisons of earnings across countries are instructive. That is, it should be asked whether the Australian wage structure—in terms of actual earnings rather than award rates—shows signs of compression. Thus, table 12 compares earnings dispersion in Australia and the United States for eleven industries.[50]

50. The industries were selected on the basis of availability in the *International Labour Yearbook*. Industries used are listed below. The industry name is followed by the international standard industrial classification (ISIC) code that appears in the

Table 12. *Changes in Wage Structure in Australia
and the United States, 1969–80*

	Dispersion[a] based on actual earnings structure	
Year	Australia	United States
1969	0.09	0.19
1970	0.10	0.20
1971	0.14	0.21
1972	0.14	0.22
1973	0.13	0.22
1974	0.12	0.22
1975	0.14	0.21
1976	0.14	0.22
1977	0.14	0.22
1978	0.15	0.22
1979	0.15	0.22
1980	0.16	0.22

Sources: Calculated from data in International Labour Office, *Yearbook of Labour Statistics* (ILO, various issues).
a. Standard deviation divided by mean for eleven industries. See note 50 for list of industries.

Comparison of the two columns in table 12 suggests that interindustry wage dispersion is narrower in Australia than in the United States. The pattern of change over time in the two countries is also instructive. Dispersion in Australia widens during the early 1970s, a period when collective bargaining held sway. Thereafter—because the arbitration authorities decided to catch up and regain control—the dispersion stabilizes. It appears that when bargaining occurs in Australia, the dispersion of interindustry wages widens—although not to U.S. levels—since the arbitration system puts a floor on the lower tier of wages. When arbitration regains authority, the wage distribution is "fixed" at existing levels and held there. The numbers reflect the "folklore" of what occurred; it is unlikely that this concurrence is mere coincidence.

Yearbook. In some cases where a source other than the *Yearbook* was used to construct the corresponding U.S. industry, the U.S. SIC code is shown in parentheses. The categories are basic metal, 37; construction, 5; fabricated metal and machinery, 381–383 (34, 35, 36); food and beverage, 31; industrial chemicals, 351; mining and quarrying, 2; miscellaneous manufacturing, 390; paper and printing, 34 (26, 27); textiles, apparel, and leather footwear, 321, 322, 324 (22, 23, 314); transport, storage, and communications, 7; and transportation equipment, 384. Apart from the *Yearbook*, data were taken from *Employment and Earnings*, various issues. The results reported in the text are basically unchanged for manufacturing industries.

Table 13. *Distribution of Weekly Earnings of Full-Time Workers, the United States and Australia, 1970–81*[a]
Percent

	Males		Females	
Year	Australia	United States	Australia	United States
1970	n.a.	75	n.a.	n.a.
1975	83	70	78	76
1977	82	66	82	76
1979	81	67[b]	81	73[b]
1980	82	n.a.	80	n.a.
1981	81	n.a.	80	n.a.

Sources: Australian Bureau of Statistics, *Year Book Australia 1982* (Canberra: ABS, 1982), p. 162, and similar tables from 1981, 1976–77, and 1975–76 issues; U.S. Bureau of Labor Statistics, *Labor Force Statistics Derived from the Current Population Survey: A Databook*, Bulletin 2096 (Government Printing Office, 1982), vol. 1, p. 728; U.S. Bureau of the Census, *Wage and Salary Data from the Income Development Survey Program: 1979 Special Studies*, Series P-23, no. 118 (GPO, 1982), table 1.
a. Ratio of first quartile of earnings distribution to median. The quartile is determined by the interpolation of available data.
b. Refers to actual earnings. Data for the United States for earlier years refer to usual earnings.

Since industry comparisons pose risks in that industry definitions are not always compatible, it is useful to consider an alternative measure of wage dispersion and compression. For example, table 13 compares the ratio of the first quartile of the earnings distribution to the median based on surveys of full-time workers in Australia and the United States in various years. A higher ratio means a narrower gap between those on the bottom of the wage distribution and those in the middle; this represents compression from below. The ratios for Australia are consistently higher than the comparable figures for the United States. In short, it appears that the arbitration system succeeds in compressing the wage distribution, even in the face of overaward pay.

Obviously, many objections could be raised to those comparisons. For one thing, factors other than the arbitration system might account for the relative compression in Australia. For another, comparisons might be made with countries other than the United States. Probably the most striking piece of evidence that the arbitration system "matters" is to be found in purely Australian data, in the movements of wage differentials between women and men (table 14). As noted earlier, during the early part of the period 1970–81, the Arbitration Commission implemented its equal pay and equal value decisions. According to the minimum-award wage rates for this period, the ratio rises from 74 percent

Table 14. *Ratios of Average Hourly Earnings to Hourly Minimum Wages and of Female Earnings to Male Earnings, 1970–81*[a]

Year	Ratio of hourly earnings to minimum hourly rates[b]		Ratio of adult female to adult male hourly wages	
	Adult males	Adult females	Minimum rates	Hourly earnings[b]
1970	1.40	1.23	0.74	0.65
1971	1.40	1.24	0.75	0.67
1972	1.46	1.38	0.78	0.74
1973	1.50	1.43	0.80	0.76
1974	1.55	1.44	0.86	0.80
1975	1.45	1.32	0.92	0.84
1976	1.44	1.31	0.94	0.85
1977	1.44	1.31	0.94	0.86
1978	1.43	1.33	0.94	0.87
1979	1.44	1.33	0.93	0.86
1980	1.48	1.37	0.93	0.86
1981	1.44	1.33	0.94	0.86

Source: International Labour Office, *Yearbook of Labour Statistics, 1980*, p. 441, and *1982*, p. 503.
a. Nonagricultural activities.
b. Earnings are as of October and relate to nonmanagerial employees.

in 1970 to 94 percent in 1976, after the decisions were fully implemented. Actual hourly earnings indicate that the ratio rose from 65 percent to 85 percent over the same period. Since occupational structure cannot change drastically in the space of a few years, these changes must reflect the will of the Arbitration Commission.

The first two columns of table 14 show that while the commission was pushing up the official wages of women relative to those of men, the ratio of actual to official rates changed considerably. When, in the early 1970s, arbitrated wages fell behind actual wages, the commission moved to correct the situation in 1975. These changes are reflected in table 14. However, the data suggest that the Arbitration Commission—though it controlled only official rates—was able to influence actual rates, even during a period when the two drifted apart.

Therefore, the argument that the arbitration system produces wage structures that are no different from those that market forces would otherwise produce overstates the case. The system does have noticeable effects and this has important implications for incomes policy. An arbitration system that was merely a show would be an unlikely candidate for implementing an incomes policy. The point of an incomes policy, as applied in the labor market, is to make wages behave differently. Having the ability to affect wages is a necessary, but not sufficient, condition for the Arbitration Commission to function as an incomes policy instrument.

Can the Arbitration System Impose Wage Restraint?

The evidence cited here suggests that the arbitration system can push wages *up*. It can compress the wage structure by pushing up the wages of those on the bottom; it can push up women's wages relative to men's wages, and, as noted earlier in this chapter, it can push up youth wages relative to adult wages. The key question for incomes policy is whether it can hold wages *down*. Legally, of course, it cannot, since overaward pay is permitted. Thus the question is really whether the arbitration authorities would be able to exercise a restraining influence over actual pay by implementing anti-inflationary policies over award wages.

In the short run, a decision to restrain award rates would probably affect actual rates. After the wage pause was implemented in early 1983, the average rate of wage increase slowed markedly. Ordinary-time earnings for full-time workers rose at an annual rate of 4.9 percent during the first quarter of 1983 (a period only partly affected by the pause); this figure was down from 16.6 percent of the previous year.[51] But such an impact says little about the longer-term outlook.

The record of the late 1960s and early 1970s suggests that in the face of significant demand pressures, wage restraint of award rates will tend to be overwhelmed. In such an environment, the arbitration authorities will eventually feel compelled to set award wages more "realistically," that is, closer to actual levels. However, such problems are less likely to occur through the mid-1980s, given the government's projections of unemployment rates high enough to affect core union members. The question is really whether some autonomous element of wage push might enter the system—along the lines of the mid-1970s experience—and what the arbitration commission might do to prevent it.

Without some mechanism to provide for wage restraint, the Arbitration

51. Australian Department of Employment and Industrial Relations, official release L82/266, May 31, 1983.

Commission is unlikely to want to be the central element of an incomes policy. Various approaches might be offered to create a climate of restraint. For example, there has been some discussion in Australia of implementing a "tax-based incomes policy" (TIP). Under the many variants of the TIP proposal those who exercise restraint either receive a tax subsidy of some type, or avoid a tax penalty. In the United States, the TIP idea received substantial attention in the 1970s and was even offered to Congress (and rejected) in the form of a scheme known as "real-wage insurance."

The difficulty with TIP lies in the implementation, not the theory. In the abstract, the notion of "taxing inflation" is appealing. But difficult questions arise concerning the costing of wage adjustment, which must be done precisely if subsidies or penalties are to be handed out. The presence of nonwage compensation, promotions, merit increases, variation in hours and overtime, and the like must all be dealt with in detail. Questions of equity arise for individuals who change jobs, for new firms, and for individuals who receive larger (or smaller) increases than the average in their unit. Employers would undoubtedly push for a system of advance approval of wage decisions; they would not be satisfied with after-the-fact review. And they could rightly question the equity of being taxed by one arm of government for complying with the decision of another arm (an arbitration tribunal) that compelled them to overstep the guideline.

At first blush, it might seem that Australia, which already has a detailed wage-setting mechanism, might use its arbitration machinery to deal with such problems. However, the arbitration tribunals were not designed for such tasks. They are essentially courts, not administrative and enforcement agencies.

In principle, all of these obstacles might be overcome. But in practice the choice is between a program that poses a severe administrative burden and one that is simple but inequitable. The political energy that would have to be expended in getting either version approved could be better spent on obtaining support for a "conventional" incomes policy. Such a policy might include a "deal" on taxes, but not a TIP.

Indeed, rather than take the TIP approach, the incoming Labor government decided to implement an incomes policy—using the Arbitration Commission as the central wage mechanism—supported by a social compact. This approach appears to be worth trying in the Australian context. By late 1982, Australia was suffering from both severe unemployment and inflation. There appeared to be support for far-reaching action in the labor movement, while the attitude in the employer community ranged from acquiescence to a willingness to experiment. Moreover, the government projections presented to participants in the National Economic Summit Conference indicated that government policy was not going to be strongly stimulative; the prospect of an incomes policy crumbling in the wake of excess demand would diminish when unemployment exceeded even the relatively high levels of the late 1970s and early 1980s.

A social compact, of course, depends on the delivery by government of a variety of items not directly related to wages. Most prominent of these—from the viewpoint of the ACTU—are proposals related to taxation, social welfare policy, price "surveillance," and a mechanism for industrial policy. Not all of these items may be deliverable, or deliverable in precisely the form promised. And all will take time. A key question is the degree of labor cooperation that will be forthcoming in the event that elements of the package turn out to be nondeliverable, or nondeliverable within a reasonable period of time.

The Need for a Safety Valve

The economic policy in the new Labor program was centered around social accord and incomes policy. It assumed that the accord would "work" as planned. There appeared, however, to be little contingency planning for the possibility that the plan would not work, that is, that it would break down. In an area as uncertain as incomes policy, it is obviously important to consider such a contingency.

An incomes policy typically breaks down when a visible group succeeds in violating the rules, that is, by receiving more than is allowed by the guidelines, regulations, or whatever. Most discussions of wage determination in Australia put a great deal of weight on "comparative wage justice," which basically means that traditional wage relationships should be preserved. According to this principle, a wage increase to one group—even if it violates the rules of an incomes policy—justifies similar increases for other groups. A break in the dam can quickly become a torrent under such arrangements.

Although it is true in Australia, as elsewhere, that notions of equal pay for equal work and of treating everyone "the same" are generally supported by public opinion and the rhetoric of the labor market, it is not clear that such ideas are inherently more firmly rooted in the Australian social fabric than they are in other countries. It is clear, however, that the arbitration system reinforces such notions. Like other courts, arbitration tribunals rely heavily on precedent. This is not simply a matter of equity. Setting wages for nine out of ten employees in the work force is a big job, even in a small country. Taking a follow-the-leader approach is a matter of administrative convenience for the tribunals; it reduces the effective work load to manageable proportions.

The U.S. experience with wage controls during World War II, the Korean War, and the Vietnam War is instructive. As in Australia, there is a certain amount of inherent pattern-following in U.S. wage determination. When controls were in effect, however, these patterns became enshrined and reinforced in regulations. "Tandem relationships" became convenient devices for grouping cases together, so that a relatively small number of government regulators, even in the more ambitious programs, were able to set wages throughout the economy.

Since the wage-setting system in Australia reinforces notions of comparative wage justice, incomes policy there is particularly vulnerable to erosion. One approach to this problem—which was implicitly taken in the 1983 accord—is to try to ensure that no one succeeds in breaking the rules. But this is difficult to do, particularly in a "voluntary" program where violations are not penalized. What is needed, then, is a "safety valve" that will make violations less obvious and will allow them to be more readily "explained" by special circumstances.

The more complex the wage settlement, the more difficult it becomes to make coercive comparisons. In the United States, the growth of fringe benefits—especially benefits whose cost is not easily compared, such as defined-benefit pension plans, health and welfare plans defined in terms of services rather than employer costs, and so on—has contributed to this difficulty. Fringe benefits have been growing in Australia. Where they do exist, they are often constructed in a way that makes comparison relatively easy. For example, defined-contribution superannuation schemes are more common than defined-benefit pension plans.

Creative differentiation of settlements would be helpful in prolonging the life of incomes policy in Australia, because it blurs comparisons. Indeed, the parties could negotiate about many benefits other than wages. Job-security guarantees will be of increasing concern to a work force that has experienced high unemployment. Quality-of-work-life arrangements have received some attention in Australia, but comparatively little implementation. These, too, could be added to the negotiators' menu. The fact that arbitration tribunals have not dealt with such matters in the past does not mean that they will veto new arrangements on which both labor and management have agreed.[52] Creative government policy should foster interest of the parties in nonwage issues.

Finally, it is in the interest of macroeconomic policy to encourage flexible compensation by means of the gain-sharing arrangements discussed earlier. Gain sharing would make future deflations less painful. It could be presented as an extension of industrial democracy, a variation of indexation, and a route to employment security. Even though an incomes policy might be eroded, if it left a legacy of gain sharing, it would have made a permanent contribution to economic stability.

Looking Ahead

The issues connected with the labor market in Australia are similar to those that arise in most industrialized countries. As the industrial and occupational composition of the labor force changes, labor, management, and government will place more emphasis on the need for innovative approaches. An increasingly white-collar work force can be expected to have different priorities than have traditionally risen from the industrial sector. Since the Australian labor movement has had considerable success in recruiting members in the newer sectors of employment, these priorities are likely to be expressed both in bargaining and through the arbitration system.

To the extent that the newer and younger members of the work force are interested in nonwage areas such as flexible work hours and quality of work life, their needs can be satisfied only in a climate in which labor

52. The author interviewed plant officials at the Woodlawn Mines near Canberra, an operation noted for various innovations in the quality of work life that are unusual in Australia. These arrangements were privately negotiated by the employer and the unions involved. Although an atypical compensation structure was included, the plant officials reported that they had no trouble obtaining approval from the appropriate arbitration tribunal.

and management resolve conflicts at the workplace level. The issue of centralization versus decentralization in Australia has beclouded this fact. With an arbitration system in place, Australia has always relied on a centralized system by which to determine wages. Although it has oscillated between dominance of the national arbitration authorities and dominance of a few key wage bargains, which are subsequently endorsed and spread through the arbitration system, the system has been weak in resolving nonwage, local issues, which are necessarily decentralized and difficult to deal with across the board.

The typical spell of employment for males with a particular employer in Australia is estimated to be about eighteen years,[53] which is roughly comparable to the situation in the United States. Employees do not spend their working time in a relationship with the arbitration authorities, but with their employers. In these circumstances, there is good reason to stress improvements in day-to-day industrial relations. The macro-economic need for an incomes policy should not be allowed to interfere with such developments.

Certain issues are inherently of national, rather than local, concern. The larger issues of wage determination, inflation, and unemployment clearly fall into this category, as does the promotion of widespread gain sharing. Cases in which existing social welfare policies may be influencing labor-market behavior in undesirable ways are also of national concern. The economic summit conference of 1983 was an encouraging exercise in directing the attention of the key parties toward the menu of economic choices available. Incomes policy is a central component of the national accord. If cooperation succeeds in the area of wage determination, it will no doubt be possible to reach a consensus on other social issues, too. Conversely, cooperation in other realms will assist in reinforcing an incomes policy.

53. Keith Norris, "Labour Turnover and Job Durations in Australia," working paper (Murdoch: Murdoch University, 1983).

Appendix: Statistical Tables

Table 15. *Government Employment Trends, Selected Years, 1971–81*

		Civilian government employees as a percentage of total civilian employees	
Year	Civilian government employees (thousands)[a]	Total	Female
1971	1,203.2	22	20
1975	1,436.9	25	24
1980	1,531.9	25	25
1981	1,549.3	24	25

Sources: *Year Book Australia 1982*, p. 145, and similar tables in earlier editions; *The Labour Force*, cat. no. 6204.0, and various issues. Data for government employment are as of June; total employment, as of August.
a. Including government enterprises.

Table 16. *Civilian Labor Force Trends, 1966–82[a]*
Percent

Demographic group	Unemploy- ment rate, 1980	Participation rates			Proportion of labor force	
		1966	1974	1982	1966	1982
Males	4.4	83.9	81.0	76.6	69.4	63.0
15–19	14.0	66.6	58.3	62.5	7.1	5.9
20–24	6.3	93.7	90.0	89.3	8.2	8.7
25–34	3.6	97.7	97.0	94.9	14.6	16.8
35–44	2.0	98.1	97.2	95.1	15.8	13.9
45–54	2.6	95.9	94.2	90.0	13.0	10.3
55–59	3.1	90.9	87.6	79.1	5.2	4.4
60–64	2.5	79.4	72.4	47.7	3.5	2.2
65 and over	1.6	23.3	18.4	9.2	2.0	0.8
Females	7.0	36.2	42.2	43.9	30.6	37.0
15–19	16.5	63.0	54.5	56.0	6.6	5.1
55–64	3.5	21.0	24.0	18.4	2.1	1.9
65 and over	1.4	4.4	4.0	2.5	0.5	0.3
Married	4.7	29.0	40.7	42.1	16.0	22.1
20–24	8.1	37.3	54.2	53.8	2.0	2.2
25–34	6.1	29.5	43.7	48.5	3.8	7.0
35–44	3.5	36.5	51.2	57.2	5.2	6.9
45–54	2.9	31.9	43.3	47.6	3.6	4.4
Other	10.5	49.7	45.3	47.0	14.6	14.9
20–24	9.0	90.2	80.8	82.6	3.1	4.4
25–34	6.4	81.7	81.7	75.6	1.4	2.6
35–44	4.5	70.4	72.6	63.3	1.0	1.2
45–54	5.6	62.3	60.2	59.7	1.3	1.1
All groups	5.4	59.8	61.4	60.0	100.0	100.0

Source: Australian Bureau of Statistics, *The Labour Force*, catalog nos. 6204.0, 6203.0, and various issues.
a. The unemployment rate is for November 1980; all other data are for August of the year shown.

ANDREW S. CARRON

The Australian Financial System

THE Australian financial system has changed drastically in recent years, shedding its anachronistic practices and demonstrating increasing sophistication. This evolution will continue, and will present both welcome opportunities and unfamiliar perils. Institutions will be challenged to adapt, innovate, and meet higher standards of efficiency. Government agencies face the difficult task of encouraging these developments while maintaining stability in financial markets, conducting an effective monetary policy, and satisfying society's expectations for fairness, protection against exploitation, and an equitable distribution of income.

This change has been facilitated by reforms in government regulation. As recently as the late 1970s one could have found pervasive effects from the laws and practices that governed banks and other institutions: a rigid structure often unresponsive to new opportunities, market segmentation impeding the flow of capital among sectors, and administered prices and quantitative controls that failed to clear markets. Some of these were the result of explicit social policy; others were the unintended consequences of outdated rules. One would also have found that the effectiveness of the regulations was beginning to show signs of erosion

Thomas J. Valentine, Kevin T. Davis, Peter D. Jonson, Peter Kenen, and Carol J. Austin provided helpful comments on an early draft of this chapter. Shannon P. Butler and Eva Klug provided research assistance. The author is also grateful for the assistance and advice of Richard E. Caves, Lawrence B. Krause, Fred H. Gruen, the Australian Embassy in Washington, D.C., and the Reserve Bank of Australia.

195

as financial activity shifted to unregulated institutions and as regulated firms found means of evading the constraints.

A major study of the financial system undertaken in the late 1970s, the Campbell report, did find ample scope for reform.[1] Some recommendations have already been implemented (this action may be attributable as much to the predispositions of government officials or to the exigencies of the market as to the persuasiveness of the Campbell Committee's arguments). Many other proposals are under current review.

As a result of these developments, the Australian financial system today is a complex amalgam of the old and the new. Some institutions date back to the previous century, their original goals and principal tools remaining largely intact. Unusual financial instruments are also to be found—the products of inventive minds seeking ways of circumventing government controls. And one can discern obvious progress toward a rationalized system based on market forces.

Policy and Structure

The structure of the Australian financial system is a product of government regulation. From the outset, each type of institution was intended to serve a distinct part of the economy, although the differences are less pronounced now than they once were. Certain intermediaries were closely controlled to promote economic and social objectives, and those firms were also accorded preferences and protections intended to balance the costs imposed.

The principal distinction in Australia's system is between banks, now as in the past considered to be institutions of "exceptionally high standing" and "functionally unique," and nonbanks.[2] Stringent prudential regulations, unique to banks, promote sound investment decisions. Australia's monetary authority, the Reserve Bank, provides a lender-of-last-resort facility to banks, giving the highest level of protection to bank

1. See Australian Financial System Inquiry (hereafter AFSI), *Final Report of the Committee of Inquiry* (Canberra: Australian Government Publishing Service, 1980).

2. AFSI, *Final Report*, p. 428. In this chapter "bank" refers only to a trading bank, its savings bank subsidiary, or a state-owned bank. Merchant banks and the representative offices of foreign banks are not "banks."

depositors. Being subject to controls, banks have become the principal (and often only) instruments of stabilization policy, which from 1945 to 1983 was carried out through control of monetary aggregates, exchange rates, and capital inflows from overseas.

Because banks have this special role, the government controls new entry. The Banks (Shareholdings) Act limits the ownership share that may be held by a single individual or firm and thus discourages the formation of new banks. Only one new private bank has been chartered in the past forty years.

The Australian government reviews all foreign investment and places restrictions on foreign investment in certain industries: finance, insurance, the media, air transportation, mining, and real estate. By most criteria, the limits on entry to banking have been the most restrictive regulations imposed. Although recent policy decisions indicate a willingness to accept at least partial foreign ownership of Australian banks, all the major trading bank licenses are domestically owned. Foreign banks maintain representative offices in Australia and have ownership interests in merchant banks, finance companies, and authorized money-market dealers. Nevertheless, they have long sought full banking licenses. Their primary motive is to be able to engage in foreign exchange transactions.

As a result of these restrictions and recent mergers, banking in Australia has become a highly concentrated sector—the country now has four major banks of roughly equal size that together hold about 90 percent of trading bank deposits.[3] Each has a nationwide network of branches. The Commonwealth Trading Bank is owned by the commonwealth government, whereas the other three principal banks are publicly traded corporations chartered in Australia. By international standards, this level of concentration is typical. There are fewer major banks in most of the large European countries, all of which have greater populations than that of Australia. But when viewed against the restrictions on Australia's nonbanks, not to mention the banks' ownership of savings banks and other intermediaries, the banking sector is seen to be relatively insulated.

3. *Reserve Bank of Australia Bulletin* (May 1983), pp. 739, 743. The major banks are organized as holding companies with trading (commercial) bank, savings bank, and various nonbank subsidiaries.

Banks and Monetary Policy

An important justification for the special treatment of banks in the financial system is their role in money creation. Banks alone are empowered to offer transactions accounts, an important component in the money supply. Monetary policy is conducted through controls on these and other deposits. Interest payments on transactions accounts are prohibited, for example, and up to the end of 1980 interest rates on bank deposits were subject to regulated ceilings, although this was done principally to encourage low-cost loans. The restrained level of competition resulting from the controls has allowed the banks to accumulate high levels of capital and conservative asset portfolios and thus to minimize the risk of failure.

The Liquid Assets and Government Securities (LGS) and Statutory Reserve Deposit (SRD) requirements provide the basis for a fractional reserve system. The LGS convention requires trading banks to hold a specified list of instruments equal to 18 percent of deposits. Another 7 percent of deposits must be placed with the Reserve Bank in a low-interest SRD account.[4]

The monetary authorities have also used explicit directives to control credit expansion. In the past the Reserve Bank periodically issued "lending requests" to the major trading banks that specified the government's desired percentage growth in loans.[5] Most other countries have used such controls only intermittently and gave up the practice by the mid-1970s. One exception is the United States, which resorted to credit controls in March 1980. Quantitative controls in Australia were used as late as 1982, but not subsequently.

The government also controlled foreign exchange as part of its macroeconomic stabilization efforts. Until December 1983, the value of the Australian dollar was set on a daily basis by the Reserve Bank, and there were restrictions on many types of foreign exchange transactions, which were removed several months before the exchange rate was

4. The SRD was introduced during World War II as a form of profit control. It is an instrument used only by trading banks and is based on time as well as demand deposits. Nevertheless, the Reserve Bank has relied on it as a monetary policy tool in recent years.

5. See K. Davis and M. Lewis, *Monetary Policy in Australia* (Melbourne: Longman Cheshire, 1980), pp. 32–33.

allowed to float.[6] Dealing in foreign exchange, however, is still restricted to the trading banks.

Captive Market Regulations

Among the other restrictions imposed by the commonwealth government were a number of controls on the sale of government securities, the intermediaries that handle them, and the ultimate investors. The principal objective was to maintain the stability of the financial system. But monetary control and reduction of the government's debt service costs were also important aims of the regulations.

As noted earlier, trading banks must hold government securities in their portfolios at a certain percentage of their deposits (the LGS and SRD requirements). Savings banks, meanwhile, are limited to a list of "prescribed assets." Beginning in 1956, when private savings banks were first authorized, they were compelled to hold 70 percent of their assets in liquid and public securities, principally local and semigovernment (agency) issues. At that time, the Commonwealth Savings Bank and state banks held more than 90 percent of their assets in these instruments. The balance was to be invested in housing loans. The percentage required to be invested in public instruments was subsequently reduced and eventually eliminated.

The Reserve Bank has designated nine authorized money market dealers to operate a secondary market in short-term commonwealth government securities. Their function is to provide liquidity to the financial system and to facilitate the marketing of government debt. They must hold 70 percent of their assets in government securities and are required to observe strict capital and reporting requirements. In exchange, the dealers are accorded access to the Reserve Bank for short-term borrowing, and the Reserve Bank provides the dealers with advance notice of its actions, which makes their task easier and enables them to earn adequate profits with a manageable degree of risk.

The "30/20" requirement on life insurance companies and private pension funds has had considerable influence on the government secu-

6. These restrictions are described in detail in AFSI, *Interim Report*, pp. 203–16, and *Final Report*, pp. 138–55; A. M. Cohen, "Exchange Control and the Campbell Report," *Economic Papers*, special edition: *The Campbell Report* (April 1983), pp. 133–43.

rities market. At the end of World War II, retirement portfolios held substantial quantities of government securities. In time, these were replaced with private issues. Concern about the market's ability to absorb government debt led to the imposition of new tax rules in 1961. Life insurance offices and pension funds that did not hold at least 30 percent of their assets in government securities, of which 20 percent of assets had to comprise commonwealth government issues, would lose their favored tax treatment. This provision halted the decline in government securities holdings by life insurance companies and pension funds.

Income Distribution and Social Goals

Historically Australian governments have pursued policies that create low interest rates. This was done to encourage investment, of course, but it had its roots in the populist reaction to the banking crises of the 1890s and 1930s. When macroeconomic policies eventually proved incapable of maintaining low interest rates, direct means were used. The Reserve Bank has for many years set the maximum interest rate that may be charged on overdraft loans, the principal form of bank lending to business in Australia; after 1976 that limit applied only to loans drawn under overdraft limits of less than $100,000.[7] The corresponding "benefit" provided to the banks in compensation for this "burden" was a pattern of controls on deposit interest rates—at the expense of depositors—designed to ensure a cost of funds low enough to allow sufficient profit on operations. Although the ceilings on bank deposit rates have been lifted, those on loan rates have continued to depress some deposit rates. This practice has not been unique to Australia. National loan rate ceilings existed in Canada, France, West Germany, and Japan up to 1970. Deposit ceilings have been slower to disappear outside Australia. Some controls remain in France, Japan, Sweden, and the United States.

The most widely discussed issue in the debates over financial reform is the desirability of using direct credit allocation. The controversy surrounding this topic highlights the inconsistency between market efficiency and social goals—that is to say, a community must be willing to accept lower efficiency (higher costs) if it is to meet its distributional

7. From 1972 to 1976 the threshold limit was $50,000. See AFSI, *Interim Report*, p. 248.

priorities. Specialized lending institutions and informal suasion have been the tools most commonly employed to bring about such credit allocation. The "lending requests" have included qualitative as well as quantitative guidelines. Statutory authority exists to compel credit allocation through the banking system. Part 4 of the Financial Corporations Act, passed in 1974 but not implemented, extends authority to impose direct controls on nonbanks as well; the current government promised during the election campaign to use this authority to promote housing, small business, and the rural sector, but has chosen not to do so.

Sectoral credit is most widely allocated in the promotion of housing. Australia's housing finance system has a special role in society, as is evident from a number of its features.[8] Most mortgages are made by specialized portfolio lenders—savings banks and building societies. Mortgages for owner-occupied housing are long-term, level-payment, fully amortizing instruments. Interest rates on both new and existing loans, however, may be adjusted at the discretion of the lender, subject to commonwealth or state government ceilings. A notable government intervention in housing finance took place in March 1982 after market interest rates had risen substantially above the mortgage rate ceiling. Officers of the major savings banks met with government officials and agreed that in exchange for a 1 percentage point increase in rate ceilings the banks would lend $400 million more for housing than they had planned.[9]

The commonwealth government has established a number of specialized lenders to channel finance to certain sectors. The Commonwealth Development Bank, for example, lends to small businesses. Initially it focused on the agricultural and livestock sector, but in recent years it has been giving equal weight to nonrural borrowers. Loan terms are intended to be equivalent to those available from private lenders, but in

8. A more complete description may be found in Warwick Temby and John L. Goodman, Jr., "Coping with Volatile Financial Markets: Australia's Experience," *Federal Home Loan Bank Board Journal*, vol. 16 (March 1983), pp. 2–5.

9. Estimates of supply elasticity indicate that the increase in lending would have come about voluntarily. See Robert Albon and John Piggott, "Some Aspects of the Campbell Committee's Case for Housing Finance Deregulation," *Economic Papers*, special edition: *The Campbell Report* (April 1983), p. 45; and Reserve Bank of Australia, "Bank Interest Rates: Statement by Sir Harold Knight, Governor of the Reserve Bank of Australia," press release, March 18, 1982.

fact the bank lends on concessional terms. Another such lender is the Australian Industry Development Corporation, which serves firms that require longer-term credits than banks are willing to provide but that are not large enough to tap the domestic institutional investors or overseas capital markets directly. In its early years, before the corporation developed this market, loans went to projects on terms that did not fully incorporate the risk of default. The corporation's operations now reflect largely commercial considerations.

Structure and Performance

Financial markets exist to facilitate the movement of funds within and among sectors of the economy. Institutions develop to provide payment mechanisms and investment vehicles. These intermediaries are also a means of pooling and diversifying default and liquidity risks and of achieving the economies of scale that come with specialization. As financial systems evolve, the transmission of information on prices and quantities improves, the costs of transactions go down, and resources are allocated in the economy more efficiently. Unfortunately, the effect of financial intermediation on real economic activity has been difficult to measure, despite research efforts going back twenty-five years.[10] Nonetheless, a few general observations can be made about Australian financial markets.

Several features of the saving and investment practices in the Australian economy stand out immediately. One is the relatively high savings rate—which has stood at a level of 20–25 percent for the entire postwar period, exceeding that of the United States and the United Kingdom and approaching that of France and Germany.[11] Another remarkable feature is the substantial share of funds that comes from overseas, despite strong domestic savings (table 1). The household sector supplies a major portion of investment funds.[12]

10. The work of Raymond Goldsmith, Simon Kuznets, and others is described in Robert M. Townsend, "Financial Structure and Economic Activity," *American Economic Review*, vol. 73 (December 1983), pp. 895–911.

11. AFSI, *Interim Report*, p. 10.

12. In the Australian accounts, unincorporated businesses are included with the household sector.

Table 1. *Intersectoral Saving, Investment, and Flows of Funds, 1977–78 to 1981–82*[a]
Percent

Sector	Share of gross saving	Share of gross capital formation[b]	Net lending or borrowing[c]
Households[d]	46.1	31.3	15.0
Overseas	14.2	. . .	14.2
Corporate trading enterprises	17.7	26.9	−9.2
Financial institutions	5.7	8.4	−2.7
Government	16.3	32.7	−16.4
Statistical discrepancy	. . .	0.8	−0.8
Total	100.0	100.0	0.0

Source: *Reserve Bank of Australia Bulletin Supplement* (March 1983), pp. 13–17.
a. Average.
b. Includes capital transfers.
c. Share of total saving or investment. Borrowing is indicated by a minus symbol.
d. Includes unincorporated enterprises.

Commonwealth government deficits rose sharply after 1974 and then dropped just as rapidly by the early 1980s. Deficits of the state and local governments also increased from 1974 to 1980 but have remained at high levels since then.[13] Although government borrowings have varied greatly from year to year, the government sector in recent times has borrowed (gross) an amount equal to double its own savings, and therefore is the largest net borrower in the economy.

EXTENT OF INTERMEDIATION. Whether such high levels of savings and investment require comparable amounts of financial intermediation depends on the extent of internal and direct financing in the economy. One large net saver, the household sector, is a principal user of intermediaries. From mid-1977 to mid-1982, 98.3 percent of net acquisition of financial assets by the household sector was composed of claims on intermediaries. This use of intermediaries by households is greater than that of the United States (87.3 percent) and the United Kingdom (92.4 percent). The overseas sector, however, relies almost entirely on direct investment in both countries: only 10.6 percent of net acquisitions in Australia and −0.8 percent in the United States were claims on interme-

13. Calculations are based on Reserve Bank of Australia, *Bulletin Supplement: Financial Flows* (March 1983), pp. 34–35.

diaries.[14] Total assets of financial institutions ranged from 105 to 120 percent of gross domestic product (GDP) and then rose to 120–140 percent of GDP in the 1970s and early 1980s. This jump suggests that the growth and increasing complexity of the financial system have led to a shift from internal and direct financing to the use of intermediaries. Despite these relatively high levels of claims on intermediaries in Australia, assets of financial institutions due from nonfinancial sectors were equal to a modest 100 percent of GDP, compared with 140 percent in the United States and slightly higher levels in the United Kingdom and Japan.[15] But some transactions arranged by intermediaries, such as commitments by trading banks to endorse or discount commercial bills, do not appear on the balance sheets of the financial institutions. The growth of such instruments in recent years suggests that the calculated increase in intermediation may be understated. If bank bills were included, approximately 5 percentage points would be added to the ratio of financial assets to GDP for the early 1980s.[16]

Although obviously not conclusive, the data suggest that the Australian financial system has grown apace with the economy as a whole. Moreover, throughout its development the system has demonstrated an ability to adapt to changing conditions within the general constraints imposed by government regulation. The increases in the use of intermediaries, both in absolute and in relative terms, indicate that institutions have accommodated customers' changing demands. Most of these changes have been met by less regulated intermediaries, which conse-

---

14. Ibid., pp. 37–38; Board of Governors of the Federal Reserve System, flow-of-funds accounts, unpublished data (1983); and Bank of England, *Quarterly Bulletin*, various issues. Data for Australia and the United States are for July 1977 through June 1982. Data for the United Kingdom are for March 1978 through June 1982; data on overseas sector transactions are not regularly published for the United Kingdom. In Australia, the household sector is defined as households and unincorporated enterprises; in the United Kingdom, as individuals, unincorporated business, and nonprofit-making bodies; and in the United States, as households, personal trusts, and nonprofit organizations.

15. AFSI, *Interim Report*, pp. 11–12.

16. Calculations based on Reserve Bank of Australia publications: W. E. Norton, P. M. Garmston, and M. W. Brodie, *Australian Economic Statistics, 1949–50 to 1980–81: I. Tables*, Occasional Paper 8A (Canberra: Reserve Bank of Australia, May 1982), pp. 72, 123; *Reserve Bank of Australia Bulletin* (March 1983), pp. 611, 660; and *Reserve Bank of Australia, Bulletin Supplement* (March 1983), p. 6.

Table 2. *Total Assets of Financial Institutions, 1962, 1972, 1982*[a]
Percent unless otherwise indicated

Institution	1962	1972	1982
Banks[b]	53.2	43.9	42.4
Thrift institutions[c]	4.1	7.1	10.1
Finance companies[d]	9.2	12.9	15.8
Merchant banks[e]	0.2	4.0	7.5
Life insurance offices and pension funds	26.3	25.6	19.1
Authorized money market dealers	1.7	2.6	0.8
Other financial institutions	5.3	3.9	4.3
Total assets (billions of dollars)	14.8	42.6	180.0

Sources: Reserve Bank of Australia, *Statistical Bulletin: Financial Flow Accounts Supplement 1953/54–1979/80* (June 1981), p. 6, and *Reserve Bank of Australia Bulletin Supplement* (March 1983), p. 6.
a. Percent of total industry assets on June 30. Excludes Reserve Bank assets.
b. Trading banks, savings banks, Commonwealth Development Bank, Australia Resources Development Bank, Primary Industry Bank of Australia. Data are net of interbank claims.
c. Building societies and credit cooperatives.
d. Includes general financiers.
e. Includes cash management trusts.

quently have grown more rapidly but often merely because a business has been rechanneled within a corporate family. Subsidiaries of bank holding companies include trading (that is, commercial) banks, savings banks, finance companies, merchant banks, and cash management trusts. Although banks are still the largest institutions, others have increased their share of the financial services market over the past two decades (table 2). Two reasons for this rapid growth are that innovation has led to the development of new types of intermediaries in Australia, as in other countries, and government regulations have made bank loans and deposits less attractive than the alternatives available.

DEVELOPMENT OF THE NONBANK SECTOR. Nonbanks—which in Australia include building societies, credit unions, finance companies, and merchant banks—have been adept at offering services that are close substitutes for bank offerings. As market interest rates moved well above deposit rate ceilings at banks, cash management trusts (money market mutual funds) were introduced to provide market rates on funds subject to daily access. Credit unions began to offer automatic teller machines to offset the extensive services and numerous branches made available by the banks. Merchant banks, meanwhile, developed new forms of trade finance. An unofficial hedge market grew up to provide synthetic foreign exchange cover, in competition with the official (bank) market.

Building societies have tried to get around the restrictions on demand accounts by offering to write their own checks on behalf of depositors.[17] Although these checks continue to flow through the trading banks, the deposits they represent have moved to the thrift institutions, along with the other business those customers brought with them. As a result of this shift, fewer transactions balances are covered by the monetary and prudential controls on banks, and efficiency has been impaired by the introduction of a second intermediary in the payments process.

Banks are also beginning to lose their unique role as the commonwealth-certified repositories of deposits. Many building societies have been accorded trustee status which in the past was reserved for executors and administrators of estates. Because of this new status, building societies appear to have government backing for the deposits placed there. Yet the granting of trustee status has not been accompanied by additional prudential controls, and the laws and standards for trustees have been allowed to vary across states.

ADAPTATION BY THE BANKING SECTOR. Banks have responded to the changes in the financial system by introducing sweep accounts, thereby circumventing the prohibition on payment of interest on demand deposits. They have evaded lending restrictions and reserve and liquidity requirements through off-balance-sheet transactions. Bank commitments to accept or endorse (guarantee) bills of exchange (commercial paper) reached $11.0 billion in mid-1983, and commitments to discount (purchase) bills reached $9.4 billion. Together they nearly equal the bank overdraft loan commitments that are outstanding.[18] Furthermore, banks have acquired nonbank subsidiaries of their own: all the large trading banks own finance companies and have interests in merchant banks, which are intermediaries not covered by reserve or quantitative requirements. When the banks were asked to limit credit expansion, corporations lent to each other rather than repaying their own loans from banks. Outstanding intercompany loans are estimated to be $2 billion to

---

17. It is estimated that in 1982 fifteen million such checks were written (of a total of approximately one billion checks drawn). See AFSI, *Final Report*, pp. 415, 421; and Kevin Davis, "The Thrift Institutions," in M. K. Lewis and R. H. Wallace, eds., *The Australian Capital Markets* (University of Adelaide, forthcoming 1983), p. 53.

18. As of the second Wednesday of July 1983. *Reserve Bank of Australia Bulletin* (August 1983), p. 97.

$4 billion,[19] which is approximately one-tenth the level of bank loans to businesses.

The structure of the banking industry has also been affected. In the past, lending allocations among individual banks within the overall limit were determined on the basis of deposits. Banks therefore emphasized growth over profitability to maintain loan market share, which was considered important for long-run success. Entry controls and the limitations on deposit interest rates also encouraged banks to engage in service competition, such as the establishment of extensive branch networks.[20] Although banks have improved the quality of services traditionally considered part of banking, the large banks have trailed other intermediaries in offering innovative services.

The Process of Regulatory Reform

The need for financial reform eventually came to be recognized, but was not thought to be compelling. Many groups in society—homeowners, small businesses, farmers—believed that the existing system operated to their advantage. There was little quarrel, moreover, with the goals of financial regulation. So the decision in the late 1970s to proceed with a review of the Australian financial system should not be viewed simply as a reaction to developing problems. It was also, in part, a response to promises made during a campaign. Certain individuals inside and outside the government pressed for the inquiry, and acquiescence was ultimately achieved for what was then seen as a relatively innocuous process. Thus in 1979 the government appointed the five members of the Campbell Committee.

THE CAMPBELL REPORT. Throughout its deliberations the Campbell Committee was guided by several basic principles. Belief in the virtues of a free market and in competitive neutrality among firms was high on the list. Some observers complained that social objectives (such as

19. Edna Carew, *Fast Money: The Money Market in Australia* (Sydney: George Allen & Unwin, 1983), p. 21; and AFSI, *Interim Report*, p. 196.
20. Peter L. Swan and Ian R. Harper, "The Welfare Gains from Bank Deregulation," in AFSI, *Commissioned Studies and Selected Papers*, part 1, Macroeconomic Policy: Internal Policy (Canberra: AGPS, 1982), pp. 475–512; and AFSI, *Final Report*, p. 527.

income distribution) were not going to be considered explicitly. The committee chose not to judge the merits of such objectives, but argued strongly that they should be achieved through taxing or spending programs rather than through controls on the financial system. Others complained that the committee focused too narrowly on government regulation and did not give sufficient weight to the failings of private firms or to other government interventions such as taxation, fiscal policy, or monetary policy in general.

In its final report submitted in September 1981 the Campbell Committee presented upwards of 300 specific findings and recommendations.[21] Two suggestions that generated substantial discussion in Australia were that the remaining ceilings on interest rates be removed and that the entry of foreign banks be approved. Other significant recommendations included abolition of captive market regulations, extension of Reserve Bank liquidity support to nonbank depository institutions, relaxation of exchange controls and movement to a free exchange rate, and privatization of government-owned financial intermediaries.

The Liberal-Country government of Prime Minister Malcolm Fraser received the recommendations with statements of approval and implemented a few of the less contentious proposals, but did not move on the major issues before it was turned out of office. The Labor government elected in early 1983 campaigned on a platform that opposed the entire Campbell philosophy; once in power, though, it instituted major reforms consistent with the study's market-oriented approach.

REFORMS. Even as the Campbell Committee continued its deliberations, the government began to implement some of the suggestions that had emerged from the reform process. New procedures for marketing government debt were initiated in 1979; ceilings on interest rates for bank deposits were removed in 1980; and in the private sector, margins on foreign exchange transactions apparently narrowed as the committee's investigation shed light in that area.

---

21. AFSI, *Final Report*, pp. 758–822. Reviews of the Campbell Committee's findings can be found in Fred Brenchley and P. P. McGuinness, eds., *The New Money Jigsaw: The Campbell Report on Australia's Financial Future—And What It Means for You* (Sydney: Magazine Promotions, 1981); J. O. N. Perkins, *The Australian Financial System after the Campbell Report* (Melbourne: Melbourne University Press, 1982); Malcolm Fisher, ed., *A New Financial Revolution? An International Review of the Campbell Report* (St. Leonards, New South Wales: The Centre for Independent Studies, 1982).

Further changes came in the first year after publication of the Campbell recommendations, but many of these were obvious reactions to market events. Sale of commonwealth government bonds was put on a tender (auction) basis in May 1982. The previous tap system, under which securities were continuously available at a stated rate of interest, had a number of problems: control of the monetary aggregates became complicated because quantities could not be set; the requirement that the system adhere to a constant price during the period of issue was incompatible with an environment of volatile interest rates; and the availability of securities on the primary market discouraged development of a secondary market, impairing both portfolio adjustments by holders of government debt and the government's ability to conduct open market operations. The government announced in June 1982 that it was abandoning the lending requests under which banks had been asked to limit credit expansion. Although consistent with the Campbell recommendations, the decision was attributed to the ineffectiveness of the controls over the preceding three years.

Other changes were more clearly the result of the Campbell study. In March 1982 the minimum maturity on large deposits at trading banks was shortened from thirty to fourteen days; the previous reduction, from three months to thirty days, had been in 1964. This move increased competition between the trading banks and the merchant banks. The government also announced that it would entertain applications for new bank licenses from non-Australian interests and thus opened up an opportunity for the largely foreign-owned merchant banks to acquire the advantages of conducting a general banking business. In August 1982, the prescribed assets requirement for savings banks was abolished—this action enabled them to acquire more mortgage loans and divest government securities—and they were permitted to invest up to 6 percent of assets in commercial and consumer loans.

With the election of a Labor government in 1983, it appeared that the reform process might be stopped. Indeed, a reexamination of the Campbell findings was begun (by the Martin Group). It was widely believed, in Australia and elsewhere, that the new government would be slow to implement reforms. That expectation turned out to be wildly incorrect.

In October 1983, well before the Martin review of the Campbell report was completed, virtually all of the controls on foreign exchange transactions were lifted. This action was followed in December by the floating of the exchange rate for the Australian dollar. Then in January 1984 the government announced that it accepted the principle of foreign bank entry.

The Martin Group report was released to the public in February 1984.[22] It proposed liberalization of bank entry requirements for both domestic and foreign applicants, but recommended that foreign ownership of a bank should not exceed 50 percent. The committee also suggested that additional licenses be issued to deal in foreign exchange while the applications for full banking licenses were being considered. The Martin Group concurred with the Campbell recommendations on the need to remove most remaining controls on banks, including the minimum maturity on interest-bearing deposits and the interest rate ceilings on loans. Furthermore, the Martin Group advocated elimination of the captive market arrangements such as the 30/20 requirement on life insurance companies and pension funds; the LGS ratio would be redefined to serve only as a means of promoting safety and soundness.

These deviations from the traditional Labor party position were characterized by the government as prudent responses to individual events. They were not to be seen as part of a pattern, and no inferences were to be drawn concerning further reforms. Yet there seems to be a consensus within the government and even in the opposition party that a pattern of reform is taking shape and that it is both inevitable and desirable. The goals of government financial policy may not change, but the process surely will.

The Remaining Reform Agenda

Despite the progress thus far, the accumulated web of government controls still requires substantial rationalization. The reports of the Campbell and Martin committees provide guidelines on many of the outstanding issues. Presented here are a few of the most pressing concerns.

22. Martin Group, *Australian Financial System: Report of the Review Group, December 1983* (Canberra: AGPS, 1984).

Captive Market Arrangements

The requirements that certain intermediaries hold substantial shares of government securities in their asset portfolios were not modified in the first round of financial reforms, despite substantial doubt as to the continued effectiveness of or necessity for the captive market arrangements. For example, the 30/20 requirement on life insurance companies and private pension funds is structured as a tax incentive rather than a financial regulation. In the mid-1970s, however, the tax advantages available to these institutions were reduced considerably, and thus one justification for continuing the 30/20 rule was removed. The changes also diminished the effectiveness of the 30/20 rule: by one estimate, the premium between private and government securities that offset the tax advantages was reduced from 2.5 percentage points to 0.7 percentage points.[23] If the captive market requirements are found to be ineffective in facilitating the marketing of government debt, then a strong argument exists for eliminating or modifying the rules.

In theory, the sectors required to hold government debt would affect the market price only if their specified holdings were large relative to the market and if other (noncaptive) institutions could not usurp the liability-creating function of the captive intermediaries. The first condition was satisfied: from 1961 to 1979 captive holders purchased 77 percent of the annual net increase in issues.[24] Although some funds were shifted—the trading banks, for example, channeled some of their asset growth to their finance company and merchant bank affiliates, which were not covered by LGS and SRD rules—there were few alternatives to transaction deposits at banks, and no close substitutes for life insurance and pension funds.

Captive market requirements thus may have been successful in reducing the cost of government debt. The rates on commonwealth government securities were substantially below those on comparable finance company debentures from 1965 to mid-1979.[25] The differential

23. AFSI, *Final Report*, p. 175.
24. Excludes holdings by the Reserve Bank. Estimates are based on Norton, Garmston, and Brodie, *Australian Economic Statistics*, p. 54.
25. Finance company debentures are the closest substitute for government bonds. Rates on other instruments of comparable maturity were either controlled by government regulation or not collected.

for two-year instruments averaged 1.44 percentage points during this period. A comparison of security yields of five-year maturity indicates a differential of 1.82 percentage points. Beginning in 1979, the government rates approached the private rates.

Not enough is known about the factors that determine interest rates to attribute the earlier differential to the marketing arrangements. The lack of a differential between government rates and private rates on a variety of instruments in recent years, however, indicates that captive arrangements are probably ineffective today. The share of government securities demanded by captive buyers is now too small to influence the market price. These issues must be sold on the basis of rate, maturity, and security, as with all other securities.[26] The principal effects of captive market arrangements now are to distort portfolio decisions, arbitrarily distribute costs and benefits, and reduce the efficiency of the financial system. Furthermore, captive markets are not a requisite for financial stability, and a case can be made that they retarded the development of secondary markets and the dispersion of ownership that could have improved the flexibility and resiliency of financial markets.

Seasonality and Liquidity

Cash flows in the Australian financial system exhibit a marked seasonal pattern. Interest rates, money supply, and loan demand are all affected. As a result, investors and institutions must attempt to predict the changes, differentiate between trend and cycle, and adjust their decisions accordingly. Furthermore, participants in the financial markets expend substantial resources to monitor seasonal variations. The problem distorts saving and investment decisions, creates uncertainty with regard to the condition of the economy and government policy intentions, and retards the level of economic activity.

The principal cause of seasonal fluctuations is the commonwealth government's taxing and borrowing policy. Small businesses and the self-employed are not required to make periodic payments of income taxes and typically pay all of their taxes near the April 1 deadline. Even

---

26. See W. H. Evans and H. A. Rozenstein, "The Market for Commonwealth Government Securities," Reserve Bank of Australia Research Discussion Paper 8008 (Sydney: RBA, 1980), and the references contained therein.

corporations, which since the 1978–79 financial year have been required to make quarterly installment payments, still pay about half their tax liability each year in May. Tax payments by these sectors thus depress liquidity from March to June, and in turn interest rates are forced to rise. Some seasonal government securities are redeemed as these payments are made, but the full effect of the tax payments is not offset. Tax refunds are made from July to November, and during this period the pressure on liquidity and interest rates is relaxed.[27]

The effect is substantial. Consider, for example,the monthly multiplicative seasonal factors for ninety-day bank bills in 1983 (figure 1).[28] Their actual April peak is 17 percent (roughly 190 basis points) higher than the seasonally adjusted value, while the November rate is 11 percent (120 basis points) lower. The sharp seasonal pattern is seen in the rates for most market-determined financial securities, even at longer maturities.

All market-determined interest rates in Australia are affected. Until recently, foreign exchange controls and management of the exchange rate prevented the necessary adjustments from taking place. Restrictions on investments by Australians in overseas fixed-income securities and the inability to predict government exchange rate intervention prevented arbitrage between Australian and foreign markets.[29]

A well-integrated financial system should assimilate seasonal variations without affecting interest rates. Seasonality is a feature that has been noted for years in Australia, and one not found in other well-developed financial systems.[30] Several solutions to the seasonality problem have been proposed. The most straightforward approach would be to eliminate the lumpiness of tax payments.[31] The principal objection

27. Carew, *Fast Money: The Money Market in Australia,* pp. 8–9; and A. M. Cohen, "Changing Patterns of Cash Flows and Their Implications for Financial Markets," *The Securities Institute Journal* (December 1980), pp. 14–15.

28. The factors were calculated with the X11M seasonal adjustment program on data for 1968–83. Stable seasonality was present at the 1 percent level.

29. I have benefited from discussions on this issue with Kevin Davis.

30. Cohen, "Changing Patterns," pp. 16–17; G. Clarke and T. J. Valentine, "Seasonal Liquidity Fluctuations," *Bulletin of Money, Banking and Finance, 1982–83: No. 3* (North Ryde, New South Wales: Macquarie University, Centre for Studies in Money, Banking and Finance, 1983), pp. 1–2.

31. AFSI, *Final Report,* pp. 102–12; Cohen, "Changing Patterns," p. 18; Clarke and Valentine, "Seasonal Liquidity Fluctuations," p. 28.

Figure 1. *Typical Seasonal Pattern for Short-term Interest Rates, 1983*

Percent

Source: Data are based on seasonal factors calculated with the X11M seasonal adjustment program for the period from 1968–83. Stable seasonally occurred at the 1 percent level. Data were provided to the author by the Reserve Bank of Australia.

seems to be that certain taxpayers would face a one-time shift in tax due dates that would require more than twelve months of taxes to be paid in the first year. Introduction of the new schedule in phases could moderate the impact.[32] Other solutions would be to establish government accounts at banks so that tax payments would not drain liquidity, use open-market operations to offset the effects of the tax collections, or have the government provide more timely budget information to reduce uncertainty. Although these alternatives have merit, there is no compelling reason not to treat the problem at its source.

In past years, seasonally rising interest rates in Australia combined with a managed exchange rate could be relied on to attract capital from overseas. With a flexible exchange rate, the adjustment would take place as the variations in the exchange rate (price) partly offset the inflow of funds (quantity). Such induced seasonal exchange rate fluctuations can be expected to create additional problems for the traded goods sector that are similar to those now encountered by the domestic sector.[33]

Loan Rate Controls and Housing Finance

Although ceilings on deposit rates were removed in 1980, the government retained control of the maximum rate of interest that could be charged on certain loans. These restrictions were not always binding, as the government used periods of interest rate declines to move closer to letting the market determine rates.

Ceilings on loan rates impair the efficiency of the financial system. When loan rates are below market rates, there is excess demand and banks must ration the available quantities. As a consequence, banks cannot use rate premiums to adjust for risk and the funds go to the most creditworthy borrowers. Riskier enterprises must seek funds from higher-cost providers such as finance companies and merchant banks. The composition of the portfolios of intermediaries is also affected. Risk is concentrated in the less regulated intermediaries, despite the advantages of diversification.

A below-market interest rate does not have desirable income distri-

32. See N. R. Norman, "The Campbell Process: An Appraisal" (Sydney: Committee for Economic Development of Australia, November 1982), pp. 22–24.
33. I am indebted to Tom Valentine for raising the important issue of the interactions between seasonal liquidity changes and a floating exchange rate.

bution effects and thus would appear to fail the standards set for it. Cross subsidies are involved, but since large borrowers and depositors operate in uncontrolled markets, the smaller participants are the ones who redistribute income among themselves. Undoubtedly some borrowers benefit from controlled rates, but only because some depositors are unable to place their savings in instruments that earn market rates of return. Moreover, the controls on loans can be evaded. Banks have occasionally restricted credit through the overdraft or installment loan facility while extending it to the same customers eligible for term or credit card loans.

The effect of loan rate ceilings is most obvious in housing finance. Since the mid-1970s, the ceiling on savings bank loans has almost always been binding, while ceilings on building society loans have often approximated market rates. Savings bank loans carried an interest rate of 12.5 percent in mid-1983 while building society loans averaged 14.5 percent.[34] Savings bank loans are usually available only to the bank's deposit customers, however, and then in an amount related to the size and duration of the deposit relationship; supplemental financing at much higher rates may be required. Loans (at higher rates) are readily available from building societies.

Savings banks have been able to offer low interest rates on mortgages because household depositors have accepted below-market interest rates on their savings. The total cost of a mortgage loan must take into account forgone deposit interest, higher down payments, rates on second mortgages, and waiting time when funds are scarce; this effective rate is substantially higher than the nominal controlled rate. At the other extreme, mortgage rates charged by finance companies and life insurance companies overstate the equilibrium rate by incorporating higher risk premiums and higher costs per year for the fixed charges of originating a short-term loan. Therefore deregulation of the housing finance system would probably not increase the total cost to the household sector (a view shared by the Martin Group), although nominal loan rates would certainly rise and some households would be worse off. However, the distributional aspects of this change would be favorable. Under the

34. *Reserve Bank of Australia, Bulletin* (May 1983), p. 772; and J. V. Larkey, interview with author, Australian Association of Permanent Building Societies, Deakin, Australian Capital Territory, June 29, 1983.

current system, the most creditworthy borrowers—that is,the wealthiest borrowers—are most likely to get the high value loans at low rates. And at least one group of net savers, those who have not yet acquired a home, would gain from the market rates of interest that banks pay on deposits.[35]

Elements of the housing finance system violate the efficiency criterion that transactions should be permitted to take place near the market-clearing price. Income distribution among households is affected. There is little evidence to indicate, however, that other sectors of the economy are disadvantaged by these mechanisms.

Restrictions on Assets and Liabilities

The housing finance system in Australia relies on specialized institutions, and the links within this system between the mortgage market and the capital market generally are weak. Once funds are deposited with a housing lender, they may be invested in housing loans originated by that institution or in a narrow range of alternatives—primarily government securities. There is virtually no secondary mortgage market in Australia and no secondary market for local and semigovernment securities, and until recently the market for commonwealth government securities was affected by portfolio restrictions on trading banks and retirement funds. Correspondingly few means exist for channeling capital market funds into housing. Trading banks can lend to building societies, but the housing lenders themselves have no direct access to the capital market. Up to late 1980 savings banks could not even bid for funds in the deposit market. Meanwhile, the building societies faced deposit rate restrictions in some states. Even now, loan rate ceilings constrain the deposit rates they can pay. Although the housing lenders are inadequately integrated into the capital markets, they can be affected by general financial conditions. Such institutions face potentially difficult solvency or liquidity problems in an environment of rising interest rates; the type of

---

35. Distributional issues are covered in Judith Yates, "The Distributional Impact of Interest Rate Regulation on the Household Sector," in AFSI, *Commissioned Studies and Selected Papers*, pt. 4, pp. 157–256; and Robert Albon and John Piggott, "Housing Finance and the Campbell Report: A Review of Efficiency and Supply Aspects," Discussion Paper no. 51 (The Australian National University, Centre for Economic Policy Research, September 1982), pp. 16–17.

problem depends on whether the institution increases deposit rates or not. As a result, it has been suggested that the asset powers of the housing lenders be expanded.

Despite numerous obstacles to the development of a secondary market in residential mortgages, this would be another useful mechanism for increasing the breadth of financial markets.[36] However, the mechanism for setting the mortgage interest rate would probably have to be changed from the current one, under which lender discretion is constrained by government specification, to a plan that automatically links mortgage rates with other capital market rates.[37] Even if the case for removing ceilings on mortgage interest rates cannot be made on distributional grounds, the argument that they should be removed as a prerequisite for a secondary mortgage market would appear compelling. Moreover, long-term savings can now be deposited with institutions other than savings banks and building societies. Without a means of generating liquidity, the specialized housing lenders may not be able to make the desired volume of new mortgage loans.

Certain activities remain the exclusive function of the banks, principally participation in the payments system and foreign exchange trading. The domestic thrift institutions (building societies and credit unions) would like to offer checking accounts to their customers, while foreign banks (now operating in Australia as merchant banks) are eager to provide foreign exchange services to their multinational clients. In part, decisions to change the existing structure might be based on the prospect of a more competitive and diverse financial system. Other issues must also be considered, however. For one thing, broadening the payments system could complicate monetary policy. For another, if foreign banks were allowed to operate in Australia, prudential controls would have to be revised to protect the domestic system from disturbances that might threaten the parent bank overseas. Such topics are less part of the unfinished agenda than they are concerns arising from the process of reform, which itself raises new regulatory issues.

36. See Australian Merchant Bankers Association, "Housing Finance in Australia: Development of the Secondary Mortgage Market" (May 1983); and AFSI, *Final Report*, pp. 653–63.

37. Kevin T. Davis notes that the social benefits flowing from the current system may outweigh the advantages of a secondary mortgage market.

Policy Concerns after Financial Reform

As restrictions on investments and operations are removed and firms begin to enter new businesses, traditional industry boundaries will become less distinct. The remaining rules, having to do with monetary control and prudential regulation, will thus become less effective. This situation presents a challenge. In the first instance, the gains of reform must be preserved. If that is to be done, innovation, growth, and risk-taking behavior must be encouraged. At the same time, the government must still be able to stabilize real economic activity and to maintain order in financial markets.

Structural Adjustments

Financial reform in Australia appears to be leading to major changes in the structure of the financial system. Indeed, the adjustments have been under way for several years. The owners, managers, and employees of financial institutions may be greatly affected by the restructuring, customers less so.

Deregulation of banking—that is, the reduction of direct controls on bank operations and the encouragement of new bank entry—can be expected to have profound effects on market structure. Australia's trading banks already have merged to form four large entities prepared to compete against anticipated entrants from overseas. In time private savings banks, which today have a separate identity only on paper, will be absorbed into their parent trading banks (provided that the regulations do not discriminate between the two entities). The changes elsewhere will be more substantial. Merchant banks will be compelled to seek trading bank licenses to compete effectively against the deregulated incumbents; the merchant banks would use the new authority to achieve parity in the cost of funds and foreign exchange, but would not be equally driven to offer checking accounts. (The Martin Group thought that merchant banks might alternatively withdraw from deposit competition and specialize instead in arranging mergers and acquisitions.) Finance companies will continue to have a role in a deregulated environment, although their affiliation with bank holding companies will undoubtedly require appropriate prudential controls. Because the banks have wider contact with the household sector, they might be expected to attract a greater share of the personal loan business, leaving finance companies to concentrate on higher risk-return commercial business such as loans to smaller corporations and property development.

The thrift institutions will be adversely affected by bank deregulation. Substantial consolidation is already under way. The number of permanent building societies in Australia declined by half during 1973–83, even as those institutions increased their share of total financial institution assets.[38] Just as the United States has found, building societies in Australia will require a broader range of asset powers, participation in the payments system, consolidation of the smaller firms, access to interstate markets, a deposit protection system, and new sources of capital. The close ties between credit unions and their customers give them advantages that may persist in a deregulated environment. The workplace or community affiliation affords easy access to credit information, which reduces the cost of processing a loan application. On the other hand, the "common bond" feature of the credit union—the industry's defining attribute—implies a lack of diversification that can make institutions especially vulnerable to depressed conditions at the local level. These issues have been recognized, and steps are being taken to minimize transition difficulties.

Such adjustments enable institutions to reduce unit operating expenses through the achievement of scale economies and the rationalization of overlapping branch systems. Larger firms also have a broader range of potential customers inasmuch as the maximum amount of loans to a single borrower is governed by the lender's assets and capital. Inherent in these moves are the likelihood of employment shifts and the possibility of a substantial reduction in the number of jobs at the traditional financial intermediaries. Firms seeking to reduce payroll costs will demand smaller wage increases and productivity improvements; alternatively, the industry's growth may be channeled to the intermediaries with less rigid employment structures.

Internal subsidies, service competition, and allocation through ra-

---

38. Australian Association of Permanent Building Societies, *Building Society Fact Book*, 2d ed. (Deakin, Australian Capital Territory: AAPBS, 1983), pp. 2, 8; and Reserve Bank of Australia, *Report and Financial Statements, 1983* (Sydney: RBA, 1983), p. 22; and table 2 above.

tioning will not survive the move to a deregulated environment. Since the mid-1970s savings banks have been losing a market share to competitors (primarily building societies) who have been able to provide profitable housing loans and yet avoid the extensive branch networks and high payroll costs. In fact, there has never been a de novo private savings bank; they are all affiliates of the major trading banks or are state government enterprises.

Structural adjustments are the means by which the benefits of reform are to be realized. They should be permitted to continue and financial companies should be subject only to the general rules applicable to employers and providers of services to the public, provided that the adjustments are consistent with the conduct of monetary policy and the maintenance of stability.

Monetary Control

Certain stabilization policies employed in the past are incompatible with Australia's present financial system. Direct controls such as lending requests will not be effective in limiting credit expansion because the regulated intermediaries are no longer the sole sources of large amounts of funds. Even if the regulatory net were to take in all domestic financial institutions, there would still be intercompany, direct market, and overseas financing. Attempts to limit these sources would distort the economy and would necessitate the reimposition of exchange controls.

A floating exchange rate may have its limitations but it does create new opportunities. A set exchange rate has been relinquished as a tool of stabilization. At the same time, the removal of transient distortions in short-term interest rates releases short-term money market instruments for use in open market operations by the Reserve Bank. As a result, monetary policy can be geared to offsetting the seasonal contraction of liquidity.

Australian monetary policy seeks to target growth of a relatively narrowly defined money supply (M3). Alternative methods of influencing this aggregate include reserve requirements, open market operations, and lending by the Reserve Bank. These techniques do not require limitations on participation in the payments system, and so do not conflict with proposals to grant new bank licenses. Rules must be applied uniformly, of course, and it may be appropriate to bring building societies and certain other intermediaries under commonwealth government regulation. To the extent that nonbanks offer substitutes for transaction accounts, they should be required to maintain appropriate reserves; this requirement should at the same time entitle such institutions to have access to the Reserve Bank's liquidity facility.

Underlying the question of whether monetary controls should be extended to nonbanks is the important issue of how to define "money" and determine the relationship between the chosen indicator and real economic activity. Although narrowly defined quantities are relatively easy to control, the links to the real sector are tenuous. On the other hand, broadly defined quantities that are more closely related to the real sector are less susceptible to control. This situation is hardly unique to Australia; it influences monetary policy in many countries that rely on quantity targeting for economic stabilization.

Answers to the problem of money control should not be sought in the financial system. Furthermore, reform of the financial sector to improve efficiency is desirable in its own right. Market forces assure the undesirability (if not the futility) of attempts to prevent private institutions from responding to profitable opportunities. The focus of monetary policy must therefore shift to market-oriented techniques.[39]

Prudential Regulation

Traditionally, banks in Australia have been treated as the very foundation of the financial system, and they are said to have "benefits and burdens" befitting their role in the economy.[40] They have been closely regulated to assure their viability, and they have been protected by restrictions on entry to prevent them from being bruised by competition. Banks have had a monopoly on third-party payment instruments and foreign exchange trading. Moreover, the Reserve Bank stands ready

39. See K. T. Davis and M. K. Lewis, "Can Monetary Policy Work in a Deregulated Capital Market?" *The Australian Economic Review* (First Quarter 1982), pp. 9–21; Carolyn J. Moses, "Financial Innovation and Monetary Policy: A Preliminary Survey," Reserve Bank of Australia Discussion Paper 8301 (Reserve Bank of Australia, May 1983).

40. See the statement by H. M. Knight, governor of the Reserve Bank, in AFSI, *Transcript of Proceedings* (Canberra, 1979), pp. 1797–98.

to provide support in the event that a bank encounters serious financial difficulties.

This situation is beginning to change. The relaxation of controls on bank portfolios and interest rates has led some to question whether existing methods of control are adequate for the emerging financial system. In the past, rules of thumb provided adequate guidance and moral suasion was sufficient to guarantee that prudential controls would be implemented. These methods are no longer appropriate. Entry of new banks, if it has the intended effect of intensifying competition, will also lead to more risk taking. The increasing importance of nonbanks means that their problems are more likely to affect the economy as a whole; yet these intermediaries are not subject to regulation at the national level. There is also the question of ultimate regulatory responsibility for the foreign banks that will be operating in Australia. In sum, a new approach to prudential regulation is needed.

The Campbell Committee explored this issue at great length. It recommended reforms consistent with a philosophy of reducing government intervention. The committee's report advocated the elimination of portfolio restrictions on both banks and nonbanks, ease of exit for intermediaries that fail, a role for the Reserve Bank in the maintenance of liquidity (although not for insolvent institutions), and rules to prevent fraud and provide information similar to the rules that exist for nonfinancial firms in the economy.[41] The Campbell Committee stated a preference for "functional" rather than "structural" regulation (and thus urged that there be no outright prohibitions on the services that intermediaries may offer), consistent rules across states and between banks and nonbanks, and consolidation of nonbank subsidiaries with bank holding companies for purposes of prudential regulation. But the fundamental distinction between banks and nonbanks was affirmed.[42] The Martin Group, too, accepted this view.

The Campbell Committee offered three reasons for continuing the special treatment accorded banks:

Trust is a pre-condition for an efficient payments system: cheque-clearing institutions must be able to deal confidently with one another. It is widely accepted that there is a need for a safety haven for small investors, a role that

41. AFSI, *Final Report*, pp. 284–91.
42. Ibid., p. 428.

has traditionally been filled by the banks. A banking collapse which involved depositors in significant losses could be expected to create substantial disturbance in financial markets and therefore in the economy as a whole.[43]

Each of these points can be challenged. First, the operation of a check-clearing system does not depend on the unquestioned solvency of the participants. In the United States, 40,000 institutions are authorized to offer transactions accounts, and several hundred of these may fail each year. However, means exist to protect the participants. The Martin Group suggested that nonbank participation in Australia could take place through agency facilities. Institutions need not advance funds before payment is received, and reasonable precautions against fraud and theft could be developed.

As for the second point, the many changes that have occurred in the Australian financial system make it imperative to reevaluate traditional roles. Although banks could be allowed to continue to offer virtually risk-free deposits, it may be appropriate to encourage certain nonbanks to do so as well. Alternatives to banks for risk-free assets already exist in the form of government securities. Mutual funds backed by commonwealth issues, or deposits at intermediaries fully collateralized by such instruments, could provide the asset demanded without conferring on private institutions the right to issue unlimited amounts of debt with a government guarantee.

Third, banks no longer have a monopoly on deposits. Merchant banks, building societies, credit unions, and finance companies accept funds from small and large depositors, and their importance in the system is now sufficiently great to warrant concern over failures among nonbanks.

Taken together, these reasons for special treatment of banks are not persuasive. Furthermore, the differential treatment of banks and non-banks that is implied would have adverse effects on the competitiveness of the financial system. Until recently, there was a rough balance between the burdens and benefits for banks. The nonbanks grew more rapidly in percentage terms, the banks in absolute terms. With the removal of restrictions on banks, however, the scale tips in their favor. The nonbank intermediaries are still subject to asset controls and geographic limitations, and they have limited sources of capital. They cannot offer checking accounts and do not have access to the support facilities of

43. Ibid., p. 296.

the Reserve Bank. Under these circumstances it is unlikely that the nonbank depository institutions will be able to offer banks significant competition across a wide range of services.

The appropriate policy would be to recognize the evolution of financial services by extending checking account powers and Reserve Bank support to qualified nonbanks. These institutions need not have the same authority as banks in order to compete. Merchant banks would concentrate on wholesale and international banking, while building societies and credit unions would probably continue to emphasize retail (noncommercial) services and thus would not have to offer a full range of services. The problem of failing institutions could be handled within the nonbank industry, as it has been in the past, but access to the Reserve Bank could be made available in the event that problems become widespread. The establishment of an industry-operated facility for depositor protection and maintenance of liquidity, as suggested by the Campbell Committee, would be an appropriate way of recognizing the continuing differences between banks and nonbanks while permitting competition to take place between the two industries.

Although the committee insisted on distinguishing between banks and nonbanks, it did propose that prudential regulation be consistent for all. The committee's recommendations consisted of a mixture of existing regulations and market-oriented mechanisms. Although on one hand the committee said there should be no restrictions on the types of assets that institutions may hold, it recommended a continuation of capital ratio limits, risk asset limits (for example, on the amount of loans to one borrower, on the amount of nonincome property, and on loans to related entities), liquidity requirements, and the like. The concession to free-market ideology, on the other hand, was that these regulations should be applied differentially, depending on the management capability, portfolio risk, and financial performance of each intermediary. The committee suggested that the discretionary power of the Reserve Bank to provide solvency or liquidity support should be maintained essentially in its current form. Foreign banks, it was argued, should be established as subsidiaries, along with guarantees of support by the parent comparable to those provided to a branch, so that government control could be assured.

The approach suggested by these recommendations is cumbersome and suggests an ambiguity in the goals of prudential regulation. The information requirements, for one thing, are overwhelming; it is not possible to evaluate the riskiness of particular portfolio choices ex ante with sufficient precision to make capital or risk asset controls effective but not burdensome. With respect to foreign banks, one can opt for the greater control that would be maintained over a subsidiary or the greater support that would be provided to a branch, but not both.

Some prudential controls seem designed to maintain the availability of banking services by protecting institutions from failure. Others provide assurance to small depositors. Another rationale for providing deposit guarantees is based on the government's superior ability to collect and assimilate information on the operations of financial institutions; the government has the ability to make its assurances credible and has the incentive to disseminate widely the information that it collects. A private agency, with finite resources, could not make such guarantees; nor could it internalize the value of the information, and so would have no incentive to collect it.

These arguments for prudential regulation can be countered by two substantive objections. First, the protections that are provided remove some of the incentives for efficient resource allocation that the market would otherwise present. This point is self-evident. Second, these suggested goals can be met through means that do not require government involvement in the operations of financial intermediaries. For example, the possibility that inadequate banking services might arise from the failure of incumbent firms can be averted through a more liberal procedure for licensing banks; both entry and exit should be made easier. Government securities (purchased directly or through an intermediary) would provide a risk-free asset with minimal controls on banks.

The case for prudential regulation should not rest on its ability to smooth the daily operations of financial institutions. The primary role—and, arguably, the only role—for government control of intermediaries is to prevent speculative runs on healthy institutions that might lead to instability, illiquidity in the financial system, and rapid deflation. This risk is not diversifiable for individual institutions. The actions of one firm can adversely affect the economy as a whole. A run would affect the government's ability to stabilize the economy through monetary policy. This is the basis on which prudential regulation should be designed.

It is not necessary to go far beyond the Campbell proposals to develop a plan for regulation that achieves the desired objectives. In principle, financial institutions should be given market-oriented incentives for prudent behavior. Such incentives would be present if these institutions could be assured of receiving timely, accurate, and useful information on the operations and investment policies of agencies that solicit funds from the public. In addition, there must be private funds at risk, in the form of capital, subordinated debt, or long-term uninsured deposits. The combination of information and risk capital would lead investors to demand prudent behavior of financial intermediaries. Liquidity support, provided under explicit authority by the Reserve Bank, would be needed to assure the availability of deposit funds in the event of financial difficulties throughout the economy. To prevent such support from being used to prop up failing institutions, the regulatory agency must have the power to put an institution into receivership while sufficient assets remain to cover deposit liabilities.

This is not a prescription for deposit insurance, which can create perverse incentives for risk taking in the absence of rigid controls on permissible activities. Nevertheless, it would be possible to have de facto insurance for certain classes of deposits. Small depositors could be given precedence over others in the event of liquidation so that, given the intention to close failing institutions while assets still exceed deposits, it would not diminish incentives for prudent operation. Furthermore, since only a small buffer of funds need be at risk—probably no more than 20 percent of liabilities—the guarantee could be extended to another class of deposits in the interest of promoting stability. Demand accounts are the most readily withdrawn, and the lowest interest rate penalty is associated with such withdrawals. Higher required reserves against all insured deposits would help to prevent exploitation of the guarantee. With demand deposits and all small accounts protected by the government against loss, the likelihood of speculative runs is substantially reduced while incentives are preserved. Moreover, this structure would enhance system liquidity in the event of a run, because investors would shift funds into demand accounts (the risk-free investment) rather than out.

Foreign banks should be chartered in Australia as majority-owned subsidiaries of the parent holding company. This would be the best way to attract needed capital, apply comparable rules to domestic and foreign banks, and insulate the Australian operation from the problems of the parent company. The ability to monitor and control the daily actions of foreign banks is more important than the need for parent support in the event of difficulties, the reason being that foreign banks are principally interested in wholesale operations and prefer to deal with large firms that can evaluate their bank's soundness on their own. Foreign banks would also be inclined to deal primarily with firms that have interests in both Australia and the country of the parent bank. The parent would therefore be unlikely to abandon a failing subsidiary because of the repercussions from its multinational customers. It may be appropriate, when issuing licenses to foreign banks, to establish one set of rules for a strictly wholesale operation and a more stringent set of requirements for institutions that seek to offer a full range of retail services as well.

Conclusions

Australia's financial markets have developed to meet the varied needs of savers and borrowers. Large corporations have access to direct markets for equity and debt, and intermediaries supply funds under a wide range of conditions. Smaller firms have fewer options, although the trading banks are able to meet most financing requirements. Households can place their savings in depository institutions, money market mutual funds, or other intermediaries at virtually any desired maturity. Their access to loans is equally diverse and includes housing finance, consumer installment loans, and credit card debt. Secondary markets exist for government debt, commercial paper, bank certificates of deposit, and other widely held instruments.

These institutions have shown an ability to adapt to changes in the flow of funds over time. Government demand for funds, for example, increased sharply beginning in the mid-1970s; the supply of savings from overseas rose in the early 1980s as the share provided by households declined. Such shifts have been handled without disruptions.

Financial markets in Australia have always been well integrated geographically because banks, merchant banks, and finance companies have branches throughout the country. Building societies and credit unions are restricted to operations within states, but these institutions have never been marginal sources of funds. Although Australia lacks a well-developed secondary mortgage market, the principal portfolio lenders, the savings banks, offer nationwide services.

Despite substantial reforms in recent years, further work remains to be done. In the first instance there are the remnants of obsolescent government controls. More important are the issues emerging from the deregulation process itself. These have to do with monitoring and controlling a financial system that is more flexible and diverse than the earlier system, is more susceptible to events elsewhere in the world, and is continuously changing in response to market events.

The goals of financial stability, monetary control, and income redistribution cannot be faulted. Indeed, these have been the objectives of direct controls on the structure and operation of financial intermediaries, but such controls have been only intermittently successful in achieving these objectives, and relatively less so in recent years. It has been argued that these desired ends come at excessive cost, and that they can be achieved more effectively by other means. There is a strong case for eliminating many of the remaining regulations that govern the banking system.

The Campbell Report provides a clear agenda for reform of the Australian financial system. Its approach is generally sound and consistent. Nonetheless critics have complained that the report is preoccupied with government regulation and have argued that private and other government actions are also important.[44] However, the focus of the report must be seen as correct. The committee rightly noted the effects of inflation, high interest rates, and economic growth, but analysis of these issues was clearly beyond its capability. Although the private sector was found wanting in numerous respects, the effect of government regulations overwhelms these other considerations. The Martin Group report essentially concurred in these conclusions. All the evidence suggests that the private sector stands prepared to meet the financial requirements of the Australian economy.

---

44. P. J. Sheehan and B. Derody, "The Campbell Report: A Critical Analysis," *The Australian Economic Review* (First Quarter 1982), pp. 35–62; and Peter Sheehan, "The Campbell Report: An Overview," *Economic Papers*, special edition: *The Campbell Report* (April 1983), pp. 194–205.

EDWARD M. GRAMLICH

"A Fair Go": Fiscal
Federalism Arrangements

THE Australian belief in equality and apparent fear of market outcomes
are evident in the system of fiscal relations between the commonwealth
and the state governments. From the standpoint of equality Australia
has the most equalizing federalist system in the world. Grants intended
to remove disparities in incomes and to alleviate the enormous costs of
providing public services are large, respected, and longstanding; such
grants have existed in some form for over fifty years. But from the
standpoint of protection from market outcomes there are many inefficiencies in the Australian system, many cases in which bureaucratic
controls are used to allocate resources in preference to market-like

I am indebted to Fred H. Gruen for his advice and help in arranging interviews, and
to my conference discussants, Professors Russell L. Mathews and Clifford Walsh, for
their helpful (and extensive) comments. Among the federal officials who were helpful
at the interview stage were Carol J. Austin, Vincent C. Blackburn, Ian Castles, Judge
R. Else-Mitchell, V. W. J. Fitzgerald, Peter D. Jonson, and William E. Norton. Among
the state treasury officials were Peter Emery, John Hall, Barry Nicholls, and Norman
Oakes. Among the academic economists were Peter D. Groenewegen, Nanak Kakwani,
Ronald Lane, Russell L. Mathews, Michael G. Porter, Jeff Richardson, Peter L. Swan,
Thomas J. Valentine, and Clifford Walsh. Among the economists from private business
were James Catterall, John Donovan, Brian Hamley, John McLeod, and Donald
Stammer. I owe special thanks to those who read and commented on early drafts of the
manuscript—Ted Bergstrom, Peter D. Groenewegen, Brian Hamley, Peter J. Lloyd,
Barry Nicholls, John Niewinghuysen, Joseph A. Pechman, John Yinger, and the other
authors whose chapters appear in this book. Finally, I thank the Alfred P. Sloan
Foundation for financing some of my work on the project.

mechanisms, and many other instances in which the system does not let public officials bear the full responsibility for their decisions. As Russell Mathews, the guru of Australian federalism, puts it: "The Australian fiscal system which has evolved since World War II may then be seen as one which maximises the amount of political noise and minimises the degree of electoral accountability, financial responsibility, economic efficiency and effective policy choice."[1]

These two partly conflicting themes imply that the Australian system will have a better score when evaluated on grounds of equality than on economic efficiency. In this paper I develop this theme. I first discuss fiscal federalism in general—in contrast to a purely centralized scheme for the provision of public services, what does a federal scheme try to accomplish? I then describe the Australian system, with relatively little emphasis on the historical origins of the system, a topic amply covered by others.[2] I also discuss a particularly interesting, and underresearched, question, the extent of diversities in the Australian system—how federal is it?

The next sections of the paper turn to various policy considerations. I first analyze the Australian system of intergovernmental grants. I also address a series of selected tax issues that illustrate close involvement with fiscal federalism. Several suggestions for reforming or improving Australia's fiscal arrangements are made and evaluated in both of these sections.

Fiscal Federalism

Most countries have adopted a centralized system of government for the financing and provision of public services. A few—prominently Australia, Canada, the United States, and West Germany—have opted for more decentralized provision, here called fiscal federalism. As compared to a centralized system, a federal system will typically entail less equal provision of public services. Subnational governments, free

1. Russell Mathews, "The Commonwealth-State Financial Contract," in Jennifer Aldred and John Wilkes, eds., *A Fractured Federation? Australia in the 1980s* (Sydney: George Allen & Unwin for the Australian Institute of Political Science, 1982), p. 48.

2. One of the best sources is U.S. Advisory Commission on Intergovernmental Relations, *Studies in Comparative Federalism: Australia* (Washington, D.C.: US ACIR, 1981), especially the articles by Russell Mathews, R. Else-Mitchell, and W. R. C. Jay.

to decide how much to tax their citizens and spend on public services, typically select dissimilar amounts, so that citizens in different jurisdictions receive different amounts of public services. Since preferences for public services vary, a more decentralized system should achieve a higher rating on grounds of economic efficiency. Citizens in subnational jurisdictions can decide on their preferred array of public services. They can also move to jurisdictions that provide arrays closest to the ones they prefer.

It follows that a federal system can be evaluated for the equality and efficiency with which it provides public goods. On the question of equality, in Australia, as in many other countries, there is a basic tax-transfer redistributive system that is operated almost entirely by the central government to reduce the variance of spending power among individual families. But as long as income, wealth, and relative prices vary by community or by state, the income, sales, or property tax rates necessary to provide a standard menu of public services (the so-called tax price of public services) also vary. One problem this introduces is that it creates an incentive to move to affluent communities where public goods are cheap, bidding up land prices, pricing the poor out of these communities, and increasing the amount of income segregation of communities. Another problem is that the basic economic and social opportunities available to citizens—such as for education and health care—may depend on public services because the variance in tax price may cause poor areas to spend less on education and health than more affluent areas, thereby adding to the other disadvantages faced by the poor. Hence the variance in tax prices provides a rationale either for centralized financing and provision of public services, or for decentralized provision with equalizing transfers among communities. How well the transfers do equalize opportunities among communities or states is the first criterion by which a federal system can be evaluated.

The second criterion is economic efficiency. In market economies governments should seek to minimize unnecessary distortions in the pattern of resource allocation and relative prices. One way to minimize these distortions is for local governments to provide the array of public services desired by their electorates. The closer is the array to that desired by voters, the more efficient the system. A second way is to select taxes that involve minimum economic distortions to pay for these public services. A third way is to avoid wasteful duplication and

234 *Edward M. Gramlich*

inconsistency on both the tax and expenditure sides of the budgets that can result when the actual providers and financers of public services are subnational governments. Rail lines extending across state lines can be standardized; one state's highways can start where another state's leave off; taxing conventions can minimize compliance and paperwork costs for the private sector.

Subsequent sections of the paper analyze the Australian federal system in terms of the one equality criterion (how well it equalizes the tax price, or expected expenditures on public services, in the face of income and wealth differences) and the three efficiency criteria (how large the excess burden is in the provision of public services, how distortionary the tax system is, and how significant duplication and coordination costs are across states).

The Australian Federal System

The basic outlines of the Australian federal system were set down in the Constitution of 1901. The Constitution gave the central government (Commonwealth of Australia) responsibility for defense, foreign affairs, international and interstate trade and commerce, maritime activities, currency and banking, and old-age and invalid pensions. An amendment in 1946 extended this pension responsibility to cover all forms of social security payments to families. The six signatory states retained most other responsibilities such as the provision of education, health, public safety, transport, and community and social services. States were also given control of their local governments and to this day have retained that control, though localities had some responsibility delegated to them for road systems, recreation and cultural services, and services to property.[3]

3. One examining a map of Australia may be confused by exactly what areas are states and what are not. There have always been six official states in Australia. Ordered as they usually are in government documents (by population, except in one case), and with the capitals in parentheses, they are New South Wales (Sydney), Victoria (Melbourne), Queensland (Brisbane), South Australia (Adelaide), Western Australia (Perth), and Tasmania (Hobart). The Northern Territory (Darwin) will eventually be independent, but not before the mid-1980s. Because administrative and financial arrangements for the Northern Territory are sui generis, I generally do not discuss Northern Territory relationship in this chapter.

The Australian Constitution empowered the central government to impose all forms of taxation, but not to discriminate among states. States were given concurrent powers of taxation, except that they were not permitted to collect customs and excise duties. In later years this exclusion was interpreted by Australia's High Court to mean that virtually all forms of sales or other indirect taxes on goods were considered to be excise duties and were unavailable to the states, a fact that takes on fundamental importance in an evaluation of the Australian system.[4]

The system of grants from the central to state and local governments has changed over time much more than the tax system. In the early days the Constitution made provision for the sharing of customs and excise duties with the states. Under Section 96, it also empowered the commonwealth to grant financial assistance to any state, basically on any terms. This provision was eventually interpreted to enable the central government to provide both general-purpose equalization grants among the states and specific-purpose, or categorical grants, to achieve particular expenditure objectives.[5]

This granting authority has its origin in the period just before World War I when the states of Tasmania and Western Australia sought and obtained special grants to help balance their budgets; they were joined by South Australia just before the Great Depression. When economic disparities widened in the depression, the commonwealth responded to threats of secession by creating in 1933 a unique body, the Commonwealth Grants Commission (CGC).[6] The CGC, an independent statutory authority, was to report on application of any state for special assistance. Over time this authority has developed into a responsibility to recommend the level of equalization grants to be paid to individual states. Currently this commission computes what are known as grant "relativities," the ratios that determine the relative amounts of general-purpose

4. R. Else-Mitchell, "Constitutional Aspects of Commonwealth and State Taxing Laws," in Dean Jaensch, ed., *The Politics of "New Federalism"* (Adelaide: Australasian Political Studies Association, 1977), pp. 37–42.

5. R. Else-Mitchell, "The Australian Federal Grants System and Its Impact on Fiscal Relations of the Federal Government with State and Local Governments," in US ACIR, *Studies in Comparative Federalism: Australia*, p. 30.

6. Western Australia went so far as to vote for secession by a two-thirds margin, but the petition was denied by the British parliament because the rest of Australia had not approved.

assistance received by states to equalize their tax prices for public services.

World War II brought another important change. To finance the war the government passed the Uniform Tax Scheme, which excluded states from individual and company income taxes. In return, the central government supplemented and eventually replaced the previous special-assistance grants with unconditional grants that are now referred to as tax-sharing grants. These grants have grown through time and are now the main form of central government aid to states; they also constitute the means by which interstate equalization is accomplished. As noted above, the CGC became the agency that made recommendations about relativities for tax-sharing grants and its importance has grown along with those grants.

This evolution of the grant system was paralleled by an increase in central government supervision of the capital accounts of states and localities. In the 1920s there were fears that certain states would not be able to repay their large outstanding debts (with New South Wales later defaulting on some bonds in the 1930s), and that the Commonwealth would become liable for these repayment obligations. For this reason, and also to rationalize and coordinate state offshore borrowing, in 1928 a constitutional amendment created another unique body, the Australian Loan Council (ALC), to regulate the floating of this debt. Although the prime minister is represented on the ALC (with the treasurer normally serving as chair), and the six state premiers also serve, the central government has increasingly dominated the ALC. Through the ALC, the central government now does all the borrowing for state general governments, and these governments repay the ALC. The central government domination of the ALC began in the 1950s, when it began to make special loans to the states to finance their capital projects. By the early 1970s the states had become heavily in debt to the central government, which then took over $1 billion of state debt and the interest charges on it. In 1975 this arrangement was transformed into an interest-free capital grant to state governments of one-third of the ALC borrowings on their behalf.

The ALC also regulates the borrowing of most "semigovernmental" authorities (quasi-governmental bodies engaged in revenue-raising operations for electric power, public utilities, and transportation) under what is known as the "gentlemen's agreement" of 1936. This control has been gradually relaxed in very recent years.

The modern history of the Australian grant system resembles that of the U.S. grant system. During the 1972–75 regime of Labor party Prime Minister Gough Whitlam, specific-purpose grants grew from 2.1 percent of GDP to 5.8 percent in three short years (similar to what happened in the United States during the Great Society years). This growth reflected the declared intention of the Labor party to standardize public services among states with highly restrictive specific-purpose grants even in functional areas for which states had formal constitutional responsibility.

Just as the Great Society was eventually followed by a retrenchment labeled "the new federalism" in the United States, similar events occurred in Australia. In 1976 the Liberal-Country party government of Malcolm Fraser proposed a series of measures to decentralize the system by insuring automatic growth of tax-sharing grants, computing relativities for all states (not just those that had been applying for special assistance), and cutting out or scaling back many of the rapidly growing specific-purpose grants (similar to the proposals for special revenue-sharing and block grants made by Republican Presidents Nixon and Reagan in the United States). States were also given more revenue-raising capability by being allowed to attach a surcharge or a rebate onto the national income tax rate, though for good economic and political reasons to be discussed below, no state has ever used this power. As a result of Fraser's initiatives, the growth of tax-sharing grants has far exceeded that of specific-purpose grants since 1975, and by 1981 the former accounted for about 4.5 percent of GDP. But the specific-purpose grants were not cut back either, at least in nominal terms, and they still constitute 4 percent of GDP (the lack of a sharp cutback in these grants is also similar to what the United States has experienced). Hence attempts to change the system by both the Labor party and Liberal-Country party prime ministers have expanded the system—specific-purpose grants grew and tax-sharing grants did not decline under Whitlam, and the latter grew while the former did not decline under Fraser.

Some broad summary indicators of this growth and development in the postwar period are given in table 1. During the 1970s direct (nongrant) expenditures by the central government increased by 2.6 percentage

Table 1. *Government Expenditures, Grants, Taxes, and Surplus, by Level of Government, Selected Years, 1950–80*

	Commonwealth government					State and local governments			State and local taxes as percent of revenue[d]
Year	Expenditures	Grants	ALC advances[a]	Taxes	Surplus[b]	Expenditures	Taxes	Surplus[c]	
Amount ($ millions)									
1949–50	763	202	36	1,000	−1	651	196	−217	45.2
1959–60	1,794	649	397	2,827	−13	1,979	842	−91	44.6
1969–70	4,551	1,637	680	7,157	289	4,935	2,256	−362	49.3
1974–75	9,992	5,194	1,225	15,272	−1,139	11,876	4,622	−835	41.9
1979–80	20,023	10,662	896	29,627	−1,954	22,894	9,186	−2,150	44.3
Share of GDP (percent)									
1949–50	15.0	4.0	0.7	19.6	−0.0	12.8	3.8	−4.3	...
1959–60	13.1	4.7	2.9	20.6	−0.1	14.4	6.1	−0.7	...
1969–70	14.9	5.4	2.2	23.4	1.0	16.2	7.4	−1.2	...
1974–75	16.2	8.4	2.0	24.7	−1.9	19.2	7.5	−1.4	...
1979–80	17.5	9.3	0.8	25.9	−1.7	20.0	8.0	−1.9	...

Source: W. E. Norton, P. M. Garmston, and M. W. Brodie, *Australian Economic Statistics, 1949–50 to 1980–81:1. Tables*, Occasional Paper 8A (Canberra: Reserve Bank of Australia, May 1982), tables 2.16, 2.17, 2.19, 2.20, 5.1, pp. 47–48, 50–51, 116.

a. Australian Loan Council advances.
b. Net of ALC advances—that is, commonwealth taxes minus the sum of commonwealth expenditures, grants, and ALC advances.
c. Net of ALC advances—state and local taxes plus commonwealth grants plus ALC advances minus state and local expenditures.
d. State and local taxes divided by the sum of grants, ALC advances, and state and local taxes in percentage terms.

points of GDP, and grants increased by 3.9 percentage points of GDP as a result of the developments discussed above. The 1970s brought economic pressures to limit government borrowing, so the ALC has tightened up, and ALC advances have actually fallen as a share of GDP. Both the central and the state and local government taxes have risen as a share of GDP, but not as much as expenditures, and particularly at the central government level the deficit has grown. The other fact to note is how small state and local taxes are. By 1980 they accounted for only 23 percent of total tax revenue and only 44 percent of the revenue available to the states and localities (that is, the sum of grants, ALC advances, and taxes). This latter phenomenon has led many observers to suggest that the heavy reliance on grants eliminates some of the responsibilities for sound budgetary management at the subnational level.

The Extent of Diversity

The historical evolution of Australian federalism toward a more centrally controlled system might imply that state and local differences in services are gradually being eliminated. Those observers, mainly in the Labor party, who believe in standardizing public services across areas will generally not lament the passing of these differences; those firmly committed to the federalism goal of accommodating differences in tastes for public services on the part of citizens will lament the passing.

But before any funerals are held, it makes sense to see just how great are these differences in public services. And, for all the rhetoric about the growth in central control and the standardization of public services, the differences in these public services levels turn out to be surprisingly great. Table 2 shows public consumption outlays per capita by state. The overall national average in the first row is $761 per capita, ranging from a high of $1,010 in Tasmania to a low of $659 in Queensland. Tasmanians spend 50 percent more on public services than do Queenslanders. Although it might be thought that income differences could explain some of the disparities, they do not. To begin with, state incomes do not vary much in Australia—Victoria, the highest income state, has a personal income per capita 1.05 times the national average, while

Table 2. Expenditures for Public Services, by State, 1980–81

Dollars per capita unless otherwise indicated

Item	Weighted average[a]	New South Wales	Victoria	Queensland	South Australia	Western Australia	Tasmania	*Comparative statistics* Weighted standard deviation[b]	Coefficient of variation[c]	Standardized coefficient of variation[d]
Total public consumption outlays[e]	761.0	738.0	755.0	658.7	850.4	889.0	1,010.0	76.9	0.101	0.077
Primary and secondary education	229.1	218.3	260.7	181.1	257.0	226.0	266.5	28.2	0.123	0.098
Public safety	76.5	78.3	66.0	73.2	83.5	93.5	97.5	8.7	0.114	0.135
Health and hospitals	202.2	206.0	186.9	165.7	218.0	269.4	248.2	27.8	0.138	0.143
Social services	13.5	9.6	15.3	17.4	16.0	14.4	13.9	3.1	0.230	...
Community development	2.2	2.2	3.7	...	3.1	1.4	1.6	0.9	0.409	...
Recreation and culture	10.7	7.7	8.5	8.6	18.7	18.5	31.5	5.4	0.505	...
Total public consumption outlays as a share of disposable income (percent)	12.7	12.0	12.0	12.0	14.6	15.5	17.9	1.5	0.118	0.057
Addendum										
Percentage share in the United States[f]	11.8	...	...	...	...	...	...	2.1	0.175	...

Sources: State expenditures—Australian Bureau of Statistics. *State and Local Government Finance in Australia, 1980–81* (Canberra: ABS, 1981), tables 17, 26, 35, 44, 53, 62; population—Treasury Department, *Payments to or for the States, the Northern Territory, and Local Government Authorities, 1982–83*, Budget Paper 7 (Canberra: Australian Government Publishing Service, 1982), table 6, p. 19. Also Russell Mathews, "Federalism in Retreat: The Abandonment of Tax Sharing and Fiscal Equalization," reprint 50 (Canberra: Australian National University, Centre for Research on Federal Fiscal Relations, 1982), table 3, p. 26; Russell Mathews, "Regional Disparities in Australia," in U.S. Advisory Commission on Intergovernmental Relations, *Studies in Comparative Federalism: Australia* (US ACIR, 1981), table 1, p. 3; "National Income and Product Accounts Tables," *Survey of Current Business*, vol. 62 (August 1982); and Norton, Garmston, and Brodie, *Australian Economic Statistics*, table 5.18, p. 147.

a. Weights based on population shares.
b. Square root of weighted average squared error.
c. Weighted standard deviation divided by the weighted mean.
d. All calculations redone with public spending standardized for differences in population structure and dispersion, climate, and topography.
e. Components do not add to total because only selected consumption items are shown.
f. Total public consumption as a share of U.S. personal income, excluding Alaska and Hawaii.

Queensland, the lowest income state, is at 0.91 of the national average.[7] In the case at hand, Queensland, with low spending, does have the lowest income; but Tasmania, with high spending, has the second lowest income. The comparison can be made more formally by computing public consumption as a share of disposable income, as in the last row. When this is done, Tasmania is still spending 50 percent more than three other states, and the coefficient of variation actually increases.

The other rows of the table show that this variation is not a result of the functional aggregation scheme, but exists across the board. For every category of public consumption the coefficient of variation exceeds 0.1, and it rises to quite high levels exactly where it might be expected to—in the less standard categories like community development and recreation and culture where statewide taste differences might be significant.[8]

As a standard for comparison, the last row of table 2 gives the statewide coefficient of variation of public consumption divided by income for the United States, a country in which public spending differences are perceived to be very great. The standard deviation and coefficient of variation are greater in the United States than in Australia, but not by very much. Roughly there appears to be about two-thirds as much expenditure diversity in supposedly homogeneous Australia as in the supposedly heterogeneous United States.

It is impossible to compare Australian statewide figures with those in the United States beyond this point, but it is possible to refine the Australian calculations. As part of its calculations for grant relativities, the CGC measures public spending as standardized for differences in population structure and dispersion, climate, topography, and other factors. The last column in table 2 repeats the Australian calculations with these standardized expenditures, both gross and as a share of

7. Russell Mathews, "Regional Disparities in Australia," in US ACIR, *Studies in Comparative Federalism: Australia*, table 1, p. 3.
8. Some critics have objected to these calculations because they ignore equalization transfers. Although this is true, one would think that eliminating them would make my point even stronger—if anything, there should be more of a difference between high- and low-income states and even more diversity. On the other side, there is one sense in which the variation does depend on the aggregation scheme. Since Queensland is the normal outlier, calculations done with Queensland excluded do lower the coefficient of variation, usually by about 15 percent.

Table 3. *Measures of Local Government Diversity in Expenditures, Australia and the United States, 1979–80*
Dollars

Suburban area[a]	Mean current expenditure	Standard deviation	Coefficient of variation
Sydney, New South Wales	145	33	0.228
Brisbane, Queensland	99	28	0.282
Victoria	155	48	0.310
Detroit, Michigan[b]	223	70	0.312

Sources: For Australia—Australian Bureau of Statistics, *Local Government Finance: New South Wales, 1980* (ABS, New South Wales Office, 1981); *Local Government: Victoria, 1980–81* (ABS, Victoria Office, 1981); and *Local Government: Queensland, 1980–81* (ABS, Queensland Office, 1981). For the United States—U.S. Bureau of the Census, *1977 Census of Governments*, vol. 4: *Governmental Finances*, and *Finances of Municipalities and Township Governments* (GPO, 1979).
a. Suburban areas with populations of 20,000 or more, excluding central cities.
b. Excludes two cities with their own public hospitals and a domed sports center.

disposable income.[9] While the coefficient of variation does increase for certain types of spending, it declines for the largest public education category and for the overall total, and especially for the overall total as a share of income. It is clear that these other factors do partly explain interstate expenditure diversity. But whether the two-thirds ratio would be raised or lowered with these added controls will remain a mystery until the same calculations are done for the United States.

Of course, the reason for having diverse public services is to accommodate differences between citizens' tastes. When a comparison of services is made among Australian states, one cannot be sure that is the proper inference. Australia's states are large and far apart, with dramatically different labor markets (so that many households do not have a realistic option of whether to live in various states). A more meaningful comparison would then be to show diversity within cities in the same area, or the same labor market. Such a comparison cannot easily be made for Australia because only three states publish data on local government expenditures, and no states publish data on local incomes. But those data that are available, shown in table 3, for the suburbs of Sydney, Brisbane, and the large cities of Victoria still indicate significant diversity. Now the coefficient of variation has risen to between 0.23 and

9. The figures are taken from Russell Mathews, "Federalism in Retreat: The Abandonment of Tax Sharing and Fiscal Equalization," reprint 50 (Canberra: Australian National University, Centre for Research on Federal Financial Relations, July 1982), table 3, p. 26.

0.31, the latter being just that for the Detroit suburbs.[10] Adjusting for income differences might lower the coefficient of variation (though surprisingly it does not for Detroit), but such an adjustment could not possibly eliminate the large amount of expenditure diversity shown.

It is easier to report these numbers than to interpret them. One point is obvious. Despite most commentators' emphasis on the centralist drift of Australian federalism, this system is federalist in more than name. Expenditure differences between states and communities are quite large, almost as large as in the diverse United States, and the dislocations involved in moving to a much more centralized system would be nontrivial. Beyond that, state expenditure differences seem by and large to be unexplained by differences in incomes or spending power or by differences in population structure and climate. That is a healthy sign, for it indicates that the system appears to be accommodating taste differences and is not just passing along income or cost differences. Moreover, if anything, differences are largest in areas in which tastes might be expected to vary and play a strong role, such as culture and community development, and for localities within urban labor markets. While fiscal federalism in Australia is perhaps a shadow of the system that might have existed in 1901, it is still thriving, and in some gross sense it might even be reasonably efficient in accommodating taste differences that apparently do exist in Australia.

The System of Intergovernmental Grants

The centerpiece of any federalist system, Australia's included, is the system of intergovernmental transfers from the central to subnational governments. There are three basic components of the grant system: unrestricted tax-sharing grants (4.8 percent of GDP in 1982), advances from the ALC (0.9 percent of GDP, 0.7 percent when repayments are excluded), and categorical specific-purpose grants (3.4 percent of GDP). With each component a set of policy issues has developed in recent years, and this section comments on these issues.

10. I hesitate to call Detroit a typical U.S. city, but it is one for which I have data readily available.

Tax-Sharing Grants

As described above, these grants are the lineal descendants of the sharing of customs duties originally envisaged by the Australian Constitution. Two important issues keep reappearing in discussions of them— their size and how they are distributed among states.

A series of conferences for the premiers of the six states held at the onset of the Liberal-Country party administration in 1975 established that the tax-sharing grants would be equal to 40 percent of personal income tax collections in the previous year. Although the number of these grants has grown at a reasonably adequate rate since that time (holding steady as a share of GDP), the central government has moved unilaterally to reduce them below the 40 percent standard. This was costly to the states in two ways: there was a loss of money and, since the level of funding is now considered by many as not guaranteed, there was also a loss of financial autonomy. This unilateral action has worked, in a small way to be sure, to enhance what is perceived as domination of the system by the central government. This point is brought up again below in the discussion of the appropriate government body to take responsibility for imposing taxes.

But the procedure for splitting up this grant money is what gives the Australian federalism system its unique character. The Personal Income Tax Act of 1978 provides one of the clearest imaginable statements of the objective of equalizing the tax price of public services:

the respective payments to which the states are entitled . . . . should enable each state to provide, without imposing taxes and charges at levels appreciably different from the levels of *taxes and charges imposed by the other States*, government services at standards not appreciably different from the standards of the government services provided by the other States (italics added).[11]

The question of how these equalizing payments are to be determined has been given to the CGC, and then to the premiers of the states for agreement. Because equalizing payments by their very nature involve taking from some states and giving to others, gaining agreement on a set of relativities has been difficult. But in 1982 the commonwealth did institute changes in the relativities written into the 1976 act, and by 1985

---

11. *Payments to or for the States, the Northern Territory, and Local Government Authorities, 1982–83*, Budget Paper 7, prepared by the Treasurer of the Commonwealth of Australia (Canberra: Australian Government Publishing Service, 1982), p. 13.

the shares will be adjusted in part according to the plan recommended by the CGC.

To understand how the CGC establishes relativities, some algebra is necessary. The CGC tries to equalize what it calls (mistakenly, I argue below) fiscal capacity. If the per capita revenue base in the ith state is denoted by Y_i and that for the commonwealth average is $\overline{Y}$, the CGC defines a concept of revenue needs, T_i, that is approximately equal to

(1) $$T_i = \overline{t}(\overline{Y} - Y_i),$$

where $\overline{t}$ is the average tax rate applied to the base in all states (with $\overline{t}\overline{Y}$ then yielding the revenue of a standard tax system, or "taxes and charges imposed by the other states" in the above quotation). Expenditure needs, E_i, are approximately equal to

(2) $$E_i = \overline{e}(C_i - \overline{C}),$$

where $\overline{e}$ is a standard level of public services, C_i is a vector of the costs of providing these services in a particular state, net of specific-purpose grants, and $\overline{C}$ is the representative cost vector for all states.[12]

Tax-sharing grants could be open-ended, as was the case in earlier days when particular states could apply for special assistance; in that case the CGC just computed the deficit for each state as the sum of revenue and expenditure needs, added a basic entitlement constant across all states, G^*, and determined each state's tax-sharing grant, G_i, by

(3) $$G_i = E_i + T_i + G^*.$$

Because of budgetary stringency, these grants have not been treated as open-ended by the central government, and it has been necessary to scale back G_i so that the sum of these grants is consistent with desired overall budgetary totals for the central government. One way to do this is simply to reduce G^* by an appropriate amount, thereby giving a

---

12. The exact formulas used by the CGC are not always written down and change from time to time. In one recent year, for example, the CGC defined $\overline{t}$ and $\overline{e}$ by first doing the calculations with each state excluded and then defining standardized tax revenues or costs as a population-weighted average of these values. My formulas give numbers very close to theirs but are simplified approximations.

constant per capita reduction in all states.[13] Another way is to make proportional reductions by the factor $(1 - \alpha)$; thus

$$(4) \qquad A = \overline{G}N/\sum_{i=1}^{6} G_i N_i,$$

where $\overline{G}$ is the predetermined amount of assistance per capita made available by the central government, N is total population, and N_i is population in each state. After lengthy arguments, what the CGC has in fact done is to take the average of the two amounts.[14] Even these shares are only those recommended by the CGC—the commonwealth and the premiers of the states then negotiate the final shares.

This attempt to equalize public spending capacity across states is the most explicit and comprehensive in the world, and after fifty years the CGC now has extensive experience at trying to measure true cost differences, as opposed to policy or efficiency differences that are not adjusted for. Moreover, while CGC members and economists often are frustrated by the slowness of changes,[15] the fact is the CGC is powerful, is listened to, and even makes fairly significant changes in the equalizing provisions that are eventually adopted. Any flaws in the system should then be viewed against a background of its notable achievements.

Nonetheless, the system is not perfect, and various kinds of criticisms can be made. The most basic has been raised by Walsh, and it involves the G^* term in equation 3.[16] He argues that the mix of expenditure diversity and revenue centralization creates a revenue cartel that damages effective government. If states had to rely more on revenues that they themselves raised, consistent with any overall level of equalization, they would spend more time and effort managing their government and less lobbying for their relativity or their basic entitlement. To put this point in terms of the new "rent-seeking" literature, while the basic

---

13. A supporting argument is given by Nicolaas Groenewold, "The 'New Federalism' and Horizontal Equalization," *The Economic Record*, vol. 57 (September 1981), pp. 282–87.

14. As described in Commonwealth Grants Commission, *Report on State Tax Sharing and Health Grants, 1982*, vol. 1 (Canberra: AGPS, 1982), pp. 23–24.

15. See, for example, the lengthy and detailed complaints of one of the CGC's two economists, Russell Mathews, in "Federalism in Retreat."

16. Clifford Walsh, "Reforming Federal Financial Relations: Some Radical (or Are They Conservative?) Proposals," presented at the Federal Finances Symposium, Hobart, Tasmania, August–September, 1983.

entitlement G^* has been treated above as predetermined, in fact it is a political rent-seeking variable; resources are used up in determining it; and there is no reason why it will be set at the level that maximizes satisfaction in various states. Walsh's solution would be to set G^* equal to zero (or drastically reduce it), and have the central government return appropriate taxing authority to the states. As will be seen below, the latter suggestion is one that makes sense even if G^* is not reduced at all, but in Walsh's argument it becomes that much more important to deal with vertical tax assignments.

A second problem can be termed the "Woop Woop" problem, after a (possibly mythical) sparsely settled town in Western Australia where the main activity after dark is listening to the "woop woop" of the frogs. There are many towns like this in Australia, and the cost of supplying them with public services is very high. The CGC mechanically tries to eliminate these cost differentials by its equalization formulas. But that just removes a disincentive that would otherwise encourage citizens to move away from these high-cost areas and in the long run raises the overall cost of providing public services (and private goods too, for that matter). When differential tax prices result from divergent resource costs, it may be better for the CGC to avoid equalizing every cost difference. Doing so mechanically obscures what should be a matter for a policy debate on equality versus efficiency.

A final criticism, perhaps mainly semantic but one about which there is a fair amount of misunderstanding in Australia, is that the CGC scheme is ultimately not an equalization scheme at all. The argument is as follows. Assume that the costs of providing public services are equal across states but that one state has an income of $900 per capita, $100 below the national average. Assume further that the tax rate in this state equals the average rate of 0.1. Without any equalization grants, the state spends $90 on public services, $10 less than the national average. The CGC then gives the state $10 (see equation 1), based on the reasoning that if the state devoted the entire $10 to the public sector, its spending would be up to the average. The CGC claims that the $10 grant gives the state "the capacity" to provide an average menu of public services. But the CGC grant is unconditional, and surely the state will use some of it (probably about $9) to cut taxes and provide more private goods and raise public spending only about $1. The CGC scheme, then, has equalized neither true fiscal capacity (which is still lower in the state, $910 versus $1,000 as conventionally measured) nor expected public expenditures ($91 versus $100). It may be a sensible scheme, but because it does not make any important variable equal, it cannot be called an equalization scheme.[17]

Should the CGC take a further step and recommend grants that make some variable equal across states? There are, as it turns out, three ways in which that could be done that are consistent with CGC traditions and logic and that seem to be consistent with Australian politics. One way that works through the price term was suggested by Martin Feldstein in his work on local school finance in the United States.[18] According to this approach, suppose that state expenditures are determined by the following illustrative expression (the logic works for any other hypothesized relation):

$$(5) \qquad E_i = a_0 + a_1 Y_i + a_2(G_i + R_i) + a_3 S_i - a_4 P_i + u_i,$$

where all symbols are as defined above, S_i represents specific-purpose grants received by the ith state, assumed to be uncorrelated with income, R_i refers to royalty payments for mineral resources, also assumed to be exogenous and uncorrelated with income, P_i is the price of public services to a state, and u_i is a random residual with a mean of zero. Feldstein's approach is to use open-ended matching grants to vary the price facing states according to

$$(6) \qquad P_i = \overline{P} + b_1(Y_i - \overline{Y}),$$

where $\overline{P}$ is the average price facing all states. According to equation 6, the grant formula would be such that prices are higher in states with high income. The way to determine exactly how much higher the prices would be is to find the price that makes expected state expenditures independent of state incomes. Formally, that amounts to substituting equation 6 into equation 5, differentiating the expression with respect to state income, setting that derivative equal to zero, and solving to find b_1, the coefficient that tells how much a state's price should be raised as its income

17. This example has focused on capacity, but one could obviously construct a symmetric example for cost.

18. Martin S. Feldstein, "Wealth Neutrality and Local Choice in Public Education," *American Economic Review*, vol. 65 (March 1975), pp. 75–89.

increases. Doing all this yields a simple expression,

$$(7) \qquad b_1 = a_1/a_4.$$

The equalizing scheme thus gives more price aid to poorer states the higher the sensitivity of expenditure demand is to income (because this sensitivity would otherwise lead to large spending differentials), and the lower is the implied price sensitivity of demand (because more aid is necessary to get the state to spend more to offset its income deficiency). It is important to note that this scheme equalizes only expected expenditures on public services, not actual expenditures. In that sense, it is independent of the state's own fiscal policy, just as is the present CGC procedure.

The second approach follows the same logic but is adapted to the CGC tradition of giving only unconditional aid. It involves simply altering G_i to neutralize the income effect by replacing equation 3 with

$$(8) \qquad G_i = \overline{G} - b_2(Y_i - \overline{Y}),$$

so that states with higher income have lower unconditional grants. Solving in the same way as before yields

$$(9) \qquad b_2 = a_1/a_2.$$

A more general approach, in keeping with the CGC tradition of neutralizing all differences—income, resource income, prices, and specific-purpose grants—makes the expression for tax-sharing grants

$$(10) \qquad G_i = \overline{G} + \frac{a_1}{a_2}(\overline{Y} - Y_i) + (\overline{R} - R_i) + \frac{a_3}{a_2}(\overline{S} - S_i) + \frac{a_4}{a_2}(P_i - \overline{P}).$$

In either case (equation 9 or 10), if a state has a revenue need, as defined by $(\overline{Y} - Y_i)$, it should be reimbursed by a_1/a_2 of this need, as contrasted to t times the need (now granted by the CGC). In general, a_1/a_2 will be closer to unity than t, implying more aid to states with lower income. Indeed, in many cases a_1/a_2 will equal unity.[19] On the other hand, if a

19. The a_1/a_2 may not equal unity—that is, unconditional grants may be spent at a higher rate than income—because of what has come to be known as the "flypaper" effect (money sticks where it hits). For a discussion, see Edward M. Gramlich, "Intergovernmental Grants: A Review of the Empirical Literature," in Wallace E. Oates, ed., *The Political Economy of Fiscal Federalism* (Lexington, Mass.: D. C. Heath, 1977).

Table 4. *Tax-Sharing Grants Implied by Various Distribution*
Formulas, by State[a]
Dollars per capita

Item	New South Wales	Victoria	Queens- land	South Australia	Western Australia	Tasmania
1982 relativities	426.6	415.4	575.3	630.2	675.0	825.0
1982 CGC report[b]	431.9	424.3	649.6	594.9	580.4	674.2
1982 premiers' agreement	429.1	421.5	647.0	613.3	578.7	693.8
Power equalization						
Price only[c]	482.7	469.5	556.1	517.1	529.6	538.9
Income only[d]	475.1	455.9	581.8	525.1	543.4	556.8
Income and exogenous						
revenue[e]	496.7	435.1	634.7	511.5	445.5	536.5

Sources: Present relativities, specific-purpose grants, and population—Treasury Department, *Payments to or for the States, the Northern Territory, and Local Government Authorities, 1982–83*, Budget Paper 7 (Canberra: Australian Government Publishing Service, 1982), esp. table 6, p. 19; income—Russell Mathews, "Regional Disparities in Australia," table 1, p. 3; resources royalty—David Nellor, *Taxation of the Australian Resources Sector* (Clayton, Victoria: Monash University, Centre of Policy Studies, 1983), table 2.2, p. 2.4.

a. Assuming $500 per capita is to be distributed.
b. Commonwealth Grants Commission.
c. Based on $G - \bar{G} = 0.11\ (\bar{Y} - Y)$, where the coefficient of 0.11 comes from Blackburn's work (see note 20).
d. Based on $G - \bar{G} = 0.16\ (\bar{Y} - Y)$, where the coefficient of 0.16 also comes from Blackburn's work.
e. Based on $G - \bar{G} = 0.16\ (\bar{Y} - Y) + (\bar{R} - R) + 1.68\ (\bar{S} - S)$, where the 1.68 coefficient also comes from Blackburn.

state receives fewer exogenous royalty payments or specific-purpose grants, or pays higher prices for its public services, it should receive more G_i, again with a higher multiplier.

These formulas determine the extra payments made to a particular state: as with the present system, the basic entitlement can then be determined by taking the total amount of grant money made available by the central government, determining needs-related payments, and spreading the remaining funds among all people to determine the G^*.

Table 4 shows how all these approaches work in practice. All six rows show results for an overall distribution of $500 per capita, roughly the amount to be allocated in 1982 once specific-purpose grants for health are converted to general-purpose assistance. The first row shows the results of distributing these funds by the 1982 relativities, close to those initially agreed on in 1976. These relativities ranged from a low of 1.0 for Victoria to a high of 1.87 for Tasmania, and the results reflect that fact, giving almost twice as much per capita to Tasmania. The second row shows what the distribution would have been if the relativities proposed by the CGC had been in existence. The CGC relativities reduce the variance of the distribution somewhat: Victoria is still normalized at 1.0, but now Tasmania is cut to 1.59. Both Western Australia and South Australia have reduced shares under this scheme, and more money is left for Victoria. The third row gives the results of the political compromise established at the 1982 Premiers' Conference, to be phased in gradually by 1985. The numbers are fairly close to the CGC recommendations, though the gap between those recommendations and the preexisting relativities is not closed entirely.

The last three rows give some illustrative calculations that show how my suggested equalization approaches work. The fourth row is based on the price version of equalization described in equation 6. To present numbers comparable to the rest of the table, I show only how much money would go to various states to offset the impact of income on spending for public services: as described by equation 6, the effect on the price itself would be inversely related to the sensitivity of expenditures to price, a_4. The fifth row is based on equation 8, in which unconditional grants adjust only for the income differentials. There is a slightly wider range between the high- and low-income states in this row than in the fourth row because unconditional grants have a smaller effect per dollar on spending for public services, and hence more money is necessary to bring the spending of low-income states up to the average.[20] Were the impact of unconditional grants on spending even lower, on the order of that for income, this disparity would become wider still. The bottom row of the table makes allowance for exogenous sources of funds such as specific-purpose grants and minerals royalties, as described by equation 10. Although some observers believe that such an adjustment would help Victoria, the state with the highest income, and hurt Queensland, with the lowest income but the home of large deposits of resources, the ironic result is that funds go the other way because Victoria receives

20. The coefficients used in the calculations are based on pooled state budget data, given in V. C. Blackburn, "The Effect of Commonwealth Payments on the Financial Position of State Governments in Australia," presented at the Fiftieth Conference of the Australia and New Zealand Association for the Advancement of Science, Adelaide, May 12–16, 1980, appendix 2, p. 42. They are $a_1 = 0.11$, $a_2 = 0.68$, and $a_3 = 1.14$. According to these coefficients, there is a significant "flypaper effect." A similar set of coefficients, based on estimation of tax functions, is given by P. Bernd Spahn, "Federal Grant Policy and State-Local Taxation," in Russell Mathews, ed., *State and Local Taxation* (Canberra: Australian National University Press for the Centre for Research on Federal Financial Relations, 1977), table 7-3.

specific-purpose grants that are above average and Queensland, grants that are well below average.[21]

The criticisms raised in this section about present CGC procedures thus involve each of the terms of the basic CGC equation 3. One proposed improvement is to have the central government remove itself, partially or completely, from the revenue-raising business by allowing each state to raise more of its basic entitlement, G^*, on its own. Another is to weigh efficiency against equality in determining the public service cost-adjustment terms, E_i. A third is to alter the capacity-adjustment terms, T_i, to make expected expenditures on public services independent of state income; so if the authorities decide the optimal equalization scheme should be partial, it should at least be described as that.

The Loan Council

The second fifty-year-old unique institution in the Australian grant system is the Australian Loan Council (ALC). As stated above, this was started in 1928 to regulate the borrowing of state and local governments. But despite this rationale, it is probably true that any agency established to deal with a problem that happened once fifty years ago had better be reexamined. The ALC is essentially a credit-rationing scheme operated by the central government on one set of borrowers who happen to be in the public sector, leaving alone all other borrowers who happen to be in the private sector. The usual argument against such a scheme would be that capital markets are efficient, and that rationing by price incentives (that is, high interest rates) is effective not only in limiting the overall amount of debt floated, but in channeling them to those borrowers most willing to pay. Formal, government-imposed credit rationing schemes such as the ALC would have no role in such a view of the world. Are there any redeeming features of the ALC?

21. I argued above that public-service price differentials could be ignored in these calculations and followed that convention here. A question remains about private-goods price differentials. Should they be used to deflate money incomes? One argument might be to use them and do all adjustments in real terms. Another might be to adopt the same view as for public-service prices, to discourage households from moving to areas having high transportation and distribution costs, and hence to ignore private-goods prices. If I were a member of the CGC, I would probably vote for splitting the difference. As an author, I was not able to find such numbers by state, so I ignored the problem and simply used money values everywhere.

Three years ago the Campbell Committee of Inquiry investigated this matter and gave a mixed verdict. They recommended that semigovernments—those public authorities engaged in commercial operations such as for transport, harbors, rail, and electricity and brought under the ALC by a gentlemen's agreement—be released from it and allowed to borrow on their own. As a response to this recommendation, in 1982 state electric power authorities were given such freedom for a three-year trial period, and in 1983 the ALC relaxed its constraints on other semigovernmental borrowing. For state and local general governments that would still come under the ALC, the Campbell Committee recommended that the so-called 30–20 rule be eliminated. It required certain financial institutions to hold 30 percent of their assets in public securities, of which 20 percent had to be commonwealth securities. This change has not yet been implemented, though the growth in so-called noncaptive holdings of government securities has been so rapid since that time that such a change would probably have little effect on the pattern of interest rates today.[22] But the Campbell Committee still called for continuation of the ALC, mainly because it believed that without the ALC there would be no discipline on the borrowing of state general governments.[23] The most commonly heard justification is that politicians (in state governments) have short horizons and cannot be relied upon to worry about overborrowing when they themselves will not be in office when the interest is due. A subsidiary rationale is that foreign borrowing must be controlled by the commonwealth.

One could certainly question control of foreign borrowing and arguments on its behalf. Free capital markets for subnational securities do seem to work well in other countries, such as the United States. And although a large share of state and local funds comes from grants, the size of the state need not imply less discipline: *at the margin* states do have to finance their expenditures and borrowing by raising taxes. Their central government grants are fixed in amount, and cannot be boosted to cover unwise capital investments. The profligate state must raise taxes. The incentive for sound capital investments is therefore stronger than might at first be apparent. And this is doubly true if states borrow

22. The data for this statement were supplied by Donald Stammer of Bain & Co., Sydney.

23. See Australian Financial System Inquiry, *Final Report of the Committee of Inquiry* (Canberra: AGPS, 1980), chaps. 10, 12, and the recommendations there.

from abroad. If states do not hedge against exchange rate risk (the risk they will have to repay in appreciated currency if the Australian dollar depreciates), they will have to pay for this gamble.

A related matter that receives remarkably little attention in these debates (not even mentioned by the Campbell Committee) is that since 1975 the commonwealth has given capital grants equal to one-third of the total amount borrowed on behalf of state general governments. Hence if a state requested a $100 million capital program and the request was approved, the ALC would borrow $100 million for the state and the state would actually repay only $66 million to the ALC. Not only is the borrowing done at subsidized interest rates because the central government guarantees repayment of the bond, but the state also receives $34 million free and clear, with no interest or repayment obligations. It is no wonder that state general government borrowers have to be rationed through nonprice methods. If the goal is to convince states to pay attention to the market, a first step might be to eliminate these large subsidies for capital borrowing.

One final point, also not stressed by the Campbell Committee, seems to grow more important every day. The more stringent are the ALC restrictions on governmental borrowing, the more do states contrive creative financing schemes to circumvent the ALC. Queensland has always led in this area. One of its favorite schemes involves "security deposits." When a rail or other capital facility is to be built to transport resources to port, Queensland may force the company to make a loan of the construction costs, called a security deposit, to the state. The state then builds the facility and nominally repays the principal and interest out of freight rates. Mining companies allege that Queensland in fact raises its rates to provide revenue to repay the company's loan. The result of all this paper shuffling is not a reduction in borrowing at home or offshore—private companies have to do that to provide their security deposit—but a form of hidden taxation of resources companies; these companies must provide capital to build a railroad but do not own it or receive a return on it.

An even more creative scheme was devised by New South Wales. Called "leverage leasing," it is a first cousin to the recently limited safe-harbor leasing in the United States. When a public facility is to be built, a private company is formed to build and own it. Since this company is private, it can claim depreciation allowances and the investment allowance on the new construction expenses. It then leases the facilities to the government, which charges rates in the usual way. Again the ALC has been circumvented—the private company had to borrow internally or externally to build the facility, and total borrowings are unaffected. But this time a tax loophole is created; it costs the federal treasury in company tax reductions that would not have been made had the facility been built by public borrowing. Again there is no reduction in total borrowing, but some new tax loopholes are created by the government's attempt to regulate borrowing.[24]

When these kinds of factors are added, the normative case for the ALC seems weak and becoming weaker. The recent relaxation of the gentlemen's agreement seems a step in the right direction, and this agreement could be abolished altogether. And to put it in even more radical terms, while the ALC itself cannot be abolished without a constitutional amendment, the treasurer could, on his own, begin providing more routine approvals for state general government borrowing—and at the same time eliminate the large subsidy so that states themselves would be more concerned about borrowing costs and would ration themselves.

Specific-Purpose Grants

The other leg of the Australian grant triad is the set of specific-purpose grants. While there are many of these specific-purpose grants, the largest sums are concentrated in primary and secondary education, higher and technical education, housing, roads, and, until recently, health. These grants, like categorical grants in other federal countries, are characterized by tight categorical requirements on how the money is spent. Except in the case of health, specific-purpose grants have always been limited in amount by the central government.

Both in the United States and in Australia the main problem with categorical grants is that they are not set up so as to lead to efficient spending outcomes. In the United States federal matching shares are quite high—the federal government pays about 80 percent of the cost of a project on a typical grant, much more than the share of marginal

---

24. Tax authorities eventually disallowed the tax advantages on the leased equipment, but this still does not stop circumvention of the ALC.

benefits likely to be realized by citizens in other states. Thus states find these grants advantageous, tend to subscribe very heavily to them, and even establish offices in Washington to seek out and lobby for more grants. The federal government then must limit the size of the grants administratively, usually to an amount that is small relative to what the states would otherwise have spent in the relevant program area. It becomes easy for states to claim that the expenditures they would have incurred in the case were under the supposedly categorical grant and then divert the grant money to their own purposes. This phenomenon, known as grant displacement, explains why most U.S. federal categorical grants result in state-local tax reduction, and why the efforts of Presidents Nixon and Reagan to convert the grants to general-purpose assistance have probably resulted in little real change in state-local spending.[25]

In Australia, circumstances are much the same. Australian federal matching ratios are even higher than they are in the United States, 100 percent for most specific-purpose grants, and the incentives for states to overspend are that much greater. Again, the central government is forced to limit spending administratively, though this time to amounts that seem to be larger relative to the normal expenditures of state governments. Observed grant displacement is thus less, at least as perceived by two authors who have studied the problem, V. C. Blackburn and Bernd Spahn. Their results indicate a lack of displacement for specific-purpose grants. A dollar of these grants raises state spending by more than a dollar and hence raises state taxes a small amount, while a dollar of general-purpose assistance raises state spending less than a dollar and lowers state taxes.[26]

But although the observed level of displacement is smaller in Australia, that changes only the symptoms of the problem, not the problem itself. In Australia, as in the United States, the central difficulty with specific-purpose grants is that the matching shares of the central government are too high, so that states have no incentive to limit their use of the grants

    25. See Edward M. Gramlich, "An Econometric Examination of the New Federalism," *Brookings Papers on Economic Activity,* 2:1982, pp. 327–70.
    26. The relevant numbers for Blackburn were given above in note 20. He finds that $1.00 of specific-purpose grants raises spending by $1.14 and (implicitly) raises taxes by $0.14, while $1.00 of general-purpose aid raises spending by $0.68 and (implicitly) lowers taxes by $0.32. Spahn finds that $1.00 of specific-purpose grants raises taxes by $0.36 and (implicitly) spending by $1.36, while $1.00 of general-purpose aid lowers taxes by $0.12 and (implicitly) raises spending by $0.88.

and overspend unless arbitrary limitations are imposed by the central government. The obvious solution to the problem is for the central government to lower its own matching shares until the marginal external-internal cost ratio corresponds to the marginal external-internal benefit ratio—hence taking the pressure off administrative mechanisms to ration expenditures. If this is not done, the block-grant approach followed in the United States may still be preferred to making no changes at all, but it is definitely a second-best reform if specific-purpose grants are being used in project areas in which there are some out-of-state benefits.

While the Australians have not adopted the block-grant solution on anything approaching the scale used in the United States, they have followed the model in one crucial program area—health. In this case the reform does appear likely to succeed, for reasons that are somewhat idiosyncratic but nevertheless instructive.

By the early 1970s Australia had developed a system whereby state governments ran inexpensive public hospitals (free, without any means test, in Queensland), and the central government made a small payment to the hospitals based on numbers of patients. During the Whitlam administration this policy was changed to require Australian states to provide free care regardless of means in the standard care wards of their public hospitals, with the central and state governments each paying half of the expenses. In the jargon of grants, this amounted to a categorical open-ended grant with a central government matching share of 50 percent. The free hospital care led to a rapid escalation in costs, which caused central government outlays for specific-purpose health grants to triple as a share of GDP (0.4 percent to 1.3 percent) in just one year.[27] This also led to another commission of inquiry, the Jamison Committee, to find ways of improving the efficiency of the system.

The Jamison Committee recommendations, most of which were adopted by the Fraser government, were to put a cap on the specific-

27. Similarly, it might be imagined that health expenses would have been higher in Queensland, where public hospitals have been free since World War II, than in other states. This is clearly not the case. Queensland has the lowest per capita expenditures on this budget item by a large amount, as is shown in table 2. Moroever, nobody has yet produced any quantitative evidence that service levels of public hospitals in Queensland are substandard, or even below those in other states. Since Queensland hospitals have always been free, that state has learned how to manage hospitals more cheaply by centralizing control, putting doctors on salaries, and reimbursing hospitals by group session hours and not by the number of visits.

purpose grant and to convert it to a general-purpose grant. The aggregate amount of the grant would eventually be indexed for cost changes in some way, and its distribution would be determined in a manner like that used by the CGC.[28] But while their funds would be set in this manner, states themselves would continue to operate their public hospitals. Under the subsequently passed States (Tax Sharing and Health Grants) Act of 1981, states were not required to spend their health grants on hospitals—these were general-purpose grants—but they had to make free health care available to low-income groups, pensioners, and others in special need. Implicitly states were free to devise fee schedules for others.[29]

Soon after the Jamison Committee made its recommendations, as a result of an election, Fraser was out of office and Labor party prime minister Robert Hawke was in. One of the important election campaign platforms of the Labor party was to return to the 1975 scheme of free health care in the public hospitals, this time to be financed by an income tax surcharge of 1 percent. Such a change is now being planned and is slated to be made in early 1984. There is an important difference, however, between the Whitlam health grant and the plan presently envisaged by the new Labor government. As under the Fraser administration the health grant will still be capped, but it will be larger by an amount equal to the 1 percent income tax surcharge. States will still be responsible for their public hospitals and now will be free to control everything but the fee schedule. Hence states will still have an incentive to manage their hospitals cheaply—they still save $1 if they can cut costs by $1.

28. See Commission of Inquiry into the Efficiency and Administration of Hospitals, *Report of the Commission of Inquiry into the Efficiency and Administration of Hospitals*, vol. 1 (Canberra: AGPS, 1981).

29. A much more detailed examination of these issues is given in a joint paper by the Commonwealth Treasury and Health Departments, "Hospital Funding Arrangements: A Historical Perspective," paper presented at the Research Advisory Committee Seminar of the Centre for Research on Federal Financial Relations (Canberra: Australian National University, May 19, 1983). See also the discussion in George Palmer, "Commonwealth/State Fiscal Relationships and the Financing and Provision of Health Services," in P. M. Tatchell, ed., *Economics and Health, 1981*, Proceedings of the Third Conference of Australian Health Economists (Canberra: Australian National University, 1982).

Table 5. *Tax Revenues for Governmental Units, 1981–82*
Millions of dollars

Item	Common- wealth	States	Localities	Total
Individual income tax	21,224	. . .	. . .	21,224
Company income tax	5,215	. . .	. . .	5,215
Excise duties[a]	6,090	. . .	. . .	6,090
Sales tax	2,854	. . .	. . .	2,854
Customs duties	2,060	. . .	. . .	2,060
Payroll tax	16	2,398	. . .	2,414
Stamp duties	11	1,350	. . .	1,360
Motor taxes	10	1,009	. . .	1,020
Property taxes	21	370	1,718	2,109
Other	491	1,976	88	2,555
Total	37,992	7,103	1,806	46,901

Source: Russell Mathews, "Federal-State Fiscal Relations in Australia," paper presented to Workshop on Australia's Federal System, Resource Development and Resource Trade (Canberra: Australia-Japan Research Centre and the Australian National University, November 1983), table 1, p. 9.
a. Includes natural gas and crude oil levy and coal export duty.

Taxation Responsibilities

The other important aspect of Australia's fiscal federalism system is the sharing of tax responsibilities. The broad detail on how taxing responsibilities are shared is given in table 5. Commonwealth taxes amounted to four-fifths of total taxes in 1981–82. The Constitution, along with subsequent High Court interpretations, gave the central government exclusive right to impose customs, excise, and sales duties. The Uniform Tax Scheme of the World War II years gave the central government control over both the individual and company income tax. Partly because of this revenue imbalance, states were given exclusive access to the payroll tax (on employers only) in the early 1970s. In addition, states impose various types of stamp duties and other miscellaneous taxes. Just as in the United States, local Australian governments have one main tax, the property tax.

In this section, I discuss three tax-policy questions with strong federalism overtones. I first discuss a problem that has arisen in connection with the individual income tax, the largest and most important tax in Australia. This problem turns out to be related to the lack of death duties in Australia, so I then do an autopsy on the death of these death duties. Finally, I examine some options for taxing Australia's significant earnings from natural resources.

Individual Income Taxes

For many years now the individual income tax has been Australia's primary means of raising revenue. One virtue usually attributed to the income tax is that it has desirable consequences both for horizontal equity—taxpayers with the same incomes are treated equally—and for vertical equity—since the progressivity of the schedule can be varied, any amount of income redistribution can in principle be accomplished. The individual income tax is also acknowledged to distort people's choices between work and leisure and between consumption and saving, but this distortion is not obviously larger than the distortion implicit in other taxes.

None of this is inappropriate for Australia, but there is a cancer that is greatly eroding support for the income tax, or at least support for further increases in the income tax. The problem is that Australia's income tax is one with fairly high marginal rates—now 30 percent of income up to a level just above the median income, then 46 percent, then 60 percent. In addition to this there is a state payroll tax, paid by the employer at a rate of 5 percent in most states. But there are almost no other supporting taxes. There is no capital gains tax for assets held more than a year. There is no death duty. There is no broad-based retail sales tax. That means that a very strong economic incentive is created for avoiding or evading the income tax. If one can convert income from relatively completely taxed wage and salary income to capital gains income, one can save up to $0.60 on each $1.00 ($0.65 with the payroll tax included). In the United States, no model for an ideal system, the differential is less than half that.[30]

How important are tax avoidance and evasion? The figures available are sparse for avoidance (legal activities) and even sparser for evasion (illegal underreporting). There are some data, however, and several

---

30. A taxpayer in the highest marginal income tax bracket in the United States pays $0.50 out of each dollar; the same taxpayer pays $0.20 in capital gains tax. From the remaining $0.30 of the dollar, another few cents are lost to the retail sales tax.

Australian economists have come up with numbers suggesting that a striking share of the tax base is lost through simple tax evasion, either illegal underreporting of income or overreporting of deductions.

Using time-series data, Russell Mathews gives figures indicating that between 1965 and 1979 the share of tax revenues resulting from wage and salary income has risen steadily, from 67 percent to 81 percent. Had this share not changed at all, income tax revenues would have been $2.7 billion, or 21 percent higher.[31] Such a calculation could be biased high or low. On the one hand, it may be an underestimate of the amount of evasion because it assumes there was no evasion in 1965. On the other hand, it could be an overestimate because it attributes all change in the distribution of tax revenues to the tax law, and there could be a number of alternative explanations.

But the results obtained by Mathews are supported by two different calculations of Neville Norman. Norman first modifies a procedure that has been used to estimate the size of the underground economy in the United States—analyzing changes in the currency-deposits ratio, which in Norman's case is corrected for changes in that ratio due to inflation. The currency-deposit ratio has risen from 27 percent to 43 percent in Australia since 1965. On the basis of his econometric analysis Norman estimates that 10 percentage points of this increase are due to inflation, leaving 6 percentage points to be explained by the shift toward nonreportable income activities. Applying the same money velocity for the nonreported sector as for the reported sector, Norman then gets an estimate of lost income tax revenues of $3.5 billion in 1981, 21 percent of revenues, exactly the same share that Mathews found for an earlier year.[32]

Norman also has one other method, which makes inferences on the basis of the commissioner of taxation's "honors list"—a sample of returns of apprehended evaders. Using this sample, Norman found that detected evaders did not report about half of their income in 1973–74. Extrapolating this forward and assuming on the basis of other calculations that 7 percent of potential taxpayers were evaders, Norman finds

31. Russell Mathews, "The Structure of Taxation" (Canberra: Australian National University, Centre for Research on Federal Financial Relations, 1980), table 4.

32. See Neville R. Norman, "The Economics of Tax Evasion," paper presented at the Eleventh Conference of Economists (Bedford Park, South Australia: Flinders University, August 1982).

Edward M. Gramlich

a 1978–79 income tax loss of $2.7 billion, again just Mathews's 21 percent share.

Each of these methods has its weaknesses, but the fact that all three suggest one-fifth of potential income tax revenues is being lost through simple tax evasion is surely meaningful. And one-fifth is a large share indeed. If the true amount of tax revenue lost through simple evasion is anything like this, many of the claims usually made on behalf of the income tax have a very hollow ring. Because Norman also found evasion to be concentrated at the top of the income scale, the tax is promoting less vertical equity than might be imagined. Because many evaders are not apprehended, the tax is not conferring horizontal equity. And because resources are devoted both to evasion and to entirely legal avoidance schemes, the tax also seems to be generating substantial economic inefficiencies.

There might then be some sense in altering the overall mix of Australian taxes to place less reliance on the income tax (implying lower marginal rates for those who pay), and more reliance on other taxes (implying higher tax rates for those who evade). Recently at least four economists, two from the right and two from the left, have so argued in Australia.[33]

It may seem that evasion of the federal income tax would have little to do with fiscal federalism. Nothing could be further from the truth. Because states are excluded by a constitutional interpretation from imposing broadly based retail sales taxes, they can raise more revenue only through a surcharge to the income tax, a higher payroll tax, or various narrowly based, nonneutral taxes such as stamp duties, financial assets charges, or taxes and charges on the resource industry. Given the taxing situation, all options are likely to generate economic inefficiencies.[34] The obvious solution is either to change the constitutional interpretation or otherwise empower states to use a retail sales tax.

33. The two convervative authors are Geoffrey Brennan, "Tax Reform Australian Style" (Canberra: Australian National University, 1980); and Peter L. Swan, "Reforming the System: An Economist's View," address given to the Economic Society of Australia, Sydney, March 4, 1983. The two liberal authors are Russell Mathews, "The Case for Indirect Taxation," Endowed Lecture in Taxation Law and Policy, Taxation Institute of Australia, May 5, 1983; and Peter D. Groenewegen, "Rationalizing Australian Taxation Revisited," Shann Memorial Lecture (Nedlands, Western Australia: University of Western Australia, 1983).

34. Given the high rates of income tax, one might at least imagine that states would make use of their freedom to lower these rates and recover the revenue in other ways.

The "Death" of Death Duties

While the main problem today in the Australian federalism arrangements seems to be the states' lack of access to desirable sources of revenue on equity or efficiency grounds, there is one potential counterexample. Formerly the states imposed death duties; in 1977–78 the states raised $240 million from this source, about 5 percent of their revenue. But then states began lowering their death duties until finally, in 1982, the last one was abolished. Why?

An important lesson of local public finance is that income redistribution cannot be done at the subnational level. If one state imposes higher death duties than another without correspondingly augmenting public services, the high-income elderly tend to migrate to the low-tax state, thereby reducing revenues in the high-tax state and effectively forcing it to lower its death duties. Although migration between subnational districts is normally desirable for efficiency, it can frustrate attempts of subnational governments to redistribute income. Hence most income redistribution needs to be done at the national level.[35] For this reason, of all the taxes that the Australian central government could have left to states, the death duty was precisely the wrong one.

The lesson was borne out quite predictably. Most Australian states in the late 1970s had rather imperfect systems of death duties that were potentially evadable by the very wealthy with clever lawyers. These states imposed fairly stiff taxes on small estates and featured long waiting periods and unexpected fluctuations in real tax levels as asset values fluctuated. An early salvo in the campaign against death duties was fired in 1970, when Sydney Negus was elected senator from Western Australia as one of the first single-issue candidates. He ran on a shoestring and had one campaign platform, to try to abolish death duties.

State treasury officials gave two political reasons why they would not seriously entertain such a measure. One is that states would be worried that the CGC would think they had enough money. Another is that states would be prevented from advertising the income tax as that tax paid to Canberra (as they do now). As soon as states cut rates once, it would become apparent to voters that they could do so again, and they could no longer insulate themselves from criticism of the income tax.

35. A colleague, Deborah Laren, and I have tried to show the truth of this lesson for some policies operating on the other side of income and age distribution (for U.S. public assistance policies) on the other side of the globe in "Migration and Income Redistribution Responsibility," *Journal of Human Resources* (forthcoming, Fall 1984).

The election of Negus resulted in no legislation, but soon afterward the premier of Queensland (ever the maverick in the Australian federation), Joh. Bjelke-Peterson, picked up the issue. At the time, high capital gains on family farms were causing both farmers and other small entrepreneurs to fear the loss of family holdings to death duties. Rather than index brackets for inflation or make other incremental changes, as his own treasurer urged, Bjelke-Peterson pushed ahead and by 1977 had totally abolished Queensland's death duties. Parts of Queensland have some of the nicer beaches and climate in Australia, and either for this reason, the lack of death duties, or some combination, the elderly began to flood from the other states to Queensland. A study of Australian migration patterns by Graeme Hugo shows that between 1976 and 1981 Queensland was the only Australian state to have a net gain of persons over fifty years old as a result of internal migration, with a large share of those migrants coming from New South Wales and Victoria.[36]

At that point the other states began tripping over one another to follow Queensland's lead and abolish their own death duties. The game of "follow the leader" is shown in table 6, which shows death tax rates from 1976, when Queensland made its move, to 1983, when Victoria's duty was finally phased out. Since the central government also lowered its own smaller death duties over this time (for reasons not explained by my story), Australia now stands without any death duties. Untaxed long-term capital gains and estates and the possibility for nonwage earners to avoid the income tax poke a large hole in the achievement of the equality objective that many Australians hold so dear. As the tax system stands now, those beginning life with wealth can accumulate even more by capital gains and pass it through to the next generation without ever being taxed. But those who start without much wealth and work in wage or salaried jobs may never get ahead because of the high marginal income tax rates. For these groups, it is not such a "fair go."[37]

36. Graeme Hugo, "Interstate Migration in Australia, 1976–81," *Australian Bulletin of Labour*, vol. 9 (March 1983), pp. 102–30.

37. So, at least, was the argument given by several different tax commissions analyzing the Australian system in the mid-1970s. See, for example, Australian Treasury Taxation Paper, *Estate and Gift Duty, Purposes and Rationale 14*, December 1974; or Taxation Review Committee, *Full Report of the Taxation Review Committee*, January 31, 1975 (Canberra: AGPS, 1976).

In a paper written about that time, Geoffrey Brennan argues a contrary case. See H. G. Brennan, "On the Incidence of Estate and Gift Duties: A Theoretical Analysis,"

Table 6. *State Estate Tax Rates, 1976–83*[a]
Percent

Type of inheritance and state	1976	1977	1978	1979	1980	1981	1982	1983
Estate passing to spouse								
New South Wales	27.0	...	...	...	...	...	...	...
Victoria	26.0	...	...	...	...	...	...	...
Queensland	20.0	...	...	...	...	...	...	...
South Australia	27.5	...	...	...	...	...	...	...
Western Australia	25.0	25.0	...	...	...	...	...	...
Tasmania	26.0	26.0	...	...	...	...	...	...
Estate passing to child								
New South Wales	27.0	27.0	27.0	27.0	27.0	27.0	...	...
Victoria	26.0	26.0	26.5	26.5	26.5	34.0	22.0	...
Queensland	20.0	...	...	...	...	...	...	...
South Australia	27.5	27.5	27.5	27.5	...	...	...	...
Western Australia	25.0	25.0	25.0	12.5	...	...	...	...
Tasmania	26.0	26.0	26.5	26.5	26.5	26.5	...	...

Source: Commonwealth Grants Commission, *Report on State Tax Entitlements* (Canberra: AGPS), appendixes, 1977–82.

a. Data for years shown are for June. For June 1976, June 1977, and June 1978 a child is defined as under age twenty-one. Beginning in June 1979 no age distinction is given.

Two interpretations are possible. One was given above: an attempt to devolve redistribution responsibilities to the subnational level was totally frustrated by migration or the anticipation of it. But an alternative explanation holds that the prevailing death duty was simply unpopular: Senator Negus and Premier Bjelke-Peterson showed how unpopular. The speed of events and the coarseness of migration data probably preclude finding the true explanation. But one tax that states apparently cannot use is the death duty.

As a postscript on this matter, a recent development does give signs of mitigating the imbalance in the way income from labor and capital are taxed, at least for those with a long-run view of things. Henry J. Aaron's

---

in R.L. Mathews, ed., *State and Local Taxation* (Canberra: Australian National University Press, 1977). He makes the point that if the income of the donor was subject to income tax, estate taxes could be viewed as a form of double taxation, with concomitant inefficiencies. While Brennan's model seems convincing as far as it goes, there are two practical problems with the argument: to the extent that estates are accumulated by long-term capital gains, they would not have previously been subject to any tax at all; and efficiency is not everything. One of the goals of estate taxation is to even out disparities in economic opportunities across generations. Hence even a double tax may at times be appropriate.

chapter in this book describes the Hawke government's recent law to raise taxes on superannuation payments — private lump-sum pension benefits — to rates of 15 percent on the first $50,000 and 30 percent thereafter for all accumulations, beginning in 1984. Revenues from this tax will obviously grow quite slowly. But it should gradually close a major loophole in the income tax law by, in effect, giving taxpayers the option of choosing expenditure tax treatment. If workers want to save in the form of private pensions (currently their contributions to super-annuation are limited, but the employers' contributions are not), they will be taxed henceforth at 30 percent on their accumulations, or at their marginal income tax rates if they convert their lump sums to annuities. The 30 percent tax treatment resembles a flat rate expenditure tax applied also to bequests; the marginal rate treatment, a progressive income tax. In either case, the lack of a death duty is made irrelevant and a major gap in the present revenue system of Australia is closed.[38] But this neat device for closing the loophole still does not solve the revenue problems of the states.

Resources Rent Taxes

One important actual and potential source of revenue for the states is that derived from exploitation of natural resources. All six states have some mineral resources and gain revenue from them. The second row of table 7 indicates that in 1978–79, the latest year for which complete data are available, the states raised between $3 and $43 per capita through various charges and bidding fees paid by the mineral resources industry, amounting to between 2 and 20 percent of their total revenues. The central government taxes exploration of mineral resources too and thus raises $137 per capita, 9 percent of its revenues, through schemes for leasing offshore oil drilling rights, company taxes on resource developers, a coal export duty, and a natural gas and crude oil levy. Moreover, the Hawke government is now considering proposals for replacing the natural gas and oil levy with what is known as a resources rent tax on the petroleum sector.

The question of the proper taxation of rents from natural resources raises many issues—defining rents and proper deductible expenses, determining discount rates, international harmonization of taxation of

38. This point was called to my attention by John F. Helliwell.

Table 7. *Resources Taxes and Royalties, by State, 1978–79*
Dollars per capita

Item	Commonwealth duty[a]	State royalty	Total
Weighted average, all states	137.1	16.8	153.9
New South Wales	137.1	6.7	143.8
Victoria	137.1	22.1	159.2
Queensland	137.1	24.9	162.0
South Australia	137.1	3.2	140.3
Western Australia	137.1	43.0	180.1
Tasmania	137.1	5.1	142.2
Addenda			
Weighted standard deviation	. . .	11.7	11.7
Coefficient of variation	. . .	0.697	0.076

Sources: Nellor, *Taxation of the Australian Resource Sector*, tables 2.2 and 2.3; pp. 2.4 and 2.8 (inflated to 1978–79 prices by using an inflator of 1.487); and Treasury Department, *Payments to and for the States, the Northern Territory, and Local Government Authorities, 1982–83*, table 6, p. 19.
a. Includes company taxes (34 percent), natural gas and crude oil levy (60 percent), coal export duty (5 percent), and a small amount of royalties.

multinational resources companies—and I make no pretense of giving this complex subject a careful treatment. Some of these topics are considered in the chapter by John F. Helliwell. But in the Australian context, the resources tax is complicated by two factors: there are a lot more earnings from resources to tax than there are in most countries; and the federal-state tax issue is unusually complex.

Even the discussions that do try to come to grips with the optimal tax treatment of resources rents typically assume the existence of one government, something that must strike practical persons in Australia as akin to the economist's "can opener" assumption. In fact, there are two governments that impose a tax, the state and the commonwealth, and makers of resources tax policy must worry about how the two fit together, a matter infrequently addressed by Australian economists.

The reason both governments can impose taxes is a provision in the Australian Constitution of 1901 that gives states title to mineral rights located within their borders—the state in effect becomes the landowner. To a limited degree the commonwealth is a landowner too—it holds title to resources in the mineral-rich Northern Territory and offshore oil properties, but most of the commonwealth revenue derives from its power to assess company income taxes, export duties, and other special imports. As long as this fundamental aspect of property rights in Australia is not changed and there are income taxes, there will be two governments that tax.[39]

Dual taxing authorities create two types of inefficiencies. First, both domestic and international resource companies must incur the numerous practical problems of dealing with the disparate taxing procedures of seven governments instead of one. Second, the state and federal governments compete for these apparently rich sources of revenue. Cassing and Hillman have developed one realistic example to illustrate what can happen. They assume that the commonwealth wants to maximize revenue from a coal export duty, the optimal rate of which depends negatively on the rail freight that Queensland charges coal producers to transport coal to port. The state of Queensland (always Queensland!), the home of this coal deposit, finds that its monopolistic price for these rail services depends negatively on the federal duty. As long as the two governments do not cooperate, the state and federal governments will compete for tax revenues, and this competition increases deadweight inefficiencies, drives down total output, and reduces joint federal-state revenues.[40] Vertical tax competition yields many similar inefficiencies.

If a mine or a well could be made operational with no uncertainty, it would be possible to design efficient schemes of taxation—schemes that tax away some revenue without interfering with the pattern of development. But there is a great deal of uncertainty in the resources sector—about the geological information, about world prices once the resources are produced, and about production costs—and any taxation scheme for resources (unless it confers full tax credits for losses, which are not even feasible if drillers go broke and leave the industry) will then lower the net expected return from a venture and provide some disincentive to exploration and development. Although Australia's interest is generally in maximal exploration and development (the reasons, and caveats, are given in the chapters by John F. Helliwell and by Rudiger Dornbusch and Stanley Fischer), one could not argue seriously that the earnings from these resources should go untaxed. If other forms of income are

39. Indeed, there is also a third. Local governments also assess taxes and charges on minerals companies, but to keep the discussion manageable, I consider those charges as user fees and do not include them.

40. J. H. Cassing and A. L. Hillman, "State-Federal Resource Tax Rivalry: The Queensland Railway and the Federal Export Tax," *The Economic Record*, vol. 58 (September 1982), pp. 235–41.

taxed, presumably earnings from resources should be too. The important question is how these earnings can be taxed with the least inefficiency.

If there were just one government imposing a tax and certain strong assumptions held, the most efficient tax would be none at all on earnings from production. Firms should bid for rights to explore property, and in the competitive limit they will bid away all their expected profits.[41] But such a scheme may not be practical in Australia for two reasons. First, a bidding scheme implies releasing mineral resources firms from the company tax—something that is again likely to be politically infeasible and certainly will cause difficult problems of transfer pricing for firms that are engaged in mining and other industries. Second, a complete royalty bidding scheme may not raise much revenue in Australia because the mining companies do not appear to trust the states. Repeatedly the representatives of mining companies point to the fate of minerals properties that proved more lucrative than expected: rather than let the firms keep the winnings from their gamble, the states boosted rail charges or imposed some other tax, hidden or not.[42] As long as firms expect this behavior to be possible, and governments cannot commit themselves to forswear it, firms will underbid on the competitive auctions and revenues from resources will not be maximized.

Another possibility, called a Leland tax in Australia, is a two-part tariff. One part, the bid tax, should be independent of the profits of mining firms. The other part, the profits tax, should be a function of the present discounted value of expected profits from minerals.[43] As before, the royalty bid is to compensate the landowners for their property. But, as returns are earned, the government also receives a share of these

41. This point is argued by Ted Bergstrom, "Property Rights and Taxation in the Australian Minerals Sector," in L. Cook and M. G. Porter, eds., *The Minerals Sector and the Australian Economy* (Sydney: George Allen & Unwin, 1984).

42. This point was made most forcefully by John MacLeod of CRA Ltd., an Australian mining firm. Bergstrom recognizes and discusses it. See ibid.

43. The scheme takes its name from H. Leland, "Optimal Risk Sharing and Leasing of Natural Resources, with Application to Oil and Gas Leasing in the OCS," *Quarterly Journal of Economics*, vol. 92 (August 1978), pp. 413–38. It is also described in detail by Craig Emerson and Peter Lloyd, "Improving Mineral Taxation Policy in Australia," Discussion Paper 36 (Canberra: Australian National University, Centre for Economic Policy Research, October 1981); and by Peter L. Swan, "A Review of the Northern Territory Government's Green Paper on Mining Royalty Policy for the Northern Territory," Discussion Paper 39 (Canberra: Australian National University, Centre for Economic Policy Research, December 1981).

earnings from the profits tax. Although the Leland scheme formally taxes the present discounted value of present and future minerals profits, in the real world a tax system that cannot tax future values can come very close just by taxing profits as properly defined.[44]

Australian taxes on minerals are imposed variously on volume, value, or profits, based on royalties at the state level and company duties and special duties at the commonwealth level; all are assessed at widely disparate rates.[45] Nobody would describe them as efficient or neutral. But it does not seem difficult to move from this hodge-podge system to an efficient set of taxes and straighten out the state-federal problem simultaneously. The strategy would be to allow states, the landowners, to assess royalties as lump-sum amounts, bid competitively. The federal government could then assess its present proportional company tax, allowing deduction of all royalties, expensing other capital and exploration costs, but *not* allowing the deduction of interest payments (because the proceeds of the loan for which interest is paid are not taxable). The company tax should allow full loss offsets—that is, potential tax credits—to maintain neutral treatment over time.[46] Applying the same marginal

44. This can be seen as follows. According to the Leland scheme, there is a tax on the present and future value of profits, V,

$$V = \sum_{j=0}^{L} v_j/(1 + r)^j,$$

where v_j represents annual profits in real terms, r is the real interest rate (or the nominal interest rate if v_j is expressed in money terms), and j designates the year until the resource is exhausted in year L. To simplify the algebra, set $L = 1$ and assume that profitability is expected to grow at rate g in this second year. If taxes are levied at the proportional rate, t, the present value of a Leland tax is $\hat{T} = tV$; the present value of all present and future company taxes, T, is

$$T = tv_0 + \frac{tv_0(1 + g)}{1 + r} = t\left[V_0 + \frac{V_0(1 + g)}{1 + r}\right] = tV = \hat{T}.$$

45. See, for example, two interesting tables that try to characterize the schemes in Emerson and Lloyd, "Improving Mineral Taxation," tables 2 and 3.

46. These ideas go back to the work of E. Cary Brown, "Business Income Taxation and Investment Incentives," in Lloyd A. Metzler and others, *Income, Employment, and Public Policy: Essays in Honor of Alvin H. Hansen* (Norton, 1948). Because any loan has a present market value of zero, the discounted tax liabilities on it should also be zero. This can be accomplished by adding the proceeds of the loan to taxable income and then later allowing the deduction of interest and principal payments from taxable income, or by not adding the proceeds of the loan and then not allowing for any interest or principal deductions. Both the Australian company tax and the U.S. corporate tax do not add loan proceeds but do allow for interest deductions, so they both can be said to subsidize debt finance at the expense of equity finance.

company tax rate of 46 percent imposed on other sectors would then attain neutral treatment among all sectors of Australian industry.[47] A more pragmatic reason for keeping the same marginal rate is to avoid the transfer pricing difficulty. The central government's particular levies such as those on natural gas, crude oil, and coal would have no place in such a scheme and should be abolished.[48] The scheme would reasonably approximate the Leland tax, and the lines of taxing authority between the states and the commonwealth would be clear.

If such a scheme were adopted, the CGC could operate just as it does now. Already states earn royalty income that the CGC takes into account in determining its needs variable, T_i. The CGC does not compensate deficiencies in the tax base dollar for dollar, although it does attempt to compensate deficiencies in potential royalties dollar for dollar. But note the word "potential." The CGC correctly realizes that if it compensated actual royalties dollar for dollar, states would have no incentive to maximize their actual resource earnings. Hence the CGC goes through a complex calculation to estimate potential royalties on the basis of the underlying profitability of a resource deposit, and it even tries to calculate whether states are assessing hidden royalties in setting unusually high rail charges. All these procedures could and should remain in this version of the Leland tax scheme.

The final option worth considering is the resources rent tax (RRT), tentatively described in a December 1983 discussion paper published by the Hawke government. The RRT is planned to apply only to natural gas and oil, and to replace the admittedly cumbersome excise taxes the commonwealth now imposes. The present tax requires a distinction between new and old oil (new oil is that discovered after 1975 and taxed at a lower rate to encourage production), and is based on production levels instead of profitability. As such, it discourages production from wells that are marginally profitable.

The RRT, on the other hand, is designed to tax only extraordinary

---

47. In the strictest sense, the optimal tax literature does not suggest tax rates that are constant across all sectors, but rather rates that vary depending on elasticities of supply. In real world applications, however, the one-tax-rate standard is usually defended as the best that can practically be done.

48. Two papers have recommended reforms along these lines, although not identical to these. See Craig Emerson and Peter Lloyd, "Improving Mineral Taxation"; and David Nellor, *Taxation of the Australian Resources Sector* (Clayton, Victoria: Monash University, Centre of Policy Studies, 1982), chaps 6 and 7.

profits from resources, those beyond the level necessary to encourage production, in a way that represents an "equitable sharing of economic rents between the community and investors in the petroleum sector."[49]

The government provides some calculations that illustrate the basic idea, if not the precise details. In the illustrations tax rates vary between 10 and 40 percent, with early year losses carried forward at a "threshold" rate or rates (interest rates, for purposes of calculating tax liability) that vary between 20 and 40 percent. In other respects, the tax base closely resembles that of the Leland tax. An important decision yet to be made is whether to apply one threshold rate and one tax rate to all projects, or to use multiple rates, designed in effect to tax more profitable projects but at the cost of added administrative difficulties.

To the extent that the loss offsets in the RRT are incomplete, and it is too early yet to tell how much, there will be an inevitable reduction in the net profitability of petroleum development and in the development itself. On the other hand, the RRT will rationalize petroleum taxation, base taxes on underlying profitability, and provide tax reductions and incentives for greater development of marginal wells.

The RRT, if and when adopted and extended to other resources, will raise some difficult issues of fiscal federalism. In setting heavier taxes for the most profitable wells, the RRT will in all likelihood reduce the states' potential royalty earnings. Were just one state affected, but not the average, the CGC would compensate the state dollar for dollar and that would be the end of it. But in this case average potential royalties for all states will decline, and even with present compensation arrangements, states in the aggregate will lose revenue from the RRT. The Hawke government has promised to negotiate further compensation arrangements with the states, presumably increasing the G^* (in equation 3) by an appropriate amount, but at this point states might be forgiven for fearing that a bird in the hand is worth two in the bush. Moreover, with the G^* raised appropriately, the disparity between revenue respon-

---

49. The Hawke government's tentative proposal can be found in Treasury Department, *Discussion Paper on Resource Rent Tax in the Petroleum Sector*, December 1983. It follows a long discussion in the Australian literature, initially started by Ross Garnaut and Anthony Clunies-Ross, "Uncertainty, Risk Aversion, and the Taxing of Natural Resource Projects," *The Economic Journal*, vol. 85 (June 1975), pp. 272–87, and later, "The Neutrality of the Resource Rent Tax," *The Economic Record*, vol. 55 (September 1979), pp. 193–201.

sibility and expenditure responsibility is made that much greater, with possibly damaging consequences for states' abilities and capabilities to manage their own affairs.

Summary—Equality and Efficiency Reconsidered

Overall the Australian system of fiscal federalism receives high marks for equality, although not for efficiency. The CGC is a remarkable institution for the amount of equalization it achieves, for its respectability and longevity, and for the degree to which analysts and politicians work together until agreements are reached. One can quibble with its precise procedures, arguing that there should be less equalizing for the cost of public services and more with regard to income, but these are relatively minor criticisms.

The system is less admirable from an efficiency standpoint. The CGC's basic entitlement is set at a high level, divorcing taxing responsibility from expenditure responsibility and placing an extraordinary premium on states' ability to lobby for grants. Moreover, its equalization for public service price differences can cause people to locate in areas quite costly to supply, and there are vast stretches of such areas in Australia. The ALC, while it still has its Australian defenders, has the look of an anachronism, emphasizing as it does nonprice political rationing and encouraging costly schemes to circumvent it. The specific-purpose grants have matching shares designed to encourage their over-utilization by states and intended to force the commonwealth into still more administrative rationing schemes. The taxing imbalance almost ensures that state taxation will cause excessive distortion. And the mélange of competing resource taxes and unclear lines of demarcation between the state and federal authorities risks overburdening one of Australia's most promising growth industries.

Postscript

As an outsider from the United States, a country that worries perhaps excessively about its federalist institutions, I could not help but be struck by how little most public servants and economists in Australia appear to care about fiscal federalism. Many observers seem to want a centralized system, even though the historical differences between states, the vast distances, and the existing spending disparities suggest that such a hope is a pie in the sky. Thoughts about whether states are given enough freedom to manage their own budgets rarely come up. Perhaps this explains why the same people who trust federal bureaucrats in Canberra to control public spending and borrowing do not trust state authorities because they have "short horizons," and why some proposals for taxing mineral resources have not considered the state-federal ramifications of their proposals. With a few notable exceptions, very little economic research is done on federalism. The Australian federal system has its strong points, it could be improved, and there is no shortage of interesting analytical issues. Somebody ought to take it seriously.

LAWRENCE B. KRAUSE

Australia's Comparative Advantage in International Trade

THE world economy is changing rapidly. Leading those changes have been the countries in the Pacific basin. International trade has been intimately involved, having grown faster than output, particularly in the fast-growing countries during the 1960s and 1970s. However, international trade contracted when the world economy suffered recession. Thus trade may have been both the handmaiden of growth and the mechanism spreading economic distress. This chapter analyzes the role that Australia has played in these developments. It examines the basis for Australia's comparative advantage and relates changes in trade to factors within the Australian economy. The policy stance of Australia with respect to both trade and direct investment is also investigated.

International Trade and the Economy

It is often said that Australia has always been a trading nation and that is no doubt true. However, if one measures commitment to inter-

Among the many Australians who assisted the author, special recognition should be given to Peter J. Lloyd and Wolfgang R. Kasper, who served as discussants of the chapter at the Brookings-Canberra Conference, William Charmichael, W. M. Corden, Thomas G. Parry, and several people at the Reserve Bank. Julia A. Henel provided very able research assistance.

Table 1. *Imports and Exports, Annual Averages, 1949–83*

Item	1949–50 to 1953–54	1954–55 to 1958–59	1959–60 to 1963–64	1964–65 to 1968–69	1969–70 to 1973–74	1974–75 to 1978–79	1979–80 to 1982–83
Amount (millions of Australian dollars)							
Imports	1,369	1,539	1,975	2,952	4,139	10,117	19,691
Exports	1,554	1,647	2,138	2,857	5,122	11,086	19,295
Trade balance	185	108	163	−95	983	970	−434
Share of GDP (percent)							
Imports	19.3	14.0	12.8	12.9	10.6	12.3	14.2
Exports	21.7	14.9	13.7	12.4	13.0	13.5	14.1

Sources: W. E. Norton, P. M. Garmston, and M. W. Brodie, *Australian Economic Statistics, 1949–50 to 1980–81: I; Tables,* Occasional Paper 8A (Canberra: Reserve Bank of Australia, 1982), p. 3; Australian Bureau of Statistics, *National Income and Expenditure 1982–83,* Budget Paper 10, prepared by R. J. Cameron (Canberra: Australian Government Publishing Service, 1983), p. 6; and *Budget Statements 1983–84,* Budget Paper 1, prepared by the Treasury of the Commonwealth of Australia (Canberra: AGPS, 1983), p. 42.

Table 2. *Exports as a Share of GDP for Selected Industrial Countries, 1958 and 1982*
Percent

Country	1958	1982
Australia	12.8	13.9
Canada	14.5	23.8
France	8.8	17.8
Germany	16.0	26.7
Sweden	17.3	27.1
United States	4.0	7.0

Source: International Monetary Fund, *International Financial Statistics, Yearbook 1983,* vol. 36 (1983), based on calendar years.

national trade by the ratio of exports and imports to domestic production (GDP), then Australia has become less of a trading nation during the postwar period; this is quite the reverse of other industrial countries. As seen in table 1, Australia's exports and imports of merchandise, measured at current prices, were each about 20 percent of GDP or even higher in the early 1950s than they are today. But those shares of GDP declined rapidly, and by the late 1960s and early 1970s they were no higher than 11 to 12 percent. The picture is not greatly altered if goods and services are considered together rather than goods alone. Subsequently the trends were reversed but not appreciably; in 1982–83, exports were 12.9 percent of GDP and imports 13.4 percent. As seen in table 2, exports as a share of GDP almost doubled between 1958 and 1982 in

Table 3. *Share of Australian Exports to and Imports from Selected Trading Partners, 1949–81*

Annual average, percent

Item and country	1949–50 to 1953–54	1954–55 to 1958–59	1959–60 to 1963–64	1964–65 to 1968–69	1969–70 to 1973–74	1974–75 to 1978–79	1979–80 to 1980–81
Imports							
United Kingdom	46.9	41.8	31.1	23.9	19.3	12.3	9.3
European Community[a]	8.8	10.1	11.2	12.2	13.4	14.1	12.6
Japan	1.9	2.7	5.8	10.1	15.5	18.8	17.4
South and South-east Asia[b]	13.2	12.0	9.7	7.2	7.0	9.6	12.4
United States	11.1	12.9	20.0	24.9	23.0	21.2	22.1
Exports							
United Kingdom	35.9	31.3	21.3	15.4	9.7	4.4	4.4
European Community[a]	21.7	21.4	16.2	13.2	9.9	10.5	8.9
Japan	6.7	11.6	16.4	19.8	28.5	31.2	27.1
Pacific basin[c]	8.7	9.6	9.0	11.8	12.9	14.2	16.0
United States	9.6	6.8	9.6	12.3	12.2	10.3	11.0
Canada[d]	1.5	1.5	1.7	1.7	2.7	2.5	2.1
New Zealand[d]	3.5	5.7	6.0	5.7	5.4	5.2	4.7

Sources: Norton, Garmston, and Brodie, *Australian Economic Statistics: 1949–50 to 1980–81*, pp. 6, 9; and Department of Trade and Resources, Economic Policy Division, *Pattern of Australian Exports, 1970–71 to 1980–81*, Internal Information Paper (April 1983), pp. 19–22. For Canada and New Zealand before 1974–75, see International Monetary Fund, *International Financial Statistics, Yearbook 1979*, vol. 32; and International Monetary Fund, *Direction of Trade Statistics*, computer tapes.

a. The European Community excludes the United Kingdom. Ireland, and Denmark are included beginning in 1973–74.

b. South and Southeast Asia include Bangladesh, Brunei, Burma, Hong Kong, India, Indonesia, Kampuchea, Laos, Macao, Malaysia, Maldive Islands, Pakistan, Philippines, Singapore, Sri Lanka, Taiwan, Thailand, and Vietnam.

c. The Pacific basin includes Taiwan, Hong Kong, the Republic of Korea, Indonesia, Malaysia, the Philippines, Singapore, Thailand, and Papua New Guinea from 1970–71. Before 1970–71, countries included are those listed in note b above.

d. Data for Canada and New Zealand before 1974–75 are in calendar years beginning in 1949.

many European countries and rose about 70 percent in the United States and Canada, but hardly at all in Australia.

A second major development has been change in Australia's trading partners, as seen in table 3. In the early 1950s trade with the United Kingdom made up about 40 percent of Australia's exports and 50 percent of its imports. By 1980 less than 5 percent of Australia's exports went to the United Kingdom. Japan had become the principal market in the mid-1960s and in the early 1980s was taking almost 30 percent of the total and the United States about 10 percent. In recent years, however, it has been the developing countries whose markets have been growing for Australian products; these markets are absorbing about one-third of Australia's total exports, with the Association of Southeast Asian Nations (ASEAN) and the OPEC countries being particularly important. The picture is only slightly different on the import side. The United Kingdom's share has dropped to less than 10 percent and has been replaced by Japan and the United States, each of which has a 20 percent share of the Australian market in the early 1980s. Australia is also buying more from developing countries—17 percent of the total in 1982, with the OPEC countries being somewhat more important than the ASEAN countries.

From a regional viewpoint, it is the developed and developing countries of the Pacific basin that are Australia's largest trading partners. They have provided markets for about 60 percent of Australia's exports since the early 1970s. Australia is also buying more from the Pacific basin; the import share has risen from about 49 percent in the early 1970s to 59 percent recently, about the same as exports. In the early 1950s it was Europe that had 60 percent of the shares.

A third characteristic of Australian trade that has changed is its commodity composition, as seen in table 4. In the early 1950s wool alone made up about half of Australia's exports, and other agricultural products took about another 30 percent of the total. By the early 1980s mining and fuels were 30.7 percent of Australian exports; rural products were down to 45.0 percent; and manufactures, 20 percent (special transactions, 4.2 percent). Changes in the composition of imports were much less marked. Capital goods remained about 20 to 25 percent of the total. However, the share of finished consumer goods and motor vehicles did rise and producers' materials fell. Of course, more dramatic changes would appear with a disaggregated commodity classification.

Explaining the Trends

What accounts for these major changes in Australian trade? McColl and Nicol have taken a close look at exports; they applied a constant market shares (CMS) analysis to Australian trade for the period 1963–66 to 1975–77.[1] The CMS method attempts to separate causative factors into growth of world trade, commodity compositional effects, market distributional effects, and competitive effects (measured as a residual).

1. G. D. McColl and R. J. Nicol, "An Analysis of Australian Exports to its Major Trading Partners: Mid-1960s to Late-1970s," *The Economic Record*, vol. 56 (June 1980), pp. 145–57.

Table 4. *Distribution of Exports and Imports, by Commodity Group,
1950–81*
Annual average, percent

Type of trade and commodity	1950–51 to 1954–55	1955–56 to 1959–60	1960–61 to 1964–65	1965–66 to 1969–70	1970–71 to 1974–75	1975–76 to 1979–80	1980–81
Imports[a]							
Food, drink, and tobacco	6.7	6.3	5.4	4.9	5.0	5.1	4.3
Minerals, fuels, and other basic materials[b]	19.7	21.1	18.5	14.3	11.6	14.6	18.4
Manufactured goods[c]	68.9	67.7	70.9	75.6	79.2	77.6	74.7
Other	4.7	4.9	5.2	5.2	4.2	2.7	2.6
Exports							
Meat	6.2	8.2	9.2	9.5	10.3	9.0	8.3
Cereals	12.8	9.9	15.6	12.4	12.1	12.1	12.1
Wool	50.7	43.2	33.9	24.3	13.8	10.3	9.8
Other rural	12.1	13.9	13.3	11.7	11.0	10.0	11.8
Unprocessed and processed minerals[d]	. . .	. . .	. . .	. . .	15.9	18.7	17.7
Coal	0.1	0.4	1.3	3.1	5.6	10.8	10.3
Metals	5.3	7.1	7.1	9.8	10.0	9.8	8.8
Simply transformed manufactures[d]	. . .	. . .	. . .	. . .	9.1	9.0	7.9
Elaborately transformed manufactures[d]	. . .	. . .	. . .	. . .	13.9	10.4	12.2

Sources: Norton, Garmston, and Brodie, *Australian Economic Statistics: 1949–50 to 1980–81*, pp. 5, 8; Department of Trade and Resources, *Pattern of Australian Imports*, pp. 23–36.

a. After 1965–66 the classification of imports was changed from the statistical classification of imports to the Australian import-commodity classification. See notes b and c.

b. Data from 1950–51 through 1964–65 include basic materials, fuels, and lubricants. Data after 1965–66 include crude materials (inedible), mineral fuels, and lubricants.

c. Data from 1950–51 through 1964–65 include textiles, base metals, motor vehicles, electrical machinery and equipment, other machines and machinery, and other manufactures. Data after 1965–66 include chemicals, manufactured material, machinery (electric and otherwise), transport equipment, and miscellaneous manufactured articles.

d. Data begin in 1970–71.

While there are legitimate criticisms of CMS methodology, particularly in its interpretation of the meaning of competitiveness, it does identify certain obvious variables affecting trade.

The facts are that Australian exports did not grow as fast as world trade. In 1938, Australia supplied about 2.2 percent of world trade, and this share rose to 3 percent in the early postwar period. However, by the late 1950s it had dropped to 1.5 percent, reversed slightly to 1.65 percent in 1963–66, but declined further to 1.27 percent in 1975–77. McColl and Nicol confine their detailed analysis to the eleven industrial countries that bought two-thirds of Australia's exports. In those countries Australia's share was 2.3 percent in 1963–66, 1.95 percent in 1967–69, 2.05 percent in 1970–72, and only 1.7 percent in 1975–77. If Australia had exported the same share of domestic production in 1975–77 as it had in 1963–66, exports would have been 1.5 percent greater. If Australia had managed to increase its exports in line with world trade, exports in 1975–77 would have been 30 percent greater.

The findings of the CMS analysis are that all Australia's lost market shares can be attributed to an unfortunate commodity composition of its exports. Specializing in wool, meat, and grains was very unlucky. Australia's market distribution was positive on balance as the slow-growing United Kingdom market was more than counterbalanced by the fast-growing Japanese market. The competitiveness measure was also positive, particularly in Japan. It should be noted, however, that during the end of the period from 1970–72 to 1975–77, Australia's competitiveness seemed to decline.

Export successes were achieved in minerals in which Australia increased its market share in Japan and in alumina (which is classified as an industrial chemical). But at the same time, market losses were suffered for iron and steel, transport equipment, electrical machinery, instruments, and metal manufactures—most of which are so-called elaborately transformed manufactures (ETMs).

As mentioned above, the rapidly growing developing countries of Asia are buying an increasing portion of Australia's exports, but Australia's market share declined from 4.1 percent in 1964–66 to 3.4 percent in 1974–76.[2]

A similar type of analysis was conducted by Australia's Department of Trade and Resources.[3] It established that Australia's share of world

---

2. Bureau of Industry Economics, _Industrialization in Asia—Some Implications for Australian Industry_, Research Report 1 (Canberra: Australian Government Publishing Service, 1978), table 3.11, p. 31. If China is excluded, there was no decline over the ten years, but there was a decline from 1969–71 to 1974–76. See also Kym Anderson and Ross Garnaut, "Australian Protection and Trade with the Developing Countries" (Canberra: Australian National University, 1983).

3. Department of Trade and Resources, Economic Policy Division, _Australian Export Performance in the 1970s: Some Further Analysis_, no. 4, Internal Research Memorandum (August 1982); and _Pattern of Australian Exports, 1970/71 to 1980/81_, Internal Information Paper (April 1983).

markets declined further to 1.18 percent in 1980. This analysis is less satisfying than the CMS because it approaches trade only from the side of the exporters (not market by market) but it does have the virtue of separately identifying trade value and trade volume (CMS is based on value data alone). During the decade from 1970 to 1980, world trade volume increased 5.6 percent a year, but Australia's export volume increased only 3.6 percent a year. Most of the difference was attributed to the commodity composition of Australia's exports, a finding similar to that of the CMS study. Even with respect to fast growing manufacturing, Australia's exports are split about evenly between simply transformed manufactures (STMs), which are growing more slowly, and ETMs, which have large increases, whereas world exports are about 80 percent ETMs and only 20 percent STMs.

Some product disaggregation was undertaken, which indicated for the period 1971–72 to 1980–81 that world agricultural trade volume increased 4.2 percent a year but Australia had only 0.8 percent; world manufactures trade volume increased 6.7 percent a year, but Australia's was only 2.2 percent; but world mining trade volume increased only 1.4 percent a year, while Australia's rose 7.6 percent. Because of the composition of trade within mining, however, the value of Australia's mining increased less than the world average since Australia had no petroleum in its export basket—the price of which rose dramatically—although the price of its coal exports did increase.

One disturbing finding concerning Australia's market distribution was that Japan's share of Australia's exports peaked in the mid-1970s and began to decline. This reflects the fact that Australia's share of Japanese imports declined from 9.4 percent in 1972 to 5.0 percent in 1980. The slowing of Japanese growth since the first oil crisis has meant that fewer Australian natural resources are being demanded than would likely have occurred without the slowdown. Also a belief was expressed in the Department of Trade and Resources report that Japan may be intentionally trying to diversify its sources of imports away from Australia. To replace Japan, Australia must look to the newly industrializing countries of Asia; recently it is having notable success in Korea and some in Taiwan, but less in Hong Kong and Singapore.

Several hypotheses were advanced by the Department of Trade and Resources to explain the relative deterioration in Australia's export position: the inward orientation of manufacturing policy and performance, the small scale of manufacturing, a foreign investment bias toward natural resources, changes in the real exchange rate, protectionism in overseas markets, foreign ownership and control of Australian producers, international transportation costs, and the low level of R&D expenditures in Australia. Some of these hypotheses are addressed below.

The Resource Content of Australian Trade

The traditional theory of comparative advantage is still the cornerstone of accepted wisdom concerning the determination of the structure of international trade. Efforts have been made to give empirical content to the theory. One approach that is particularly useful is to expand the number of factors of production beyond the simple classification of labor, capital, and natural resources. The three-factor model has been expanded to a five-factor model that consists of unskilled labor, human capital (skilled labor), physical capital, technology, and natural resources.[4] All five factors are generally required in production and thus occur in combination. The interesting question is the relative intensity of each. Empirical implementation of the model in a straightforward manner requires data on factors according to product, and such data are not available. However, the model can be approximated by classifying products by their dominant factor input, that is, dominant from the viewpoint of location of production, which is of interest for international trade. Physical capital is internationally mobile; deficiencies can be easily remedied by inflows from abroad. Thus physical capital is dropped in this chapter as a classification item. All commodities are characterized as being intensive in unskilled labor, human capital, technology, or natural resources. Data on production processes in the United States are used to form the classification scheme.[5]

Australian exports and imports by factors for 1970–81 are shown in table 5. It comes as no surprise that Australian exports are predominantly natural resource intensive. This is by far the major characteristic of Australian exports. In the early 1970s the natural resource share was about 85 percent; it rose slightly to 87 percent in the mid-1970s and dropped to about 85 percent in 1980. Because these shares are calculated

4. For a more detailed discussion, see Lawrence B. Krause, *U.S. Economic Policy toward the Association of Southeast Asian Nations* (Brookings Institution, 1982), chap. 4.
5. See the appendix for an explanation and listing.

Table 5. *Four-Factor Analysis of Australian Trade with the World, 1970–80*
Percent

		Factor		
Item and year	Human capital intensive	Natural resource intensive	Unskilled labor intensive	Technology intensive
Exports				
1970	7.9	85.8	1.5	4.8
1971	7.6	85.4	1.3	5.7
1972	8.3	85.5	1.3	4.9
1973	7.9	84.2	2.1	5.8
1974	7.9	84.6	1.6	5.9
1975	7.5	85.0	1.2	6.2
1976	6.1	87.7	1.1	5.1
1977	6.3	87.4	1.0	5.3
1978	7.3	85.3	1.5	5.9
1979	6.8	88.1	1.7	3.4
1980	6.3	85.3	2.1	6.2
Imports				
1970	25.7	19.1	14.2	41.0
1971	28.2	18.1	14.2	39.5
1972	26.6	19.3	17.2	36.9
1973	26.5	19.3	17.0	37.2
1974	28.7	22.3	15.6	33.4
1975	29.5	21.7	13.6	35.2
1976	30.1	22.3	14.5	33.1
1977	28.1	23.2	14.2	34.4
1978	27.6	21.5	14.5	36.5
1979	26.7	22.8	14.9	35.6
1980	25.5	25.8	12.9	35.9

Source: United Nations commodity trade tapes. Figures are rounded.

from value data at current prices, a bias is introduced when relative prices change as they did during the 1970s. Hence the decline in the natural resource share may be underestimated. Australian exports that are human capital intensive also became marginally less important over the decade. At the same time, it is somewhat surprising to find that technology intensive products increased their share from less than 5 percent in the early 1970s to more than 6 percent in the early 1980s. There was little change in the labor intensive share. Technology intensive products, in general, have grown as a share of world trade, and Australian exports took part in it.

Supporting evidence is seen on the import side. Australian imports

Table 6. *Four-Factor Analysis of Japanese and U.S. Trade
with Australia and the World, Selected Periods, 1970–79*
Percent

Country and period (average)	Human capital intensive		Natural resource intensive		Unskilled labor intensive		Technology intensive	
	Australia	World	Australia	World	Australia	World	Australia	World
Japan								
Imports								
1970–72	0.4	3.5	98.6	78.1	0.3	4.1	0.7	14.3
1977–79	0.5	3.5	98.6	81.8	0.3	5.0	0.6	9.7
Exports								
1970–72	41.5	44.6	7.6	8.1	23.0	23.0	27.9	24.4
1977–79	53.8	49.8	4.1	5.3	12.4	14.2	29.6	30.7
United States								
Imports								
1970–72	3.6	33.2	91.3	38.9	1.2	12.5	3.9	15.4
1977–79	3.6	26.0	89.5	49.5	0.7	8.9	6.3	15.6
Exports								
1970–72	20.5	20.1	12.1	31.0	5.3	5.9	62.1	43.1
1977–79	18.7	18.6	10.5	32.4	6.8	5.8	64.0	43.2

Source: Same as table 5. Figures are rounded.

are split between technology goods with the largest share, human capital
intensive products next, and then natural resource and labor intensive
products. However, natural resource intensive products apparently grew
as a share of total imports during the decade (keeping in mind the upward
bias). Only a small decline was recorded in the share of labor intensive
products despite the increase in protection for such goods and the
evidence that human capital intensive products also declined slightly. A
larger decline occurred in the technology share, which went from about
40 percent in the early 1970s to about 36 percent in the early 1980s. While
too much weight should not be placed on these measurements, it does
appear that Australia's comparative advantage is changing from heavy
dependence on natural resources to somewhat greater reliance on
technology goods.

Australia's largest trading partners are Japan and the United States.
These are also the two most competitive countries in the trade of
technology goods. Thus, if there were some shift in the resource base of
Australia's comparative advantage, it should appear in Australia's
bilateral trade with them. The factor basis of Japanese and U.S. trade
was examined with respect to the world and to Australia separately, as
summarized in table 6. Japanese imports are dominated by natural

resource goods and even more so are its imports from Australia. During the decade of the 1970s, Japanese overall imports became slightly more natural resource and labor intensive and slightly less technology intensive. These trends did not appear in Japan's imports from Australia. However, Japan imports so few technology goods from Australia that little can be made from the figures.

Japan exports primarily human capital and technology intensive goods to its trading partners. This pattern was duplicated in its exports to Australia. During the 1970s Japan's overall exports became somewhat more human capital and technology intensive and somewhat less labor and natural resource intensive. These trends were almost mirrored in trade with Australia, except that the technology share of Japan's exports did not rise as much (6 percent compared to 25 percent). Thus there is weak confirming evidence of the change; Japan's export share of technology goods rose sharply, but its technology exports to Australia did not rise to the same degree.

The United States imports natural resource and human capital intensive products and to a lesser extent technology and labor intensive products. U.S. imports from Australia are predominantly natural resources, with technology goods second. During the 1970s U.S. imports of natural resource goods rose and human capital and labor intensive goods fell. However, the pattern was different with respect to imports from Australia; namely the natural resource share fell and the technology share rose, again providing some confirming evidence. U.S. imports of technology goods from Australia rose considerably during the decade of the 1970s. Large increases in percentage terms were made in U.S. imports of Australian technology goods such as aircraft, mining machinery, pumps, tractors, electrical medical equipment, medicines, electrical apparatus, and electrical power and other specialized machinery.

U.S. exports are largely technology and natural resource goods. During the 1970s there was little change in the structure of U.S. exports, although exports of these goods increased slightly. U.S. exports to Australia alone are even more heavily concentrated in technology goods, and that share rose slightly during the 1970s. However, U.S. natural resource and human capital exports to Australia declined somewhat, and the share of labor intensive products rose. Thus U.S. export shares to Australia did not confirm the hypothesis.[6]

6. Although the overall technology share of U.S. exports grew little during the decade, it resulted from very different trends with different trading partners. The

To summarize the results of examining the resource content of Australia's bilateral trade with Japan and the United States, there is weak confirming evidence that, whereas Australia's comparative advantage is still largely in natural resource goods, there may have been some shift toward greater comparative advantage in technology goods during the 1970s. Support for this hypothesis comes from observations that Japan's own improvement in technology goods was not fully reflected in its trade with Australia and that Australia was able to increase its technology exports to the United States despite the further improvement in U.S. comparative advantage in such goods.

Trends in Australia's International Trade

As noted above, a striking characteristic of Australia's international trade is the decline in exports and imports as a proportion of GDP in the 1950s and the failure of that proportion to rise subsequently. The fall in the 1950s does not appear to be surprising. The high level of trade in the early 1950s reflects the short-lived rise in raw material prices induced by the Korean War.[7] The work of Kuznets concerning structural change during the process of economic growth points in the same direction.[8] He concluded that in "young" countries such as Australia, proportions of foreign trade are expected to fall (or not rise) with rapid growth. This results from territorial expansion (extensive use of land) and the growth of services as a share of both consumption and output. Australia's population became much larger during the 1950s as a result of massive immigration, and size is inversely related to trade proportions. Indeed, according to Kuznets, it was the earlier high ratios that were the distortion when Australia was a small offshoot of Europe.

The failure of the trade proportions to rise subsequently, however,

---

technology share did rise sharply in U.S. exports to Pacific basin countries, excluding Japan. Thus the rise in Australia's share may be due to a regional effect rather than to the absence of Australia's improved competitiveness in these products.

7. This point was made to the author at the Brookings-Canberra Conference.

8. See Simon Kuznets, *Economic Growth of Nations: Total Output and Production Structure* (Harvard University Press, 1971); "Quantitative Aspects of the Economic Growth of Nations," *Economic Development and Cultural Change*, vol. 15, pt. 2 (January 1967); and *Modern Economic Growth: Rate, Structure and Spread* (Yale University Press, 1966).

does not appear to be a result of natural causes. Several hypotheses noted earlier in this chapter have been advanced to explain the phenomenon. Probably the most important explanation was the choice by Australia of an inward-oriented industrial policy, mainly a strategy of promoting manufacturing through import-substitution policies. High tariffs on imports of manufactures were the main instrument of policy, and protection was maintained as needed even after the average level of tariffs was reduced. In its historical context, this policy choice is easily understood. In the early postwar period most independent raw material producers attempted to spur manufacturing in order to become more industrialized and less dependent on the vagaries of nature and unstable world raw material prices, just as the older industrial countries had before World War II. Australia tried to maintain its war-induced growth in manufacturing through protection. Australian governments received advice on tariff making from a statutory authority, the Tariff Board. Recommendations for changes in tariffs were often made and implemented in response to requests by domestic producers. Australia took the "small country" option during the various rounds of tariff negotiations under the General Agreement on Tariffs and Trade (GATT) and offered few tariff reductions, knowing that its reluctance would not jeopardize a world agreement. Many Australian tariffs were not even bound under the GATT. Of course, few real concessions were given by others on temperate agricultural goods, the products of greatest export interest to Australia at the time. (It is doubtful whether even an aggressive effort by Australia could have changed that outcome.)

The Tariff Issue

High protection was not without its critics in Australia. Indeed, some of the most valuable work on these tariffs and their deleterious consequences has been done by economists working in Australia or by Australians abroad. The work of W. M. Corden, David Evans, R. G. Gregory, Wolfgang Kasper, and Peter Lloyd is notable in this regard.[9]

9. The works of all of these authors are so well known that references are unnecessary; however, some citations may be useful. See W. M. Corden, *The Theory of Protection* (Oxford: Clarendon Press, 1971); H. David Evans, "A Programming Model of Trade and Protection," in I. A. McDougall and R. H. Snape, eds., *Studies in International*

Table 7. *Average Effective Rates of Assistance to Manufacturing Industries, 1968–69 to 1981–82*[a]
Percent

Industry	1968–69	1969–70	1970–71	1971–72	1972–73	1973–74	1974–75	1975–76	1976–77	1977–78	1978–79	1979–80	1980–81	1981–82
Food, beverages, and tobacco	16	17	18	19	19	18	21	20	16	10	13	11	9	8
Textiles	43	42	42	45	45	35	39	50	51	52	52	55	61	54
Clothing and footwear	97	94	91	86	88	64	87	96	138	142	145	137	141	204
Wood, wood products, and furniture	26	27	26	23	23	16	18	19	18	18	16	14	13	13
Paper and paper products, printing, and publishing	52	50	50	52	51	38	31	30	30	26	29	27	26	30
Chemical, petroleum, and coal products	31	31	31	32	32	25	23	24	22	19	19	17	14	13
Nonmetallic mineral products	15	15	15	14	14	11	11	10	7	5	5	5	4	5
Basic metal products	31	30	28	29	29	22	16	16	15	12	12	12	13	14
Fabricated metal products	61	60	60	58	56	44	39	38	34	32	34	33	34	34
Transport equipment	50	50	51	50	51	39	45	66	57	57	63	74	74	79
Motor vehicles	52	...	...	51	...	41	77	116	104	108	130	149	149	158
Other machinery and equipment	43	43	43	41	39	29	24	25	22	20	21	22	22	22
Miscellaneous manufacturing	34	35	35	32	31	24	27	26	25	26	27	26	27	27
Total manufacturing	36	36	36	35	35	27	27	28	27	23	25	24	24	26

Sources: Industries Assistance Commission, *Annual Report 1975–76* (Canberra: AGPS, 1976), table 2.4.6, p. 114; IAC, *Annual Report 1978–79* (Canberra: AGPS, 1979), table 1.3.2, p. 83; and IAC, *Annual Report 1982–83* (Canberra: AGPS, 1983), table A2.1.3, p. 57.

a. The forms of assistance covered by this table include tariffs, quantitative restrictions on imports, production and export subsidies, and special pricing schemes for sugar and petroleum products. The assistance provided by the motor vehicle local-content scheme is included only in the estimates based on 1977–78 production weights. Forms of assistance not taken into account include government purchasing practices and assistance from state governments, some descriptive details about which are provided in the Industries Assistance Commission's *Annual Report 1980–81* (Canberra: AGPS, 1981), chap. 2, and apps. 2.2 and 2.3. Years 1968–69 through 1973–74 are at 1971–72 production weights; years 1974–75 through 1976–77 are at 1974–75 production weights; and years 1977–78 through 1981–82 are at 1977–78 production weights.

Several government commissions have also investigated the issue.[10]

The tariff has been a major focus of Australian policy ever since the formation of the commonwealth. Those who defend protectionism have contended that high tariffs would increase real wages, attract immigrants from Europe, and increase self-sufficiency (reduce external dependency); the traditional infant industry argument has also been offered.[11] As seen in table 7, by the late 1960s the level of effective rates of assistance to Australian manufacturing had reached 36 percent on average; this must be considered a high figure by the standard of industrial countries. Furthermore, barriers have been created by Australian state governments to limit competition from firms in other states. Devices such as discriminatory transportation rates and service, discriminatory state government purchases, assistance and subsidies, and regulations of health and the like have been used by all the state governments of Australia to favor enterprises with production facilities within their states. Thus even the unity of the national market has been jeopardized.

The trend toward greater protection of Australian industry began to be seriously questioned in the late 1960s to early 1970s, probably as a result of the rapid development of the highly competitive minerals industry. It also may have reflected the exhaustion of all reasonably easy opportunities for import replacement. Employment in Australian manufacturing peaked as a share of the labor force in the mid-1960s and was replaced at the margin by services and minerals employment. As seen in table 7, along with the high level of protection, assistance given to individual industries ranged up to more than twice the manufacturing

Economics (Amsterdam: North-Holland, 1970); R. G. Gregory, "Some Implications of the Growth of the Mineral Sector," *Australian Journal of Agricultural Economics*, vol. 20 (August 1976); R. G. Gregory and L. D. Martin, "An Analysis of Relationships between Import Flows to Australia and Recent Exchange Rate and Tariff Changes," *The Economic Record*, vol. 52 (1976), pp. 1–25; Wolfgang Kasper and others, *Australia at the Crossroads: Our Choices to the Year 2000* (Sydney: Harcourt, Brace, Jovanovich, 1980); and Peter J. Lloyd, "Protection Policy," in Fred H. Gruen, ed., *Surveys of Australian Economics* (Sydney: George Allen & Unwin, 1978).

10. Committee of Economic Inquiry (Vernon Committee), *Report on the Committee of Economic Inquiry*, 2 vols (Canberra: AGPS, 1965); Committee to Advise on Policies for Manufacturing Industry (Jackson Committee), *Policies for Development of Manufacturing Industry*, 4 vols (Canberra: AGPS, 1976); and Crawford Committee, *Study Group on Structural Adjustment* (Canberra: AGPS, 1979).

11. Lloyd, "Protection Policy."

average (clothing and footwear). There was no hiding of the level of effective protection in Australia; the information was widely available through the excellent work of the Industries Assistance Commission (IAC). Up to that point Australian protection was mainly in the form of tariffs. The work of the IAC, which measured the levels of effective protection provided by nominal tariff rates and evaluated other aids to industry, made transparent the cost of industrial assistance to Australian society.

As part of the policy initiatives of the Whitlam government in July 1973, tariffs were cut across the board by 25 percent. As seen in table 7, average effective protection for Australian manufacturing was reduced from 36 percent to 27 percent. That turned out to be a high water mark for trade liberalization. Shortly before and after the tariff cut, the Australian dollar was appreciated and the world sunk into a deep recession due to the first OPEC oil shock. These two factors plus the tariff reduction put tremendous competitive pressures on import-competing manufactures, and unemployment in manufacturing rose sharply. All of this tended to discredit tariff cutting in the eyes of the public, although the consensus of economists is that the tariff reduction was less important than changes in the exchange rate.[12]

Almost immediately, industries that faced severe competitive pressures from imports (especially textiles, clothing, footwear, and motor vehicles) received increases in assistance even though they were already the most heavily protected industries in Australia. In addition, the form of assistance changed as quotas, tariff quotas, content requirements, bounties, and export subsidies were introduced. Quotas disrupt trade more than tariffs because effective assistance rises automatically as the competitiveness of the domestic industry declines. The dispersion of assistance rates increased, both between different industries and between products within the same industry. The standard deviation of average effective rates of assistance for broad groups of manufacturing industries is shown in table 8. Since the amount of resource misallocation is positively correlated with dispersion, it is possible to argue that all the economic gains of the 1973 tariff cut were subsequently eroded. The

12. See Lloyd, "Protection Policy," p. 260. However, shortly after the cut the tariff was supported by a majority of Australians. Morgan Gallup Poll no. 16, as reported in "Twenty-five Percent Cut in Imported Duties Approved," *The Bulletin*, vol. 93 (September 8, 1973).

Table 8. *Standard Deviations of Average Effective Rates of Assistance to Manufacturing Industries, 1977–78 to 1981–82*[a]
Percentage points

Industry	1977–78	1978–79	1979–80	1980–81	1981–82
Food, beverages, and tobacco	18	18	17	17	18
Textiles	45	43	49	50	46
Clothing and footwear	38	44	37	38	49
Wood, wood products, and furniture	14	13	10	9	9
Paper and paper products, printing and publishing	14	15	15	15	16
Chemical, petroleum, and coal products	11	11	10	12	12
Nonmetallic mineral products	7	8	7	7	7
Basic metal products	8	9	9	9	8
Fabricated metal products	13	13	16	17	18
Transport equipment	45	53	62	61	64
Other machinery and equipment	13	13	13	11	11
Miscellaneous manufacturing	17	15	17	15	15
Total manufacturing	30	32	33	34	41

Source: Industries Assistance Commission, *Annual Report 1982–83*, table A2.1.3, p. 57.
a. Standard deviation of average effective rates calculated for each of the Australian SIC industries with an Australian SIC subdivision. See table 7, note a, for types of assistance included.

imports of manufactures into Australia, which rose sharply in 1974, were subsequently curtailed.

Few domestic "gains" can be attributed to the high level of assistance afforded certain industries in Australia. As compared to the industries that received less assistance for the period from 1968–69 to 1981–82, the heavily assisted industries had less growth in gross product and had five times the decline in employment. Furthermore, there was a substantial burden on consumers and consuming industries as a result of assistance to only those industries predominantly assisted by quotas; the IAC estimates that in 1981–82 the total consumer tax equivalent of this assistance alone was equal to $3.9 billion.[13] Australian consumers have

13. Industries Assistance Commission, *Annual Report 1982–83* (Canberra: AGPS, 1983), p. 11.

paid a heavy price to sustain a widely diversified manufacturing sector; because of the size of the country, most production of this sector is confined to small-scale operations. Hence inward-oriented policy does explain why imports have not risen appreciably as a proportion of the economy.

These inward-oriented policies also help explain why export shares have not risen. The CMS analysis mentioned above indicated that Australia's share of world trade declined because it specialized in products for which world demand rose very little (temperate agriculture and minerals). Why then did not Australian producers shift resources to produce products for which world demand was rising rapidly? The answer is that the structure of assistance in Australia is such that resources were directed toward industries in which Australia was unlikely to have or to create a comparative advantage. Evidence that excess protection existed suggests that there was an ongoing incentive to misdirect resources. Indeed, high protection is the antithesis of what is required to foster world-competitive industries. This is not to suggest that foreign protectionism played no role in limiting Australian exports. Australia should have a comparative advantage, for instance, in processed raw materials, but it is known that many countries, and especially Japan, escalate their tariffs (and other trade restraints) so as to confine imports of natural resources to their crudest state. Nevertheless, Australia's own policies and slower overall growth of output would seem the more important reasons since other countries did increase their exports of manufactures despite trade barriers.

Factors Affecting Exports

Given Australia's inward orientation, what explains the export success that was achieved in certain manufactures and in technology goods in particular? Table 9 lists the ten fastest-growing Australian exports of technology goods to the United States and the level of assistance they receive in Australia.[14] It is notable that the export successes are negatively related to government assistance. Without government assistance,

14. The correspondence was made through general description rather than product codes, so errors of interpretation are possible.

Table 9. *Comparison of Product Assistance Rate and the Average Effective Protection Rate for Selected Industries, 1981–82*

Industry subdivision	Product assistance rate (percent)[a]	Average effective rate for industry (percent)	Standard deviation (percentage points)
Aircraft	− 5	79	64
Pumps and compressors	16	22	11
Industrial machinery and equipment	19	22	11
Medicine	− 1	13	12
Measuring, professional, and scientific equipment	1	22	11
Electrical apparatus	27	22	11
Electrical power machinery	14	22	11
Agricultural machinery	19	22	11
Cameras and optical goods	6	22	11
Heating and cooling equipment	27	22	11

Source: Industries Assistance Commission, *Annual Report 1982–83*, pp. 57, 62–72.

a. Average effective rate for the industry subdivision (four-digit level, Australian SIC). See table 7, note a, for types of assistance included.

producers have to be able to meet foreign competition at home and thus exist in an environment that promotes competitiveness and exports. In the absence of more careful empirical work, the hypothesis must be considered tentative, but if substantiated, it would have important implications for Australian policy for it indicates a direct linkage between trade liberalization and export success.

The advantage of location appears to be a second factor that helps explain Australia's export success in manufacturing. Much of Australia's export of manufactures is sold to New Zealand and nearby Pacific island countries. Proximity does provide a basis for comparative advantage. Not only are transportation costs minimized, but ease of serving customers, speed of delivery, and cultural interpenetration are improved. The potential also exists for greater Australian exports to the ASEAN countries, although greater competition exists for those markets and Australia's import policies may stand in the way of closer trading ties.

Ever since 1966, trans-Tasmanian trade has been given special treatment under the New Zealand–Australian Free Trade Agreement (NAFTA), which was broadened and strengthened under an agreement for Closer Economic Relations (CER) that became operative in 1983. The NAFTA was only a partial free-trade agreement, which required item-by-item bargaining. The difficulties and limitations of a partial free-trade agreement have been demonstrated in South and Central America, and the New Zealand–Australian effort was not more successful.[15] The CER improves upon NAFTA because it automatically provides for eventual free trade of all goods; it covers quantitative import restrictions, export subsidies, and tariffs. Limiting provisions have been made for "unfair competition" (the meaning of which is unclear), and there are safeguards for severe material injury. Another shortcoming is that wheat, dairy products, citrus fruits, grapes, and certain other fruits are excluded.[16] Furthermore, there is no provision for the free movement of capital between New Zealand and Australia. Nevertheless, CER could become significant for New Zealand if it were used as an incentive to make the whole economy more efficient and reduce government interventions. For Australia, Tasmanian trade will remain a small share of the total but is strategic for manufactures, and CER can be helpful in this regard.

A third factor that helps explain Australia's success in exporting certain manufactures is the nature of the economy's structure and its factor endowment. Australia has a highly literate labor force with a wide variety of skills. There are also many successful Australian entrepreneurs, and foreign multinational firms operate extensively in the country. And Australian firms expend a moderate amount of their resources on research and development.[17] What this describes is a country that could specialize in middle-technology goods and specialized items. There is a tendency for economists and politicians to think only in terms of high technology at one extreme or labor intensive goods at the other. Few products or processes are regularly revolutionized in the laboratory or are made only with unskilled labor. The large middle ground is where Australia fits. Australian successes apparently have come from individual firms (entrepreneurs) making marginal improvements on existing products to fit needs they perceive—such as mining machinery—and then marketing them at home and abroad.

15. P. J. Lloyd, "Economic Relations Between Australia and New Zealand" (Canberra: Research School of Pacific Studies, 1976).

16. P. J. Lloyd, "NZ, CER, and the Pacific," public lecture at the University of Auckland Centenary Celebration, May 1983.

17. In 1973, 1.2 percent of Australian GDP went to R&D. This compares with 2.3 percent in the United States, 1.7 percent in Japan, 1.1 percent in Canada, and 0.9 percent in New Zealand. See A. T. A. Healy, ed., *Science and Technology for What Purpose? An Australian Perspective* (Canberra: Australian Academy of Science, 1979).

Exchange Rates and Trade

Exchange rates have been examined as part of the discussion of monetary policy and natural resources (the Gregory thesis). However, attention should also be drawn to the consequence of changes in real exchange rates for exports of manufactures. Concern has been expressed about the competitive position of Australian manufactures as a result of exchange rate movements or the failure of those rates to move to offset inflation differentials. Exchange rates are believed to have a greater effect in the short term on the volume of Australian manufactures trade than on minerals or agricultural trade because the prices of natural resource products are set in U.S. dollar markets and supplies of agricultural goods are inelastic (again in the short run). Thus when the Australian dollar-U.S. dollar exchange rate changes, it has little immediate effect on the volume of Australian natural resource exports, but has a large effect on profits of producers of those exports. Hence when the Australian dollar appreciates, it discourages manufactures production and exports (encourages imports) and reduces the manufactures share of the export basket. The reverse occurs when the Australian dollar depreciates.

Since the early 1970s the Australian dollar has gone through a complete cycle. In nominal terms, it appreciated sharply, if belatedly, in late 1972 and further in 1973 by approximately 16 percent.[18] Subsequently the Australian dollar was devalued until 1979, when it reached a point 27 percent below its peak value. From 1979 to the third quarter of 1981 it rose 16 percent and then began a gradual slide, which culminated in a sharp but temporary drop in the second quarter of 1983. When the nominal effective exchange rate is corrected for inflation differences between Australia and its trading partners, the size of the change is reduced by about half, but the distinct cycle remains. Because exchange rates affect trade with a lag of about a year, the loss of Australia's market shares in the mid-1970s might well be due to this cause. However, the further erosion after the Australian dollar depreciated suggests that other forces must have been more important.

---

18. The measurement described is the effective exchange rate measured by the MERM method (multilateral exchange rate model) by the International Monetary Fund.

Australian Trade and Industrial Assistance Policy

Prime Minister Robert Hawke said on August 8, 1983, "Long term growth in our living standards is feasible only if we maintain open investment and trade policies."[19] Thus he endorsed the firm conviction that is widely shared by academics and is given rhetorical support by most Australian politicians—although reality is moving in the opposite direction. As is typical in a recession and in developments in other countries, Australian industries are requesting more assistance from the government, which is questioning whether the line can be held against greater protection. In the case of steel, that protection was given. The industry was granted a subsidy of $71.6 million, distributed annually over a five-year period, and other tariff and quota measures are to be taken to ensure that Australian producers supply 80 percent of the domestic market.[20] Even the independence of the IAC is under attack by the Australian Council of Trade Unions (ACTU). The ACTU is apparently unhappy with the IAC's analysis that demonstrates societal losses from greater protection (including job losses in manufacturing).

The obvious question is what explains the persistence of Australian protection policies that cannot be justified on economic efficiency grounds. In a provocative paper, Anderson addresses this question employing some econometric techniques.[21] The study suggests that the most significant explanation of why some industries obtain greater government assistance than others is as follows: the lower the average wage per employee, the greater is labor intensity; the smaller the value-added share of output, the smaller is the number of firms in the industry; and the lower the share of output being exported, the greater is assistance likely to be.[22] This suggests that during recessions when unemployment rises and wages are threatened, it is hard to resist protectionist pressures. It is also likely that industries with a few firms employing a large number of workers are likely to be particularly inefficient in Australia.

19. Quoted in the introduction of the IAC, *Annual Report 1982–83*, p. vi.

20. *The Asian Wall Street Journal Weekly*, August 15, 1983, p. 11.

21. Kym Anderson, "The Political Market for Government Assistance to Australian Manufacturing Industries," *The Economic Record*, vol. 56 (June 1980), pp. 132–44.

22. The significant relation between high assistance and low level of exports provides some weak support for the idea that export success is promoted by low levels of assistance.

Table 10. *Australian Attitudes toward Protection from Imports of Manufactured and Farm Products, 1979*
Percent

| Population group[a] | Question in poll | | | | | |
| | Should Australian manufactured products be protected from low-priced imports? | | | Should Australian farm products be protected from low-priced imports? | | |
	Yes	No	Unsure	Yes	No	Unsure
Total (2,000)	59	38	3	73	25	2
Male (998)	56	41	3	68	30	2
Female (1,002)	62	35	4	78	20	3
University educated (192)	35	62	3	52	46	2
Primary school educated (230)	71	24	5	83	13	4
Blue-collar workers (1,084)	65	32	3	78	20	3
White-collar workers (839)	51	46	3	66	32	2
Liberal-Country party voters (700)	55	41	3	74	24	2
Labor party voters (872)	65	33	2	74	25	2
City voters (1,233)	57	39	4	70	27	3
Noncity voters (767)	63	35	3	78	21	1

Source: *The Age* (Melbourne), June 4, 1979, p. 12.
a. The numbers in parentheses indicate total number of people in each group.

Other evidence suggests that the reasons for Australian protection may go beyond the rational, self-seeking desires of certain firms and their employees and the willingness of politicians to respond to those special interests. In a poll conducted in 1979, it was determined that a clear majority of Australians support protection, as reported in table 10. With the sole exception of university-educated people, Australians believe that domestic producers of manufactured products should be protected from low-priced imports. Very likely the support for protection would be larger at current, higher levels of unemployment. This suggests that Australians are either unaware of their own best economic interests or they are willing to bear an economic sacrifice to serve some other societal goal. The fact that even city voters and those with university educations clearly support protection from low-priced farm products suggests that the latter explanation has some credibility.

W. M. Corden provides a possible explanation in what he describes as the conservative social welfare function of the Australian society.[23]

23. W. M. Corden, *Trade Policy and Economic Welfare* (London: Oxford University Press, 1974).

He suggests that society wants to avoid a significant absolute reduction in the real income of any part of the community because people think it is unfair (especially if it is the result of deliberate policy action) because they are risk averse and want government protection for themselves, because they believe it is necessary for social peace, and because they want to avoid battles among sectors of the economy. Therefore they do not want the government to reduce protection and put competitive pressures on particular economic activities, and they would support greater assistance if competitiveness were lost. This suggests that Australian society is prepared to forgo income gains to reduce the pressures and uncertainties that come from closer interdependence.

Australia has lost some historic opportunities to reduce its protection as part of past GATT negotiations. Survey data indicate that a majority of Australians did support a worldwide lowering of import duties at the end of World War II for the purpose of containing inflation and avoiding war.[24] Favorable attitudes toward international trade were also expressed at the time Australia reopened its trade with Japan.[25] However, public attitudes had shifted by the early 1960s when Australians strongly supported quotas to protect domestic industry, to prevent a "flood of imports," and to maintain full employment.[26]

If another round of multilateral negotiations were to be undertaken, public support might be easier to obtain than it would be in response to unilateral action to reduce protection. Thus Australia should be at the forefront of countries seeking a new round of trade negotiations.[27] Global freeing of trade is the optimal solution, but if that turns out to be unobtainable, regional promotion of trade within the Pacific basin may be a good second-best alternative.[28] Several Australians have been

24. Australian Gallup Polls, Release no. 213, August–September 1944; and no. 478, December 1947. The author thanks Adrian Pagan for bringing these data to his attention.

25. Australian Gallup Polls, nos. 327–334, February–March 1946; nos. 382–397, September–November 1946; and nos. 448–458, September 1947.

26. Gallup Polls, nos. 1515–1530, March–May 1961; and nos. 1592–1604, March–April 1962.

27. In fact, former Prime Minister Malcolm Fraser made an initiative to the ill-fated GATT ministerial meeting in November 1982 for a hold on new protectionist measures but was not supported by other countries.

28. On November 22, 1983, Prime Minister Hawke proposed that Pacific basin countries coordinate their efforts to promote a new multilateral round of trade negotiations. He also supported nondiscriminatory intraregional efforts at trade liberalization. *The Australian Financial Review* (Sydney: November 23, 1983), p. 1.

instrumental in promoting closer economic cooperation in the Pacific.[29] However, before levels and dispersion of assistance to industry can be reduced, Australians must be convinced that it is desirable. Clearly, more effort is required to educate the public and the opinion leaders.

Understandably, Australians would like to know where job opportunities will be created to absorb workers displaced by imports. The only true answer is that they will be absorbed by an expanding economy, but exactly where cannot be forecasted. Wolfgang Kasper, in an imaginative paper, attempts to give some general guidance toward an answer.[30] My work suggests that Australia has export prospects in middle-technology goods along with natural resource goods. Government promotion of these industries, other than through general market measures, is unnecessary.[31] Economists can be more specific about the distortions that come from protection and the costs of existing policies. The public should have more exposure to the data provided by the IAC. If all countries had equivalent IACs, educating the public would be easier still. Wider knowledge of benefits and costs of greater liberation may not be enough, but it may contribute to reversing the tide.

Foreign Direct Investment

Foreign direct investment (FDI) has made a significant contribution to Australia's economic development.[32] Australia's policy continues to provide a reasonable welcome for new FDI, but it is far from the wide-open door that it once was. During the early postwar years Australia encouraged investment, and there was even incentive for competition

29. Sir John Crawford, ed., *Pacific Economic Co-operation: Suggestions for Action* (Singapore: Heinemann Educational Books, 1981). See, in particular, references to Peter Drysdale.

30. Wolfgang Kasper, "Where Will the Jobs Come From?" *Australian Bulletin of Labour*, Supplement 2 (December 1980).

31. The large-scale assistance to high technology that is being proposed by Senator Barry Jones is not likely to be helpful. See keynote address, Sunrise Industries Conference, "Sunrise Industries: Business Opportunities in Australia," Sydney, 1983.

32. Donald T. Brash, "United States Investment in Australia, Canada, and New Zealand," in Peter Drysdale, ed., *Direct Foreign Investment in Asia and the Pacific* (Canberra: Australian National University Press, 1972).

among the states to attract new ventures from abroad.[33] What to do about foreign investment in the future is one of the issues that is likely to be addressed over the next several years.

There were two distinct phases of foreign investment in Australia. Until the mid-1960s the main investments were by U.S. and British firms in Australian manufacturing. They were attracted by prospects for growth in the Australian market, enticed by the import-replacement strategy of the government, and protected from competitive imports by high tariffs. Subsequently FDI was attracted to the mining industries, and multinational firms played a predominant role in developing Australia's huge mining industry.[34] Some feeling for the extent of this investment can be obtained from examining table 11. In the late 1950s and early 1960s FDI inflow amounted to about $300 to $500 million per year or between 15 percent and 20 percent of all domestic investment. From the late 1960s to the late 1970s FDI rose from about $500 million to $1.6 billion, but the share of domestic investment provided by FDI dropped from a range of about 16 to 18 percent to a range of about 10 to 11 percent. However, several factors induced firms to shift toward debt financing for large-scale mining ventures, and much of this financing also came from abroad. The result of this investment is that about 40 percent of the total equity of Australian manufacturing and 50 percent of the mining industry is foreign owned, and possibly 60 percent of mining is under foreign control.[35] Australian firms more recently have been making their own direct investments in other countries; this direct investment grew from about $100 million in the early 1970s to between $200 and $300 million by the end of the decade. Thus the outflow of FDI amounted to about 20 percent of the inflow of FDI during the 1970s and to about 2.5 percent of total domestic investment.

High levels of foreign ownership of both manufacturing and mining have raised sensitive economic and political issues in Australia as they have in Canada and other countries. It was recognized that Australia's development was encouraged by FDI through the introduction of more

33. G. D. McColl, "Foreign Investment," in Peter J. Lloyd, ed., *Mineral Economics in Australia* (Sydney: George Allen & Unwin, 1983).

34. R. B. McKern, *Multinational Enterprise and Natural Resources* (Sydney: McGraw-Hill, 1976).

35. *The Asian Wall Street Journal Weekly*, October 10, 1983, p. 16; and G. D. McColl, "Foreign Investment."

Table 11. *Foreign Direct Investment, Outflow and Inflow, and Domestic Investment, 1949–80*

Period	Amount (millions of Australian dollars)			FDI outflow as a percent of domestic investment	FDI inflow as a percent of domestic investment
	Australian FDI outflow	FDI inflow	Domestic investment[a]		
1949–50	6[b]	130	454	1.3	28.6
1950–51	7[b]	134	649	1.1	20.7
1951–52	10[b]	161	787	1.3	20.5
1952–53	10	42	780	1.3	5.4
1953–54	11	137	939	1.2	14.6
1954–55	18	198	1,062	1.7	18.6
1955–56	18	224	1,204	1.5	18.6
1956–57	23	191	1,275	1.8	15.0
1957–58	16	192	1,355	1.2	14.2
1958–59	25	208	1,372	1.8	15.2
1959–60	15	530	1,571	1.0	20.4
1960–61	19	375	1,742	1.1	21.5
1961–62	20	221	1,725	1.2	12.8
1962–63	14	384	1,917	0.7	20.0
1963–64	13	425	2,146	0.6	19.8
1964–65	32	540	2,493	1.3	21.7
1965–66	38	512	2,745	1.4	18.7
1966–67	37	363	2,838	1.3	12.8
1967–68	47	561	3,044	1.5	18.4
1968–69	60	599	3,434	1.7	17.4
1969–70	127	728	3,674	3.5	19.8
1970–71	72	897	4,302	1.7[c]	20.9
1971–72	121	870	4,551	2.7	19.1
1972–73	97	391	4,564	2.1	8.6
1973–74	244	618	5,191	4.7	11.9
1974–75	94	657	6,103	1.5	10.8
1975–76	166	578	7,022	2.4	8.2
1976–77	255	1,081	7,738	3.3	14.0
1977–78	198	1,052	8,735	2.3	12.0
1978–79	224	1,437	10,455	2.1	13.8
1979–80	333	1,637	n.a.	n.a.	n.a.

Sources: J. S. Metcalfe and R. Treadwell, *An Overview of Australian Direct Foreign Investment,* Working Paper 18 (Canberra: Bureau of Industry Economics, 1981), p. 32; Norton, Garmston, and Brodie, *Australian Economic Statistics, 1949–50 to 1980–81,* p. 23; Commonwealth Treasury, *Overseas Investment in Australia,* Treasury Economic Paper 1 (Canberra: APGS, 1972), p. 148; and Foreign Investment Review Board, *Foreign Investment Review Board: 1982 Report* (Canberra: AGPS, 1982), p. 28.
n.a. Not available.
a. Private gross fixed capital expenditure, excluding dwellings.
b. Excludes undistributed profits of subsidiaries.

capital, new products, and management, advanced technology, and possibly improved foreign market access, but concern was also raised by the prospect of firms making decisions on a global basis, which may have adverse consequences for Australia.[36] The country became sensitized to some FDI issues in the mid-1960s because of apparently huge profits reported by some foreign subsidiaries and the balance-of-payments strain therefrom.[37] Subsequently concern was aroused by the attempted takeover of a well-known Australian insurance company by a foreign interest. Also the possibility was raised that foreign firms were avoiding Australian taxes through transfer pricing of bauxite. More generally, however, Australians reflected the concerns felt elsewhere that foreign control might not adequately support Australian national interest, whether it be because of excessive profits, inadequate local employment, too few exports, inappropriate technology, or simply reduction of competition.

Previous research has not established a case against FDI in Australia. In fact, the reverse is more likely the case. Foreign firms appear to have had a positive effect on technical efficiency.[38] The profit levels in industries in which multinational firms are significant are not excessive and the foreign firms are less inwardly oriented than Australian-owned firms.[39] Evidence suggests that multinational firms are more dominant in industries with high concentration ratios and with significant product diversification, but causation cannot be inferred. These studies point more toward excessive levels of government assistance to industry and to protection from imports than to improper behavior of foreign firms. Protection is distorting and if foreign owners are beneficiaries at the expense of domestic consumers, legitimate concerns can be raised.

36. See Thomas G. Parry, "Arguments for and against Foreign Investment in Australia," Discussion Paper 6 (Parliament of the Commonwealth of Australia, Legislative Research Service, 1983).

37. At that time the Holden subsidiary (Australia) was reported to be the most profitable division of General Motors (United States).

38. Richard E. Caves, "Multinational Firms, Competition and Productivity in Host-Country Markets," *Economica*, vol. 41 (May 1974).

39. Thomas G. Parry, "Structure and Performance in Australian Manufacturing, with Special Reference to Foreign-Owned Enterprises," in Wolfgang Kasper and Thomas G. Parry, eds., *Growth, Trade, and Structural Change in an Open Australian Economy* (Canberra: Australian National University, 1978); and Donald T. Brash, *American Investment in Australian Industry* (Canberra: Australian National University Press, 1966).

However, regulating FDI is clearly a much less desirable solution to the problem than minimizing the distortion directly.

Policy toward Foreign Direct Investment

The first comprehensive policy toward FDI was introduced in 1972 at the end of the McMahon government, which began a screening procedure to prevent takeovers of Australian companies unless the national interest of Australia was advanced.[40] The replacement of the Liberal-Country government by the Whitlam Labor government saw a significant tightening of controls on FDI in 1973, particularly in the minerals industries. Complete Australian ownership was considered desirable for the energy industries, as was greater Australian participation in nonenergy minerals. A period of confusion followed these proposals as they were contested by foreigners and by Australians, including some state governments. Meanwhile, new explorations came to a halt. Some order was restored in 1975 when the Foreign Takeovers Act of 1975 was enacted, which regularized a screening procedure and notification requirement. Under this policy total Australian ownership was required only for new uranium ventures, and foreigners were limited to 50 percent for other mining projects.

The Fraser government proceeded further to regularize the screening process and established the Foreign Investment Review Board (FIRB). The purpose of review was to ensure that Australians had the maximum opportunity to participate in investing in their own country. Thus public notification has to be given of foreign takeovers to determine if there is an Australian alternative. Some economic benefit must be indicated by the investment, but a wide variety of indicators is accepted, such as increased employment or greater opportunity for exports. As a guideline, 75 percent Australian equity and Australian control is required of uranium projects and 50 percent for other natural resource projects. These are targets that need not be achieved immediately. It should be noted that there is no theoretical basis for fixing any particular level of domestic ownership; rather, the requirement is in response to visceral nationalistic feelings. Projects are evaluated on a case-by-case basis,

40. G. D. McColl, "Foreign Investment."

and frequently negotiations on Australian equity participation, taxation, and transfer pricing matters are required.

During its seven-year history the FIRB has been given better marks by foreign observers than has the Foreign Investment Review Agency in Canada. Decisions are made promptly—average processing time is only thirty days. About 30 percent of applications are approved without conditions, about 64 percent are approved with conditions (mainly relating to Australia equity participation), about 4 percent are rejected, and 2 percent, withdrawn. Even the rejections are processed on average in less than two months. These numbers may be somewhat deceptive because some preapplication discussions may take place that could take a period of several months. Indeed some applications may never be submitted if these discussions indicate a negative response.

Foreign concerns in 1983 were aroused by the election of another Labor government. Although Prime Minister Hawke and Treasurer Paul Keating have stressed continuity in policy, the concerns have not been put to rest. This is only to be expected since the national conference of the Labor party in July 1982 announced a policy to reverse the trend toward more foreign domination of the country's economy by increasing Australian ownership and control of resources and enterprises and by closer regulation of foreign investment.[41] The concern has been heightened by the apparent doubling of the rejection rate by the FIRB in the latter part of 1983. Finally, the rejection of the proposal by Citibank to take over an existing totally foreign-owned bank (Grindlays Australia) and to sell its share of another bank to an Australian interest seemed to be a new departure in policy.

If the government wants to maintain Australia's acceptance of FDI, there are few grounds for preventing foreign banks from establishing full-service branches. This was the recommendation of the Campbell Committee.[42] Alternatively, if the government chooses to become more intrusive in the economy and rely less on market mechanisms, then FDI is likely to be further curtailed. More restrictive performance requirements are likely to be added to the review process—such as targets for exports and R&D, which are part of policy in some other countries.

41. *The Asian Wall Street Journal Weekly*, October 10, 1983, p. 16.
42. See the chapter by Andrew S. Carron.

Conclusions

Australia faces a major choice between outward- and inward-oriented policies. The differences are profound. Consequences are likely to be found in the domain of domestic politics and foreign policy as well as economics. If the choice is to be inward-directed policies, then levels of assistance to industry and degrees of dispersion will continue to rise. Temporary measures to sustain threatened industries during the recession will become permanent. Policies controlling FDI will likely become more intrusive and more discriminatory. And immigration policy is likely to become more restrictive.

The economic costs of inward policies are mainly forgone opportunities; however, they may become visible if countries such as Japan or even Korea surpass Australia in per capita income. The economy in a relative sense would become more inefficient than it is today. Australia would become more of a rent-seeking society, with individuals and groups increasingly relying on the government, and the political process would be absorbed in determining relative shares. Furthermore, Australian society would become more of a hostage to powerful domestic vested interests such as labor unions or monopolistic business firms whose political clout could not be overcome. In the realm of foreign policy, Australia would find itself isolated from other countries in the Pacific basin. Australian initiative, for example toward ASEAN, would be less credible because those countries are so concerned with their own economic progress.

Outward-oriented policies, on the other hand, would require facing up to adjustment problems rather than avoiding them. As a result, efficiency would be promoted, but the adjustment costs could be quite substantial and might well fall unevenly on different social groups and geographic regions. Not so long ago it was estimated that as much as 60 percent of the labor force in Australian manufacturing worked for firms that depended on protective tariffs for their survival.[43] However, this gives an impression of a larger adjustment problem than was intended

43. W. M. Corden, "Australian Economic Policy Discussion in the Post-War Period: A Survey," *American Economic Review*, vol. 58 (June 1968), pp. 88–138.

and one very much greater than actually exists today. Automatic adjustments including changes in exchange rates, expansion of exports, and the like could be initiated by trade liberalization itself. Indeed it has been estimated that the structural adjustment that would be required following a 25 percent reduction in protection would cause only minor disruptions in the labor market.[44]

Within the Pacific basin Australia is not a small country. Its policy with respect to both trade and direct investment will be noted by other countries and it will affect their policy choices. For example, the expansion of Australian direct investment abroad, which has been undertaken in part to promote exports of manufactures from Australia, might not be accepted if Australia is not hospitable to FDI itself.[45] Australia has been a positive force for peace and prosperity in the Pacific basin. Its behavior toward Papua New Guinea is the most notable, but not the only example of this positive influence. Australia's influence and leverage within the Pacific basin, however, will be directly related to how outward looking its economic policy is.

Australia needs no guidance on how to become more inward-looking; however, if the choice is an outward orientation, the question is when and how fast to attempt adjustment. During the downward stage of a recession is a bad time to adjust, but when is a good time? A case can be made that the bottom of a cycle is the optimum point to affect resource allocation decisions. That is when resources can be redirected with least cost. Moreover, if trade liberalization is to be attempted, should it be done quickly or gradually?[46] Welfare considerations often come down on the side of gradualism. This permits more orderly adjustment by individuals, which minimizes adjustment costs, and may even avoid unnecessary adjustments if basic factors in the environment should change. However, in the Australian circumstances, a strong argument for sudden change can be made. On efficiency grounds, it is better to reach a new equilibrium point quickly even with adjustment costs than

44. This result was obtained by simulation of the ORANI model. See Peter B. Dixon, B. R. Parmenter, and Alan A. Powell, "Trade Liberalization and Labour Market Disruption," impact project General Paper G-46 (University of Melbourne, Impact Centre, July 1983).

45. R. B. Bennett, J. E. Merchan, and J. S. Metcalfe, "Motives for Australian Direct Foreign Investment," Working Paper 23 (Canberra: Bureau of Industry Economics, 1981), revised February 1982 by Denis Waters.

46. This subject was vigorously discussed at the Brookings-Canberra Conference.

never to reach it at all. With a three-year electoral cycle it is too easy to get policy reversals because the pain of adjustment often comes before the policy payoff. This raises doubt as to whether the objective will ever be reached and may even slow adjustment behavior. Possibly an optimum solution would be to have a two- to three-year lead time before liberalization is implemented but then to institute it completely in one step.

Appendix: Commodity Classification System[47]

International trade in commodities is classified by the United Nations into ten broad groups, labeled by the one-digit numbers 0 to 9 (standard international trade classification, or SITC). These categories, when finally disaggregated, number approximately 1,300 basic items, each of which is identified by a four-digit or, in some cases, a five-digit code. These basic items, when summed, compose total commodity trade for a given reporting country and partner country.[48]

To create a manageable data bank, the UN trade data were initially aggregated into 106 commodity groups, which taken together represent total trade. For the purposes of this study, the category "goods, not elsewhere specified" (SITC 09 excluding 951) was then excluded because it is composed of goods without any common traits.

To test the Heckscher-Ohlin theorem the 106 commodities were classified into four groups according to their relative factor intensities. These groups are natural resource intensive, unskilled labor intensive, technology intensive, and human capital intensive goods (table 12).

The commodity classification procedure was used sequentially by initially categorizing the commodities whose factor intensities are most apparent. First, the natural resource-based goods were identified. This group consists of all commodities within SITC section 00–04 (that is, food and live animals, beverages and tobacco, crude materials, mineral fuels, and animal and vegetable oils), and SITC classes 513 (inorganic elements, oxides, and so on), 61 (leather), 63 (plywood), 68 (nonferrous

47. This appendix is taken from Lawrence B. Krause, *U.S. Economic Policy toward the Association of Southeast Asian Nations.*

48. A detailed listing of the classification system used in this study is presented in the United Nations, *Standard International Trade Classification, Revised,* series M, no. 34 (New York: UN Statistical Office, 1961).

Table 12. *Standard Industrial Trade Classification Designations*
for Products in International Trade

Factor and commodity	SITC, revised	Factor and commodity	SITC, revised
Natural resource intensive		Unwrought nonferrous metals	681, 6831, 6851, 6861, 6871
Meat	00, 01		
Dairy	02		
Fish	03		
Wheat	041	Unwrought copper	6821
Rice	042	Copper manufactures	6822
Other cereals	043, 045–47	Nonferrous manufactures	6832, 6852, 6862, 6872, 688, 689
Corn	046		
Prepared foods	048, 0713, 09		
Fruit	051–53		
Vegetables	054, 055	Unwrought aluminum	6841
Sugar	06	Aluminum manufactures	6842
Coffee	0711, 0712	*Unskilled labor intensive*	
Cacao	072–75	Yarn	651
Feed	08	Fabrics	652, 653
Beverages	11	Textile products	654–57
Tobacco	12	Glass	664–66
Hides	21	Ships	7353, 7358, 7359
Soybeans	22		
Crude rubber	23	Firearms	7351, 951
Wood	24	Furniture	82
Pulp	25	Clothing	84
Cotton	263	Footwear	85
Fibers	261, 262, 264–69	Miscellaneous consumer products	81, 83, 893, 895, 899
Iron ore	281, 282		
Nonferrous ore	283–86	Toys	894
Crude materials, not elsewhere specified	29	*Technology intensive*	
Coal	32	Chemical elements[a]	51
Gas, natural and manufactured, and electric current	34, 35	Medicine	54
		Fertilizer	56
		Plastics	58
Crude petroleum	331	Other chemicals	52, 57, 59
Petroleum products	332	Power-generating equipment	7111–13, 7116–18
Animal and vegetable oils	4		
Inorganic elements, oxides, and so on	513	Jet engines	7114
Leather	61	Car engines	7115
Plywood	63	Tractors	7125
Mineral manufactures	661–63	Agricultural machinery	7121–23, 7129
Diamonds	667	Office machinery	7141, 7149
Pig iron	671	Computers	7142, 7143

Table 12 *(continued)*

Factor and commodity	SITC, revised	Factor and commodity	SITC, revised
Metal-working		*Human capital intensive*	
machinery	715	Paints	53
Textile machinery	717	Perfumes	55
Mining machinery	7184	Rubber	62
Other industrial		Paper	64
machinery	718, 7194–98	Steel	672–79
Heating and cooling		Metal manufacturing	691–94,
equipment	7191		698
Pumps	7192	Hand tools	695
Fork lifts	7193	Cutlery	696, 697
Electric power		Machine parts	7199
machinery	722	Televisions	7241
Telecommunications		Radios	7242
equipment	7249	Domestic electrical	
Electrical apparatus for		apparatus	725
medical purposes	726	Trains	731
Transistors	7293	Cars	7321
Electrical measuring		Trucks	7322–25
equipment	7295	Road motor vehicle	
Electrical apparatus	723, 7291,	parts	7326–28,
	7292, 7296,		7294
	7297, 7299	Motorcycles	7329
Scientific equipment	8617–19	Trailers	733
Optical equipment	8611–13	Watches	864
Aircraft	734	Phonographs	891
Cameras	8614–16	Books	892
Film	862, 863	Jewelry	896, 897

Source: SITC numbers from United Nations, *Standard International Trade Classification, Revised,* series M, no. 34 (New York: UN Statistical Office, 1961). This classification scheme was in effect from 1960 to 1975.
 a. Excluding SITC 513.

metals), 661–63 (mineral manufactures), and 667 (diamonds). In previous studies SITC class 513 was not included in this group; however, it was found that Australian exports of technology intensive goods are dominated by SITC class 51 (chemical elements). Through the investigation of the subclasses included under 51 it was noted that by far the largest export in the technology intensive category was SITC class 51365 (aluminum oxide, hydroxide). This commodity is more correctly classified as a natural resource intensive good. SITC class 513 was included rather than just SITC class 51365 because the data for 51365 were not consistent. In the natural resource intensive goods group there are forty-three commodities.

Second, by using the groupings of commodities according to their respective value added per worker, as presented by Garnaut and Anderson,[49] eleven goods were classified as unskilled labor intensive. These commodities, representing those with the lowest value added per worker, are the same goods appearing in Garnaut and Anderson, except in cases when the commodity aggregations precluded further separating of goods. Included in this group are such SITC classes as 65 (textiles and fabrics), 664–66 (glass), 735 (ships and boats), 81–85, 893–95, 899 (miscellaneous consumer goods, furniture, clothing, footwear, and toys), and 951 (firearms).

The remaining commodities were divided into technology intensive and human capital intensive categories by selecting as technology intensive those goods with the highest ratios of R&D expenditures to value added.[50] Ratios were calculated by industry, classified according to two- and three-digit standard industrial classifications (SIC), for the average of the years 1967–68 and 1975–76. The SIC classes were then cross-classified by using Balassa's system correlating SIC and SITC.[51] There are thirty commodities in the technology intensive category, including SITC divisions 51 (chemical elements, excluding commodity 513, as explained above); 54 (medicine); 56 (fertilizer); 58 (plastics); 52, 57, 59 (other chemicals); 71 less 7199 (machinery); 7249 (telecommunications equipment); 726 (electric apparatus for medical purposes); 7293 (transistors); 7295 (electrical measuring apparatus); 723, 7291, 7292, 7296–99 (electrical apparatus, not elsewhere specified); 734 (aircraft); 861 (scientific, medical, and optical measuring apparatus); and 862–63 (photographic supplies).

49. Ross Garnaut and Kym Anderson, "ASEAN Export Specialisation and the Evolution of Comparative Advantage in the Western Pacific Region," in Ross Garnaut, ed., *ASEAN in a Changing Pacific and World Economy* (Miami: Australian National University Press, 1980), p. 411. The presentation in Garnaut and Anderson is based on work in Bela Balassa, "A 'Stages' Approach to Comparative Advantage," World Bank Staff Working Paper 256 (May 1977), appendix table 1.

50. R&D figures are taken from National Science Foundation, *Research and Development in Industry, 1978* (National Science Foundation, 1980); value added data are from Bureau of the Census, *Annual Survey of Manufactures.*

51. See appendix table 2 in Balassa, "A 'Stages' Approach to Comparative Advantage."

Human capital intensive goods are those that have relatively lower ratios of R&D expenditures to value added than do technology intensive goods. Among the twenty-two commodities falling under the human capital intensive rubric are SITC groups 53 (paints), 55 (perfumes), 62 (rubber), 64 (paper), 672–79 (steel), 69 (manufactures of metal, not elsewhere specified), 7199 (machine parts), 7241 (televisions), 7242 (radios), 725 (domestic electrical apparatus), 7294 (automotive electrical equipment), 735 (trains), 732 (trailers), 864 (watches), 891 (phonographs), 892 (books), and 896–97 (jewelry).

RICHARD E. CAVES

Scale, Openness, and Productivity in Manufacturing Industries

AUSTRALIA has long been concerned about the efficiency of its manufacturing sector because of the small operating scales that manufacturers can attain in the country's small and isolated markets. The national market is limited to a population of 15 million, and even that is fragmented among the distant capital cities that dot the edges of this thinly populated continent; and a great distance separates Australia from traditional exporters of manufactures and from potential customers for its exports. These conditions probably provide enough natural protection to support a diversified, small-scale manufacturing industry. The small scale and diverse composition of Australia's manufacturing industry are to a significant degree the result of natural forces.

But unnatural forces are present as well. Throughout much of its history Australia has imposed protective tariffs that have roughly dou-

Many Australians contributed data to this investigation and discussed the hypotheses that were tested. Special thanks are due to Brian L. Johns and his staff at the Bureau of Industry Economics, to the Industrial Assistance Commission, to the Australian Bureau of Statistics, and to W. M. Corden, R. G. Gregory, Fred H. Gruen, and P. J. Williamson. Research assistance was provided by Alejandro Jadresic. The data base was organized through the Project for Industry and Company Analysis, Harvard Business School. John J. Beggs and Brian L. Johns were the assigned discussants for this chapter at the Brookings-Canberra Conference.

313

bled the isolating effects of international transport costs. Other policies have preserved regional fragmentation and promoted the decentralization of manufacturing industries. To appraise the effects of these policies, we need to determine the degree to which natural and artificial forces constrain the scales and productivity levels that can be attained in Australian manufacturing.

The prospect of booming exports of natural resources underlines the importance of these long-term constraints on productivity. Even though Australia can draw freely on international capital markets to finance massive investments in the production of natural resources, this sector competes with the manufacturing and rural sectors for the services of the Australian labor force. (It also competes for labor with the large services sector, but that sector is, for the most part, sheltered from international competition and hence is likely to expand in response to the increased demand associated with the nation's growing income.) Although the nation as a whole enjoys improved terms of trade, these increase the force of international competition in some parts of the manufacturing sector and frustrate hopes for expansion into export markets in others.

This chapter is built around a statistical analysis of productivity and scale in Australia's manufacturing industries. The ideal way to measure the effect of these forces would be to compare total factor productivity in Australian manufacturing to world "best practice" in an economy that was not subject to scale constraints (or other impediments that may stem from Australian institutions). But such an economic utopia does not exist in the markets of other nations. The alternative is to repeat a research maneuver employed recently in studies of Canada and Great Britain.[1] I proceed as follows: match as many Australian manufacturing

1. See A. Michael Spence, "Technical Efficiency," in Richard E. Caves, Michael E. Porter, and A. Michael Spence, *Competition in the Open Economy* (Harvard University Press, 1980), pp. 257–74; Ronald Saunders, "The Determinants of Productivity in Canadian Manufacturing Industries," *Journal of Industrial Economics,* vol. 29 (December 1980), pp. 167–84; Irwin Bernhardt, "Sources of Productivity Differences among Canadian Manufacturing Industries," *Review of Economics and Statistics,* vol. 63 (November 1981), pp. 503–12; Richard E. Caves, "Productivity Differences among Industries," in Richard E. Caves and Lawrence B. Krause, eds., *Britain's Economic Performance* (Brookings Institution, 1980), pp. 135–92; S. W. Davies and R. E. Caves, "Inter-Industry Analysis of United Kingdom-United States Productivity Differences," Discussion Paper 61 (London: National Institute of Economic and Social Research, June 1983).

industries as possible to their counterparts in the United States; form variables that indicate the productivity levels and operating scales of the Australian industries relative to their U.S. counterparts; test hypotheses about what factors have influenced Australian productivity (or scale) by their association with variations in the relative performance levels of individual industries. Before turning to the details of the statistical design and the results of the analysis, however, I should discuss the prevailing evidence on these hypotheses.

Strategic Influences on Productivity

The strangling limitation on productivity for Australian manufacturing is thought to lie in the difficulty of attaining economies of scale. Research into industrial organization has indeed shown that returns increase in essentially all manufacturing production functions over a certain range of output, although for most products these returns stop increasing in plants or firms that are modest in size by the standards of the U.S. market. Modesty in the United States, however, is extravagance in Australia: minimum efficient scales in most manufacturing industries account for large shares of the Australian market.[2] Likewise, the unit costs associated with operating at small (suboptimal) scales may be only slightly inflated in some industries but greatly enlarged in others. Scale economies might seem to pose no problem for a small economy that is open to international trade, because activities will be carried on either at efficient worldwide scales, with part of the output exported, or not at all. The problem arises with respect to Australian products that local buyers consider to be imperfect substitutes for goods produced elsewhere in the world. Such products can be anything from nontraded goods—bricks and haircuts—to tradable homogeneous manufactured goods for which the local producer may gain some advantage because of delivery flexibility or the provision of auxiliary services.

2. Minimum efficient scale refers to the smallest output at which average unit cost reaches its minimum value. The evidence on scale economies devolves from various research techniques (engineering estimates, various statistical approaches to ex post data); the findings differ somewhat with respect to particular industries but agree fully in the conclusions just stated. For a survey, see Donald A. Hay and Derek J. Morris, *Industrial Economics: Theory and Evidence* (Oxford University Press, 1979), pp. 83–142.

Where Australian goods are imperfect substitutes for imports, Australian producers as a group face a downward-sloping demand curve. Furthermore, if the domestic producers' outputs are differentiated from each other (by product characteristics or location), *each* Australian producer faces a downward-sloping demand curve. If scale economies in production are significant, the plant scales selected by producers are unlikely to exhaust them. Many advocates of tariff protection acknowledge this problem but then leap to the conclusion that tariffs help to solve it, arguing that raising the delivered price of imports shifts the demand curves for Australian substitutes outward and increases their scales of production. That outcome is possible but not necessary. If the product is indeed differentiated, then excluding imports simply makes room for more domestic substitutes produced at small scale to replace varieties produced at efficient scales abroad.[3] What deters efficient-scale production, then, is a combination of substantial scale economies, differentiation of domestic from foreign producers, and (artificial or natural) protection of domestic producers. I shall test the hypothesis in just that interactive form.

The evidence suggests that this model fits Australia's manufacturing sector comfortably. First, it implies that the size distribution of manufacturing plants is biased toward small scales. Data on plant-size distributions by employment for the United States, the United Kingdom, and Canada are compared to the data from Australia in table 1, which concentrates on 1977 but also presents an unpublished tabulation for 1972–73 because the published Australian data are severely aggregated in the upper tail. The most interesting comparison is between Australia and Canada, nations of similar size. Canada has 70.3 percent of its manufacturing employment in plants employing 100 or more, whereas Australia has only 61.9 percent; comparable figures for the United Kingdom and the United States are 79.8 and 74.6, respectively. Industry size and census definitions may account for part of the difference, but certainly not for all of it. Conlon's investigation of matched Australian and Canadian industries confirms this difference: he found that small plants are significantly more prevalent in the Australian industries, along

---

3. See Caves, Porter, and Spence, *Competition in the Open Economy*, pp. 3–20. Their empirical analysis of Canadian manufacturing led them to conclude that international competition truncates the small end of the domestic plant- and firm-size distribution.

Table 1. *Size Distribution of Manufacturing Establishments in Australia and Selected Industrial Countries, by Employment, Selected Years, 1972–73 to 1977–78*
Percent

Employment size category	Australia 1972–73	Australia 1977–78	Canada, 1977	United Kingdom, 1977	United States, 1977
0 – 19	14.13	13.20	6.74	6.94	6.51
20 – 49	12.10	12.67	10.74	6.18	8.74
50 – 99	11.43	12.24	12.20	7.05	10.10
100 – 199	14.87		16.97	9.37	18.02[a]
200 – 499	20.07		21.31	16.19	15.59[a]
500 – 999	10.59	61.89	13.75	13.28	13.54
1,000 +	16.81		18.29	40.99	27.50

Sources: Australian Bureau of Statistics, unpublished tabulation for 1972–73; ABS, *Manufacturing Establishments: Selected Items of Data Classified by Industry and Employment Size, Australia, 1977–78* (Canberra: ABS, 1978), p. 18; Statistics Canada, *Manufacturing Industries of Canada, National and Provincial Areas, 1977*, catalog no. 31–203, pp. 184–85; U.K. Department of Industry, Business Statistics Office, "Report on the Census of Production, 1977, Summary Tables," *Business Monitor* (London: Her Majesty's Stationery Office, 1978), p. 126; and U.S. Bureau of the Census, *1977 Census of Manufactures*, vol. 1: *Subject Statistics* (Government Printing Office, 1981), pp. 1–59.

a. The break in the U.S. distribution comes at 250 rather than 200.

with other marks of small size and isolation such as higher ratios of wages and salaries to value added and of inventories to shipments.[4]

Some would add that productivity in Australian manufacturing also suffers from excessive diversification and short production runs. Unfortunately, the lack of detailed data makes it difficult to compare the output diversities of plants in different countries. Nonetheless, one analytical point almost suffices to confirm the proposition. Building a small plant and building a diversified plant are alternative ways to adapt to limited demand in a small market. If Australian plants of a given size are more diversified than plants of similar size elsewhere, that is because the other

4. R. M. Conlon, "International Transport Costs and Tariffs: Their Influence on Australian and Canadian Manufacturing" (Kensington: University of New South Wales, 1980), pp. 115–45. A comparison based on 1948 gave similar results; see Pat Brown and Helen Hughes, "The Market Structure of Australian Manufacturing Industry, 1914 to 1963–4," in Colin Forster, ed., *Australian Economic Development in the Twentieth Century* (London: George Allen & Unwin, 1970), pp. 193–95. Brown and Hughes showed that plant concentration had not changed much in Australian manufacturing over the period from 1914 to 1963–64 that they examined, a finding which suggests that the sizes of plants and markets increased at similar rates.

alternative open to Australian managers is to make their plants more specialized but smaller still.[5]

Now we turn to some strategic influences on scale and productivity in Australian manufacturing. The first is the protection accorded Australian manufacturing—both natural protection from transportation costs and artificial protection from trade restrictions. Although the costs of ocean transportation do not increase strongly with distance, Australia's distance from major exporters of manufactured products is great enough to make natural protection quite substantial. Thus in 1974 the median manufacturing industry received international transport-cost protection equivalent to a 14.4 percent tariff (the weighted mean was 13.6 percent). Australian exports are similarly constrained: transportation costs to the United States have been estimated to impose twice as large a barrier to Australian exports as do U.S. tariffs. The ad valorem tariff equivalents of transport costs tend to be lower on more highly fabricated goods. Therefore, in contrast to the typical tariff structure, effective rates of natural protection (that is, the protection of Australian value added) are lower than nominal rates. The median (weighted mean) in 1974 was 10.3 (9.7) percent.[6]

Once again, the comparison with Canada is revealing: in eighty-five matched manufacturing industries, both nominal and effective rates of transport-cost protection are more than three times as high for the Australian industries.[7] These rates of natural protection dropped slightly in the 1970s, however, even though energy prices were rising.[8]

Australia has chosen to heap artificial tariff protection on top of this

5. Peter H. Karmel and Maureen Brunt, *The Structure of the Australian Economy* (Melbourne: F. W. Cheshire, 1962), pp. 90–91. Statistical evidence affirming this trade-off in Canada appears in Richard E. Caves, *Diversification, Foreign Investment, and Scale in North American Manufacturing Industries* (Ottawa: Information Canada, 1975), pp. 34–46.

6. R. M. Conlon, "Transport Costs as Barriers to Australian Trade," Paper 8 (Kensington: University of New South Wales, Centre for Applied Economic Research, 1979), especially p. 27. See also Gary P. Sampson and Alexander H. Yeats, "Tariff and Transport Barriers Facing Australian Exports," *Journal of Transport Economics and Policy*, vol. 11 (May 1977), pp. 141–54.

7. Conlon, "International Transport Costs and Tariffs," table 7.5, p. 112. These differences apply to the median and the weighted or unweighted mean figures.

8. A. E. G. Walker and K. M. Schneider, "Transport Costs and Australia's International Trade in the 1980s" (Canberra: Industries Assistance Commission, 1980). The containerization revolution has recently affected most of Australia's manufactured imports, greatly changing the interindustry pattern of rates of transport-cost protection.

Table 2. *Imports-Weighted Averages and Standard Deviations of Tariff Rates on Manufactures, Australia and Selected Industrial Countries, 1975*
Percent

Country	Average MFN rate, weighted by country's imports	Standard deviation of MFN rates weighted by country's imports
Australia	13.4	20.6
Canada	7.5	8.2
European Community	7.5	5.9
Japan	11.0	18.4
Sweden	5.4	4.5
United States	5.8	7.3

Source: Information from General Agreement on Tariffs and Trade (GATT) compiled by Industries Assistance Commission, *Annual Report: 1977–78* (Canberra: Australian Government Publishing Service, 1978), p. 78.

high natural protection. Consider, for example, that the weighted average and standard deviation of tariff rates in 1975 were substantially higher in Australia than in five other countries, among which only Japan was close (table 2). The Australian tariff has generated a hill of evidence and a mountain of controversy; from the evidence I extract a few examples that illustrate the effects tariffs have had on Australia's productivity.[9] Until a decade ago, the country embraced the principle of made-to-measure protection, freely sheltering manufacturing industries with tariffs that would let some domestic producers cover their costs in the competition with imports. That practice implies that the tariff rate of any given sector should be higher whenever the country is less well suited for the activity in question. As the country's wealth of resources and thin population lead us to expect, studies of interindustry differences in protection have found higher assistance going to low-skill, labor-intensive industries with simple technologies.[10] Also, higher protection has gone to large industries, perhaps because of their weight in the political calculus.

9. A convenient brief review is provided by R. G. Gregory and J. J. Pincus, "Industrial Assistance," in L. R. Webb and R. H. Allan, eds., *Industrial Economics: Australian Studies* (Sydney: George Allen & Unwin, 1982), pp. 113–62.

10. John Conybeare, "Public Policy and the Australian Tariff Structure," *Australian Journal of Management*, vol. 3 (April 1978), pp. 49–64; and Kym Anderson, "The Political Market for Government Assistance to Australian Manufacturing Industries," *The Economic Record*, vol. 56 (June 1980), pp. 132–44.

When the Industries Assistance Commission replaced the Tariff Board in 1974, the government committed itself to rates of duty that were both lower and less varied among industries (and thus caused less distortion of the interindustry allocation of resources). An across-the-board cut of 25 percent put the principle into practice. As the 1970s proceeded and economic conditions deteriorated, Australia along with other countries slipped into providing distressed sectors with expedient protection by means of quantitative restrictions that were said to be a temporary measure. Nonetheless, average effective rates of assistance (covering the gamut of tariffs, quotas, subsidies, and so on) did fall from 36 percent in 1968–69 to 26 percent in 1977–78.[11] Without the replacement of tariffs by quotas, the fall would have reached 24 percent, and the 12-point decline would have been largely due to the across-the-board reduction. Thus the average level of protection has been lowered somewhat, although stopgap measures have probably kept its variance from shrinking appreciably.[12]

International comparisons provide clinching evidence on the wide dispersion of Australian tariff rates. For other countries the correlations between tariff rates and import shares of domestic markets are typically positive and thus imply that the higher tariff rates only partly offset the comparative disadvantage of the most sheltered domestic producers. For Australia, however, the association runs in the opposite direction: imports claim smaller shares in the most protected markets.[13] Made-to-measure protection has thus survived with a vengeance, and the highest tariff rates have been set at prohibitive levels. Even with the decline in average rates of assistance, the ratio of total trade to gross domestic product is low in Australia compared with that in other OECD countries. Moreover, between 1960–62 and 1973–75 the ratio fell in Australia, whereas it rose in all the other OECD countries.[14]

11. Gregory and Pincus, "Industrial Assistance," p. 137 (data from Industries Assistance Commission). The decline stopped in 1977–78; exact figures on a comparable production-weighted basis are not available for later years.

12. Indeed, the coefficient of variation rose from 0.83 in 1968–69 to 1.31 in 1977–78.

13. Thomas G. Parry, "The Structure and Performance of Australian Manufacturing Industries" (Canberra: Industries Assistance Commission, 1978), p. 37; and Industries Assistance Commission, "Trends in the Structure of Assistance to Manufacturing: Approaches to General Reductions in Protection," Information Paper 1 (Canberra: Australian Government Publishing Service, 1980), appendix 2.3.

14. David H. Robertson, "Australia's Growth Performance: An Assessment," in

The final twist to this tale of small size and restricted trade is the Australian market's regional fragmentation, which protects the various state-capital manufacturing centers from one another. Once again, a combination of natural and artificial forces is at work. The basic problem is the small population is spread around the edges of the continent, but this problem has been compounded by policy choices. Coastal shipping, it has been argued, has suffered from high costs and cartelization that result from excluding international competition, and the railroad system is said to have been balkanized under the control of the state governments.[15] The transport system's inefficiencies have been partly sorted out, but its influence on industrial location, which goes far back in time, will long persist. State policies of subsidizing local industrial development have promoted branches of each industry in each manufacturing sector.[16] As a consequence, Australia's manufacturing centers are surprisingly nonspecialized, and the typical industry is spread rather evenly among them.[17] These factors add another important deterrent to efficient scales of production.

Industrial Organization and Competition

Competitive conditions require a gingerly treatment in the Australian context because they depend on the factors of size and openness already discussed. Those factors limit both the numbers and absolute sizes of firms operating in Australian markets. Accordingly, producer concentration is higher than it would be in larger markets, such as those in the United States, although not as high as it would be if Australian and U.S. firms were the same size. For each of 120 industries used in the statistical analysis that follows, we calculated the ratio of the share of shipments

Wolfgang Kasper and Thomas G. Parry, eds., *Growth, Trade and Structural Change in an Open Australian Economy* (Kensington: University of New South Wales, Centre for Applied Economic Research, 1978), pp. 69–89.

15. George R. Webb, "Transport, Growth and Trade," in Kasper and Parry, *Growth, Trade and Structural Change*, pp. 372–83; and Committee to Advise on Policies for Manufacturing Industry, *Policies for Development of Manufacturing Industry: A Green Paper* (Canberra: AGPS, 1975), pp. 71–72.

16. Industries Assistance Commission, *Annual Report, 1975–76* (Canberra: AGPS, 1976), pp. 9–10; *Annual Report, 1980–81* (Canberra: AGPS, 1981), pp. 39–42.

17. Joan Vipond, "The Regional Consequences of Structural Change and the Scope for Regional Adjustment Policies," in Kasper and Parry, *Growth, Trade and Structural Change*, pp. 348–68.

originating with the four leading Australian producers to that originating with the four leaders in the U.S. counterpart industry. The mean of these ratios is 1.78; that figure is biased downward.[18]

The statistical evidence affirms that producer concentration depends on plant scale economies (relative to market size) and on import competition. However, contrary to what one might expect, plant scale economies do not account for much of the high producer concentration found in Australia.[19] The leading firms in many industries operate more than one plant, in part because of scale economies that extend to multiplant operation (that is, to the firm's nonproduction activities, and to multiplant coordination). Empirical evidence also indicates that the more concentrated the industry, the *smaller* are plants of the leading firms relative to other plants in the industry, and the *smaller* the difference is between the extent of multiplant operations among leading firms and other firms.[20] This pattern, also found in Canada,[21] implies that the more concentrated the industry, the more likely it is that the leading firms and their smaller rivals are operating similar numbers of similar-sized plants. That inference is consistent with the hypothesis that economies of scale to either plant or firm impose a tighter constraint on minimum firm size in the more concentrated industries.

This pattern has several consequences. First, high producer concentration should exhibit at most a weak association with excess (monopoly) profits, because potential profits may be squeezed out between high costs (diseconomies of small scale) and demand rendered elastic by import competition. That prediction is consistent with the erratic statistical significance found for concentration in applications of the conven-

18. U.S. industries' concentration ratios were weighted and averaged to make the comparison. The average will typically exceed a concentration ratio calculated directly for leading-firm shipments in the combined market.

19. David K. Round, "Plant Size, Scale Economies, and 'Optimum' Concentration Levels in Australian Manufacturing Industries," *Weltwirtschaftliches Archiv*, vol. 116, no. 2 (1980), pp. 341–52. He compared actual four-firm concentration ratios in 139 industries to the minimum ratio that would prevail if each leading firm operated only one plant equal in size to the average plants of leading firms. The median concentration ratio then would be around 20 percent, whereas the actual median is about 48 percent.

20. David K. Round, "Concentration, Plant Size, and Multiple Plant Operations of Large Firms in Australian Manufacturing Industries," *Nebraska Journal of Economics and Business*, vol. 20 (Winter 1981), pp. 19–29. The latter relationship is not robustly significant statistically.

21. Caves, Porter, and Spence, *Competition in the Open Economy*, pp. 41–56.

tional (large-economy) model of profit determinants to the Australian manufacturing sector.[22] It is also consistent with the evidence that the intensity of international competition affects the process of price adjustment in the short run, after the competitive structure of domestic sellers has been taken into account.[23]

Producer concentration wields a complex influence on productivity. Given scale economies and other influences, high concentration implies that more efficient scales of production and higher productivity are being achieved. At the same time, productivity can be adversely affected by patterns of market behavior to which highly concentrated producers are prone. Collusive price fixing was by and large free of legal restraint in Australia at least up to 1974, and thus a history of easy access to price fixing lay behind the market conditions prevailing at the time chosen for our statistical analysis, 1977–78.[24] Agreements to fix prices and divide markets have been widespread.[25] Such agreements can have many adverse effects on productivity: they enable inefficiently small competitors to enter the market beneath the fixed-price umbrella; capacity is allowed to expand in the wrong locations or in increments that are too small; excess capacity is retained to exploit collusively inflated price-cost margins; and various other forms of nonprice competition that drain resources are encouraged.[26] In conclusion, many industries are concentrated enough to have the potential for noncompetitive market behavior. And high concentration bears an uncertain relationship to relative

22. For example, S. A. Leech and J. McB. Grant, "Profitability and Concentration in Australian Manufacturing Industries, 1970–71 to 1972–73: A Further Examination," *The Economic Record*, vol. 54 (December 1978), pp. 397–400; and David K. Round, "Concentration and the Level and Variability of Rates of Return in Australian Manufacturing Industries," *Antitrust Bulletin*, vol. 24 (Fall 1978), pp. 573–94.

23. Robert G. Gregory, "Determination of Relative Prices in the Manufacturing Sector of a Small Open Economy: The Australian Experience," in Kasper and Parry, *Growth, Trade and Structural Change*, pp. 219–38; and R. Dixon, "Industry Structure and the Speed of Price Adjustment," *Journal of Industrial Economics*, vol. 32 (September 1983), pp. 25–37.

24. We leave open the question of what changes have since resulted from the Trade Practices Act of 1974 and the Prices Justification Tribunal that was installed in 1973. See J. P. Nieuwenhuysen and N. R. Norman, *Australian Competition and Prices Policy: Trade Practices, Tariffs, and Prices Justification*, Studies in Australian Economics 1 (London: Croom Helm, 1976).

25. Karmel and Brunt, *The Structure of the Australian Economy*, pp. 94–100.

26. Ibid., pp. 98–99. Karmel and Brunt confirmed the prevalence of excess capacity in moderately concentrated Australian oligopolies.

productivity because noncompetitive behavior in concentrated industries can impair productivity, while concentration as a response to a given state of scale economies can improve it.[27]

Productivity can also be affected by other aspects of business organization such as the motives and qualities of business management. The balance of evidence from other countries favors the view that closer control of large enterprises by cohesive owners or groups leads to closer supervision of managers and less inefficiency due to slippage in the "agency" relation. Because Australia's leading firms are smaller and apparently less diversified than the largest enterprises in other industrial countries, one expects fewer of them to have escaped from effective control by their owners. Many enterprises are controlled from overseas, however, and the published estimates cannot be compared with those for (say) the United States or the United Kingdom. All the same, it can be pointed out that only 35 percent of 226 large companies were under managerial control in 1974–75, 34.5 percent fell under minority or majority owner control, and the remaining 30.5 percent were controlled by other corporations (foreign or domestic). In the United States, 82 percent of the 200 largest nonfinancial publicly held companies were under management control in 1974.[28] Even without formal control by owners, executive compensation schemes may serve to motivate business managers to maximize profits (minimize costs). In Australia, however, executive compensation does not seem to hinge on the enterprise's profits to the extent that it does in the United States.[29] Thus managerial motives may or may not pose a problem for productivity.

The fact that in 1975–76 foreign-controlled members of the largest

27. These tendencies should not be entirely collinear. Suppose that scale economies and market size interact to allow room for only a few producers in Australia, but constrain them to a Chamberlin-type monopolistic-competition equilibrium with their overseas competitors. Then they have no room for dysfunctional noncompetitive behavior. Conversely, as the minimum-scale constraint is relaxed and potential excess profits become available, the scope for strategic behavior expands.

28. Michael Lawriwsky, "Ownership and Control of Australian Corporations," Occasional Paper 1 (University of Sydney, Transnational Corporations Research Project, 1978); and Edward S. Herman, *Corporate Control, Corporate Power* (Cambridge University Press, 1981), pp. 58–59. See also Michael L. Lawriwsky, "Some Tests of the Influence of Control Type on the Market for Corporate Control in Australia," *Journal of Industrial Economics*, vol. 32 (March 1984), pp. 277–91.

29. Michael L. Lawriwsky, "Objectives and Internal Organisations of Firms," in Webb and Allan, *Industrial Economics: Australian Studies*, pp. 29–30.

200 enterprise groups accounted for 22 percent of all value added in manufacturing suggests that their net effect on productivity is important. However, the direction of that effect is ambiguous. What has been documented is their favorable effect in speeding the transfer of overseas technology and the diffusion of efficient methods of business operation.[30] The evidence confirms the expectation that technology reaches Australia more freely through intracorporate transfers than through the imperfect market for technology transfers at arm's length.[31] On the other hand, the facility with which multinational enterprises operate at small scales behind the Australian tariff is not in their favor. Their presence is fostered by trade barriers that discourage foreign companies from serving the market through exports, and their possession of proprietary intangibles (marketing skills, trademarks, technical knowledge) make them viable at smaller scales of operation than native firms would be. Because of that prowess, they might on balance lower productivity.[32]

Research and Technology Transfer

Productivity in Australia is linked to research and the international transfer of technology in many important ways. Nations' policies toward technology typically focus on domestic research activities. However, the majority of the technology used by most countries originates abroad: in Australia's case, more than nine-tenths of the patents issued and payments made for technical knowledge goes to foreigners.[33] There is no evidence to suggest that Australia lags behind other countries in the diffusion of new ideas, and much of the research and development undertaken commercially in Australia serves to adapt technology from

30. Richard E. Caves, "Multinational Firms, Competition, and Productivity in Host-Country Markets," *Economica,* vol. 41 (May 1974), pp. 176–93; and Donald T. Brash, *American Investment in Australian Industry* (Canberra: Australian National University Press, 1966), pp. 157–202.

31. W. P. Hogan, "British Investment in Australian Manufacturing: The Technical Connection," *Manchester School of Economic and Social Studies,* vol. 35 (May 1967), pp. 133–66.

32. Suggestive evidence appears in Brash, *American Investment in Australian Industry,* pp. 34–52, 162, 165; studies of productivity in Canada and Britain have leaned toward ascribing a negative effect to multinationals.

33. For a survey see Brian L. Johns, "The Production and Transfer of Technology," in Kasper and Parry, *Growth, Trade and Structural Change,* pp. 239–53.

abroad, especially that secured from foreign affiliates.[34] Some 70 percent of the funds spent on research and development goes toward development; meanwhile, independent firms undertake even less basic research than do foreign subsidiaries. Australia's rate of spending on research and development at the national level is typical of the small industrialized countries. That aggregate rate suggests no particular problems for the contribution of local research to productivity. However, a controversy circles around the question of how much money the government contributes to research and development and the extent to which these activities are carried on in government laboratories. The dominant organization, Commonwealth Scientific and Industrial Research Organization, has been criticized for lacking a mechanism that will enable it to interact with users of the technology, and for spreading its resources thinly (agricultural research excepted) over a number of industrial areas.[35] Thus, one does not expect Australian productivity to be more deficient in high-research sectors than in others, but it may nonetheless be true that national research outlays are not ideally allocated.

Labor Relations

Unsatisfactory labor-management relations clearly have a negative influence on productivity—as has. been confirmed statistically in the United Kingdom.[36] Observers familiar with the U.K. scene have suggested that labor relations in Australia may have a similar effect on productivity in sectors subject to high levels of union membership.[37] Although Australia's highly unionized manufacturing sector does not suffer the wastage of resources due to long strikes, it does experience

34. Peter Stubbs, *Innovation and Research: A Study in Australian Industry* (Melbourne: F. W. Cheshire, 1967), pp. 73–99; and Thomas G. Parry and J. F. Watson, "Technology Flows and Foreign Investment in the Australian Manufacturing Sector," *Australian Economic Papers*, vol. 18 (June 1979), pp. 103–18.

35. C. A. Tisdell, "Research and Development Services," in K. A. Tucker, ed., *The Economics of the Australian Service Sector* (London: Croom Helm, 1977), chap. 8; and K. Gannicott, "Does Australia Need an Innovations Board?" *Australian Economic Review*, no. 47 (Third Quarter 1979), pp. 31–36.

36. Caves, "Productivity Differences among Industries"; and Davies and Caves, "Inter-Industry Analysis."

37. H. A. Turner, "The Australian Disease and Its Doctor," *Australian Bulletin of Labour*, vol. 3 (September 1977), pp. 28–44.

many short strikes, which (in the United Kingdom, at least) seem to impair productivity by increasing the uncertainty of plant scheduling, inflating needed inventory levels, and the like. Also, the fragmentation of Australia's unions generates friction over jurisdictional issues. The arbitration system may contribute to a productivity problem by putting wage determination in a different sphere of decisionmaking from non-wage questions, which tend to have a greater effect on productivity. Wage determination is swept up into the arbitration mechanism while the nonwage issues, often specific to the workplace environment, are left aside.[38] Thus troubled labor relations may be associated with impaired productivity in Australian industries.

Labor market conditions are sometimes said to affect another aspect of Australia's productivity performance—the ease with which resources can be reallocated among sectors. An economy's allocation of resources among sectors is efficient if the rates of return to units of a given factor of production are equalized in its various uses. In the short run, the rates at which divergences are eliminated also have a bearing on efficiency. If sticky resource misallocation persists, the blame can rest on several doorsteps—labor, management, capital markets, or public policy. The ability to allocate resources to their best uses affects not just the maximum income the economy can generate but also the rate at which it can grow, since the effective seizure of expanding high-return opportunities then translates into high marginal returns to increases in the economy's stock of factors of production.

Australian observers have recognized this point and have undertaken some research on structural adjustment in the economy.[39] By and large, it turns up no specific malfunctions. True, the variability of the industry mix in the manufacturing sector from year to year seems to have shown a decline, over the long run at least up to 1973–74.[40] And over the period 1963–73 the dispersion of the growth rates of ten major manufacturing sectors was smaller for Australia than for most other countries, although

38. These points are discussed in the chapter by Daniel J. B. Mitchell.

39. Industries Assistance Commission, *Structural Change in Australia* (Canberra: AGPS, 1977), pp. 16–17.

40. R. Dixon, "Variations in the Composition of Manufacturing Employment in the Australian Economy," *Australian Economic Review*, no. 59 (Third Quarter 1982), pp. 33–42.

the conclusion ceases to hold if one moves the starting point back to 1950.[41] To the extent that an international difference in resource mobility exists, a sufficient explanation can be found in Australia's high levels of natural and artificial protection, which force sectoral growth into closer alignment with the generally stable growth of domestic demand. It is not clear whether the decline in intersectoral movement over time is unique to Australia or typical of maturing industrial economies. In any case, research specifically addressed to the intersectoral movement of labor has established an apparently high level of interindustry mobility, which appears to be unrelated to rates of assistance (tariffs, subsidies, etc.) among industries.[42] Accordingly the statistical analysis of productivity determinants in this paper will not develop this angle of adjustment capacity beyond the static role of tariff protection already outlined.

Determinants of Relative Productivity

The hypotheses outlined above were tested by matching as many Australian manufacturing industries as possible to their U.S. counterparts and testing for the factors associated with good or poor relative performance. The standard industrial classifications for the two countries match fairly well and provide a total of 138 paired industries, although missing data leave many fewer usable observations. Data for 1977 are used to analyze the determinants of their relative levels of labor productivity.[43] Productivity is a relation between output and the inputs producing it when all are valued at their social opportunity costs. Conceptual problems arise in measuring productivity and testing its determinants within a consistent framework. The solutions employed in this chapter are taken from previous research and are only briefly explained here.

41. These conclusions are based on coefficients of variation calculated among growth rates presented in Industries Assistance Commission, *Structural Change in Australia*, pp. 14, 65, 67, and 69.
42. Ibid., pp. 48–55; see also Robertson, "Australia's Growth Performance: An Assessment."
43. Typically an Australian industry is matched to several U.S. industries at the four-digit level of the U.S. standard industrial classification. Industry shipments were used throughout as the weighting variable for constructing weighted averages. Details of the procedure and of definitions and sources of variables appear in an appendix to the version of this paper issued by the Australian National University, Centre for Economic Policy Research.

Research Design

The first question that arises in implementing this design is how to evaluate output at social opportunity cost when tariffs permit domestic prices to be inflated above the world prices. I assume (provisionally) that each domestic price in equilibrium equals the world price plus the nominal tariff for each output and purchased input.[44] Then the following relation can be shown:

$$\frac{e_d}{e_w} = \frac{V_d}{V_w(1 + t_d)},$$

where e_d = physical productivity per employee (with inputs and outputs valued at world prices) in the protected industry
e_w = physical productivity in some external "world industry"
V_d = value added per employee as measured in the protected industry
t_d = the protected industry's effective rate of tariff protection.

If the comparison is made not to value added per employee in some mythical world industry, V_w, but to a specific foreign country with its own tariff structure, then the relation becomes

$$\frac{e_d}{e_u} = \frac{V_d(1 + t_u)}{V_u(1 + t_d)},$$

where u indicates the foreign reference country.

The assumption that domestic producers always set prices equal to the world price plus the tariff is, of course, one that should be verified rather than taken on faith. Depending on the industry's comparative disadvantage, its competitiveness, and the elasticity of demand that it faces, the equilibrium domestic price may fall below this benchmark in industries for which competing imports in equilibrium are in fact small.

Two strategies are available for dealing with this problem. Some investigators have had access to actual market prices in the economy under study and thus have been able to convert relative outputs directly into real terms. Others have not had access to such data and have constructed their basic dependent variable by the procedure just out-

44. See Spence, "Technical Efficiency," pp. 257–74; and Saunders, "The Determinants of Productivity."

lined, but then tested the significance of explanatory variables indicating the degree that domestic sellers fail to price up to the world price plus the tariff (and therefore appear less productive than they really are).[45] I follow the second strategy in this study. Thus the dependent variable is the ratio of value added per employee in the Australian industry to that of its U.S. counterpart (converted to Australian dollars), and the effective protection rate used for Australia includes transportation costs and nontariff barriers. (The rate for the United States includes only tariffs.)

The second question that arises with the research design is how to reconcile the productivity measure of net output per unit of labor input with the presence of other inputs in the production function. One expects producers to employ labor, capital, and other inputs so as to minimize the costs of whatever outputs they choose to produce. Other inputs need to be taken into account and the cross-section statistical analysis reconciled with the presumption that each industry has its own function. The solution developed by Davies and Caves is described here in general terms.[46] Assume that each industry (in Australia or the United States) operates on the same Cobb-Douglas production function, written in terms of net output, capital, and labor.[47] Divide through by labor input, so that the net output per unit of labor input is related to the capital-labor ratio. Control for the possibility that returns to scale in the plant are not constant (that is, the output elasticities of the Cobb-Douglas function do not sum to 1.0) by allowing net output per unit of labor input to depend on the size of the typical plant as well as the capital-labor ratio and the catchall efficiency term. Now, divide the equation for the Australian industry by the corresponding one for its U.S. branch. For the ith industry in question, one has

$$VPW_i = (EFF_i)(CAP_i)^\alpha (TP_i)^{\alpha+\beta-1},$$

45. For Canada, it was found that the degree to which domestic producers price up to the tariff can be explained by the industry's market structure. See Tim Hazeldine, "Testing Two Models of Pricing and Protection with Canada/United States Data," *Journal of Industrial Economics,* vol. 29 (December 1980), pp. 145–54. Another problem without a ready solution is that differentiated goods may be priced above the world price plus tariff.

46. Davies and Caves, "Inter-Industry Analysis," app. A. Formal derivations are set forth in the extended version of this chapter (see note 43).

47. The usual procedure of netting out purchased materials inputs is followed. This practice can be justified where there is no substitution between them and primary factor inputs to the production process, or where they are perfect substitutes.

where VPW_i = value added per employee in the Australian industry divided by value added per employee in the U.S. counterpart

$\quad CAP_i$ = assets per employee in the Australian industry divided by assets per employee in the counterpart

$\quad TP_i$ = median plant size in the Australian industry divided by median plant size in the counterpart[48]

$\quad EFF_i$ = the ratio of the two efficiency terms, which accounts for all labor-productivity differences between the two countries that are not due to capital inputs or plant scales.

This equation provides an attractive starting point for the cross-section analysis of the determinants of relative productivity. The role of relative plant size, emphasized in the preceding discussion, enters in a natural way through TP_i, and the term EFF_i can be expanded to include the other hypotheses about the determinants of relative efficiency. If one can justify applying the model to a sample of diverse industries, one need only add a disturbance term, take logarithms, and readily estimate the model statistically. However, as the equation makes clear, such a procedure amounts to assuming that all industries in both countries share a common production function. That assumption is open to question. It cannot be abandoned totally, but one can relax it a good deal without greatly complicating the statistical procedure.

First, suppose that all industries in Australia share the same Cobb-Douglas production function, as do all industries in the United States, but that the Australian and U.S. functions differ. Only two more terms need to be added to the model—the values of TP and CAP for Australia alone, alongside the ratios. Significant regression coefficients for the Australian terms will indicate the differences between the Australian and American values of α and β. Second, suppose that each industry's Australian and U.S. branches share the same production function, but that the coefficients for some industries differ from the common values of α and β. This difference can be handled by adding slope shifts to the model for those industries thought to differ from the typical patterns of

48. Monetary values are expressed in a common currency. Typical plant size, here measured in terms of employment, summarizes the size distribution of plants in an industry. Davies and Caves showed that a suitable approximation is midpoint plant size—the scale of the plant accounting for the fiftieth percentile of output when plants are ranked from the largest to the smallest.

factor intensity and returns to scale. For example, one might draw on general knowledge to suggest which sectors are especially labor intensive and free of scale economies, and which are especially capital intensive and prone to scale economies. Of course, one cannot deal with the possibility that every industry's production function might differ from all others, because the cross-section model would then break down.

Thus far I have treated capital as the assets shown on the books of producers—I have used this as the basis for measuring the variable CAP empirically. However, the model neglects another element of capital in the form of human resources; that is, it makes no allowance for differences among industries in the average skills and training of employees, or, for that matter, in the amount of time they work. These factors can be incorporated in various ways. For example, skills and training can be counted as intangible stocks of capital by capitalizing their rents and adding them to the physical asset stocks. However, an alternative procedure employed by Davies and Caves seems more attractive. The production function can be written in terms of effective labor L^* rather than the body-count L. The L^* is a weighted sum of labor types with different skills or training. When I estimate the model using the inappropriate L rather than L^*, it is possible to avoid bias by including terms that recognize the different weights applied to different labor groups when they are aggregated into L^*. Suppose, for example, that the distinction between production and nonproduction workers captures some of the difference in the amounts of human capital that industries employ. Then it can be shown that the difference between the percentage of nonproduction workers employed in the Australian industry and the percentage employed in its U.S. counterpart should be added to the model. One can treat any other binary distinction between labor groups having to do with skill or quality in the same way.[49]

Although short supplies of human capital have not been recognized as a drag on Australian productivity levels, they may in fact exert one. The country does not invest heavily in secondary education, and the expansion of higher education is a recent development. In comparing

49. As a method of incorporating human capital, this strategy offers several advantages. It permits the analyst to assume that workers of different qualities may be good substitutes for one another (although not one for one), while human capital and physical capital may be relatively poor substitutes. Also, it avoids the problems of measuring human capital directly.

the growth of Australia's real gross domestic output per capita to other OECD countries, the Industries Assistance Commission found the nation ranked at about the bottom quartile, not because total output had grown slowly but because population had grown fast. The increasingly large female and immigrant components of the labor force may be lowering the average skill level. Parry's investigation of interindustry differences in labor productivity found positive influences for the proportions of technical and managerial personnel and negative influences for the proportions of female employees and persons born overseas.[50] If Australia's stock of human capital is on the low side relative to that in the United States *and* if the shortfall varies among industries, then skill and quality differentials should prove significant in the basic model. The difference between the Australian and U.S. ratios of nonproduction workers to total employees, *NPW*, should take a positive coefficient.

Influences on Relative Efficiency

The preceding variables complete what can be considered as the core of the model for explaining relative productivity and bring the discussion to the variables that should indicate relative efficiency (EFF_i in the basic model). The first of these, described in general terms previously, takes account of the interacting effects of scale economies, small market size, and tariff protection. A subtle interaction is required, because Australia's potential productivity disadvantage increases with minimum efficient scale and the disadvantage of suboptimal-capacity producers as long as tariff protection makes inefficient capacity viable. If protection is inadequate to shelter suboptimal-capacity producers, however, the relation turns around, and "severe" disadvantages of small scale will force viable local producers to achieve efficient operating scales. A suitable form for this interaction, suggested by Saunders, is

50. It should be stressed that negative influences for these latter groups are expected on the basis of less extensive training and (in the case of females) a larger proportion of employees working part-time. See Industries Assistance Commission, *Annual Report, 1981–82*, pp. 13–18; and Thomas G. Parry, "Structure and Performance in Australian Manufacturing, with Special Reference to Foreign-Owned Enterprises," in Kasper and Parry, *Growth, Trade and Structural Change*, pp. 184–89. Parry's design resembles that employed in this chapter, but he did not use an international comparison for control or a consistent production-function framework.

$$SCLA = (K - EFFA)(MESU/CDRU)(DDU/DDA),$$

where $EFFA$ = the Australian sector's rate of effective protection
           $MESU$ = minimum efficient scale inferred from data for the
                    U.S. counterpart industry
           $CDRU$ = an (inverse) indicator of the disadvantages of sub-
                    optimal-scale production (also inferred from U.S.
                    data)
      DDA/DDU = the size of the Australian relative to the U.S.
                    market (measured by domestic disappearance)[51]
              K = a constant that must be determined inductively; it
                    implicitly determines the protection level at which
                    inefficient-scale domestic production becomes vi-
                    able for any given state of scale economies and
                    market size.

Saunders secured a significant regression coefficient for this variable
(positive, as expected) and concluded that the best fit resulted from
$K = 0.25$ (with 0.3 about equivalent statistically) as a threshold for
effective protection in Canada. Appropriately, given Canada's geog-
raphy, he did not consider transportation costs. The variable $EFFA$
includes natural as well as artificial protection. I searched for the value
of K that yields the most significant coefficient for $SCLA$ by starting with
that mean and then raising it by small fractions.

In the preceding discussion some skepticism was expressed about
disentangling the complex influence of competitive conditions on efficiency. On the one hand, producer concentration in Australia is itself
determined by forces (embodied in $SCLA$) that should strongly affect
efficiency. On the other, incomplete collusive bargains that can impair
efficiency have been widely legal in Australia, and so their presence may
be fairly independent of Australian producer concentration above a low
threshold. If noncompetitive behavior creates a drag on efficiency, it
should be evident in those industries where concentration is not only
high but also above a minimum threshold determined by scale econo-

51. Saunders, "The Determinants of Productivity," pp. 172–74. For the United
States, we substituted industry shipments for domestic disappearance in order to avoid
a large number of missing observations.

mies.[52] I employed *CONC,* equal to *C4A*CDRU*EFFA;* and *CNRS,* residuals from a logarithmic regression of *C4A* on *MESU,* expressed as a fraction of U.S. industry shipments and *CDRU* multiplied by *EFFA.* In these definitions, *C4A* is the share of turnover in Australia accounted for by the industry's four largest producers; *MESU* is the ratio of shipments by the median-sized plant in the U.S. counterpart industry to total shipments by the U.S. industry (a proxy for minimum efficient scale); and *CDRU* is the ratio of net output per employee in U.S. plants smaller than the industry median to output per employee in larger plants (an inverse proxy for the cost disadvantage of suboptimal scale). Thus the value of *CONC* increases with Australian producer concentration, with the extent of tariff protection in Australia, *EFFA,* and with the relative productivity advantage of small units. Its coefficient should be negative.

The alternative variable, *CNRS,* seeks by another route to identify Australian industries that are unconcentrated relative to the floor imposed by scale economies apparent in the United States. *CONC* embodies the assumption that an Australian industry's concentration must be high relative to the scale-economies threshold before it permits collusion that is dysfunctional for efficiency; *CNRS* assumes that the problem may arise for any Australian industry that is less concentrated than a constraint based on U.S. scale economies would suggest. I expect a negative regression coefficient for *CNRS.* Nonetheless, because *CNRS* and *CONC* both involve producer concentration, they must receive two-tail tests in recognition of another behavioral factor. The concentration ratio could correct for an error in my assumption that each Australian industry raises its price to the world price plus tariff and transportation costs. A competitive industry with not too great a comparative disadvantage might set a lower price and as a result appear inefficient by the test of the dependent variable. A term reflecting the concentration ratio, if it corrects for this factor, would take a positive coefficient.

A number of other hypotheses about relative efficiency were tested. Since none of them proved statistically significant, however, the tests are summarized briefly here. Economic growth in Australia before 1977 should influence the distribution of plant scales existing in that year.

52. The logic of this statement follows from the justification for the variable *SCLA.* Saunders employed a variable constructed like *CONC* in his study of the efficiency of Canadian industry and failed to confirm the hypothesis.

Suppose that an enterprise cannot efficiently alter the scale of a plant, once it is built, and therefore chooses the plant's initial scale in consideration of the time expected to elapse before the plant can be fully utilized. Then the faster the market grows, the less incentive will prevail for putting suboptimal plants in place. This hypothesis was tested with negative results by means of the ratio of the absolute growth of the Australian market over 1967–77 to apparent minimum efficient scale. The available data restrict me to this shaky embodiment of the hypothesis, which covers too short a period and employs no control for the ease of enlarging established plants.

Several hypotheses address the role of multinational companies. They may exploit superior efficiency or transfer technology from abroad, earning rents that show up as higher relative productivity in Australia. Or they may exacerbate problems of inefficiently small scales, with the opposite result. As it turned out, no significant relationship emerged between relative productivity and the share of the Australian market accounted for by foreign subsidiaries (either that variable taken by itself, or in interaction with the industry's research intensity or rate of productivity growth).[53]

Finally, I hoped to test the influence of divisive labor relations on Australian productivity. The absence of any appropriate data at the industry level forced me to omit this potentially important factor and thus to inflict omitted variable bias on the model. I made a crude attempt to approach the issue by inquiring whether relative productivity is lower in those Australian industries whose counterparts are heavily unionized in the United States; this approach rests on the defensible assumption that the state of an industry's labor relations depends heavily on its production technology, and that as a consequence an industry with divisive labor relations in one country is prone to the same problems elsewhere. However, the data offer no support for this supposition.

It should be emphasized that the omission of these also-ran hypotheses has no substantial effect on the magnitude and significance of the coefficients reported. This assurance does not extend, however, to the untested hypothesis about the effect of labor relations on the productivity of the economy.

53. Bernhardt, in "Sources of Productivity Differences," found a positive influence for foreign investment interacted with research intensity for Canada; Saunders found a negative influence mitigated in research-intensive sectors.

Statistical Results

The data base containing the variables listed above was prepared as a cross section of Australian and U.S. manufacturing industries centered on the year 1977 (1977–78 for Australia). Different years were tolerated for variables not collected in the reference year. Although most variables come from standard government statistical sources, missing observations proved to be a serious problem—because of nondisclosure in the published source or difficulties in matching different statistical classifications. The fact that different industries tend to be missing for each variable greatly reduced the number of degrees of freedom available. Hence for a few important variables, ad hoc procedures were used to plug these gaps, but this was not done across the board.[54]

The most revealing results appear in the following equations:

$$VPW = -0.659 + 0.099 \; CAP - 0.298 \; CAPL - 0.065 \; CAPA$$
$$(1.58) \quad (1.48) \qquad (4.35) \qquad (0.93)$$

$$+ \; 0.008 \; TP - 0.076 \; TPA + 0.449 \; NPW$$
$$(0.24) \qquad (2.23) \qquad (0.67)$$

$$+ \; 0.823 \; SCLA + 0.174 \; CONC,$$
$$(3.27) \qquad (1.14)$$

Degrees of freedom $= 64; \bar{R}^2 = 0.424$

$$VPW = -0.574 + 0.086 \; CAP - 0.302 \; CAPL - 0.049 \; CAPA$$
$$(1.51) \quad (1.30) \qquad (4.55) \qquad (0.74)$$

$$- \; 0.023 \; TP - 0.065 \; TPA + 0.456 \; NPW$$
$$(0.56) \qquad (2.04) \qquad (0.69)$$

$$+ \; 0.764 \; SCLA + 0.194 \; CNRS.$$
$$(3.09) \qquad (1.81)$$

Degrees of freedom $= 64; \bar{R}^2 = 0.441$

I consider first the neoclassical core of the model, which encompasses the ratios VPW, CAP, TP (expressed in logarithms), and the difference in nonproduction worker share, NPW, defined above. It also includes

54. Compare Caves, Porter, and Spence, *Competition in the Open Economy*, pp. 31–36.

three slope-shift variables: *CAPL*, the logarithm of *CAP* entered again for a group of the more labor-intensive industries, to allow for a slope shift; *CAPA*, the logarithm of the capital-labor ratio for the Australian industries only, to allow for a systematic difference between Australian and U.S. production functions; and *TPA*, the logarithm of the typical plant size for the Australian industries only, to allow for a systematic difference in revealed scale efficiency between Australia and the United States.

The estimated neoclassical core behaves in a peculiar fashion. Relative labor productivity, *VPW*, is positively related to relative capital intensity, *CAP*, although the coefficient's significance is weak. However, the coefficient of the slope shift that allows for different production technology in the more labor-intensive industries is negative, large, and highly significant. The coefficient of *CAPA* indicates that the output elasticity of capital is lower (that of labor is higher) in Australian industries than in their U.S. counterparts, although the difference is not statistically significant. Thus these coefficients suggest strongly that the same Cobb-Douglas technology does not apply to labor-intensive industries as to other industries, and it weakly suggests that Australia obtains relatively higher labor (lower capital) productivity in the typical manufacturing industry.

A somewhat similar pattern arises for the variable indicating relative typical plant size, *TP*. It is quite insignificant, suggesting by itself no plant-level scale economies in the typical industry. However, the slope shift for typical plant size in the Australian industry, *TPA*, takes a significant negative coefficient. A possible interpretation is that, faced with operating in a small and protected market, Australian manufacturers have adapted so as to minimize their intrinsic productivity disadvantage in industries best suited to small-scale and (perhaps) labor-intensive operations.[55] The *NPW*, which indicates differential use of nonproduction workers, has the right sign but does not increase the model's explanatory power. If Australia underinvests in human capital, the effect does not show up in productivity differentials among manufacturing industries.

55. I experimented with a variable analogous to *CAPL* that permitted a slope shift in capital-intensive industries. However, the data base did not include many industries in the highly capital-intensive sectors, and perhaps for that reason the variable proved insignificant.

SCLA—which indicates the combined influence of artificial and natural protection, minimum efficient scale, and market size—is highly significant in both equations. The value of the constant embedded in *SCLA* that yields the most significant regression coefficient is 0.30, which is approximately the mean of the rate of effective protection (natural plus artificial) for industries in the sample. That is, for any given incidence of scale economies, protection above the mean has a negative effect on productivity, and that effect grows larger as the importance of the scale economies increases. Saunders obtained similar results for Canada, except for a slightly lower apparent threshold of 0.25 for protection's negative effect.[56]

I tested the hypothesis that the effect of *SCLA* should be weaker in industries where product differentiation supplies some insulation for domestic producers. I calculated mean values of several variables indicating the intensity of differentiation of an industry's products and tested whether the coefficient on *SCLA* is higher in industries with below-average differentiation. For a composite criterion reflecting structural differentiation (customization, importance of auxiliary services, infrequency of purchase), the hypothesis was supported, and the coefficient on *SCLA* was two-thirds larger in the less differentiated industries. When the differentiation criterion is the importance of research and development, the hypothesis is again confirmed, and the difference in coefficients becomes fourfold. However, when the importance of media advertising becomes the differentiation criterion, the coefficient on *SCLA* is two-thirds larger in the differentiated industries. That apparent exception, rather than undermining the hypothesis, may affirm the importance of scale economies of sales promotion in high-advertising industries.

The only other variable to affect relative efficiency in these equations is the one representing the influence of producer concentration in Australia (*CONC* or *CNRS*). The coefficients would be negative if concentration led to producer behavior that depresses productivity (after one controls for the lower limit that scale economies impose on producer concentration). A positive coefficient might be given the opposite interpretation. However, a still more attractive interpretation of a positive coefficient is that concentration increases the likelihood

---

56. Saunders adjusted the relative weight of the tariff and scale-economy terms where the product is *SCLA* by attaching an exponent to the former. My experimentation indicated that, for Australia, the best fit results when that exponent is equal to 1.0.

that Australian prices are pushed up to (or beyond) the level warranted by protection. The positive coefficients of this variable (significant at 10 percent in the second equation) make one inclined to prefer this hypothesis, which has previously been confirmed for Canada.

The chief finding here is that relative productivity is affected by the interaction of protection, scale economies, and product differentiation: Australia's average productivity disadvantage is greatest for industries marked by substantial scale economies, large cost disadvantages of suboptimal-scale production, high protection (natural or artificial), and extensive structural product differentiation. With these factors controlled, there is weak evidence that concentrated industries in Australia are more likely to elevate their prices relative to the limit set by international competition; put the other way around, fairly strong evidence exists that their potential rents are not all squandered in cost-increasing activities (nonprice competition, for example). These findings agree with similar research on the Canadian economy. I find no evidence that productivity in manufacturing suffers from short supplies of non-production-labor skills or an inappropriate amount of foreign investment. My confidence in these conclusions is limited by the peculiar result for the model's neoclassical core, which, however, suggests the plausible hypothesis that Australian industry has had some success in adjusting its production technology to operate at small scales.

Determinants of Relative Scale

The preceding model allowed for several types of shortfall in relative productivity. Those in the basic model are neoclassical sources associated with input combinations and scales of production. Those picked up in the efficiency term are more varied—some are related to scale, some to inefficiencies associated with the excess cost of producing Australia's level of output. Because the influence of the size of Australian production units is diffused through several variables, we append a direct investigation of what determines the scale of Australian production units relative to their counterparts in the United States. I am concerned here with the scale economies of plants, although scale economies also accrue to the multiplant firm.

Australia's plant-size distribution can be measured and evaluated in various ways. A particularly attractive measure is the proportion of an industry's employment in plants larger than the median plant in the U.S. counterpart industry.[57] The published data on the plant-size distributions of Australian industries are too coarse to permit a calculation of this variable with any accuracy, but there are data on the companies assigned to each Australian industry finely disaggregated by size class. The extent of multiplant operation by the leading companies is also known. Therefore, one can calculate as the dependent variable the proportion of Australian employment in companies larger than the median U.S. plant size and control for the plant-company discrepancy by including as a regressor the number of plants per company for the four leading Australian firms.[58] To indicate the notation, one regresses *RELS* and *MLTP* on other variables to be explored.

Hypotheses about Relative Size

These hypotheses were explained earlier in the chapter, so they can be set forth briefly. The first of them concerns the viability of suboptimal-scale production—that is, the influences operating through *SCLA*, the variable defined as a determinant of relative productivity. A similar variable for explaining relative size can take a slightly simpler form:

$$SCLB = RMSU*CDRU*EFFA,$$

where *RMSU* is median plant size in the U.S. counterpart industry (that is, *MESU*) divided by U.S. industry shipments. As defined above, *CDRU* and *EFFA* are the inverse indicators of the productivity disadvantage of small plants (U.S. data) and the overall Australian rate of effective protection (natural or artificial). The predicted negative influence of *SCLB* on *RELS* thus implies that Australian plants should be smaller (relative to the U.S. median) in industries that have a large minimum efficient scale in the United States but low drawbacks to suboptimal scale, and in industries that receive high protection in Australia.

57. This variable was analyzed for Canada by Caves, Porter, and Spence, *Competition in the Open Economy*, pp. 270–73.
58. A more sophisticated correction could be obtained for some industries by fitting some functional form to the published data on multiplant operation by several size classes of leading firms. I did not expect that the gain would be worthwhile.

The market-size constraint on plant (or company) size of course assumes that the production unit is tied to a national or smaller market. Any manufacturing industries that have attained significant exports should escape the constraint and exhibit larger plant sizes—a hypothesis confirmed for Canada. Thus, one includes *EXPA* as the ratio of exports to turnover for the Australian industry.[59] It should obtain a positive coefficient. However, so few Australian industries attain significant exports that the prospects of *EXPA* are modest.

The presence of foreign subsidiaries is another potential influence on *RELS: FCTA* is equal to share of turnover in the Australian industry accounted for by foreign-controlled companies. The sign expected for its coefficient is ambiguous. If the proprietary assets of multinational comapnies help them to obtain a large share in an Australian industry, then they will choose to build large plants, enlarging the size of that industry's typical plant. However, the relation could go the other way where products are highly differentiated or where multinationals serve the Australian market partly with imported articles and partly with goods produced locally. The first relation may hold for some industries, the second for others, so that the absence of a significant relation need not mean "no influence." The ambiguous effect of multinationals is in part the result of differences in the degree to which nonproduction activities are integrated into plant operations. Such overhead activities may be more prevalent in the United States, and may be enlarging U.S. plant sizes. If technological and marketing knowledge is imported (via multinationals or otherwise) into Australia, local production units will be smaller. Because nonproduction workers produce most of these intangibles, one can test the effect by including *NPW*, the difference between the nonproduction-worker proportions of the Australian and U.S. labor forces. Its coefficient should be positive. Yet another version of this hypothesis, specified more narrowly, is that *RELS* is negatively related to *RNDU*, research and development outlays as a proportion of sales in the U.S. counterpart industry. One needs to control for the regional fragmentation that confines some producers in many Australian manufacturing industries to local markets. The best available measure of regional fragmentation comes from data on the interstate dispersion of

---

59. I assume that the exports-shipments ratio for the U.S. counterpart industry may be neglected because of the U.S. market's large size.

production among the Australian states. Specifically, for each industry I calculated *REGH*, the Herfindahl index of concentration of the industry's employment among the states.[60] The lower the value of *REGH*, the more evenly is an industry's employment dispersed among regions. Therefore, I presume, the more localized the markets, the smaller the plant sizes should be.

Statistical Results

The data base employed to estimate this model is the same as that used in the previous section to explain relative productivity, but missing values in this case leave a smaller number of observations. Also, multicollinearity proved a more serious problem here, rendering the model somewhat sensitive to small changes in specification. The hypotheses about *RELS* were tested (in the first instance) in a linear additive model; no formal framework offers itself that is comparable to the neoclassical core determinants of *VPW*. The three versions reported in table 3 embody some interactions that will be explained along with the results.

First, the coefficient of export activity, *EXPA*, takes a perverse sign but is quite insignificant—this is not surprising in view of the small share of output exported by most Australian manufacturing industries. I wondered if the expected effect might turn up in the more capital-intensive resource-processing sectors, and accordingly allowed the coefficient of *EXPA* to take different slopes in the capital-intensive (*EXPAK*) and labor-intensive (*EXPAL*) industries (the sample industries were split around mean capital intensity; *KD* is an intercept shift for capital intensity). As equation 3-1 in table 3 shows, this maneuver failed to alter the negative results. The conclusion reached was that export markets have yet to influence the structure of Australia's manufacturing industries (contrary to their Canadian counterparts), and *EXPA* was dropped from the model. Its removal had no substantial effect on other coefficients, as equation 3-2 shows.

The *SCLB*, which combines influences of scale economies and the

60. The Herfindahl index is calculated by squaring the fraction of national employment in each state and summing the fractions. It can range from 0.167 (even distribution) to 1.0 (all in one state). Its sample mean is 0.33.

Table 3. *Determinants of Sizes of Australian Production Units Relative to U.S. Midpoint Plant Size (RELS)*[a]

Independent variable	Equation		
	3-1	3-2	3-3
MLTP	0.010	0.011	. . .
	(2.22)	(2.60)	
SCLB	−0.205	−0.217	0.223
	(1.59)	(1.75)	(1.72)
NPW	1.438	1.686	1.819
	(1.89)	(2.54)	(2.63)
REGH²	−1.847	−1.923	−2.412
	(1.72)	(1.89)	(2.33)
REGHHF	2.292	2.471	2.623
	(1.99)	(2.29)	(2.34)
FCTA	0.285	0.300	0.321
	(3.30)	(3.70)	(3.82)
FCTRD	−0.273	−0.287	−0.309
	(3.27)	(3.65)	(3.79)
EXPAK	−0.304	. . .	. . .
	(0.25)		
EXPAL	−0.653	. . .	. . .
	(0.65)		
KD	0.044	. . .	. . .
	(0.35)		
Constant	0.194	0.137	−0.047
	(1.11)	(0.94)	(0.38)
Degrees of freedom	36	39	40
$\bar{R}^2$	0.302	0.343	0.251

a. The numbers in parentheses are *t*-statistics. The variables are described in the text.

tariff, takes the appropriate negative coefficient but is only marginally significant in a one-tail test. The relative prevalence of nonproduction workers in Australian plants, *NPW*, is positive and significant. The regional-dispersion variable, *REGH*, when entered in its original form (not shown), took a perverse negative coefficient that was nearly significant statistically. To explore this anomaly, I first squared the variable in order to give more dispersion to the highly fragmented industries—a move that only mitigated the perversity. Then I tested the hypothesis that regional dispersion is associated with smaller scales more strongly in those industries with above-average levels of foreign investment (*REGHHF* allows a slope-shift for *REGH²* in those industries). As table 3 shows, regional dispersion is significantly more associated with small scale in those industries, although the basic perverse result (negative coefficient of $REGH^2$) remains unexplained. Foreign investment, $FCTA$, itself has a significant positive influence (two-tail test), whereas $RNDU$, when entered as an additive regressor, wields a significant negative influence. However, a positive correlation between $FCTA$ and $RNDU$ proved to be an important source of multicollinearity in the model. In table 3, $RNDU$ is entered interactively with $FCTA$ by means of the variable $FCTRD$, which is defined as $FCTA$ $(1 + RNDU)$.

Finally, the extent of multiplant operation in Australian industries, $MLTP$, took the significant positive coefficient expected for cleaning up the mismeasurement of relative plant size. Because multiplant operation may be associated behaviorally with other variables in the model (notably $REGH$), I was concerned that its inclusion might affect the interpretation of other variables. Therefore, in equation 3-3, I suppressed its interaction with the other regressors by first regressing $RELS$ on it, then taking the residuals from this regression as the dependent variable in equation 3-3; as the table shows, this change has little effect on the magnitudes and significance levels of the other regression coefficients.

To recapitulate these conclusions, tariff protection does increase the viability of small-scale production to the degree that scale economies permit. Tariffs, as well as inducements that encourage multinational companies to disperse their plant locations, are flagged as policies aggravating the economy's problem of small-scale operation. But Australian plants are small partly because they forgo in-plant nonproduction activities, and because they import the services of nonproduction workers (the negative influence of U.S. research and development). Foreign investment itself is associated with larger plant sizes, but this influence has strong negative offsets in research-oriented industries (here, product differentiation is surely at work) and in industries subject to geographic fragmentation. Although this interpretation has a satisfying coherence, it must be discounted because of the multicollinearity of the regressors and the amount of manipulation that followed upon the initial results.

The two dependent variables, VPW and $RELS$, are different measures of the same general phenomenon—the displacement of scale and productivity by structural conditions and policies prevailing in Australia. The two variables are only seemingly unrelated and therefore should be estimated by generalized least squares for greater efficiency. This maneuver failed to be helpful because of the missing observations, which yielded somewhat fewer degrees of freedom for *RELS* and many fewer for *VPW* than in the ordinary least squares equations reported above. Because the qualitative interpretation of the significance of key variables remained unchanged, we do not report the results.

Conclusions

The most important normative question about Australian industrial organization, I submit, is the degree to which its efficiency and productivity are constrained by serving small and isolated markets, and the degree to which public policy has worsened this problem—or could relieve it. The strategy used in this paper has been not to study the relevant policies directly but to delve into the underlying question of how important these constraints are. Once that is known, quantified estimates of the effects of tariff protection and other relevant policies come into reach. This paper has attempted a first step at this quantification by applying a coherent framework to analyze the productivity of Australian manufacturing industries relative to their counterparts in the United States. The analysis covers outright differences in average productivity and also differences in scale of operation.[61] The statistical findings suggest the following conclusions about economic behavior and policy.

Small market size and isolation do constrain both the overall productivity and the scale efficiency of Australian manufacturing industries. This problem will be mitigated by long-run economic growth. It may be exacerbated by the general equilibrium adjustment of an expanding resources sector, insofar as it makes suboptimal scale of operation more attractive in some industries.

High levels of tariff protection impose an economic cost that consists mainly of making suboptimal scale production feasible. In so doing, Australian protection acts like amplified international transportation costs.

Australian manufacturers have apparently made the best of the

---

61. Ideally, it should also incorporate what is customarily called "technical inefficiency," that is, the degrees to which productivity levels in individual plants and
companies in each country fall short of the highest level obtainable within that country's
economic structure. Research of this type is under way in both countries.

opportunities open to them, in the sense that their "revealed" production function claims a relative productivity advantage in activities that are small scale and not capital intensive. This behavioral finding may have implications for the allocation of investments in the development and adaptation of production technology.

Previous research has indicated many public policies that account for the geographic fragmentation of manufacturing industries, notably a fragmented transportation system and plant-location inducements by the states. The results of this paper are consistent with the finding that state policies have contributed to geographic dispersion and small scale in industries where foreign subsidiaries are prevalent, and suggest that these inducements may frequently have been aimed at the multinationals.

This paper has not directly addressed competition policy in Australia, but it does provide some relevant conclusions. First, I do find some evidence that concentrated industries with only moderate comparative disadvantages (in international trade) are more likely to "price up to the tariff." This finding in turn implies some loss due to allocative ineffi-ciency. Second, the conclusions reached about scale and productivity are highly cautionary with respect to the technical inefficiency (lower productivity) that might occur as a result of any attempt to improve allocative efficiency by fragmenting production. Third, these results by no means rule out the possibility that collusive agreements and practices in concentrated industries impose efficiency costs, but they do suggest, albeit weakly, that not all the monopoly rents claimed by more concen-trated industries are dissipated in this fashion—a finding relevant to the unresolved debate concerning the concentration-profits relation in Australia.

HENRY J. AARON

Social Welfare in Australia

AUSTRALIA'S social welfare system is different from that of any Western European nation, the United States, or Canada. Australia relies mainly on income-tested benefits, not only for the nonaged poor—who receive such benefits in many other countries—but also for the aged and the unemployed. Furthermore, Australian tax laws encourage employees to take most private retirement benefits as lump-sum payments rather than as pensions. Somewhat paradoxically, most public transfer payments are fully taxable, whereas most private retirement benefits are substantially free of tax.[1]

Any social welfare system modifies the distribution of income that market forces alone would generate. All actions of government, from the establishment of property rights and the maintenance of national defense to cash grants to indigents, have such an effect. Hence, the designation of some programs, but not others, as "the social welfare system" is necessarily arbitrary. Furthermore, the number and size of social programs a nation finds desirable depend in part on the degree to which private arrangements have evolved to meet the same objectives. To complete the circle, private social welfare activities—charities, pensions, and individual saving—depend both on tax laws and other government regulations, and on "need," which may be ameliorated by

I thank Ian Castles, Daryl A. Dixon, Chris Foster, Edward M. Gramlich, Fred H. Gruen, Ian Manning, Neville R. Norman, Andrew S. Podger, and Glenn A. Withers for their constructive comments. Andrew Podger and Philippa Smith were the assigned discussants for this chapter at the Brookings-Canberra Conference.

1. Legislation foreshadowed in 1983 will tax a gradually increasing proportion of lump-sum retirement benefits, but it will be many years before even half of them are subject to tax.

government social services and transfer payments. In short, one cannot understand the Australian social welfare system, or indeed any other, if one does not go beyond government social welfare programs, to private retirement benefits and insurance, and to those elements of the tax system that bear on public and private transfers.

To understand the effects of a social welfare system on individual welfare, it is also necessary to understand how people respond to it. Government and private programs alike influence labor supply, saving, and other economic decisions of individuals and businesses. The net effect on the incomes of recipients may be greater or less than the direct public expenditures. Pensions for the aged, for example, may cause private saving to rise or to fall.[2] In evaluating the desirability of government programs, one is presumably interested more in the effects of government spending combined with the induced changes in behavior than in the former alone. If pensions caused changes in private behavior that offset all or most of the direct effects of the government program, they might be of great political importance, but they would have no immediate effect on the income of the aged.

This discussion of the social welfare system in Australia is concerned with two principal topics: the structure of the system, and the approach to social welfare that it represents. Thus the first section of the chapter describes the main components of the system and recent changes in their size and form. It also examines a number of significant issues connected with retirement policy, health insurance, and unemployment benefits. The second section compares attitudes toward social welfare programs in Australia with those in the United States.

Three key areas of the discussion focus on the interactions between tax policy toward private retirement benefits and public retirement income programs; the implications of the reintroduction of national health insurance by the Hawke government; and certain aspects of unemployment benefits that deserve to be reexamined in the light of trends in labor force participation.

Perhaps the most idiosyncratic aspect of this review is its relative neglect of family assistance of various kinds, of programs intended to

2. For a review of evidence of the effects of old-age pensions on saving, labor supply, and income distribution, see Henry J. Aaron, *The Economic Effects of Social Security* (Brookings Institution, 1982).

supplement incomes of low earners, of the Australian debate about the measurement of poverty, and, except for brief mention in the conclusion, of the private and public programs to aid people who are disabled or injured. Any brief survey of a social welfare system as sophisticated and complex as that in Australia must of necessity be selective. I have chosen to focus on the programs that do what social insurance does in most other countries, and I apologize for neglecting efforts to help the poor. My justification is that of Willie Sutton, the notorious bank robber, who, when asked why he robbed banks, replied: "That's where the money is."

The Social Welfare Menu

Australians are quick to tell an outsider that their attitudes toward social welfare have been shaped by their nation's early history: Australia originated as a penal colony in which the government provided many of the social services. The typical Australian, they report, continues to expect the government to guarantee a basic income and certain social services and feels entitled to claim available benefits whenever conditions for eligibility are satisfied. There is little or no stigma associated with accepting benefits under most programs. Indeed, people believe that by paying income taxes, they earn the right to most benefits. At the same time, they do not begrudge benefits to those who may have earned too little to pay taxes.

These generalizations have exceptions. A minority of Australians object to large parts of the system, and many grumble about "dole bludgers" who freeload unemployment benefits or the aid available to single parents.[3] Nevertheless, the contrast between the general attitude in Australia and the scorn for welfare recipients and persistent concern about abuse of unemployment insurance in America is striking.

The belief in Australia that the government is obliged to provide cash assistance and that people have every right to claim it without loss of

---

3. The original meaning of "bludger" is one who lives on the immoral earnings of women. More recently the word has taken a meaning roughly equivalent to the American word "freeloader." There is no implication of dishonesty, just antisocial slothfulness.

pride is limited, however, to benefits designed to prevent destitution. It has led to programs that provide flat benefits unrelated to previous earnings. The implicit view is that government is obliged to prevent utter indigence or to assure people compensation for accidental injury, but not to assist people in sustaining their customary living standards during retirement, sickness, disability, or unemployment.

Aggregate Expenditures

Social welfare expenditures in Australia have nearly tripled in real terms since 1970–71 (see table 1).[4] The increases are evident in all program categories:

Age pensions increased most in the early 1970s, when benefits were raised and eligibility liberalized.

Veterans' service pensions, which had earlier been negligible, rose when large numbers of World War II veterans reached the age of eligibility.

Family assistance jumped in 1976 to offset repeal of tax concessions for children.

Unemployment benefits have risen from negligible amounts to become the second largest program of cash assistance. Most of the increase is attributable to the rise in unemployment from 78,000 in 1970, when many were out of work too briefly to bother claiming benefits, to an estimated 680,000 in 1983–84, when most are projected to be out of work for many weeks, months, or even years.

Health expenditures first increased with the introduction of universal, budget-financed health benefits and then receded as these benefits were reduced or moved off budget. Nearly all cash benefit levels were increased sharply during the tenure of the Whitlam government.[5]

---

4. Table 1 refers only to commonwealth outlays. It omits sizable outlays by the states and by private charitable entities.

5. For excellent histories of public expenditures during the 1970s, see R. B. Scotton and Helen Ferber, eds., *Public Expenditures and Social Policy in Australia*, vol. 1: *The Whitlam Years, 1972–75* (Melbourne: Longman Cheshire, 1978), and *Public Expenditures and Social Policy in Australia*, vol. 2: *The First Fraser Years, 1976–78* (Melbourne: Longman Cheshire, 1980). For a comprehensive legislative history covering the twentieth century, see Department of Social Security, *Developments in Social Security: A Compendium of Legislative Changes Since 1908*, Research Paper 20 (Canberra: Australian Government Printing Service, June 1983).

Table 1. *Social Welfare Expenditures, by Broad Category, Selected Years, 1970–71 to 1983–84*
Billions of Australian dollars

Category	1970–71	1974–75	1979–80	1982–83	1983–84
Current dollars					
Assistance to the aged	0.6	1.7	3.6	5.0	5.5
Veterans' service pension	a	0.2	0.5	1.1	1.3
Assistance to the handicapped	0.1	0.3	0.9	1.2	1.4
Assistance to widows and single parents	0.1	0.3	0.8	1.5	1.7
Family allowances and other assistance to families	0.2	0.2	1.0	1.5	1.7
Unemployment benefits and other aid to unemployed and sick	a	0.5	1.1	2.6	3.7
Health	0.6	1.3	3.2	3.4	4.3
Net state and local health outlays	0.54	1.4	3.4	. . .	. . .
Administration and other	0.2	0.5	0.8	1.2	1.6
Total	2.0	5.1	12.0	17.5	21.2
Constant dollars					
Age pension	2.2	4.1	5.2	5.4	5.5
Veterans' service pension	0.1	0.5	0.7	1.2	1.3
Assistance to the handicapped	0.5	0.8	1.3	1.3	1.4
Assistance to widows and single parents	0.4	0.7	1.2	1.6	1.7
Family allowances and other assistance to families	0.8	0.6	1.6	1.8	1.7
Unemployment benefits and other aid to unemployed and sick	0.1	1.2	1.6	2.8	3.7
Health	2.7	3.3	4.6	3.7	4.3
Administration and other	0.9	1.2	1.2	1.3	1.6
Total	7.6	12.5	17.4	18.8	21.2

Sources: Current dollar estimates, 1982–83 and 1983–84—*Budget Statements, 1983–84*, Budget Paper 1 (Canberra: Australian Government Publishing Service, 1983), pp. 113–14. "Other" includes assistance to veterans and their dependents other than service pensions, other welfare programs, aboriginal advancement programs not classified elsewhere, and recoveries and repayments. Data for 1979–80—*Budget Speech 1980–81*, Budget Paper 1, pp. 90, 104–05; for 1974–75—*Budget Speech 1976–77*, Budget Paper 1, pp. 39, 47–48; and for 1970–71—*Budget Speech 1973–74*, Budget Paper 1, pp. 27, 34–35. Net state and local health outlays received from Andrew Podger in correspondence dated March 15, 1984. Constant dollar estimates are based on the general consumer price index except for health. Health is based on consumer price index for health and personal services through 1980–81 and is chained to the general index for later years.

a. The value is less than 50 million Australian dollars.

Assistance to the Aged

Men sixty-five or older and women sixty or older are entitled in fiscal year 1983–84 to receive an "age pension" of $368 a month if they are single or $614 a month if they are married; veterans are entitled to identical benefits five years earlier.[6] The basic entitlement in Australia

6. Benefits are payable weekly and the amounts are stated in weekly quantities for all programs. I have translated them into thirty-day equivalents and have rounded them to the nearest Australian dollar.

is the same for everyone, although extra supplements are payable for child support, rent assistance, and other "fringe benefits."[7] The basic age pension is payable to residents and in certain circumstances to Australians abroad. Previous earnings history or even labor force participation have no bearing on the amount. Benefits are reduced, however, if current income exceeds specified levels. In 1983, 60 percent of the aged received full pensions.[8] As in the United States, benefits in Australia are indexed for inflation as measured by the consumer price index.

By comparison, the average monthly U.S. retirement benefit in July 1983 was $423 for single retirees and $638 for couples,[9] but the amount ranged from just over $100 to more than $900 a month for single retirees (about 50 percent more for couples).[10]

Large benefit increases were enacted in both countries in the early 1970s: a 20 percent benefit hike and indexation were introduced in the United States in 1972; a number of liberalizations were initiated in Australia by the Whitlam government. Calculations based on the exchange rate in late 1983 (with Australian dollar equal to $0.91 in U.S. currency) indicate that Australian age pensions for single retirees are 79 percent and for couples 86 percent of average U.S. benefits. Since Australian income in 1976 was about 80 percent of that in the United States, the ratio of average cash benefits for the aged to per capita income appears similar in the two countries.

RELATIVE COST. A broad measure of the cost of age pensions is the ratio of these benefits to total earnings of active workers. By this measure

7. Fringe benefits include concessionary rates on travel, telephone service, local council, property and water rates, pharmaceuticals, optometrical services, hearing aids, nursing home benefits, and (until restoration of the national health plan described below) medical care. They are currently available to pensioners of all categories (age, service, invalid, widows, and sole parents) with incomes (including age pension in Australian dollars) below $599 a month if single and $1,000 a month if married.

8. The reduction equaled 50 percent of outside income over $214 a month for couples ($129 for single persons). In all, 15 percent of the aged received no pension and 30 percent of the remainder received reduced pensions.

9. The estimate for couples in the United States presumes that only one spouse worked. If both spouses worked, the benefit could be greater or less depending on joint earnings histories.

10. U.S. benefits are unaffected by unearned income, but are reduced by 50 percent of earnings over $500 a month.

Australian age pensions cost 5.49 percent of total earnings in 1981. The U.S. system cost about 9.15 percent of total earnings in 1983.[11]

The discrepancy is attributable to a number of factors. The first is that 40 percent of Australians who are otherwise eligible for the age pension receive reduced payments or none at all because of the income test. The U.S. average refers to payments actually made. Second, the U.S. population is older than the Australian population. In 1981, 11.5 percent of the U.S. population was older than sixty-five, compared with 9.8 percent in Australia. Third, service pensions in Australia provide pensions for aged veterans; in the United States most of these benefits are provided through the social security system.[12] A number of other programs—widows' pensions, for example—provide survivors with benefits that in the United States are paid through social security. In addition, money wages on which the calculations in both countries are based form a smaller part of total compensation in the United States than in Australia, where there are few employer-financed health benefits or payroll taxes on employers.

TAX TREATMENT OF PENSIONS. Age pensions in Australia are fully included in taxable income and are subject to an income test. The combination of the income test and income tax produces an effective tax rate of 65 percent.[13] If other income exceeds $129 a month for single persons or $214 a month for couples, benefits are reduced by 50 percent of the excess. For purposes of the income test, all earnings, periodic pension payments, and repetitive income from capital are included. But gifts, capital gains, inheritances and lump-sum "superannuation" payments do not count in the income test. More than one-third of age pensioners in 1981–82 received reduced benefits because of the income

11. This estimate is based on the U.S. Social Security Actuary's estimate that old age and survivors' insurance cost 10.28 percent of *covered* payroll, and that 89 percent of all earnings were included in covered payroll.

12. Both countries have separate systems to provide compensation for service-connected disabilities.

13. Andrew Podger and others carefully examine this question in "Relationships between Social Security and Income Tax Systems—A Practical Examination," Research Paper 9 (Canberra: AGPS, 1980). See also Andrew Podger and others, "The Finance of Social Security: Some Implications of the Interaction between Social Security and Personal Income Tax," Department of Social Security, Research Paper 11 (Canberra: AGPS, 1980).

test.[14] The combination of income tax, income test, and the reduction of a pensioner tax rebate causes an effective marginal tax rate of 71¼ percent for many pensioners.[15] When the interaction of pensions with benefits in kind is taken into account, the effective rates of tax become erratic and over some ranges exceed 100 percent.[16]

INCOME AND MEANS TEST. The financial test for age pension has a long and complex history that is still being written.[17] The Fraser government in 1978 arrested the trend toward removal of the financial test for benefits when it reversed a 1975 decision to exempt persons aged seventy or older from any test. Henceforth, all inflation adjustments or other subsequent increases in benefits were to be subject to an income test. In 1983 Hawke's Labor government took two further steps in this direction. It restored the income test for the entire benefit payable to persons seventy or older. In addition, it announced its intention to restore sometime after fiscal 1984 a test for all pensioners that is based on both earned income and asset holdings.

Superannuation

Nearly half of Australian workers are covered by privately financed plans that promise superannuation benefits when they leave their current jobs if certain conditions are satisfied. In fact, roughly 80 percent of the

14. Correspondence with Daryl Dixon.

15. For a proposal to subject income from all sources to one tax schedule, see Daryl Dixon and Chris Foster, *An Alternative Path to Integration of Social Security and Personal Income Tax Arrangements*, Occasional Paper 1 (Sydney: Australian Tax Research Foundation, 1983).

16. See Meredith Edwards, "The Income Unit in the Social Security System: Explanation and Evaluation," paper prepared for the Fifty-third Australian and New Zealand Association for the Advancement of Science Congress, May 1983.

17. Up to 1969 benefits were subject to a means test that was based on earnings plus a percentage of countable assets. If the sum exceeded a low level, benefits were reduced dollar for dollar. In 1969 the tax was changed from dollar for dollar to one dollar for every two dollars, and in 1972 the threshold above which pension was reduced began to be increased. From 1973 up to 1978 the financial test was relaxed in two ways. In 1973 persons seventy-five and older were exempted from the means test. At the same time age pensions were made taxable. In 1975 the exemption age was lowered to seventy. In 1976 the means test was replaced by a pure income test; that is, actual income from capital was counted, rather than an imputed amount based on an arbitrary rate of return applied to measured assets. Because many assets yield little current money income and

number of payments from these funds occur when workers quit, are fired, or otherwise leave their jobs before they are fifty-five. The 20 percent who receive retirement benefits, however, account for more than 80 percent of the payments from these funds.[18] Most superannuation benefits for employees in the private sector are payable as lump sums, whereas most commonwealth and some other public sector employees are required to take all or part of their benefits in the form of pensions. In contrast to many private pension plans in the United States, virtually all Australian plans are reported to be fully funded, in the sense that each has sufficient book reserves to pay off vested benefits. However, lax rules about pension reserves permit heavy investment of pension funds in stock or other assets of the firm in which employees are covered; thus pension security is diminished should the firm go bankrupt. In addition, there are few legal restrictions on the conditions employers may establish for vesting, and most plans return only the employee's own contributions with interest if that employee leaves before an extended period of service.[19]

COVERAGE. The coverage of the work force by superannuation plans is highly uneven (see table 2). In general, coverage increases with age and earnings. Men are more likely to be covered than are women. Civil servants and employees of publicly owned companies (such as utilities) are highly likely to be covered, as are employees of large private companies. Coverage of small private companies, however, is spotty.[20]

It is widely reported that Australians treasure lump-sum superannuation payments because they provide the only occasion when most people will have at hand sufficient cash to make a large expenditure without

---

capital gains are not counted, this switch relaxed the financial test for eligibility for most affected persons. For the few whose assets earned more actual income than was imputed under the means test, this change was a deliberalization. Taken together, these changes may be seen as part of a gradual trend toward a system of flat-rate pensions for the aged payable to all, regardless of circumstances.

18. Correspondence with Howard C. Prott, federal secretary of the Association of Superannuation Funds of Australia, September 15, 1983.

19. Association of Superannuation Funds of Australia, *1980 Survey of Superannuation Funds*, No. 11 (Sydney: ASFA, December 1981). This survey oversamples larger pension funds.

20. The proportion of various groups covered at retirement by a superannuation plan may differ greatly from these proportions.

Table 2. *Coverage of Superannuation Plans, by Age, Sex, Occupation, and Earnings, 1979*[a]

Category	Percentage of persons covered by superannuation plans	Category	Percentage of persons covered by superannuation plans
Age		*Occupation*	
15–19	17	*(continued)*	
20–24	32	Transport and storage	50
25–34	46	Communications	77
35–44	49	Finance	52
45–54	52	Community services	43
55–59	53	Entertainment	16
60 or over	46	Public administration	75
Sex		*Weekly earnings*[b]	
Men	50	Less than $120	15
Women	26	120–140	20
Occupation		140–160	26
Agriculture	14	160–180	38
Mining	58	180–200	44
Manufacturing	40	200–250	53
Utilities	67	250–300	66
Construction	30	300–350	71
Trade	27	$350 or more	75

Source: Australian Bureau of Statistics, *Employee Benefits, Australia, February to May 1979* (Canberra: ABS, 1980), catalog no. 6334.0.

a. Coverage for all categories is 42 percent.

b. Australian dollars.

going into debt. In any event, there is little evidence that a significant proportion of these payments is used foolishly.[21]

TAX ASPECTS. The apparent preference of Australians for lump-sum payments rather than periodic pensions may arise simply from incentives in both tax and pension laws. Up to 1983 only 5 percent of lump-sum payments, taken at retirement or at job termination before retirement, was considered taxable income. Because most people are taxed at a marginal rate of 30 percent and the top marginal rate is 60 percent, the tax rate on lump-sum payments ranged from 1.5 percent to 3 percent. In

21. David M. Knox reviews the evidence from a number of surveys of the uses to which lump-sum benefits are put in his Ph.D. dissertation, "The Efficacy of Employer-Sponsored Occupational Superannuation in Australia" (North Rhyde: Macquarie University, July 1983). He reaches the conclusion stated in the text.

contrast, all pensions were included in taxable income, other than the portion that returned the contributions made by employees from fully taxable earnings. The pension laws reinforced the incentives in the income tax to take lump-sum benefits by counting all repetitive payments (such as superannuation pensions) in the income test, but omitting one-time receipts (such as lump-sum payments, gifts, or inheritances).

As a result, it was possible for rather wealthy people to receive large lump-sum superannuation payments, to pay negligible tax on them, to invest the proceeds (possibly along with abundant other wealth) in assets yielding little cash income, and to remain eligible for income-tested age pensions. The apparent unfairness of this arrangement was compounded by the fact that Australia has never taxed capital gains and has repealed its tax on wealth transfers by gift or bequest.[22] The so-called income test was in fact an earnings-plus-part-of-capital-income test.

INITIATIVES OF THE HAWKE GOVERNMENT. When it assumed power in 1983, Hawke's Labor government faced a dilemma. Social welfare ideology of the left and policies of the previous Labor government both pointed to further relaxation and possibly to the eventual elimination of the income test on the ground that assistance should be available without socially stigmatizing conditions. Such a move would have increased budget outlays, however, and the Hawke government faced deficits of unprecedented size. Furthermore, the added benefits from such a step would flow largely to the wealthy, among whom relatively few Labor party constituents would be found.

The new government quickly resolved this dilemma at the expense of ideology by calling for restoration of the means test to take effect not earlier than fiscal year 1985. In addition, it secured enactment of a tax on lump-sum superannuation payments at the rate of 15 percent on the first $50,000 and 30 percent of additional amounts paid to people after the age of fifty-five.[23] This tax promises eventually to narrow the advantage of lump-sum payments over ordinary pensions, whose taxability as ordinary income was to remain unchanged. For many years, however, most lump-sum distributions will remain untaxed as the new

22. For state actions in this area, see the chapter in this book by Edward M. Gramlich.

23. Except for the nonproportional rate, the burden of this tax resembles that of a proportional expenditure tax.

rules are to be applied only to future accumulations.[24] For people with sufficient retirement income to be taxed at more than 30 percent, lump sums may continue to have advantages over pensions.[25] Even with the tax on lump-sum payments, all workers continue to face enormous tax incentives to save through tax-favored superannuation schemes (lump-sum or pension), rather than on their own. In fact, the value of tax concessions under the pre-1983 law to a person who set aside enough current earnings to accumulate $100,000 exceeds the value of age pension for single males.[26]

Although the Hawke government moved to increase taxation of lump-sum superannuation benefits and to tighten the test for age pension, it did nothing major to subject capital gains to income taxation or to require that they be included in the income test for programs other than age pension.[27]

24. The tax is imposed on a portion of the payment equal to the ratio of the number of years after the effective date of the tax to the total number of years that a person was under his or her superannuation plan. This ratio is far below the actuarial value. A person who is covered for ten years before and ten years after the imposition of the tax and whose plan accumulates contributions at 10 percent should pay tax on nearly three-quarters of any payment. (This fraction disregards the effect of mortality, which would boost the fraction even more.) In fact, the tax will be levied on only half of the payment.

25. The advantage does not hold in all cases. Lump sums must be distributed on retirement, precipitating immediate tax liability. Because the corpus out of which pensions are paid is not distributed until the payment of the pension, tax is deferred. Which of these advantages is greater will depend on interest rates, life expectancy, and the marginal tax rate on retirement income.

26. If one assumes that the rate of return to saving before deduction of taxes is 10 percent, a person who would have accumulated $100,000 before passage of the new rules would have netted $98,500 (after paying $1,500 in taxes) if he was in the 30 percent bracket or $97,000 (after paying $3,000 in taxes) if he was in the 60 percent bracket. In contrast, if the earnings from which retirement saving was made and all interest earnings were fully and currently taxed, if the saving was carried out over twenty-five years, and if the person allocated the same amount of before-tax income to savings, he would have accumulated $43,800 in the 30 percent bracket, or $16,160 in the 60 percent bracket. Under the Hawke reform, a person who set aside the same amount of pretax earnings would accumulate $77,500. Thus, the reform corrects 38 percent of the undertaxation for people in the 30 percent bracket, but only 24 percent of the undertaxation for people in the 60 percent bracket. These percentages are larger the greater the amount saved, and are lower the longer the period over which saving occurs. In contrast, the age pension for a single male subject to the 30 percent tax rate has a present value of approximately $37,000 ($27,000 for a person subject to the 60 percent tax rate).

27. Small changes were proposed affecting the definition of when gains from the sale of property are exempt from income tax. In particular, income tax is meant to apply

Income Assistance to the Elderly: Policy Issues

The fundamental policy issues with regard to income assistance for the elderly revolve around whether such benefits should be mandatory or voluntary, what levels are appropriate, and whether they should vary with past or current income. All of these issues are under debate in many developed nations because slowed economic growth has heightened concern about the sustainability of commitments to future benefits.

The Australian system of income assistance to the elderly provides relatively generous benefits to those who had much-below-average earnings during their working lives. At the lower end of the earnings distribution, about one-third of U.S. social security beneficiaries receive smaller benefits than they would under the Australian age pension.

The Australian system gives meager age pensions to workers who earned much more than average, but large tax benefits to those who receive some kind of superannuation benefit (see table 2). As indicated above, current tax concessions combined with age pensions may mean more generous treatment of high-bracket earners in Australia than in the United States.[28] In addition, the absence of taxation on capital gains, gifts, bequests, inheritances, or wealth greatly encourages asset accumulation. In the United States, some saving is sheltered from tax, but only until it is paid out in pensions or as lump sums; and modest taxes are imposed on capital gains, gifts, and bequests.[29] Taxes on real property are much higher in the United States, accounting for 2.7 percent of gross national product, compared with 1.5 percent in Australia.

---

to gains from the sale of property acquired with the intent of selling it for gain. Before 1983 a person could avoid this tax by giving the property away, say, to a spouse or child, who then sold it. Because Australia taxes individual, not family incomes, it was held that the seller (the spouse or child) had not acquired the property for the purpose of selling it for gain, but rather had received it as a gift. And, of course, they could give back the proceeds, also free of tax. The 1983 proposals, among other things, would prevent use of such procedures for tax avoidance.

28. The treatment of pensions in the United States is less generous than the pre-1983 system in Australia. The tax system put in place in Australia in 1983 is more generous than the U.S. system for some taxpayers, less generous for others.

29. The difference between the treatment of capital income in Australia and the United States should not be exaggerated, however. Only 40 percent of realized capital gains is taxable in the United States. Excessive depreciation deductions and the investment tax credit available in some activities generate losses for tax purposes when

Thus, the Australian system is probably more generous to aged workers who have had low earnings than is the U.S. system. In contrast, the Australian system gives far less to those at the middle-income levels than do U.S. and other social insurance systems. The average U.S. social security recipient receives more, and those who had above-average earnings receive much more, than they would receive from age pensions in Australia. At the top, the extraordinarily generous pre-1983 tax treatment of superannuation provided upper-bracket earners with indirect benefits that may have more than offset the relative meagerness of the Australian age pension relative to social security. As the tax on lump-sum superannuation takes effect, the difference in taxation of pensions will narrow, and the Australian system will become less generous than the U.S. system both at the top and in the middle-income levels.

These differences should show up in the income distributions of the elderly in Australia and the United States. In particular, the Australian age pension can be expected to truncate the lower tail of the income distribution. Unfortunately, published data on the income of the elderly are sparse and do not permit a direct comparison.[30] Published data do document that the elderly in the upper one-third of the income distribution in the United States received 40 percent of their income from public cash transfers in 1980, and that the corresponding fraction for Australia was 14 percent in 1975–76. The sources of income of the middle or lower third are not made clear, however.

DISADVANTAGES OF THE PRESENT SYSTEM. From the standpoint of assisting the low-income elderly, the Australian system of age pensions rates high marks when compared with social insurance. By another criterion, however, the present Australian system appears somewhat anachronistic. A flat benefit, income-tested system seems appropriate for a country in which few people spend much time in retirement or in

---

real economic incomes are being earned. The deductions for mortgage interest and property taxes on owner-occupied housing allowed in the United States are not permitted in Australia. George Cooper found the estate and gift taxes, even before liberalizations enacted recently, to be "voluntary" tax. See George Cooper, *A Voluntary Tax? New Perspectives on Sophisticated Estate Tax Avoidance* (Brookings Institution, 1977).

30. Comparison of the average income of one-person elderly units in both countries with the average income of all single adults shows that Australian units are somewhat worse off relative to mean adult income than are U.S. units. Only 34 percent of such Australian units have income greater than or equal to half of mean income of single adults. In the United States, the proportion is 45 percent.

which supplementary pensions cover most workers. But Australian longevity is high, labor force participation among the elderly in Australia is low, and coverage under superannuation plans is spotty. Incomplete coverage of superannuation benefits means that many workers will suffer sharp declines in income after retirement unless they have saved extensively on their own in forms that are not sheltered from tax.

The present system has severe disadvantages. Although coverage of superannuation plans has been spreading, the tax imposed on lump-sum benefits paid from accumulations based on contributions after 1983 may retard further expansion. Large groups of workers, whole occupations, and many industries are unlikely ever to have superannuation plans unless coverage spreads. Furthermore, although superannuation plans serve less than half of the labor force, in 1981–82 they resulted in an estimated annual revenue loss of $1.7 billion to $2.4 billion that must be made up by higher rates on all.[31]

Compared with social insurance, the Australian system may have greater flexibility when fiscal difficulties arise. Because the "earned right" principle is relatively weak in the Australian system, it may be somewhat easier politically to curtail benefits than it is under social insurance systems. This difference should not be exaggerated, however, as the view is often voiced in Australia that workers have a right to pensions and benefits of all kinds earned by virtue of paying income taxes. Of greater importance, a flat benefit system combined with income testing can assign relatively generous payments to the needy few without establishing heavy obligations to the affluent. This structure maximizes the reduction in poverty attained by any given expenditure. In the achievement of this important objective, the Australian system deserves high marks. It is perhaps paradoxical that the objective of income testing advanced in the United States and some European nations by conservative critics of the welfare state is defended by supporters of the welfare state in Australia.

31. David Ingles and others, *Taxation Expenditures, Submission by the Department of Social Security to the Inquiry into Taxation Expenditures by the House of Representatives Standing Committee on Expenditure*, Department of Social Security, Research Paper 17 (Canberra: AGPS, March 1982). The range exists in part because the higher figure includes tax on previous accumulations. Some of these accumulations would not exist if a tax was in place, unless contributions were increased sufficiently to cover all tax payments.

REFORM. If Australians should decide that the status quo is unacceptable, two broad courses of action are open. First, flat-benefit age pensions could be replaced with earnings-related public retirement benefits. Supplementary private plans might survive, but their size and scope would probably diminish.[32] Alternatively, the government might require private employers to provide superannuation benefits for all workers, other than perhaps those below a certain age or with little job tenure. Such benefits would have to meet standards of safety, vesting periods (a maximum waiting period after which employees are given legal title to all or part of the employer's contribution plus interest earnings), and portability (the transfer of pension credits from one employer to another). Although this approach would require the revision of existing pension and superannuation arrangements, it would enhance rather than diminish the role of insurance companies, banks, and other private fiduciary institutions in the provision of pensions.[33]

Although the fundamental economic differences between these approaches may not be great, the political gulf between them is enormous. The major economic difference between the two approaches is that the accumulation of reserves is far more likely under a private than under a public superannuation system. Full funding of private superannuation is a tradition in Australia, but few public systems in any country have anything approaching full actuarial reserves.

The important political difference between the two approaches is that the government scheme would be financed by taxes, the private system by premiums. A government system would embrace a plank of the platforms of most social democratic parties, including those in Australia. Such a system would not be a natural part of labor-management negotiations over compensation. The mandatory private system would keep outlays off the budget, although only cosmetically. And it would encourage workers and management to negotiate the trade-off between

32. Among larger pension funds belonging to the Association of Superannuation Funds of Australia in 1980, plans covering 42 percent of employees made some kind of allowance for the introduction of national superannuation.

33. For a review of some of the arguments for and against the introduction of graduated pensions, see David Ingles, *Financing Social Security: An Analysis of the Contributory "Social Insurance" Approach,* Department of Social Security Research Paper 19 (Canberra: AGPS, June 1982).

money wages and deferred compensation beyond the legally mandated minimum.[34]

Even if Australia does not modify its pension system, but especially if it does, reform of the taxation of pensions and capital gains should also be considered. A strong case can be made for deferring tax on saving of all kinds until it is consumed.[35] But there is little rationale for taxing consumption paid for out of previous savings at a lower rate than consumption financed out of capital income or earnings.

The exclusion from taxation until 1983 of 95 percent of lump-sum superannuation payments did exactly that. Even the tax on lump-sum payments accumulated after 1983 will impose a reduced tax burden on superannuation savings of all people subject to the 46 or 60 percent tax rates on other income. Such a concession may be justified only as a political expedient to gain acceptance for some tax.[36] If one wishes to defer tax on pension accumulations until they are paid, principles of tax equity imply full taxation of all payouts at the same rate applied to ordinary income.

Whatever rule is adopted for pension saving and accumulations should be applied to other forms of saving and other capital income. It is difficult

34. One of the remarkable features of Australian labor relations to an American is the relative neglect of nonwage compensation. Numerous Australians emphasize the dominance in labor negotiations and union politics of the "hip-pocket nerve," the great sensitivity of Australian workers to changes in take-home pay, and relative indifference to pensions, health benefits, and what are called fringe benefits in the United States. They explain that Australian workers believe that the government, rather than employers, should provide such assistance.

35. The argument rests on the proposition that a tax on consumption, under certain conditions, does not distort the choice between present and future consumption. A tax on income (consumption plus saving), in contrast, favors present over future consumption. Because the base of a consumption tax is smaller than that of an income tax, however, the consumption tax requires a higher tax rate to yield a given revenue. For that reason, the direct distortion of the labor-leisure choice is more severe under a consumption tax than under the income tax. The practical question is, Which of these distortions is more serious, and are indirect distortions of the labor-leisure choice under the income tax important? See Anthony B. Atkinson and Joseph Stiglitz, *Lectures in Public Finance* (McGraw Hill, 1980); and Anthony B. Atkinson and Agnar Sandmo, "Welfare Implications of the Taxation of Saving," *Economic Journal*, vol. 90 (September 1980), pp. 529–49.

36. It might be possible to construct a case on the basis of optimal tax theory for differentiated rates on lump-sum payments, but it is quite unlikely that the system adopted in 1983 approximates them.

to fathom the justification for imposing a tax on capital gains earned by pension funds, payable when funds are distributed to pensioners, while exempting similar capital gains received by other investors. It is equally hard to understand why tax on interest income earned by a pension fund should be deferred until distribution, while interest on bank deposits or privately held bonds is taxable when earned.

Unemployment Insurance

Unemployment benefits have been the most rapidly growing form of cash assistance provided by the commonwealth government. Most of this growth reflects increased unemployment. However, unemployment benefits would have been approximately half as large as they were in 1983, given the number of beneficiaries, if real benefits had remained at 1971 levels.

Benefit amounts are based on family status, not on previous work history or earnings. For 1983–84 the benefit levels are $315 a month for unmarried persons eighteen years or older and $631 a month for married persons, plus $51 a month for each child. Single persons aged sixteen and seventeen receive a reduced benefit of $193 a month. Persons old enough to receive the age pension (men sixty-five or older, women sixty or older) are ineligible for unemployment benefits. Payments in 1984 are not reduced if the beneficiary has income of less than $86 a month; benefits are reduced by half of the next $214 a month of income, and dollar for dollar of any additional income.

In contrast, unemployment insurance averaged $528 a month in the United States in November 1982, or almost the same as the Australian benefit at that time, at an exchange rate of $0.91 in U.S. currency equals $1.00 in Australian currency. This amount varies widely across states,[37] but not with family status or age.

INCOME TEST. The income test includes spouse's income and thus effectively denies benefits to married people whose spouses are fully employed. The basic benefit, but not the bonus for children or certain other payments, is subject to income tax. In both cases, however, the

37. In 1980 the highest benefit state (Ohio) paid benefits 80 percent higher than those paid in the lowest benefit state (Mississippi). Benefits vary both because average earnings differ and because benefit formulas are disparate.

test is administered in the most liberal fashion possible. An Australian who has earned $100,000 in the previous year will be eligible just as promptly as one who earned $10,000 in the previous year.[38]

DISTINCTIVE FEATURES. Two features other than the level of benefits that mark Australian unemployment insurance strike a North American observer as particularly generous.[39] First, no employment history is necessary to establish eligibility for benefits. Since the normal school-leaving age in Australia is sixteen, this provision permits sixteen- and seventeen-year-olds to claim unemployment benefits six weeks after they leave school. Indeed, it is reported that officials visit secondary schools to inform students when and how to apply so as to minimize the waiting period for benefits after schooling ends. Second, once on the rolls, a person may receive benefits indefinitely if he or she indicates a willingness to work by registering with the Commonwealth Employment Service and accepts work if it is offered.

In contrast, both the United States and Canada require a period of work before eligibility for unemployment benefits can be established; and both set limits on the duration of payments, after which a person must work for some period of time before eligibility can be reestablished.[40] As a result, only 36 percent of the U.S. unemployed qualified for unemployment insurance in August 1983, whereas virtually all of the unemployed in Australia qualify for unemployment benefits.[41]

38. The practical administrative decision that leads to this result is the exclusive reliance on *estimated prospective* income in applying the test. The alternative is to measure income over an accounting period stretching into the past or to carry forward past income over some basic amount. Evidence from income maintenance experiments shows that total costs of a program of income assistance can be twice as high under relaxed accounting rules (such as those used in Australia) as under strict accounting rules. The strict rules raise important issues of policy as they do not permit prompt payment to many families after income declines. See Jodie T. Allen, "Designing Income Maintenance Systems: The Income Accounting Problem," in Subcommittee on Fiscal Policy, Joint Economic Committee, *Issues in Welfare Administration: Implications of the Income Maintenance Experiments*, Studies in Public Welfare Paper 5, 93 Cong. 1 sess. (GPO, 1973) pt. 3, pp. 47–97.

39. For a comparison of the Australian and Canadian systems, see Paul W. Miller and Paul A. Volker, "Unemployment Compensation in Australia" (Canberra: Bureau of Labor Market Research, 1983).

40. The amount of work experience and the additional period necessary to reestablish eligibility after exhausting benefits differs from state to state within the United States.

41. Subcommittee on Oversight and Subcommittee on Public Assistance and Unemployment Compensation of the Committee on Ways and Means, U.S. House of

Table 3. *Comparison of Insured and Uninsured Unemployment in Australia and the United States, February 1983*
Percentage of total unemployed

		United States	
Measure	Australia	Insured	Total
Duration of benefit or unemployment			
13 weeks or less	39.6	. . .	77.1
13–26 weeks	20.6	. . .	
More than 26 weeks	39.7	. . .	22.9
More than 52 weeks	20.0	. . .	11.7
Age of recipient			
Less than 18 years	11.0	} 16.2	} 37.2
18–24 years	40.7		
55 years or more	5.1	13.4	7.7

Sources: For U.S. total unemployment data see U.S. Department of Labor, Bureau of Labor Statistics, *Employment and Earnings*, vol. 30 (March 1983), pp. 31, 44; insured unemployment data are from unpublished records, U.S. Department of Labor, Employment and Training Administration. Data on Australia are from Department of Social Security, *Quarterly Survey of Unemployment Benefits* (Canberra: AGPS, February 1983).

Administrative rules guarantee that proportionately fewer people in the United States than in Australia will receive unemployment insurance benefits when young or for protracted periods. The rules, in part, reflect different judgments about the importance and appropriate way of providing cash assistance for such groups as unemployed youths. They may also reflect different appraisals of the behavioral effects of giving cash to the young or to anyone for extended periods.

More striking, however, is the fact that in 1983 the proportion of the unemployed out of work six months or more was nearly two times larger in Australia than in the United States (table 3). This difference cannot be explained in terms of the demand for labor, as unemployment rates in Australia and the United States in 1983 were similar. Geographic fragmentation may play a role, as Australian labor markets are widely separated. But it is likely that the structure of unemployment benefits also causes longer stretches of unemployment than would otherwise occur. The much more stringent U.S. system has been shown to increase the length of spells of unemployment.[42]

Representatives, *Background Material on Poverty*, WMCP:98–15, 98 Cong. 1 sess. (GPO, 1983), p. 101.

42. Finis Welch, "What Have We Learned from Empirical Studies of Unemployment Insurance?" *Industrial and Labor Relations Review*, vol. 30 (July 1977), pp. 451–61.

Table 4. *Real Value of Benefits and Pensions per Month, Selected Groups and Years, 1960–80*
December 1979 dollars

Year	Pension for couple		Unemployment benefit for 16- and 17-year-olds	Unemployment benefit for married couple	
	No children	Three children		No children	Three children
1960	285.50	350.00	48.00	153.50	201.50
1965	275.00	369.00	44.00	178.00	272.00
1970	292.00	425.00	48.00	180.50	313.50
1975	406.50	570.00	227.00	406.50	570.00
1980	414.00	586.50	139.50	414.00	586.50

Source: Andrew S. Podger and others, *The Relationship between the Australian Social Security and Personal Income Taxation Systems—A Practical Examination,* Policy Review Branch, Research Paper 9 (Department of Social Security, Development Division, December 1980), tables 10, 11, 14, 15.

Pensions, Benefits, and Labor Supply

Labor force participation and the employment rates of young persons and of older men in Australia have changed considerably since the late 1960s. The proportion of men in the labor force who are sixty to sixty-four dropped from 76.1 percent in 1974 to 47.7 percent in 1982. Although the number of older men and women in the labor force in other OECD countries dropped during this period, the decline in Australia was among the sharpest.[43] The employment rate of youths aged fifteen to nineteen fell from 61.6 percent in 1966 to 54 percent in 1974 and 49 percent in 1982. Increases in school attendance rates account for no more than half of the drop in the employment rate.

REASONS FOR THE DECLINE. There are at least two "obvious" explanations for these events. The first has to do with the adverse economic environment in Australia since 1974. Weak demand for labor is said to have driven older workers out of the labor force and kept younger job seekers from finding employment. The second explanation is that the sharp increase in pensions and benefits during the 1970s (see table 4) expanded the the purchasing power of a couple's age pension. In addition, with the aging of World War II veterans the proportion of the male population aged sixty to sixty-four eligible for service pensions rose

43. See Bureau of Labour Market Research, *Retired, Unemployed, or at Risk: Changes in the Australian Labour Market for Older Workers,* Research Report 4 (Canberra: AGPS, 1983), especially pp. 125–27 for comparative graphs.

from 25 percent in 1968 to 35 percent in 1973 and to 50 percent in 1981.[44] The real value of the unemployment benefit for sixteen- and seventeen-year-olds rose sharply from 1970 to 1975, reaching more than half of the pension paid to elderly couples. Because the youth unemployment benefit was not indexed, inflation in subsequent years sharply eroded its real value.

Australian analysts have sought unsuccessfully to determine the degree to which each of these explanations accounts for the large changes in labor supply.[45] Unfortunately, not enough information is available to answer this question.[46] To confuse matters further, there is some evidence that the decline in the number of older men participating in the

44. William J. Merrilees, "The Mass Exodus of Older Males from the Labour Force: An Exploratory Analysis," *Australian Bulletin of Labour*, vol. 8 (March 1982), pp. 81–94.

45. For general background, see Bureau of Labour Market Research, *Retired, Unemployed, or at Risk*; Andre Kaspura and David Kalisch, *Some Important Features of the Australian Labour Market: 1950–1980*, Bureau of Labour Market Research Working Paper 6 (Canberra: AGPS, May 1982). See also Barry Hughes, "Labour Force Participation: What are the Issues?" (n. d.); and Bruce J. Chapman, "Comments" (n.d.).

On the decline in labor force participation of older men, see Merrilees, "The Mass Exodus of Older Males from the Labour Force"; Yvonne Dunlop and Lynne S. Williams, "Declining Labour Force Participation Rates at Older Ages" (Bureau of Labour Market Research, n.d.); P. Stricker and P. Sheehan, *Hidden Unemployment: The Australian Experience* (University of Melbourne, Institute of Applied Economic and Social Research, 1981); Ian Manning, "Inducements to Retire and Early Retirement among Australian Men 1971–81" (University of Melbourne, Institute of Applied Economic and Social Research, n. d.); and Paul W. Miller, "Explanations of Declining Labour Force Participation among Older Males: Barking up the Wrong Tree!" (Australian National University, n. d.).

On the effects of unemployment compensation and influences on labor force participation of young workers, see Miller and Volker, "Unemployment Compensation in Australia"; R. G. Gregory and R. C. Duncan, "High Teenage Unemployment: The Role of Atypical Labour Supply Behaviour," *The Economic Record*, vol. 56 (December 1980), pp. 316–30; R. G. Gregory and P. R. Paterson, "The Impact of Unemployment Benefit Payments on the Level and Composition of Unemployment in Australia," Australian National University, Centre for Economic Policy Research, Discussion Paper 11 (Canberra: Australian National University, July 1980); R. G. Gregory and W. Foster, "The Contribution of Employment Separation to Teenage Unemployment," Centre for Economic Policy Research, Discussion Paper 31 (Canberra: Australian National University, July 1981); William J. Merrilees, "The Effect of Unemployment Benefits and Unemployment on School Enrollment Rates" (University of Sydney, n.d.).

46. Analysts have had to rely on aggregate time series because no detailed microdata or panel surveys are available. But time series data do not contain enough information to distinguish betwen the two proposed explanations.

labor force is explained, at least in part, by a difference in attitudes of the cohort reaching age sixty in the mid-1970s. Even before the economy sagged or age pensions were liberalized, this cohort had declared its intent to retire earlier than older cohorts had done.[47] As already indicated, Australian age pensions are not unduly generous by comparison with benefits available in the United States. The benefits in both countries are lower, however, than benefits in Western Europe.[48]

The unlimited availability of unemployment benefits to older workers in Australia does make it possible for an older worker to receive a de facto early retirement pension, particularly when the demand for labor is weak. An older worker can quit his job, qualify for the unemployment benefit after a six-week waiting period, and receive benefits until he or she becomes old enough for age pension. When unemployment is low, that person might be officially referred to a suitable job and would have to take it or lose the unemployment benefit. When unemployment is high, the few job openings that are available will no doubt go to younger workers. Indeed, at such times successful inducement of older workers to retire may be regarded as desirable because job openings for younger workers with growing families are thereby created. The plain fact is that the early retiree receives nearly as large a pension as the late retiree and, of course, receives assistance for a much longer period.

In this fashion, the Australian system encourages early retirement. To reduce this incentive, it may well be desirable under some conditions to pay larger pensions to workers who defer retirement. No such changes are likely until the fiscal climate improves. Differentiation of benefits runs counter to the principles underlying a scheme based on flat benefits. Furthermore, any change in benefits would create a dilemma. It would either boost government spending and widen the already daunting budget deficit, or it would reduce benefits for some at a time when jobs are scarce.

EDUCATION AND UNEMPLOYMENT BENEFITS. The payment of unemployment benefits to teenagers who leave school raises issues that bear more on education policy than on income assistance. Although many teenagers

47. Miller, "Explanations of Declining Labour Force Participation among Older Males."
48. Organization for Economic Cooperation and Development, *Public Expenditure on Income Maintenance Programmes*, Studies in Resource Allocation 3 (Paris: OECD, July 1976).

Table 5. *Selected Indicators of Education,*
Selected Industrial Countries, 1975–76.

Country	Average number of years in school	Percentage of age group enrolled in educational institutions	
		Ages 16–18	Ages 19–24
Australia	12.6	40.2	7.3
Canada	14.2	66.0	16.2
France	15.5	54.0	12.3
Germany	11.5	35.2	13.9
Japan	14.0	74.8	14.7
New Zealand	13.6	40.4	7.5
Sweden	14.1	56.8	14.6
United Kingdom	13.2	37.4	9.3
United States	16.7	75.7	26.7

Source: Organization for Economic Cooperation and Development, *Educational Statistics in OECD Countries,*
1981 (Paris: OECD, 1981).

enjoy a measure of economic independence, few sixteen- or seventeen-
year-olds are family heads or are wholly independent. The central
educational question is whether Australia wishes to increase the typical
period of education. In 1982 only 36 percent of students were completing
twelve years of school.[49] The proportion of Australian sixteen- to
eighteen-year-olds in school is much lower than that in the United States,
Japan, Canada, or Sweden; and the fraction of those eighteen to twenty-
two years old who are receiving higher education is drastically lower
than that in the United States, Japan, or Canada (table 5).

The role of education in economic growth remains controversial,
although studies of the situation in the United States and Japan suggest
that education has played a large part in boosting worker output.[50]
German and Swedish economic success reminds one, however, that
lengthy schooling for the entire population may not be a necessary
condition for high labor productivity.

Should Australia wish to extend schooling, the present system of
unemployment benefits for young people sixteen and seventeen years

49. Department of Education and Youth Affairs, *Youth Policies, Programs, and
Issues* (Canberra: AGPS, 1983), p. 27.
50. Edward F. Denison and William K. Chung, *How Japan's Economy Grew So
Fast: The Sources of Postwar Expansion* (Brookings Institution, 1976); and Edward F.
Denison, assisted by Jean-Pierre Poullier, *Why Growth Rates Differ: Postwar Experience
in Nine Western Countries* (Brookings Institution, 1967).

old would have to be modified or supplemented. Some analysts favor a universal youth allowance whether or not schooling is extended. One such plan would replace both family allowances and unemployment benefits for youths.[51] If such a youth allowance were paid to sixteen- and seventeen-year-olds and it equaled unemployment benefits payable to them ($45 a week in 1983–84), the net cost of this scheme would have been roughly $1 billion per year. Other alternatives would be to curtail the duration of unemployment benefits for this age group, to require a period of work experience as a condition for eligibility, or to disqualify until age eighteen anyone who does not complete secondary school.

Health Care

The debate over health care policy has centered on three issues: (1) to what degree should the government bear responsibility for assuring that everyone has financial access to medical care? (2) how should such responsibility be divided between the commonwealth and the states? and (3) to what degree should the financing of health care be used as an instrument to alter the distribution of income? A fourth set of questions concerning how to control costs and establish incentives for the efficient production and consumption of health care has received less political attention but is significant for the long term because of the secular growth of spending on health care in developed countries.

Medical care in Australia blends characteristics of systems in the United States and Great Britain.[52] As in the United States, most Australian physicians practice privately on a fee-for-service basis, and patients are free to visit the physician of their choice. In Britain, however, patients ordinarily cannot see a specialist unless they are referred by a general practitioner. Hospital services, as in Britain, are rendered by closed panels of specialists and other personnel employed by hospitals, but other doctors can admit patients and care for them. In general,

51. Duncan Ironmonger, "How to Keep More Children at School," *Australian Society*, vol. 2 (July 1, 1983), pp. 3–5.

52. Richard Bailey Scotton describes the system before the far-reaching changes put into effect under the Whitlam government in *Medical Care in Australia: An Economic Diagnosis* (Melbourne: Sun Books, 1974). John S. Deeble describes the system in 1982, with some historical background, in "Financing Health Care in a Static Economy," *Social Science and Medicine*, vol. 16, no. 6 (1982), pp. 713–24 (reprinted by the Australian National University Health Economics Research Unit).

admission to a hospital occurs after authorization of a hospital-based specialist.

Most hospitals are controlled by the states and derive the bulk of their revenue from lump-sum appropriations from state budgets. The states, in turn, receive grants from the commonwealth to cover part of the cost of supporting hospitals and other health services. Except for changes in the commonwealth grant formula, these elements of the Australian health care system have not been fundamentally changed by the legislation enacted since 1973.

When the Whitlam government took office in late 1972, about three-quarters of all Australians were covered by voluntary health insurance plans; in Queensland, the one state where free hospital care in public hospitals was universally available, only half of the population was insured.[53] By fiscal 1972 insurance benefits covered more than 80 percent of physician fees, and more than half of these benefits were supported by government subsidy rather than by premiums directly imposed on patients.[54]

MEDIBANK. The Whitlam government in 1974 secured enactment of the Health Insurance Act, which led to the creation one year later of Medibank, Australia's first version of national health insurance.[55] Medibank had four principal effects: it extended the reach of health insurance to a

53. Although the government did not require people to buy insurance, the commonwealth government heavily subsidized and regulated it. Benefits for physicians' services were established by the commonwealth on the basis of consultations with the Australian Medical Association. Scotton, *Medical Care in Australia.*

54. In addition to these benefits, the commonwealth paid fully for physician services for pensioners. While most of the cost of physician services was covered by the commonwealth budget, states paid most of the cost of hospitals. The commonwealth paid fixed sums for each patient day and for certain other services. The commonwealth subsidy was larger for insured than for uninsured patients, an indirect encouragement for insurance. And it was larger still for certain patients, notably pensioners and recent migrants, who were treated free in public wards of public hospitals. Deeble, "Financing Health Care in a Static Economy."

55. Medibank was universal. It virtually eliminated the need for private insurance for physician services. And it transferred most of the cost of public hospitals from the states to the commonwealth. The commonwealth agreed to meet half of the net operating cost of public hospitals if states agreed to provide free ward treatment to all patients, regardless of means. In addition, the commonwealth increased the subsidy to private hospitals for each patient day. Patients were free to purchase insurance if they wished to reduce out-of-pocket expenses still further. Insurance continued to cover about one-sixth of hospital bills. All budget costs, therefore, were met through general revenues.

significant minority of the population previously without adequate protection; it simplified coverage for the rest; it shifted to the commonwealth much of the financial responsibility for medical care previously borne by the states; and it reduced drastically the importance of premiums—which did not vary with income, family size, or other personal circumstances—in the financing of medical care.

Equally striking, Medibank did nothing to alter the health care delivery system. Patients retained the right to see the doctor of their choice. Doctors remained private businessmen billing on a fee-for-service basis. The legal and budgetary control of hospitals by the states was unchanged.

Medibank survived barely one year in its original form. The Whitlam government had experienced difficulty in securing its enactment, and the Australian Medical Association remained opposed to mandatory insurance. Medibank came on line shortly after a spurt in health expenditures had begun.[56] Although much of this increase occurred just before the start of Medibank, it received part of the blame (or credit, depending on one's point of view) for subsequent increases. From 1973–74 through 1975–76 the share of gross domestic product devoted to health expenditures jumped from 6.0 percent to 7.6 percent.[57]

CREEPING REPEAL. Six months after Medibank went into effect the Whitlam government was replaced by the Liberal government of Malcolm Fraser. Despite campaign promises to preserve Medibank, the Fraser government gradually initiated a series of amendments that tended to undo each of the major changes that Medibank had wrought.

The first of these changes, enacted in October 1976, changed the form but not the substance of insurance coverage.[58] Additional amendments

---

The original Labor party proposal had called for a special tax of 1.35 percent of taxable income to defray part of the budget cost of the new plan. That tax was lost in the course of compromises deemed necessary to secure enactment of the proposal.

56. J. Richardson, "Efficiency and Equity in the Australian Medicare Health Insurance System," *Australian Health Review*, vol. 7 (February 1984).

57. Cedric C. J. Gibbs and Helen M. Lapsley, "The Health Care Cost Spiral: Monster or Myth," *The Medical Journal of Australia* (June 11, 1983), pp. 575–78. Part of this rise was attributable to a decline in growth of real national income in response to the worldwide recession of 1974–75.

58. A special 2.5 percent income tax was imposed to cover costs of Medibank, but anyone who could show equivalent private insurance coverage was exempted from the tax. The natural consequence was that persons with above-average income tended to drop out of Medibank because premiums were less burdensome than the tax. About

enacted in 1978 and 1979 reduced the fraction of the population with insurance for hospital or physician services by one-half.

In 1981 the Fraser government made two additional changes, seemingly technical but important change in the distribution formula under which the commonwealth subsidized state hospital outlays sharply alters the distribution of financial responsibilities between the commonwealth and the states. Previously the commonwealth had provided what amounted to an open-ended matching grant on behalf of each additional patient.[59] Henceforth, the commonwealth would provide the states with a block grant for health care that the states could supplement as they wished. The commonwealth continued to bear financial responsibility only for the cost of care to pensioners and other selected groups comprising about 20 percent of the population.

MEDIBANK RETURNS. In the 1982 election Fraser's Labor challenger, Robert Hawke, campaigned on a promise to restore Medibank. After electoral success, the Labor government reaffirmed its commitment in its first complete budget, submitted in August 1983. In broad outline, the new health insurance benefits were to resemble those of the original Medibank plan.[60] Although the plan increased grants from the common-

---

half of those previously covered by Medibank left the system. As a result, the apparent size of the budget fell. Advocates of balanced budget amendments or spending limits and those who tend to judge the size of the public sector by the share of gross national income spent through public budgets or collected in taxes should take note of this fiscal shell game. Such a reduction in the ratio of budget expenditures to national income signifies absolutely nothing about the size of the public sector. Similarly, legislation that shifted onto the budget a set of activities previously financed privately might indicate nothing about the size or the role of government.

59. The commonwealth grant to the states was 50 percent of net state costs of operating public hospitals based on "agreed" budgets derived from expenditures in the previous year. Although these grants were fixed once the negotiation was completed, the Jamison Commission, appointed to investigate rising hospital costs, argued that this arrangement "resulted in state governments viewing hospital expenditures at the margin as 50 cent dollars." Commonwealth Department of Treasury and Commonwealth Department of Health, "Hospital Funding Arrangements: An Historical Perspective," in R. L. Mathews, ed., *Hospital Funding* (Canberra: Australian National University, Centre for Research on Federal Fiscal Relations, 1983), p. 7.

60. The commonwealth would defray at least 85 percent of the cost of medical services provided by physicians and optometrists according to a fee schedule. Physicians were given the option on a patient-by-patient basis of billing the government and accepting 85 percent of the schedule fee as complete reimbursement or of billing patients their full fees. All Australians would be entitled to free care in public hospital wards. On the revenue side, the Labor plan called for a 1 percent tax on all taxable income.

wealth to the states, it preserved the principle set in place by the Fraser government that the grants should be in the form of a lump sum and that overruns of hospital budgets are the responsibility of the revenue-constrained states.

The net result of a decade of legislation has been a return to a plan much like that introduced by the Whitlam government in 1975. The Whitlam and Hawke plans differ from the voluntary insurance they replaced in two respects. First, both mandatory plans were universal and more uniform than voluntary systems. Second, mandatory systems increase the costs borne by upper-income groups, in part because costs are financed to a greater degree than under voluntary systems by general revenues drawn largely from graduated personal income taxes, and to a smaller degree by flat premiums. In part, the shift occurs because tax-financed direct government subsidies to insurance companies replace tax concessions that accrued mainly to upper-income taxpayers. The mode of physician practice and the organization and control of hospitals, however, is unchanged.

CONTROLLING MEDICAL EXPENDITURES. The Australian system of financing health care, like the systems of all other developed industrial countries, insulates patients from most costs of serious illnesses. The debate over the last decade has concerned the extent to which such protection should be mandatory and how the costs should be distributed. The fundamental principle that individuals should not be required to pay much of the cost of care at the time it is provided has never been in doubt. The net effect of legislative changes from 1974 through 1983 has been to reduce the degree to which patients are exposed to such costs.[61]

The question of whether nonpoor patients should be required to pay an increased share of the cost of care at the time they receive it remains unresolved. Advocates assert that by making patients more price conscious, cost sharing will reduce the demand for low-benefit services and will induce providers to improve efficiency. Opponents argue that the effect on outlays is likely to be small and possibly perverse, that high-

---

The yield, it was asserted, would cover the cost of added benefits. The cost of a direct commonwealth subsidy to private insurance was to be met out of savings from the repeal of tax concessions previously allowed for health insurance premiums.

61. The Hawke government's medicare plan reversed this trend to a small degree by prohibiting the purchase of supplementary insurance to pay for the portion of the physicians' fees not covered by medicare reimbursement (85 percent of scheduled fees).

benefit services will be sacrificed and low-benefit services continued, and that patients lack the information or the leverage to have much influence on the quantity or quality of care they receive.[62]

Whatever the merits of each position, the European, North American, and Australasian countries have shown little political inclination to rely heavily on direct charges to patients to control health expenditures. The rejection of significant cost sharing shifts a grave responsibility—how to determine the quantity of resources allocated to health care—to agents other than patients or providers. If patients bear little or no cost, they will seek all care, however costly, that provides any medical benefit. If physicians gain or, at worst, lose nothing from its provision, they will have every incentive to provide it. And if the list of beneficial procedures and the population to be served are growing, the natural consequence will be rapidly increasing outlays.

Precisely this result is observable in most modern industrial societies. Indeed, concern is growing that some services provide expected benefits worth less than their cost and that the proportion of health outlays that falls in this category is increasing.

Although health outlays have shot up as a fraction of national income in most countries, they have not risen in Australia since 1975. Three factors seem to be at work. Hospital budgets are stringently enforced by the states; the commonwealth grant formula puts the states at risk for cost overruns; and reimbursement for the services of physicians is governed by a fee schedule that appears to have contributed to a sharp decline in income per practitioner since 1975–76.[63] These institutional

62. For a review of the arguments on both sides, see Louise B. Russell, "Medical Care," in Joseph A. Pechman, ed., *Setting National Priorities: The 1984 Budget* (Brookings Institution, 1983), pp. 111–44; J. Richardson and R. Wallace, "Health Economics," in Fred H. Gruen, ed., *Surveys of Australian Economics*, vol. 3 (Sydney: George Allen & Unwin, 1982), pp. 125–86. J. R. Richardson, "The Use of Hospital and Medical Services in Australia: Some Policy Issues," School of Economic and Financial Studies, Research Paper 257 (North Ryde: Macquarie University, October 1982), presents estimates based on parameters from the Rand Health Insurance Study, suggesting that the reductions in spending on health that would result from the introduction of cost sharing would be small.

63. J. Richardson, "Incomes of Private Medical Practitioners in Australia and Their Control," paper presented to the Twelfth Conference of Economists, University of Tasmania, Hobart, August 28–September 1, 1983. Great Britain, like Australia, finances hospitals through fixed budgets and has experienced little growth in medical outlays as a fraction of gross national product. The United Kingdom also pays doctors on a salaried

arrangements do not guarantee slow growth in medical outlays, as indicated by the rapid increase in Australian outlays from 1973 to 1976. But if there is a collective will to restrain outlays, it provides a practical framework for doing so. This restraint may have extracted a toll in the availability of services.[64]

Australian health planners labor under special problems arising from extremely low population densities. A variety of high-technology services operates least expensively or most efficiently at larger scales than can be generated in Australia's states, other than perhaps New South Wales or Victoria. Australia's geographic isolation precludes exchange of patients with neighboring countries and makes transfers of patients even among the states costly. Some surgical procedures require a large number of operations to keep surgical teams expert and mortality rates low that is greater than can be generated by most Australian states. Thus, many costly new procedures are even costlier or may be less beneficial in Australia than elsewhere because they must be provided at suboptimal scale or because patients or hospitals must incur large transportation costs.

The central point is that Australia already has in place the institutional arrangements for making decisions about how quickly or how slowly health expenditures should be permitted to rise. Given the virtually universal policy of not using price to ration care, this is a great boon.[65]

---

basis. In addition, British patients cannot see a specialist unless referred by the general practitioner with whom they have enrolled. For details on the British system and on the choices that sustained tight budget limits have forced, see Henry J. Aaron and William Schwartz, *The Painful Prescription: Rationing Hospital Care* (Brookings Institution, 1984).

64. Gibbs and Lapsley, "The Health Care Cost Spiral."

65. Prepaid group health plans are another way of insulating patients from the cost of care at the time they need it, while simultaneously subjecting providers to budget limits. Some U.S. analysts believe that the proliferation of such plans would result in the provision of low-benefit care without the need for bureaucratic control. See Alain C. Enthoven, *Health Plan: The Only Practical Solution to the Soaring Cost of Medical Care* (Sydney: Addison Wesley, 1980). For a more restrained appraisal of the benefits to be derived from health maintenance organizations, see Harold Luft, *Health Maintenance Organizations: Dimensions of Performance* (New York: Wiley, 1981). Despite the rapid growth of such plans, they continue to cover a small number of U.S. residents. In any event, they do not exist in Australia. J. Richardson points out that one consequence of the 1983 medicare plan will be the suppression of any tendency for such prepaid group plans to arise (see Richardson, "Efficiency and Equity in the Australian Medicare Health Insurance System").

Because states are so small, however, uncoordinated decisions about the provision of services are likely to result in duplication and inefficient use of facilities. To avoid these problems, the commonwealth may have to play an increased role in coordinating or controlling medical investments to minimize duplication and in helping patients move across and within states to obtain services.

Family Assistance

Like most developed countries other than the United States, Australia pays cash to parents and guardians on behalf of their minor children. Unlike most developed countries, Australia does not allow income tax exemptions for children. These two features of Australian social legislation are related. In 1976 the Fraser government repealed the income tax exemption for each child and increased family allowances. The rationale for the switch was and remains that exemptions reduce tax and increase disposable income more for people in high- than for people in low-income brackets, and that they provide no help for people too poor to pay tax. This tax saving, it is held, constitutes an "upside-down" subsidy for the support of children.[66] Family allowances, in contrast, provide the same increase in disposable income regardless of parental income. In 1983–84 the allowance was $22.80 a month for the first child, increasing with the number of children to $45.55 a month for the fifth and later children. Although this benefit is low by comparison with OECD countries, it exceeds the value of tax exemptions for dependents that can be claimed in the United States.[67]

In contrast to most other forms of cash assistance, family allowances are subject to neither income test nor income tax. This feature, combined with the fact that payments are made to the mother, converts family

---

66. This argument is not dispositive. Most tax systems exempt a basic amount of income from tax on the ground that people with that income alone have no taxable capacity. The exempt amount is larger for two people than for one. If such an exemption is legitimate (and Australia has it), then it should be larger if children are present than if they are not. This line of reasoning indicates the appropriateness of a child deduction. Family allowances may be desirable on other grounds.

67. OECD, *Public Expenditure on Income Maintenance Programmes*, pp. 26–27. U.S. taxpayers save at most $41.67 a month in reduced taxes from income tax exemptions of $1,000 a year for each child; the average tax saving is somewhat less than half of that amount.

allowances from a simple program to help families with children into a base of economic power for women, especially those not employed outside the home. If an income test were applied, one of two effects could follow. If earnings of both spouses were counted in the test and the amount that could be earned without loss of benefits were similar to that in other programs, most families would be denied benefits. If only the mother's income were counted, greater assistance would be provided on behalf of children whose mothers did not work outside the home than to those whose mothers did.

The government also provides income-tested assistance under two other programs to single parents with children. Widows' pensions are payable to women (but not to men) who are widowed, divorced, or deserted. The benefit is the same as the age pension for single aged persons, plus $51.00 a month for each child.[68] About half of the recipients have children (class A widows). The other half are widows fifty or older who are eligible although they do not have minor children (class B widows). Equal benefits are paid under the supporting parents benefit program to single parents, men or women, with children in their care. These payments are made whether or not the parents were ever married. The widows' pension and the supporting parents benefit are income tested in the same way as age pensions. Both benefits are included in taxable income. In combination, these two programs in 1983–84 provided $1.7 billion in assistance to families with children, approximately 8.0 percent of all social welfare spending, 3.0 percent of the budget, and 1.8 percent of the gross domestic product.

Compensation for Injuries

This survey has omitted a number of important aspects of the Australian social welfare system, the most notable being financial assistance to the injured or disabled. These programs include government pensions to invalids, sheltered employment allowances, rehabilitation allowances, sickness benefits, and workers' compensation. The workers' compensation system consists of two parts, a set of no-fault benefits paid by the states, and a common-law system supported by premiums

---

68. This amount is in addition to family allowances.

paid by employers. In addition, compensation is available for product-related injuries and for automobile injuries.

This system is undergoing extensive reexamination because of a sense that workers' compensation is being abused and that the whole system is expensive, fragmented, and uncoordinated.[69] Because part of the workers' compensation system is based on the common law, litigation is costly unless out-of-court settlements are made. Furthermore, compensation covers not only injuries directly related to employment, but also accidents only tenuously connected with work. For example, an automobile injury is covered if the injured person was driving to or from work. A fall on the front steps is covered if the person was on his way to or from work. If such injuries are included under workers' compensation, why should the burn a person suffers while preparing breakfast before going to work be excluded? In fact, what logically defensible boundary exists for distinguishing covered from uncovered injuries?

The cost of assistance to the handicapped is budgeted for $1.4 billion in 1983–84 (see table 1), and private workers' compensation premiums reached more than $1.3 billion in 1981–82 and have been rising sharply since then.[70] Premiums run to more than 30 percent of wages in some industries.[71] These figures do not include state workers' compensation, product liability and automobile injury settlements, or other federal programs for the disabled or sick. I have neglected these programs despite their high cost because they involve complex legal provisions and benefit rules that vary among the states.

Even a cursory knowledge of the existing Australian programs, however, makes clear that the workers' compensation system is far more generous than the U.S. system, both in the range of contingencies covered and in the amounts paid. Furthermore, the heavy reliance on a common law system in both countries, as opposed to administrative determinations or no-fault payments, tends to boost the proportion of

69. New South Wales Law Reform Commission, *Issues Paper: Accident Compensation* (Sydney: 1982); and *Accident Compensation Working Paper No. 1, A Transport Accidents Scheme for New South Wales* (Sydney: May 1983). For an analysis of the U.S. system, see Richard B. Victor and others, *Workers' Compensation and Workplace Safety: Some Lessons from Economic Theory* (Santa Monica, Calif.: Rand, 1982).

70. Australian Bureau of Statistics, *General Insurance, Australia, 1981–82*, table 2, catalog no. 5620.0 (April 1983).

71. Tony Thomas, "The Crippling Costs of Compo," *Business Review Weekly*, July 23–29, 1983, pp.12–18.

gross program costs absorbed by legal fees and investigatory expenses. In 1974 a national committee recommended adoption of a no-fault scheme for all injuries, similar to that adopted by New Zealand, but no action was taken.[72] Reforms proposed by the New South Wales Law Reform Commission in 1983 would move a step in that direction.[73]

The other pensions and health benefits available in Australia are a special blend of generosity in coverage and duration and of illiberality in level of benefits. Sweeping changes in some programs —income-related age pensions or mandatory superannuation—are under discussion. In the case of others, such as broader taxation of capital income or limits on the duration of unemployment benefits for voluntary job leavers, there is no consensus that reform is needed. Whether and how soon any changes will be enacted are likely to be governed by the continuing effort to reduce Australia's imposing deficit and to restore economic growth. Regardless of when Australia turns to these issues, increased attention should be devoted to the likely effect of existing programs and proposed alternatives on economic incentives.

Alternative Perspectives on Reform of Social Welfare Policy

Three broad issues lie behind the debates on social welfare policy in Australia and elsewhere: What is the proper role of the state in assuring social welfare? What are the relative strengths of financial incentives and other pressures on the behavior of beneficiaries? How broadly should the term "social welfare program" be construed in policy debates?

At first glance these issues seem unrelated. Closer inspection reveals that they are intertwined. Furthermore, the differences between the general view of analysts and political leaders in the United States and Australia seem large enough that a failure to make them explicit would hinder Americans from understanding the debate in Australia; it would also handicap Australians in understanding American reactions to their system.

72. National Rehabilitation and Compensation Scheme Committee of Inquiry, *Compensation and Rehabilitation in Australia* (Canberra: AGPS, 1974).
73. New South Wales Law Reform Commission, *A Transport Accidents Scheme for New South Wales*.

The Role of the State

In principle, the state can be asked to play widely different roles in trying to assure adequate income for the elderly, sick, and disabled; the unemployed; and single parents, widows, and orphans. At the one extreme, the state can be viewed as a repairman, called in to fix problems when some people find themselves with less income than society is prepared to tolerate. In this view, the state is an agent-of-last-resort, called upon to act only if all voluntary or private measures have failed. Under this principle, cash assistance and social services are provided only for the truly needy as measured by an income or means test. Benefits would be designed to prevent utter destitution, but not much more.

Alternatively, the state might not require a demonstration of need for at least some benefits. Under this policy some and perhaps all assistance would be available as a matter of right. How far away from the model of the state-as-repairman society moves clearly depends on the number and generosity of benefits available as a matter of right, and on whether payments are generous or derisory. Indeed, benefits may be so generous or income tests so lax that virtually everyone qualifies.

The Australian system is unusual because all payments are flat and, except for children's allowances, most are income tested, as the repairman model suggests. But some benefits under some programs (age pension, for example) are high enough so that most people eligible on noneconomic criteria also qualify on economic grounds. Other programs (unemployment benefit and supporting parent benefit, for example) have some features that are quite generous, at least by U.S. standards.

The central point is that the debate over whether benefits should be available independent of a demonstration of economic need or only after satisfaction of an income or means test is more widespread in Australia than in the United States. The commitment to universality—that is, the payment of benefits without economic tests—assumes transcendent importance in Australia, particularly for the political left.[74] A leading

74. During the interview carried out in preparation for this paper, I asked four persons, all of the political left, a hypothetical question based on the premise that a small sum was available to liberalize age pension: given the choice between raising benefits or relaxing the income test, the interviewee was asked which he would prefer. The answers were evenly divided. One person resisted answering it directly until the question was put to him three times. I believe that had I put the same question to

Australian writer on the left infers from one's position on this issue whether one embraces a pessimistic or an optimistic view of social and economic evolution.[75] In general, if one believes that the results of market processes are fundamentally immoral or unjust, one is likely to urge radical reform of those processes or to favor public programs that simply override market outcomes. The position of the government-as-repairman would then be difficult to embrace, because it implies that most results of market processes are acceptable and that only modest adjustments or repairs are necessary. The person who rejects the repairman role for government is unlikely to support tests for eligibility based on the outcomes of immoral market processes.[76]

No more than echoes of this rejection of market outcomes may be heard in the United States, where the issue of income testing is discussed largely in practical terms. Do income tests carry a stigma, and, if so, does it significantly reduce applications for benefits? Do income or means tests improve the distribution of benefit payments sufficiently to justify the extra administrative costs? Can a program geared entirely to the poor be in good political standing?

In the United States different programs have resolved these issues in different ways. Cash and medical assistance for the elderly and disabled, for example, are available without any income or means test.[77] Cash and medical assistance for the nonelderly are available only upon satisfaction of strict income and asset tests. The frontiers of where income tests

---

members of the political left in the United States, nearly all would have chosen the increase in benefits.

75. Adam Graycar, *Welfare Politics in Australia: A Study in Policy Analysis* (South Melbourne: The Macmillan Company of Australia Pry Ltd., 1979), p. 6.

76. I am not arguing that the image of government-as-repairman is *logically* inconsistent with the view that capitalism produces immoral outcomes, as some discussants of an earlier version of this paper inferred. There is no logical inconsistency. One might conclude without violating logic, as did one correspondent, "If the market is fundamentally immoral you should undo its resulting inequalities with income and means-tested welfare payments and not squander public monies on those not needing public assistance." My assertion is simply that such a view has been, is, and will be infrequently held and that it will appeal principally to scholars. A call to replace or radically alter a supposedly malign economic system commands more widespread support than a plea to keep repairing the damage it causes.

77. Old age, survivors', and disability insurance are payable only if the beneficiaries have earnings below stipulated levels, but they may have any amount of unearned income without loss of benefits.

should and should not be applied seem relatively well accepted in the United States.[78]

Financial Incentives

As for the question of the relative strengths of financial and other incentives in governing people's behavior, this issue has great bearing on program design. If labor supply, for example, is highly sensitive to the net wage from an additional hour of work, one must beware of exposing large numbers of potential workers to high benefit-reduction rates because such rates would cause large reductions in labor supply.[79] To the extent that labor supply fell, cash assistance would not raise the spendable cash income of those who were assisted. Or if cash assistance or social services were to discourage saving, this distortion of private decisions would be a cost of such benefits and might discourage their expansion.

The issue of how tax and transfer policies affect saving has received less attention in Australia than in the United States.[80] The impact of these policies on labor supply has received more attention, but the degree of controversy, especially in the political arena, is startlingly slight in view of the massive shifts in labor supply. Whether this comparative lack of interest is attributable to a belief that incentive effects are not important, to a lack of data to carry out research, or to both factors is

78. It is hard in the United States to find significant interest in doing away with existing income or means tests. One leading opponent of these tests, frustrated at the lack of such interest, was led to organize a conference built around this issue. See Irwin Garfinkel, ed., *Income-Tested Transfer Programs: The Case For and Against* (Academic Press, 1982).

79. In certain cases, lowering the benefit-reduction rate increases work disincentives. This counterintuitive effect is the result of two factors: the income effect of lowering the benefit-reduction rate reduces work incentives for all beneficiaries other than those with zero earnings; and lowering the benefit-reduction rate at any given guarantee or basic benefit exposes additional taxpayers to the implicit tax of the assistance system. These two effects may overpower the work incentives for initial beneficiaries of an increased net wage rate. How work incentives are changed depends on the relative size of income and subsitition elasticities and the shape of the income distribution. See Robert A. Moffit, "A Problem with the Negative Income Tax," paper prepared for the Southern Economics Association meeting, November 1983.

80. I reported in an earlier draft of this paper that I had found no studies of the effects of age pension on national saving. In correspondence, Daryl Dixon informed me of one such study.

hard to judge. A few Australian studies have sought to discover whether the liberalization of age pension in the mid-1970s contributed to the large drop in labor force participation of older males that began at that time; others have tried to determine whether unemployment benefits paid to sixteen- and seventeen-year-olds contribute to low school-continuation rates.[81]

One possible explanation for the lack of attention to these issues is the high cost of collecting data.[82] Although the United States is more than ten times as populous as Australia, the laws of probability decree that the cost of amassing sufficient data to yield statistically reliable estimates of behavior in the two countries is almost identical. Thus, the per capita cost of collecting data in Australia is more than ten times greater than it is in the United States. Experiments or surveys may seem prohibitively costly in Australia. In the absence of indigenous data, simulations based on foreign studies would be informative.

Even if reliable research is unavailable, people must and do decide whether or not they think incentive effects are important. Although opinion is divided, many Australian analysts or officials seem to think they are not. An objective review of the results of income maintenance experiments in the United States and Canada concludes with a summary of Australian views on attitudes toward graduated income assistance:

The Commission of Inquiry into Poverty felt that its proposed [program of income support] would not damage work incentives because "Australians have no respect for the bludger," and nobody is anxious to acquire such status, and argued that this assessment was confirmed by the results of the New Jersey [Income Maintenance] Experiment. The Priorities Review Staff also considered that the U.S. evidence showed that the number of hours worked by primary wage earners was not significantly affected by income supplements. More recently concern with work disincentives has been described as "that favorite chestnut of taxation reform." In contrast the Report of the Taxation Review Committee argued that a [guaranteed minimum income] would seem likely to have consequences for incentives to work and save which make it impossible to consider such a scheme seriously.[83]

81. See note 46 above.
82. One Australian critic of this paper acknowledged that there is some truth in this explanation, but went on to say that "it is more because we do not have a tradition of using empirical research for policy purposes."
83. Peter Whiteford, "Work Incentive Experiments in the U.S.A. and Canada," Department of Social Security Research Paper 12 (Canberra: AGPS, June 1981), p. i of foreword.

Concerning the effects of the existing social welfare system, Labor Minister for Social Security, Senator Don Grimes, in 1983 wrote:

The final pattern of production and consumption that emerges after transfers take place may well differ from the one which would have arisen in their absence, but within very wide limits there is no reason to suppose that the overall "cake" being divided up will be any smaller, or that society as a whole will be worse off as a result.[84]

These statements reinforce a visitor's impression that Australians, on balance, are less concerned than Americans about the effect social welfare legislation has on economic efficiency.[85]

Whatever one's views on transfer payments, the idea that they have little or no effect on economic behavior is no longer defensible, if it ever was.[86] Comments such as "Australians have no respect for the bludger" are not even relevant to the issue. Most people are in some degree "bludgers," in the sense that they adjust their behavior in response to economic incentives. Work incentive problems may be significant even if few rest easy on state largess. Important changes in labor supply may occur even if those who respond simply reduce the number of hours worked or slightly extend the number of weeks between jobs. This is the lesson of the income maintenance experiments in the United States and of studies of the effects of unemployment insurance. Although the earliest income maintenance experiment indicated that cash transfers had negligible effects on labor supply, later results from the Seattle-Denver experiment found changes in labor supply large enough to cause

---

84. Senator Don Grimes, "Supportive Policies—The Role of Social Security," speech delivered at the Economic Summit, April 12, 1983.

85. Peter Allen cites the trade-off between the goals of equality and economic efficiency explored at length by Arthur Okun in *Equality and Efficiency: The Big Tradeoff* (Brookings Institution, 1975). But instead of drawing the inference that programs to advance equality may reduce economic efficiency, he veers away from this issue, asserting that the trade-off arises "as much as anything out of the contradictions between the political principles of democracy and the principles of capitalism." He goes on to say that "if we are to achieve more equitable distribution of such basic goods and services as housing and medical care, governments will have to ensure at least a minimal level of service to all through the public sector," but says no more about the possibility of a trade-off between the goals he sets forth and economic efficiency. See Peter Allen, "Poverty Policy Issues," in Ronald Mendelsohn, ed., *Australian Social Welfare Finance* (George Allen & Unwin, 1983), pp. 102–03.

86. Sheldon Danziger and others, "How Income Transfer Programs Affect Work, Savings, and Income Distribution: A Critical Review," *The Journal of Economic Literature*, vol. 19 (September 1981), pp. 975–1028.

U.S. planners to propose work requirements and the creation of public service jobs as part of welfare reform.[87]

What Is a Social Welfare Program?

The third issue of interest here concerns the breadth in which social welfare programs should be examined. Suppose, for example, that market forces, even as modified by existing tax laws and direct government expenditures, are believed to contribute to excessive income inequality. What view should one take, say, toward the introduction of age pensions graduated with respect to past earnings?

If age pensions alone are considered, such a change would seem unattractive, because it would pay more to the relatively well-to-do than does the present flat-benefit, income-tested program. An issues brief prepared for the commonwealth Parliament endorses this view without qualification, stating "there is a moral objection to government bothering about the middle- to high-income earners" with graduated retirement benefits, because such a system "implies the perpetuation into old age of those very inequalities in income that one normally expects governments to try to mitigate. There would appear to be little justification for the general community going to the administrative trouble and fiscal expense of helping to prop up the post-retirement incomes of the better-off."[88] This view implicitly denies the possibility that helping the relatively well-to-do elderly maintain their preretirement incomes may be intrinsically desirable or that it may be useful in avoiding means or income tests. It fails to allow that other instruments, such as tax reform, may be superior devices for dealing with excessive concentrations of wealth. Even if one acknowledges that compensating changes in other programs may be difficut to bring about, this view represents a particu-

87. According to the Seattle-Denver experiment, for example, one-fourth to one-half of increments in cash assistance to two-parent families would replace reductions in earnings from decreased labor supply if there was no work requirement. See Henry Aaron and John Todd, "The Use of Income Maintenance Experiment Findings in Public Policy 1977–78," in Industrial Relations Research Association series, *Proceedings of the Thirty-First Annual Meeting* (Madison, Wisc.: IRRA, 1979), pp. 46–56.

88. Roy Forward, "Income in Old Age: Is National Superannuation the Answer?" Parliament of the Commonwealth of Australia, Current Issues Brief 4 (Legislative Research Service, 1983), p. 15. This passage is not quoted to suggest that quite different views are not widely held in Australia. The National Superannuation Committee in 1976 endorsed graduated superannuation benefits and the platform of the Labor Party included such a plank in 1983.

larly hard-line assertion of the preeminence of distributional considerations over all other possible objectives of public policy.

A broader approach, however, makes it easier to accommodate the fact that many individual programs advance several objectives and that a desirable program may even cause unwanted side effects that other programs can correct. The person who believes that the moral order is disturbed when age pensions are allowed to sustain preretirement living standards of the nonpoor might be mollified if taxes on income and wealth were modified to discourage the perpetuation of excessive inequality. But this linkage presupposes that the tax system is a potent social welfare policy and that other public expenditures—including education, training, and cash assistance—can be used to improve the earning prospects and incomes of the nonaged poor.[89]

That is to say, any program to reform the system of social welfare that ignores tax reform is incomplete.[90] A comprehensive examination of retirement policy must go beyond age pensions and "fringe benefits" to the effects of the virtual exclusion of capital gains from taxation that makes it possible for some to shield labor income from taxation by converting it into capital gains.

Summary

The three issues sketched in this section are related. If the state influences the generation of primary incomes—through tax laws, tariffs, agricultural policy, labor market interventions, licensing, and other industrial regulation—then the image of the state as a repairman undoing the unfortunate consequences of a process in which it is not a direct participant has no relation to reality. Practical questions concern how the state, as an active economic participant, can shape a wide range of policies—including but going far beyond those customarily regarded as social welfare—to deal with the problems outlined at the start of this chapter. If such policies are to be efficient, attention must be paid to how people respond to the economic incentives they face.

89. One might even broaden one's focus to include tariff policy, as is suggested in the introduction to this book.

90. See Daryl Dixon and Chris Foster, *Social Welfare for a Sustainable Society*, prepared for the 1980 Australia and New Zealand Association for the Advancement of Science congress, May 1980.

Conclusions

THE cross-currents of inference that connect the authors' discussions are the subject of this chapter. These themes supplement the preceding chapters' conclusions, and together they constitute the principal findings of the volume. They may not capture all the distinctive features or major problems of the Australian economy, but then the individual contributions did not attempt "wall to wall" coverage of significant economic issues. Another point to remember here is that an outsider bringing a fresh perspective and independent judgment may flush out some conclusions of value, but he also incurs the risk of trading on the tourist's incomplete perceptions and overvaluing conclusions that may have grown commonplace in Australia.

Unemployment with Inflation

As Rudiger Dornbusch and Stanley Fischer point out, the shift from low inflation and low unemployment to high levels of both has been more grievous in Australia than in other OECD countries. This fall from grace and the resulting dilemma for Australia's policymakers have dominated public discussions of economic policy and have been among the main topics considered in this volume. The decay in macroeconomic performance does not appear to stem from any obvious change in Australia's wage-setting institutions. Nonetheless, the role of wage explosions in inflationary bouts from 1973 on has brought attention to these institutions.

What, then, actually happened to the macroeconomic behavior of wages and unemployment in Australia during this period? Dornbusch and Fischer conclude that the Phillips-curve relationship between wages and unemployment persisted, but that the trade-off between wage inflation and unemployment grew more unfavorable after 1978. An obvious explanation for the worsening trade-off is that wages became highly sensitive to expected inflation. However, competing hypotheses have been advanced. Some argue that wages have come to vary with the typical firm's utilization of its current labor force rather than the pool of unemployed outside the factory gate. The econometric results of Dornbusch and Fischer do not strongly support that view, but they do accord with another hypothesis: that a drastic adverse shift occurs in the Phillips relationship when real wages fall below their previous level, so that a large increase in unemployment is then required to keep the rate of wage inflation constant. These hypotheses all cast doubt on the concept of a stable "natural rate of unemployment" and suggest that the natural rate wanders around in the wake of the actual unemployment rate. Henry J. Aaron points to another factor that may be involved in the shift: unemployment benefits have grown more generous and are subject to easy conditions for eligibility (they are less stringent in Australia than in the United States).

Many observers agree that explosions of nominal wages took place in 1973–75 and 1981–82 and were then temporarily locked in as real increases through indexation. Public policy evidently had a hand in these episodes, according to Daniel J. B. Mitchell and Dornbusch and Fischer, who see them in the context of Australia's distinctive wage-setting institution, the Conciliation and Arbitration Commission. These authors agree that the commission's decisions have at times exerted or transmitted upward pressure on money wages. Mitchell confirms its effect on the structure of wages; the commission, he argues, is responsible for the reduced variance of wages among sectors and occupations in the economy.

If the Conciliation and Arbitration Commission is partly to blame for the problem, can it also be instrumental in implementing a solution? Some observers think the commission is the logical institution to administer an incomes policy that would put the inflation-unemployment trade-off on a more favorable course, but the negative evidence is weighty. Mitchell, however, is quite pessimistic, noting that in its normal role the commission can only raise wages; it cannot limit or lower them. It performs basically a judicial, not a policymaking function. Furthermore, its main task is to implement "comparative wage justice"—that is, to maintain traditional relationships among the wages of differently situated groups. If a conspicuous group manages to violate a prevailing incomes policy, then the commission's policies on relative wages assure that the violation will be transmitted. On the other hand, the commission did play a role in the social compact surrounding the wage freeze of 1982, and Dornbusch and Fischer express guarded hopes that it might be able to deal with the externalities involved in the wage-setting process. Mitchell is pessimistic about involving the commission in the conventional wage-guideline approach to incomes policy but believes that it could act to foster gain sharing as part of a social compact.

Arising out of the dispute over wages and inflation is the question of whether Australia's recent high unemployment has been a Keynesian or a classical phenomenon—that is, whether it has been the result of inadequate demand or of real wages being above their long-run equilibrium level. No definitive test is available, but Dornbusch and Fischer do not rule out the classical explanation. Productivity growth—a potential bail-out of classical unemployment—is not very high, although in Australia it deteriorated less drastically after 1973 than it did in the average OECD country. Accordingly, these authors consider the resistance to real-wage reductions a serious obstacle to resolving the current macroeconomic problem. Unlike some observers, they do not believe that one can count on increasing marginal returns to labor that might accrue to blunt the inflationary pressures generated in a short-run move toward full employment. The recent depreciation of the Australian dollar will help, so long as the indexation of wages is not too sensitive to the resulting increase in the domestic prices of tradable goods.

Macroeconomic Policy in a Society Dependent on Natural Resources

The policy dilemmas of the moment should not obscure the more enduring problems of macroeconomic policymaking that are inherent in Australia's economic structure. Although for its size Australia trades a rather small proportion of its output of goods and services, its prospects for economic growth and stability lean heavily on occurrences in the international economy. John F. Helliwell's analysis of the development of Australia's natural resources reminds us that primary export specialties involve the hazard of short-run economic destabilization. Given the massive scale and lumpiness of such projects, the construction phase in a resource boom requires a large but temporary reallocation of capital and labor. Although capital inputs are frequently secured from abroad, the labor inputs are not. Once in production, a natural resource project generates exports that may be subject to large fluctuations in both price and volume in response to changes in the world economy. In this respect, these exports are similar to the traditional exports of Australia's rural industries. Large disturbances in resource development and the terms of trade have often struck Australia in the past and can be expected to return.

Such disturbances make it all the more difficult to manage macroeconomic policy. Not only are they large and unpredictable, but they also produce changes in government revenue that generate political pressures for parallel adjustments in government expenditures, without regard to the goals of economic stabilization. However, fiscal measures to stabilize a resource-dependent economy will require wide swings in the federal government's net deficit. The government must recognize that exports of nonreproducible resources represent a draft on the nation's capital, and thus during a resource boom it is reasonable to use the tax proceeds to draw down overseas debt. In a downswing, large deficits must be contemplated. However, such deficits engender the "deficit hysteria" and inflationary expectations discussed by Dornbusch and Fischer. Although Australia's deficits have been large in several recent years, outstanding federal government debt is not large in relation to GNP, and the high prevailing levels of unemployment lead Dornbusch and Fischer to be relatively unconcerned about the prospect of future large deficits or of a slump in overseas earnings from resource exports.

Stabilizing a resource-dependent economy has implications for monetary as well as fiscal policy. Dornbusch and Fischer argue that monetary growth is not necessarily tied to the government's deficit position, at least if the foreign-exchange rate is allowed to vary. They approve of Australia's overall flexible approach to monetary targeting, which adjusts money growth to exchange-rate developments. But they also note that because Australia's financial markets are well integrated with those of the rest of the world, the exchange rate can overshoot in response to disturbances and thus leave the monetary authorities with a touchy control problem.

Resource booms and busts create other tactical problems of managing macroeconomic policy. As Dornbusch and Fischer point out, the exchange rate tends to appreciate in a boom year, and the adjustment can be taken in the form of an actual appreciation or an increase in money wages. Appreciation has in its favor the fact that downward rigidity may be less troublesome in any subsequent adjustments of the exchange rate. Appreciation has the virtue of reducing the real debt burden of a country with high overseas debts denominated in foreign currency. Australian manufacturers abhor the squeeze that appreciation puts on that sector, but a squeeze will come from higher real wages if not from exchange rate appreciation.

The Effect of Resource Development on Sectoral Composition

Australia, as Helliwell points out, is like other small, resource-rich countries faced with the pressures that resource development exerts on the factors of production employed in other sectors of the economy. The nontradables sector, of course, is protected by its status and tends to expand when the proceeds of development are spent. However, the import-competing manufacturing sector and the traditional rural export industries suffer to the extent that the construction and operation phases of resource development draw upon the available stock of capital and labor. These needs can be met through immigration and capital inflow. The more Australians tend to prevent the shrinkage of the manufacturing and rural sectors, the more appropriate it is to meet fluctuations in the resource sectors' input needs through international flows of capital and labor.

As might be expected, the existing econometric models reviewed by Helliwell support the conclusion that, with full employment, the expansion of natural resources output brings about an expansion of the services sector and a contraction of manufacturing and the rural sector. However, when the real wage is fixed and labor is unemployed, the models imply a mining boom raises outputs in all sectors except parts of the rural sector and the export-oriented manufacturing industries. These models are ultimately fairly uninformative, Helliwell concludes, because they lack feedbacks that allow changes in potential output and capacity utilization to influence wages and prices; the relative validity of the full-employment and rigid-wage assumptions is therefore left up in the air.

Trade Structure and Tariff Protection

This volume has not covered the long-standing controversy over tariff protection in Australia because the skirmishes have already dug up every inch of that territory. Nonetheless, several points that pertain to Australia's trade structure and trade policies should be mentioned here. The first is that Australia's economy has become less open to trade since World War II, whereas the exposure to trade of other developed economies' markets has increased rapidly. This difference can be attributed in part to structural factors. Lawrence B. Krause shows, for example, that shortly after World War II Australia's exports were concentrated in slow-growing products and markets, and they provided no terms-of-trade inducement for increased participation in trade. Dornbusch and Fischer point out that the share of (nontraded) services in Australia's output—although it was below the OECD average before 1960—caught up during 1960–80. However, Krause stresses, industrial policy has been broadly hostile to increased imports, and reductions in the average level of tariff protection and other forms of assistance to domestic producers have been offset by an increasing variance in the protection rates of industries and by quicker resort to made-to-measure protection.

A traditional justification for Australia's high tariff protection is that its goal has been to expand the labor-intensive manufacturing sector. Formerly, the underlying motive proclaimed for the policy was to support an increased population and to gain certain economies of scale in settling a continental area. Within manufacturing, as Krause notes, protection still tends to favor labor-intensive and low-skilled manufacturing industries, and nowadays perhaps aligns itself more with the goal of income redistribution than with the desire to reach optimum population. According to Richard E. Caves, the tariff certainly has not given rise to a productive or large-scale manufacturing industry. The productivity levels of Australia's manufacturing industries tend to be low where scale economies are important and protection (both artificial trade barriers and natural transportation costs) is high. That is, the disadvantage is mitigated either where protection is low or scale economies are modest to mute the disadvantages of a small domestic market. Similarly, plants in Australia are relatively small where protection is high and small-scale operations incur only a modest cost disadvantage.

Although Krause does detect limited evidence of export prospects in middle-technology products, this advantage probably applies only to trade in the Asian region. Moreover, Caves suggests that export activity in manufacturing is still too limited to influence the distribution of plant sizes (as it regularly does elsewhere). Whether such export specialties will develop will depend on what resources exports materialize.

Australia has traditionally been quite open to another form of international commerce—direct foreign investment. Here, however, it has faced tightening restrictions from the Foreign Investment Review Board and assorted public concerns about the development of resources by foreign multinationals. According to Caves, the presence of foreign subsidiaries does not appear to affect the overall productivity of manufacturing industries in the long run, possibly because of the complex influence that foreign investment wields on the size of Australian production units. That is to say, foreign investment generally promotes larger production units and efficient transfer of technology from abroad in Australia's manufacturing industries, whereas it runs toward small sizes in research-intensive industries (because research supports product differentiation and makes smaller production units viable) and in regionally fragmented industries (multinationals may have been induced by the states to spread small plants around the capital cities).

Krause's summary of public policy toward foreign investment shows that Australia's concern, like that of other high-income host countries, lies less in maximizing the contribution of foreign investment to national income than in diluting foreign equity control and increasing the stock of investment opportunities for Australian capitalists. Interest in maximizing the take from foreign capital through the tax mechanism arises only in the resources sector, as the next section points out.

The Savings-Investment Nexus

The issue of Australia's public policy toward the savings-investment process has been touched upon by several chapters in this volume, which show that the tax structure has been relatively kind to personal saving. For the past five years there have been no death duties (Edward M. Gramlich explains the circumstances), many Australians have been able to avoid the income tax by shifting to nontaxable forms of income, and some have even practiced outright evasion. In addition, capital gains have not been subject to personal income tax. Furthermore, Henry J. Aaron notes, lump-sum superannuation payments from pre-1983 accumulations largely escape taxation if reinvested in assets that yield little cash income. At the same time, the financial system has tended to discriminate against the small-scale personal savers. As Andrew S. Carron shows, various policies have helped to depress the interest rates paid to small savers. This discrimination has served several purposes, explicit or revealed: it has reduced the cost of government borrowing by requiring banks to hold government securities and thus effectively limiting the interest rates they would bid for deposits; it has permitted restrictions (effective at times) on the maximum interest rates charged to borrowers (which favored the small borrowers not rationed out); and it has fostered nonprice competition in the banking sector through a proliferation of retail branches. Carron also points out that the intermediation undertaken by Australian financial institutions is comparable to that in other countries, given the extent of foreign investment and off-balance-sheet financing by banks. Overall, Australia has realized relatively high rates of domestic saving, consistent with a congenial tax system and a well-developed though somewhat imperfect financial sector.

Carron's generally favorable opinion of the financial sector's efficiency is not contradicted by the large inflows of capital from abroad. Much of this has taken the form of direct foreign investment. In manufacturing and other home-market sectors, this is motivated not by capital arbitrage but by entrepreneurial profits to be gained from transferring to Australia the corporate skills gained in differentiating products or supplying novel technologies and organizational skills. This proposition yields various corollaries that are confirmed by Caves's analysis of productivity and scale in manufacturing industries. In large-scale re-source developments the prevalence of overseas capital reflects the sheer scale of projects relative to the absorptive capacity of Australian financial markets, as well as the entrepreneurial role of foreign capital.

Federal-State Relations and Economic Development

Australia's federal structure has greatly influenced public finance, government expenditure, and policies toward economic development. One important element of this structure is the elaborate arrangement by which the federal government rebates tax revenues to the states and monitors their borrowings. Gramlich questions both the efficiency and equity of the system. He has reservations about the coherence of the egalitarian objectives behind federal tax-sharing grants to the states. They are not, he argues, clearly connected to economic welfare. Fur-thermore, basing equalization on actual differences in the cost of providing public services in various locations will only dampen the incentive for economic activity wherever these services can be supplied most efficiently. Notwithstanding the equalization objective, Gramlich finds that Australian states remain relatively heterogeneous in the levels of public services that they supply.

The extent to which the states rely on federal grants for revenue and the federal subsidy implicit in state borrowing tend to encourage political rent-seeking and to remove from the states some of the responsibility for sound budgetary practices. However, Aaron notes, there is one bright spot in the conversion of health-related grants from the open-ended form to block grants; apparently it has had a moderating effect on the upward trend in hospital costs.

By preempting most revenue sources, the federal government leaves the states to scrounge among various nuisance taxes for incremental revenues. However, the problem of the breadth of tax instruments affects not only the states. The entire system concentrates on the personal income tax, particularly on wage and salary income, for the bulk of its revenue, and on property taxes for local government revenue; because the federal government makes little effort to consider other broad-based taxes, the marginal rates of income taxation are necessarily high, and

the public's incentive to seek out opportunities to avoid taxes is strengthened accordingly.

State-federal relationships also play a role in the development of
natural resources. The states have traditionally been active in promoting
economic development, using uncoordinated policies that no doubt
distorted the location of investment and thus affected the well-being of
the country as a whole. Recently the point of friction has been the rents
expected to flow from the development of natural resources. To the
extent that these are captured by a commonwealth resources rent tax
(just now passed for petroleum industries), there could be some gains in
efficiency over the present hodgepodge of overlapping, competing, and
inefficient state-federal taxation. (Helliwell argues that efficiency could
be improved by combining this tax with a front-end bid for the privilege
of developing resources.) At the same time, the resources rent tax does
tend to centralize revenue even more, encourage political rent-seeking
through the quest for grants, and leave the states less incentive to manage
their fiscal affairs efficiently.

Public Attitudes and Public Policy

Several chapters suggest that Australia's public policies are greatly
influenced by the national distrust of market outcomes and a strong
belief in equality. The efficiency of market and nonmarket allocation
processes is open to empirical test, and so the distrust of market outcomes
should be subject to modification if the evidence warrants. However,
the belief in equality is a collective preference that economic analysis
can only take as given. Economic research can quote the going price in
efficiency of obtaining more equality and perhaps suggest ways to cut
that price, but it cannot prescribe the social choice between perceived
equity and real income. Several chapters review policies that implement
the trade-off.

Carron shows, for example, that both a distrust of markets and a
preference for equity are reflected in the regulations on banks and other
financial institutions. The distrust of market outcomes here does have
some economic foundation, although Carron adds that Australia's recent
shift toward less intensive and more efficient prudential regulation is

welcome. He also notes that because competition among banks has been suppressed, the banks have been encouraged to maintain excessive and unprofitable branches and to apply the same charges to differently situated customers despite different costs of serving them. Locational equality of this type has fairly high real costs. The preference for equity shows up in policies that channel funds toward the mortgage market in that they too respond to the demand for equalizing household situations.

A strong egalitarian cast, Aaron argues, can also be seen in the country's disposition toward means-tested pension benefits and a wide range of other social-welfare policies. Krause notes in addition that tariff protection strongly favors industries employing low-skill and low-wage workers. This is another example of an inefficient method of income redistribution, if that indeed is the tariff's primary social objective.

Gramlich concludes that Australia has the most equalizing federalist system in the world. The federal government collects most of the tax revenue, but grants to the states large rebates calculated to equalize their abilities to provide the same level of service at the same level of tax effort. As noted earlier, equalizing on the basis of the actual cost of providing public services is a form of geographic egalitarianism that has its costs in economic efficiency. Gramlich observes, for example, that the formal credit rationing scheme in operation for fifty years (the Loan Council) seems to have lost all touch with an efficient allocation of public investment funds.

Several authors notice that equitable interferences in market processes tend to cumulate. The pursuit of equity through public policy is a never-settled issue that continually brings forth new claims from groups that think they have suffered from incidental consequences of the last equitable policy measure, not to mention the inevitable winds of economic disturbance. Furthermore, the willingness of the public sector to respond to forceful claims in equity yields a high return to rent-seeking behavior and helps to divert resources in that direction. As a result, Krause points out, Australia's industrial policy is slanted toward the restriction of international commerce. Made-to-measure protection both increases real costs and offers rent-seeking opportunities. Each change in protectionist policies inevitably reduces the welfare of some groups while improving that of others, thus touching off new claims for equity. And the general disposition of Australian society to resist international competition makes it hostage to politically powerful vested interests at home such as labor unions and monopolistic business firms. Although equity is an eminently worthy social preference, the economist cannot help noting that its zero-sum nature renders its pursuit an unending task that has open-ended costs.

Conference Participants

with their affiliations at the time of the conference

Henry J. Aaron *Brookings Institution*

Carol J. Austin *Australian Industries Development Association*

Bruce R. Bacon *Australian Bureau of Statistics*

Peter D. Bearsley *ANZ Bank*

John J. Beggs *Australian National University*

Hector M. Boot *Australian National University*

Harold G. Brennan *Australian National University*

Andrew S. Carron *Brookings Institution*

Ian Castles *Department of Finance*

Michael G. R. Carter *Australian National University*

Richard E. Caves *Harvard University*

Bruce J. Chapman *Australian National University*

David T. Charles *Department of Employment and Industrial Relations*

Anthony H. Chisholm *Australian National University*

Kenneth W. Clements *University of Western Australia*

Andre M. Cohen *Citicorp*

W. M. Corden *Australian National University*

Michael R. Cronin *Bureau of Industry Economics*

Kevin T. Davis *University of Adelaide*

Robert Z. DeFerranti *Esso Australia, Ltd.*

Daryl A. Dixon *Social Welfare Policy Secretariat*

Owen D. Donald *Department of Social Security*

Rudiger Dornbusch *Massachusetts Institute of Technology*

Meredith A. Edwards *Department of Education and Youth Affairs*

E. A. Evans *Department of Treasury*

Norman W. F. Fisher *Bureau of Labour Market Research*

Robert M. Fisher *Australian National University*

V. W. J. FitzGerald *Department of Finance*

M. Gawan-Taylor *Australian National University*

R. J. Graham *Westpac Banking Corporation*

Edward M. Gramlich *University of Michigan*

Malcolm R. Gray *Australian National University*

Peter D. Groenewegen *University of Sydney*

Fred H. Gruen *Australian National University*

Ian R. Harper *Reserve Bank of Australia*

R. J. A. Harper *University of Melbourne*

David S. Harrison *National Institute of Labour Studies*

D. R. Harvey *Australian National University*

R. G. Hawkins *Department of Housing and Construction*

John F. Helliwell *University of British Columbia*

Helen Hughes *Australian National University*

Joseph E. Isaac *Australian Conciliation and Arbitration Commission*

P. N. James *BP Australia, Ltd.*

Brian L. Johns *Bureau of Industry Economics*

H. N. Johnson *Department of Treasury*

Paul A. Johnson *Reserve Bank of Australia*

Peter D. Jonson *Reserve Bank of Australia*

Peter H. Karmel *Australian National University*

Wolfgang R. Kasper *University of New South Wales*

Michael S. Keating *Department of Employment and Industrial
Relations*

Judith Kleinman *University of New South Wales*

Lawrence B. Krause *Brookings Institution*

John V. Langmore *Office of the Minister for Employment and Industrial Relations*

Paul L. Lasse *Counsellor for Economic Affairs, U.S. Embassy*

A. R. Lawson *Industries Assistance Commission*

Peter J. Lloyd *University of Melbourne*

N. V. Long *Australian National University*

Jim L. Longmire *Bureau of Agricultural Economics*

John D. S. MacLeod *CRA, Ltd.*

Rodney R. Maddock *Australian National University*

Alan K. Marshall *BP Australia, Ltd.*

Russell L. Mathews *Australian National University*

P. P. McGuinness *Australian Financial Review*

Ian W. McLean *University of Adelaide*

Geoff L. Miller *Economic Planning Advisory Council*

Daniel J. B. Mitchell *University of California, Los Angeles*

David R. Morgan *Department of Treasury*

Don C. Morrison *MIM Holdings, Ltd.*

John W. Nevile *University of New South Wales*

Neville R. Norman *University of Melbourne*

Adrian R. Pagan *Australian National University*

Brian R. Parmenter *University of Melbourne*

Thomas G. Parry *University of New South Wales*

John R. Piggott *Australian National University*

John R. Pinkerton *Westpac Banking Corporation*

John D. Pitchford *Australian National University*

Andrew S. Podger *Department of Finance*

Michael G. Porter *Monash University*

Donald W. Rawson *Australian National University*

Edward W. Shann *Department of the Prime Minister and Cabinet*

Philippa Smith *Consultant, NSW Department of Health*

Ralph E. Smith *Australian National University*

Andrew B. Stoeckel *Bureau of Agricultural Economics*

Greg F. Taylor *Office of National Assessments*

Richard D. Terrell *Australian National University*
Thomas J. Valentine *Macquarie University*
E. M. W. Visbord *Department of the Prime Minister and Cabinet*
Clifford Walsh *University of Adelaide*
Owen J. West *MIM Holdings, Ltd.*
Ross A. Williams *Australian National University*
Glenn A. Withers *Australian National University*

Index

Britain's Economic Performance
Richard E. Caves and Lawrence B. Krause
Editors

Why does British productivity still lag behind that of most other industrialized countries? Can Britain's financial structure or tax system or trade unions be blamed for the continued slow rate of growth of its economy? Will income from the sale of North Sea oil really improve Britain's economic situation in the 1980s?

The six papers in this book address these and other important questions about the British economy and about economic policies that have been in flux or subject to controversy. In the first paper, Rudiger Dornbusch and Stanley Fischer survey the behavior of the current account and the exchange rate during the 1970s and discuss the prospects for the U.K. economy in the next decade. The next two papers are primarily concerned with the problems of British industry: David C. Smith examines the relation of economic conditions to the growth and militancy of trade unions in recent years, and Richard E. Caves presents a statistical analysis of the productivity differences among U.K. industries, comparing them with their U.S. counterparts. In the fourth paper, Joseph A. Pechman appraises the economic effects of the British tax system. Marshall E. Blume then analyzes the British financial structure and its ability to direct savings into appropriate investment channels. Finally, Hendrik S. Houthakker discusses the use and management of North Sea oil.

The papers and the commentary on them were originally presented at a May 1979 conference in Ditchley, England, that was jointly sponsored by Brookings and the National Institute for Economic and Social Research in England and attended by about thirty prominent British, American, and Canadian economists. The book opens with an introduction and summary by the editors.

Richard E. Caves, professor of economics at Harvard University, was the principal author of *Britain's Economic Prospects* (Brookings, 1968). Lawrence B. Krause, a senior fellow in the Brookings Economic Studies program, was also a contributor to that volume.

388 pp./1980/cloth and paper